TREASURED BOOKS VOLUME 1: THE APOCRYPHA

SHEM QADOSH VERSION

Textual Research Institute, L.L.C
P.O. Box 384
Youngsville, NC 27596

Treasured Books Volume 1: The Apocrypha *~ Shem Qadosh Version*

www.shemqadoshversion.weebly.com
shemqadosh@outlook.com

Cover art & Design by J.A. Brown

First printing, 2016

ISBN-13: 978-0-9961717-1-7

1 Esdras taken and edited from the World English Bible (WEB), which is in the public domain.

1 Maccabees taken and edited from the (WEB), which is in the public domain.

2 Maccabees taken and edited from the (WEB), which is in the public domain.

Prayer of Azarias taken and edited from the (WEB), which is in the public domain.

Susanna taken and edited from the (WEB), which is in the public domain.

Bel and the Dragon taken and edited from the (WEB), which is in the public domain.

Additions to Esther taken and edited from the (WEB), which is in the public domain.

1 Baruch taken and edited from the (WEB), which is in the public domain.

Tobit taken and edited from the (WEB), which is in the public domain.

Judith taken and edited from the (WEB), which is in the public domain.

Prayer of Manassas taken and edited from the (WEB), which is in the public domain.

Sirach [*Ecclesiasticus*] taken and edited from the (WEB), which is in the public domain.

Wisdom of Solomon taken and edited from the (WEB), which is in the public domain.

2 Esdras taken and edited from the (WEB), which is in the public domain.

Editor's Preface

Introduction

Apocrypha. Many know the word, though sadly, few fully understand it. Amid the myriad of arguments and debates regarding its canonicity, one fact remains: it is greatly beneficial to the reader. Most Protestants are never exposed to the Apocrypha, since it is not present in their canon, and most Catholics never read it, despite it being available. I consider this to be quite a pity, as there is a wealth of information to be gleaned from its pages. Jerome considered it useful for study, and even the British Crown ruled that no Bible could ever be printed without it![a] Luther included it in his German Bible (though he omitted 1 and 2 Esdras entirely)[b], and it was also included in the 1611 King James Version. Even the Puritans made use of the Apocrypha, though stating in the Westminster Confession of Faith that it was not to be considered divinely inspired.

In all of these examples, one is left to wonder: why do so many today ignore the Apocrypha? To some, it is out of fear that they may be led to believe something false. For others, it is merely disinterest in matters of a Biblical nature. The former is not an issue that can be addressed simply, but suffice it to say that the very way one regards the apocrypha could solve this problem. Keeping in mind the classical position of the majority of denominations from Orthodox to Protestant, one could be reminded of the Thirty-Nine Articles that define the matter quite well: that the Apocrypha should be consulted for instruction in life and manners, but not for the establishment of doctrine. The latter reason is primarily why this present volume has been produced. But perhaps first of all we should define the very word itself.

So what, then, does *Apocrypha* mean? It comes to us from Greek via the Latin *apocryphus*, meaning "hidden" or "concealed." The idea behind said appellation is that these books contain certain topics and words that are not meant for the layman. It is also worth noting that the Hebrew term for the Apocrypha is not *matmonim* ("hidden things") as some surmise, but is

---

[a] Collins, Ken. *Who Took the Apocrypha out of The Bible?* Kencollins.com. 2016.
[b] Preface to the *Revised Standard Version Common Bible*. 2016.

rather *Sefarim Hag'nuzim*, meaning "treasured books." This is where the present volume gets its name.

It should be understood that whether these "Treasured Books" should be accepted into the canon is not a debate which the Shem Qadosh Version family of texts ever intends to enter. However, just as was done with Genesis Retold, I am hoping to draw more attention to some of these lesser-known texts, in hopes of spreading more and more Biblical truth. If Context if King, certainly Culture is Queen. The Apocrypha contains both of these: culture, in that it assists with providing insight into what is known as the "inter-testamental period" (time between the end of the 'Old Testament' and the beginning of the 'New Testament'); and context, because it opens up a world of quotes and references (see Appendix C). What many fail to realize is that within the Bible itself (specifically, the 'New Testament') are many quotes and references to Apocryphal books. Sirach is quoted numerous times, both in the Gospels by Mary (Luke 1) and by James, who draws heavily from it in paraphrase. Wisdom of Solomon is likewise quoted by the Gospels, and there are possible references throughout the NT to these books and more (see Appendix C). While the Bible is fully capable of interpreting itself, it nonetheless does not include every historical book, nor every cross-reference. And *that* is why the SQV Apocrypha has been published: to bridge the gap. My desire in this work is that the reader's eyes would be opened to new areas of their Bibles, particularly in the NT, where these books can further aid us in our search for Truth.

The Names

As with every other book in the SQV family, the present volume also amends the names of all those in the text. What is different from most English Bibles, however, is that these names are in some ways further removed than they are in our standard Bibles. For example, the Hebrew name אזרא is translated as "Ezra" in the Bible. However, in the Apocrypha, this is translated from its Greek spelling, which is Εσδρας, lending an English spelling of Esdras. Similarly we can take the name אזריה. In most Bibles, this is written in English as "Azariah." In Greek, this is Αζαριας, which converts into "Azarias" in English. Just as we did with Ezra, we have taken this name back to its Hebrew original, and transliterated it accordingly: Azaryah. Nearly every name in the Apocrypha has received this treatment. A couple of exceptions include names that were probably misprinted in the Greek/Latin source, or are written in code (such as Holofernes in Judith).

Most importantly of all, the Name of our Creator received the same special care and attention as in every other SQV book. In many cases there were Hebrew fragments to work from, which yielded a couple of options. In some rare cases, these texts actually featured the Name as it stands written: יהוה. In some cases, such as many manuscripts of Ben Sira and Tobit, it appears as three dots ·.· and in a handful of places the typical Jewish placeholders ייי and/or יי were found. In all such occurrences, it was rendered here as יהוה. This was the first phase.

Next we had to consider the Syriac Aramaic texts, such as for Ben Sira, Maccabees, Wisdom of Solomon, and the Additional Psalms. In most of these cases they contained the Syriac word ܡܪܝܐ *Mar-ya*, which is a placeholder used only as a substitute for the Hebrew Tetragrammaton (יהוה). This is also true for a couple of Ge'ez (Ethiopic) texts, which read እግዚአብሔር (*igzi'a'b'cheir*), a special Ethiopic word meaning "Master of all the Land."

The task became more difficult moving away from Semitic languages, however. As most of the Apocrypha is based on the Greek Septuagint (LXX), we had to carefully review the text in each case. While the Eastern texts in Hebrew, Aramaic, Syriac, and Ethiopic utilize a placeholder for the Divine Name, the Western texts of Greek and Latin do not. In most cases, the Greek uses Κυριος (*Kurios*), meaning "Lord" or "Master." However, it also uses the word in place of the Hebrew אדון (*Adon*), which means the same. Latin likewise uses the word domini in this case, meaning these same as its Hebrew and Greek counterparts. Thus when presented with either the Greek *Kurios* or the Latin domini, they were reviewed carefully in context. If the sense, flow, and context of the passage seemed more appropriate for the place of the Tetragrammaton, it was rendered as יהוה. If not, it was rendered as "Master."

Other titles featured in the present work include *Elyon*, a Hebrew transliteration meaning "Most High." Though it was usually translated from Greek or Latin, we prefer the Hebrew terminology when possible. Thus where a traditional rendering would read, "Most High" the present text will read "Elyon." Another is *Adonai*, featured where it is found in Hebrew and in place of a certain Latin phrase, generally translated as "Lord who bears rule." This, Dr. Charles noted, is used in place of the Hebrew phrase אדני יהוה (Adonai YHWH), and as such was translated that way. One more term is also used, though it rarely appears. That is the word *Tsevaot*. This is a transliterated Hebrew term meaning "armies" or "hosts." In most traditional renderings it appears as "Lord of Hosts" or as "Lord of Armies." I have chosen instead to render it as "Tsevaot." See explanatory note for this word. The last term used somewhat frequently is *El Shaddai*. This is generally rendered "God Almighty" but again, the transliteration is preferred.

The Texts

The source texts that went into the SQV Apocrypha will seem a little bit odd. Today, nearly all available translations (WEB, ASV, KJV) are based on the Greek and Latin texts that were available to the King James translators. While these are, for the most part, solid texts, they are nonetheless relatively late. Indeed, they are also representative of only Greek and Latin. Meanwhile Tobit, Ben Sira, and the Apocryphal Psalms were all originally Hebrew, as was 1 Maccabees. Many Hebrew and Aramaic fragments of the Apocryphal texts have been discovered since the days of the KJV translation, and as such need to be consulted. Much of the work of collating and noting variances was done in the 19th Century by Dr. R. H. Charles. Further work has also been done to publish the Dead Sea Scrolls, as well as the Cairo Genizah fragments. For each book below, in order, an explanation is given of the texts consulted, as well as the emendations that were made to the base texts.

<u>1 Esdras</u> was taken from the World English Bible (WEB) apocrypha. In that edition it was edited from the Apocrypha of the American Standard Version (ASV). This version was, ultimately translated from Greek and Latin sources, being little revised since the 1611 King James. For our edition we brought the language closer in line with modern English (where the WEB missed), and altered the names. Some terms were also retranslated for the sake of accuracy and integrity to the original text.

<u>1 Maccabees</u> was taken from the WEB apocrypha. There, just as with 1 Esdras, it was also revised from the ASV. Whereas it is based primarily on its Greek source text, our edition took it even further. Utilizing the *Comprehensive Aramaic Lexicon* and its transcription of Codex Ambrosianus, we emended the text even further, noting major differences

between the Greek and Syriac (Aramaic) texts. Many are minor, though some are quite notable. In some cases, entire sections were completely retranslated to show a closer alignment with what we believe the original Hebrew text read. The Hebrew edition of Isaac Frankel was not consulted in this matter, much to the chagrin of some. The issue with Frankel's work is that he did not transcribe or copy a Hebrew text, but rather backwards translated the Greek text (and only one manuscript in particular) into Hebrew. Thus consulting his edition offers little benefit.

2 Maccabees received the same treatment as 1 Maccabees, though without the same attempt made to understand a Hebrew original. Given the style, time, and content of the book, there is little doubt among scholars that it was originally Greek. It is also at least once removed from a different work, as the author of 2 Maccabees himself states that he is merely abridging a previous multi-volume work by someone called 'Jason the Cyrene.'

Prayer of Azarias was taken from the WEB apocrypha. It received the same treatment as the previous books, being compared with the Syriac and Latin editions.

Susanna received the same treatment as did the Prayer of Azarias.

Bel and the Dragon received the same treatment as did Susanna and the Prayer of Azarias.

Additions to Esther was taken from the WEB apocrypha. It received the same treatment as the previous books, though its text was only compared between Greek and Latin. However, since these additions are found interspersed throughout the book of Esther in the Septuagint, we decided to include the entire book, rather than just these additions. This places them in their proper context and location.

Psalms 151-155 is a special case. It is not generally found among the Apocryphal works, but given its ancient history we have chosen to include it regardless. Psalm 151 was first taken from the LXX in American English, which is in the public domain. This was then compared to the Syriac edition as well as the Hebrew text from the Dead Sea Scrolls. Sections in brackets indicate these Hebrew additions. The additions are an original translation. Psalms 152-155 are not found in the LXX at all, but are best attested in the Syriac. Some are also attested in various forms among the Dead Sea Scrolls. The translation of these four is original, based on the Hebrew text when available, and supplemented by the complete Syriac text where lacking.

1 Baruch was taken from the WEB apocrypha. It received the same treatment as the previous books, though with fewer textual witnesses. In Syriac, there is only a text of chapter 6 (the Letter of Jeremiah), so chapters 1-5 were compared only between Greek and Latin.

Tobit was taken from the WEB apocrypha. It received the same treatment as the previous books, but was also heavily revised by the current editor. Fragments are now extant in Hebrew and Aramaic that were not known at the time some previous editions were published. For these sections, the Hebrew and Aramaic versions took precedence over the Greek and Latin versions. The translation of these Semitic sections are original to this volume.

Judith was taken from the WEB apocrypha. It received the same treatment as the previous books, though with fewer textual witnesses.

Prayer of Manassas was taken from the WEB apocrypha. It received the same treatment as the previous books, including being compared with the Syriac version.

Sirach [Ecclesiasticus] was taken from the WEB apocrypha. It received the same treatment as the previous books, but was also heavily revised by the current editor. Very large Hebrew fragments are now extant from the Dead Sea Scrolls and the Cairo Genizah that allow for a better reconstruction of the Hebrew original. These were primarily used when available. When they are lacking, the Syriac, Latin, and Greek were compared.

Wisdom of Solomon was taken from the WEB apocrypha. It received the same treatment as the previous books, including being compared with the Syriac version.

2 Esdras was taken from the WEB apocrypha. It received the same treatment as the previous books, including being compared with the Syriac, Arabic, and Ethiopic versions. While the majority of the book is considered by numerous scholars to have originally been Hebrew, the style shows it was translated to Greek before being translated again into Latin, Syriac, Arabic, Ethiopic, Armenian, and Slavonic. In the case of the Arabic text, there are actually two primary Arabic textual traditions. These two are denoted as Arabic^1 and Arabic^2 by Dr. Charles; I have chosen to retain the

same nomenclature. No Hebrew or Greek versions of 2 Esdras are known to exist.

Order of the Books

The order of the books is given as follows:

1. Esdras ⲁ [1 Esdras {3 Ezra}] .... Pages 1 – 24
2. Maqabiym א [1 Maccabees] .... Pages 25 – 70
3. Maqabiym ב [2 Maccabees] .... Pages 71 – 106
4. T'fillat Azaryah [Prayer of Azarias] .... Pages 107 – 110
5. Shoshanah [Susanna] .... Pages 111 – 114
6. Bel Kai Ton Drako [Bel and the Dragon] .... Pages 115 – 116
7. Hadassah [Esther] with Additions .... Pages 117 – 130
8. Tehillim [Psalms] 151-155 .... Pages 131 – 134
9. Barukh א [1 Baruch] .... Pages 135 – 144
10. Tovi [Tobit] .... Pages 145 – 158
11. Yehudith [Judith] .... Pages 159 – 178
12. T'fillat Menasheh [Prayer of Manassas] .... Pages 179 – 180
13. Ben Sira [Sirach {Ecclesiasticus}] .... Pages 181 – 241
14. Ḥokhmat Shelomoh [Wisdom of Solomon] .... Pages 243 – 264
15. Esdras ⲃ [2 Esdras {4 Ezra}] .... Pages 265 – 304
16. Appendix A: Explanatory Notes .... Pages 305 – 306
17. Appendix B: Alphabets .... Pages 307 – 308
18. Appendix C: New Testament Parallel Verses .... Pages 309 – 310
19. Appendix D: Glossary of Terms .... Pages 311 – 313
20. Appendix E: Major Textual Variants .... Pages 314 – 315

The ordering of these books is nothing if not arbitrary. Their order varies greatly going back even to ancient times, and especially between the versions. Jerome placed them in an Appendix, while Luther placed them between the OT and NT. The Septuagint contained most of them spread throughout the work. For the present volume, for the sake of creating a method to the madness, I have chosen to arrange them based on the following logic:

Historic and Historo-Legendary;

Didactic [Wisdom Literature];

Apocalyptic

Thus 1 Esdras through the Prayer of Manassas fall under Historic and Historo-Legendary; Sirach and Wisdom of Solomon fall under Didactic and Wisdom Literature, and 2 Esdras falls under Apocalyptic. Again I stress the fact that this arrangement is entirely arbitrary.

In addition to these 15 books, there are also various appendices, as shown here:

Appendix A: Explanatory Notes
Appendix B: Major Textual Variances
Appendix C: Parallel Passages in the 'New Testament'
Appendix D: Glossary of Terms

Conclusion

Overall it is the opinion of the present editor that these books hold a great deal of information that is beneficial to the serious student of Scripture, especially those that study the 'New Testament.' I would also advise a word of caution to those who would have the Biblical canon altered to include them. Of the more orthodox denominations that accept these books, there is nearly universal agreement that they are deuterocanonical (that is, "secondary canon"). For the fundamentalist, this is usually expressed by saying they are not "divinely inspired." There are issues on both theological and doctrinal grounds that many will find within these pages. Having said that, however, I believe with a careful examination one can honestly say that these books are indeed useful, for both Christians and Jews alike.

Just as no one claims divine inspiration for a history book – and yet can still glean much useful information from it – so these texts should be used without needing to bear such endorsement.

Above all else, it is my hope and prayer that these books bless you, and lead you to an ever-growing relationship with יהוה Elohim. Shalom.

ⲈⲤⲆⲢⲀⲤ ⲁ
Esdras A
1 Esdras [{3 Ezra}]

1 1 Yoshiyahu held the Pesaḥ in
Yerushalayim to יהוה, and offered the
Pesaḥ the fourteenth day of the first month;
2 having set the priests according to their
daily courses, being arrayed in their
vestments, in the Temple of יהוה.

3 And he spoke to the Levites, the Temple-
servants of Yisra'el, that they should set
themselves apart to יהוה, to place the set-
apart ark of יהוה in the house that King
Shelomoh the son of David had built. 4 And
he said, "You no longer need to carry it on
your shoulders; now therefore, serve יהוה
your Elohim, and attend to His people
Yisra'el, and prepare after your fathers'
houses and family, 5 according to the
writing of David king of Yisra'el, and
according to the magnificence of Shelomoh
his son. Standing in the set-apart place
according to the several divisions of the
families of you, the Levites, who attend the
children of Yisra'el in the presence of your
people, 6 offer the Pesaḥ in order, and make
ready the slaughterings for your people,
and guard the Pesaḥ according to the
command of יהוה, which was given to
Mosheh."

7 And Yoshiyahu gave thirty thousand
lambs and kids, and three thousand calves
to the people who were present; these
things were given from the king's portion,
as he had promised, to the people, and to
the priests and Levites. 8 And Ḥilqiyahu,
and Zekharyah, and Yeḥi'el, the rulers of
the Temple, gave the priests two thousand
and six hundred sheep, and three hundred
calves for the Pesaḥ. 9 And Konanyahu,
and Shemayahu and Nathana'el his brother,
and Ḥashavyahu, and Yei'el, and Yozavad,
captains over thousands, gave to the
Levites for the Pesaḥ five thousand sheep,
and seven hundred calves.

10 And when these things were done, the
priests and Levites, having the unleavened
bread, stood in comely order according to
their families, 11 and according to the
several divisions by their fathers' houses,
before the people, to offer to יהוה, as it is
written in the book of Mosheh; and thus did
they in the morning. 12 And they cooked
the Pesaḥ with fire, as it pertains *to it*; and
the slaughterings they boiled in the copper
vessels and pots with a good savor, 13 and
set them before all the people. And
afterward they prepared for themselves, and
for the priests their brethren, the sons of
Aharon. 14 For the priests offered the fat
until night, and the Levites prepared for
themselves, and for the priests their
brethren, the sons of Aharon.[a]

15 The set-apart singers also, the sons of
Asaph, were in their order, according to the
appointment of David, that is, Asaph,
Zekharyah, and Yeduthun, who were the
king's seers. 16 Moreover the gatekeepers
were at every gate; none needed to leave
his daily course, for their brethren the
Levites prepared *it* for them. 17 Thus were
the things that belonged to the
slaughterings to יהוה accomplished in that

---

[a] 1:14 Given the extremely large task of slaughtering and preparing so many animals, the Aharonic Priests did not have time to prepare for themselves. So the Levites prepared the Pesaḥ for themselves, and for the Aharonic Priests.

day, in holding the Pesaḥ, 18 and offering
slaughterings upon the altar of יהוה,
according to the command of King
Yoshiyahu.

19 So the children of Yisra'el who were
present at that time kept the Pesaḥ, and the
Feast of Unleavened Bread *for* seven days.
20 And such a Pesaḥ was not kept in
Yisra'el since the time of the prophet
Shemu'el. 21 Yes, all the kings of Yisra'el
had not kept such a Pesaḥ as Yoshiyahu,
and the priests, and the Levites, and the
Yehudim kept with all Yisra'el that were
present in their dwelling place at
Yerushalayim. 22 This Pesaḥ was kept in
the eighteenth year of the reign of
Yoshiyahu.

23 And the works of Yoshiyahu were
upright before יהוה with a heart full of
reverence. 24 Moreover the things that
happened in his days have been written in
times past, concerning those that sinned,
and did wickedly against יהוה above every
people and kingdom, and how they
exceedingly grieved Him, so that the words
of יהוה were confirmed against Yisra'el.

25 Now it happened after all these acts of
Yoshiyahu, that Pharaoh the king of
Mitsrayim came to raise war at Karkemish
on *the River* Perath; and Yoshiyahu went
out against him. 26 But the king of
Mitsrayim sent to him, saying, "What have
I to do with you, O king of Yehudah? 27 I
am not sent out from יהוה Elohim against
you, for my war is on *the River* Perath.
Now then, יהוה is with me, yes, יהוה is
with me driving me on. Depart from me,
and do not be against יהוה. 28 However,
Yoshiyahu did not turn back to his chariot,
but instead began to fight with him, not
heeding the words of the prophet
Yirmeyahu, spoken by the mouth of יהוה.
29 But *instead he* joined battle with him in
the plain of Megiddo, and the princes came
down against King Yoshiyahu. 30 Then the
king said to his servants, "Carry me away
out of the battle; for I am very weak." And
immediately his servants carried him away
out of the army. 31 Then he raised up upon
his second chariot; and being brought back
to Yerushalayim he died, and was buried in
the tomb of his fathers.

32 And they mourned for Yoshiyahu in all
Yehudah; and Yirmeyahu the prophet
lamented for Yoshiyahu, and the chief men
with the women made lamentation for him,
to this day; and this was given out for an
ordinance to be done continually in all the
nation of Yisra'el. 33 These things are
written in the book of the histories of the
kings of Yehudah, and every one of the acts
that Yoshiyahu did, and his glory, and his
understanding in the Torah of יהוה, and the
things that he did before, and the things
now recited, are reported in the book of the
kings of Yisra'el and Yehudah.

34 And the people took Yehoaḥaz the son
of Yoshiyahu, and made him king in place
of Yoshiyahu his father, when he was
twenty-three years old. 35 And he reigned
in Yehudah and in Yerushalayim three
months. And then the king of Mitsrayim
removed him from reigning in
Yerushalayim. 36 And he set a tax upon the
people of a hundred talents of silver and
one talent of gold. 37 The king of
Mitsrayim also made King Yehoyaqim his
brother king of Yehudah and
Yerushalayim. 38 And Yehoyaqim bound

the nobles: but Zarakes[a] his brother he
arrested, and brought him up out of
Mitsrayim. 39 Yehoyaqim was twenty-five
years old when he began to reign in
Yehudah and Yerushalayim; and he did
that which was evil in the eyes of יהוה.

40 And Nevukhadnetsar the king of Bavel
came up against him, and bound him with a
chain of copper, and carried him to Bavel.
41 Nevukhadnetsar also took of the set-
apart vessels of *the House of* יהוה, and
carried them away, and set them up in his
own temple at Bavel. 42 But those things
that are reported of him, and of his
uncleanness and irreverence, are written in
the chronicles of the kings. 43 And
Yehoyaqim his son reigned in his place; for
he was eighteen years old when he was
made king. 44 And he reigned three months
and ten days in Yerushalayim, and did that
which was evil before יהוה.

45 So after a year Nevukhadnetsar sent and
caused him to be brought to Bavel with the
set-apart vessels of *the House of* יהוה;
46 and made Tsidqiyahu king of Yehudah
and Yerushalayim, when he was twenty-
one years old; and he reigned eleven years.[b]
47 And he also did that which was evil in
the eyes of יהוה, and did not heed the
words that were spoken by Yirmeyahu the
prophet from the mouth of יהוה.

48 And after that king Nevukhadnetsar had
made him to swear by the Name of יהוה,
he swore, but then he rebelled *against his
oath*; and hardening his neck, and his heart,
he transgressed the Torah of יהוה, the
Elohim of Yisra'el. 49 Moreover the
governors of the people and of the priests
did many things wickedly, and surpassed
all the uncleanness of all the nations, and
defiled the Temple of יהוה, which was set
apart in Yerushalayim.

50 And the Elohim of their fathers sent by
His messenger to call them back, because
He had compassion on them and on His
dwelling place. 51 But they mocked His
messengers. And in the day when יהוה
spoke to them, they scoffed at His prophets.
52 So then He, being angry with His people
for their great profanity, commanded to
bring up the kings of the Kaldeans against
them, 53 who killed their young men with
the sword around their set-apart Temple,
and spared neither young man nor maiden,
old man nor child; but he delivered all into
their hands. 54 And they took all the set-
apart vessels of *the House of* יהוה, both
great and small, with the vessels of the ark
of יהוה, and the king's treasures, and
carried them away to Bavel. 55 And they
burned the House of יהוה, and broke down
the walls of Yerushalayim, and burned its
towers with fire. 56 And as for her glorious
things, they never ceased until they had
brought them all to nothing; and the people
that were not killed with the sword he
carried to Bavel, 57 and they were servants
to him and to his children, until the
Parasians reigned, to fulfil the word of
יהוה by the mouth of Yirmeyahu: 58 "Until
the land has enjoyed her Sabbaths, the
whole time of her desolation shall she keep
Sabbath, to fulfil seventy years."

[a] 1:38 Zarakes – Most likely Yehoaḥaz, his brother, who was taken to Mitsrayim by Pharaoh.

[b] 1:46 See 1 Barukh 1:8.

2 1 In the first year of Koresh king of the
Parasians, that the word of יהוה by the
mouth of Yirmeyahu might be
accomplished, 2 יהוה stirred up the spirit of
Koresh king of the Parasians, and he made
proclamation through all his kingdom, and
also by writing, 3 saying, "Thus says
Koresh king of the Parasians: יהוה of
Yisra'el, El Elyon, has made me king of the
whole world, 4 and commanded me to build
Him a house at Yerushalayim that is in
Yehudah. 5 If therefore there be any of you
that are of His people, let יהוה, even יהוה,
be with him, and let him go up to
Yerushalayim that is in Yehudah, and build
the house of יהוה of Yisra'el: he is יהוה
that dwells in Yerushalayim. 6 Therefore,
of all those who dwell in various places, let
those who are in his own place help each
one with gold, and with silver, 7 and with
gifts, and with horses and also with cattle,
aside from the other things which have
been added by vow for the Temple of יהוה
which is in Yerushalayim."

8 Then the chief of the families of Yehudah
and of the tribe of Benyamin stood up; the
priests also, and the Levites, and all those
whose spirit יהוה had stirred to go up, to
build the House for יהוה is in
Yerushalayim. 9 And those who lived
around them helped them in all things with
silver and gold, with horses and cattle, and
with very many gifts that were vowed of a
great number whose minds were stirred up
to do so.

10 King Koresh also brought forth the set-
apart vessels of יהוה, which
Nevukhadnetsar had carried away from
Yerushalayim, and had set up in his temple
of idols. 11 Now when Koresh king of the
Parasians had brought them forth, he
delivered them to Mithredath his treasurer,
12 and they were delivered by him to
Sheshbatsar the governor of Yehudah.
13 And this is how many of them there
were: one thousand golden cups, one
thousand cups of silver, twenty-nine
censers of silver, thirty vials of gold, and
two thousand four hundred ten of silver,
and one thousand other vessels. 14 So all
the vessels of gold and of silver were
brought up, even five thousand four
hundred and sixty-nine, 15 and were carried
back by Sheshbatsar, together with them of
the captivity, from Bavel to Yerushalayim.

16 But in the time of Artaḥshasta king of
the Parasians, Bishlam, and Mithredath,
and Taveel, and Reḥum the Ba'altethmos,
and Shimshai the scribe, with the others
that were in commission with them,
dwelling in Shom'ron and other places,
wrote to him against those who lived in
Yehudah and Yerushalayim the letter
following:

17 "To king Artaḥshasta our master; Your
servants, Reḥum the storywriter, and
Shimshai the scribe, and the rest of their
council, and the judges that are in the
Hollow of Aram and Phoenicia. 18 Let it
now be known to our master the king, that
the Yehudim that have come up from you
to us, and they are building Yerushalayim,
that rebellious and wicked city, and are
repairing the marketplaces and its walls,
and are laying the foundation of a Temple.
19 Now if this city gets built and its walls
are finished, they will not only refuse to
give tribute, but will even stand up against
kings. 20 And seeing as the things
pertaining to the Temple are now in hand,

we think it wise not to neglect such a
matter, 21 but to speak to our master the
king, to the intent that, if you desire, you
may search in the books of your fathers.

22 "*In them* you shall find the chronicles of
what is written concerning these things, and
shall understand that that city was
rebellious, troubling both kings and cities.
23 And that the Yehudim were rebellious,
and always raised wars there in times past;
and because of this even this city was laid
waste. 24 Therefore, we declare now to you,
O master the king, that if this city is built
again, and its walls set up renewed, you
will from now on have no passage into the
Hollow of Aram and Phoenicia."

25 Then the king wrote back again to
Reḥum the storywriter, and Ba'altethmos,
and Shimshai the scribe, and to the rest that
were in commission, and lived in Shom'ron
and Aram and Phoenicia, after this manner:
26 "I have read the letter which you sent
me. Therefore I commanded to search, and
it has been found that that city of time past
has risen up against kings; 27 and the men
in it were given to rebellion and war, and
that mighty kings and fierce were in
Yerushalayim, who reigned and exacted
tribute in the Hollow of Aram and
Phoenicia. 28 Now therefore I have
commanded that those men cease building
the city, and that heed be taken that there is
nothing done contrary to this order, 29 and
that those wicked doings proceed no further
to the annoyance of kings."

30 Then King Artaḥshasta caused his letters
to be read, and Reḥum, and Shimshai the
scribe, and the rest that were in commission
with them, hurried to Yerushalayim with
horsemen and a multitude of people in
battle array, and began to hinder the
builders. And *thus* the building of the
Temple in Yerushalayim ceased until the
second year of the reign of Daryavesh king
of the Parasians.

3 1 Now King Daryavesh made a great
banquet to all his subjects, and to all that
were born in his house, and to all the
princes of Media and of Paras, 2 and to all
the local governors and captains and
governors that were under him, from Hodu
to Kush, in the one hundred twenty-seven
provinces. 3 And when they had eaten and
drunken, and had gone home satisfied, then
Daryavesh the king went into his
bedchamber, and slept, and awoke out of
his sleep.

4 Then the three young men of the body-
guard, those that guarded the king, spoke
one to another: 5 "Let each of us say one
thing to see what *thing* is strongest, and the
one whose sentence seems wiser than the
others, Daryavesh the king will give great
gifts to, and great honors in token of
victory, 6 such as to be clothed in purple, to
drink in gold, and to sleep on gold, and a
chariot with bridles of gold, and a turban of
fine linen, and a chain around his neck.
7 And he shall sit next to Daryavesh
because of his wisdom, and shall be called
the relative of Daryavesh."

8 And then they each wrote his sentence,
and set to their seals, and laid the writing
under King Daryavesh's pillow, 9 and said,
"When the king arises, some shall give him
the writing; and the one whom the king and
the three princes of Paras shall judge, and
side with, then his sentence is the wisest,
and to him shall the victory be given, as it
is written."

10 The first wrote, "Wine is the strongest."
11 The second wrote, "The king is

strongest."
12 The third wrote, "Women are strongest;
but above all things Truth bears away the
victory.'

13 Now when the king was risen up, they
took the writing, and gave it to him, and so
he read it. **14** And sending forth, he called
all the princes of Paras and of Media, and
the local governors, and the captains, and
the governors, and the chief officers; **15** and
he sat down in the royal seat of judgment,
and the writing was read before them.

16 And he said, "Call the young men, and
they shall explain their own sentences." So
they were called, and came in. **17** And they
said to them, "Declare to us your mind
concerning the things you have written." So
the first, who had spoken of the strength of
wine, started **18** and said, "O sirs, how
exceedingly strong wine is! It causes all
men to err that drink it. **19** It makes the
mind of the king and of the orphan to all be
as one; of the bondservant and of the
freeman, of the poor man and of the rich.
20 It turns also every thought into joy and
gladness, so that a man remembers neither
sorrow nor debt. **21** And it makes every
heart rich, so that a man remembers neither
king nor local governor, and it makes to
speak all things by talents. **22** And when
they are in their cups, they forget their love
both to friends and family, and a little after
draw their swords. **23** But when they awake
from their wine, they do not remember
what they have done. **24** O sirs, is wine not
the strongest, seeing that it enforces to do
so?" And after he had said this, he held his
peace.

4 **1** Then the second, the one who had
spoken of the strength of the king, began to
say, **2** "O sirs, do men not excel in strength,
that bear rule over the sea and land, and all
things in them? **3** And yet the king is even
stronger. He is their master, and *he* has
dominion over them. In whatever he
commands them, they obey him. **4** If he
tells them to make war against one another,
they do it; and if he sends them out against
their enemies, they go, and overcome
mountains, walls, and towers. **5** They kill
and are killed, and do not transgress the
command of the king. If they get the
victory, they bring all to the king, as well
the plunder, and all other things as well.

6 "Likewise for those that are not soldiers,
and have nothing to do with wars, but are
farmers, when they have reaped again that
which they had sown, they bring it to the
king, and compel one another to pay tribute
to the king. **7** And he is but one man; if he
command to kill, they kill; if he command
to spare, they spare; **8** if he command to
strike, they strike; if he command to make
desolate, they make desolate; if he
command to build, they build; **9** if he
command to cut down, they cut down; if he
command to plant, they plant. **10** So all his
people and his armies obey him.
Furthermore he lies down, he eats and
drinks, and takes his rest, **11** and these keep
watch around him. And none may depart
and do his own business, neither do any
disobey him in anything. **12** O sirs, how
should the king be strongest, seeing that in
such sort he is obeyed?" And he held his
peace.

13 Then the third, who had spoken of
women, and of truth, (this was Zerubbavel)
began to speak. **14** "O sirs, is not the king
great, and men are many, and wine is
strong? Who is it then that rules them, or
has rulership over them? Do not women?

15 Women have borne the king and all the
people that bear rule by sea and land.
16 They came forth from them; they
nourished them that planted the vineyards,
from where the wine comes. 17 These also
make garments for men; these bring glory
to men; without women, there can be no
men. 18 Yes, and if men have gathered
together gold and silver and any other good
thing, and see a woman who is well-
favored and beautiful, 19 they let all those
things go, and stare after her, and even with
open mouth fix their eyes fast on her; and
they desire her more than gold or silver, or
any good thing whatsoever. 20 A man
leaves his own father that brought him up,
and his own country, and clings to his wife.
21 And with his wife he ends his days, and
remembers neither father, nor mother, nor
country.

22 "By this also you must know: that
women have dominion over you. Do you
all not labor and toil, and give and bring it
all to women? 23 Yes, a man takes his
sword, and goes forth to make expeditions,
and to rob and to steal, and to sail upon the
sea and upon rivers. 24 And *he* looks upon a
lion, and walks in the darkness; and when
he has stolen, plundered, and robbed, he
brings it to his love. 25 Therefore a man
loves his wife more than father or mother.
26 Yes, there have been many that have
gone out of their minds for women, and
become slaves for their sakes. 27 Many also
have perished, have stumbled, and sinned,
for women. 28 And now do you not believe
me? Is not the king great in his power? Do
not all regions fear to touch him?

29 "Yet I saw him and Apame the king's
concubine, the daughter of the illustrious
Bartakos, sitting at the right hand of the
king; 30 and taking the crown from the
king's head, she set it upon her own head.
Yes, and she struck the king with her left
hand, 31 and then the king stared and gazed
upon her with open mouth. If she laughed
at him, he laughed also; but if she took any
displeasure at him, he was pleased to flatter
her, that she might be reconciled to him
again. 32 O sirs, how can it be, but that
women should be strong, seeing they do
thus?"

33 The king and the nobles looked at one
another, so he began to speak concerning
truth.

34 "O sirs, are not women strong? Great is
the earth, high is the heaven, swift is the
sun in his course, for he encircles the
heavens round about, and fetches his course
again to his own place in one day. 35 Is He
not great, the One who makes these things?
Therefore great is truth, and stronger than
all things. 36 All the earth calls upon truth,
and the heavens bless her. All works shake
and tremble, but with her is no unrighteous
thing. 37 Wine is unrighteous, the king is
unrighteous, women are unrighteous, all the
children of men are unrighteous, and all
their works are unrighteous, and there is no
truth in them; in their unrighteousness also
they shall perish. 38 But truth remains, and
is strong forever; she lives and conquers
forevermore. 39 With her there is no
accepting of persons or rewards; but she
does the things that are just, and refrains
from all unrighteous and wicked things,
and all men do well to perform works like
her *works*. 40 There is no unrighteousness
in her judgment, and she is the strength,
and the kingdom, and the power, and the
majesty, of all ages. Blessed be the Elohim
of Truth."

41 And with that he held his tongue. And all
the people then shouted, and said, "Great is
truth, and strong above all things."

42 Then said the king to him, "Ask what
you desire more than is appointed in
writing, and we will give it you, since you
are found wisest; and you shall sit next to
me, and shall be called my relative."

43 Then he said to the king, "Remember
your vow, which you vowed to build
Yerushalayim, in the day when you came
to your kingdom, 44 and to send away all
the vessels that were taken out of
Yerushalayim, which Koresh set apart,
when he vowed to destroy Bavel, and
vowed to send them again there. 45 You
also vowed to build up the Temple, which
the Edomites burned when Yehudah was
made desolate by the Kaldeans. 46 And
now, O master the king, this is that which I
require, and which I desire of you, and this
is the princely generosity that shall proceed
from you: I ask that you make good on the
vow, the performance of which you have
vowed to the King of Heaven with your
own mouth."

47 Then Daryavesh the king stood up, and
kissed him, and wrote letters for him to all
the treasurers and governors and captains
and local governors, that they should safely
bring on their way both him, and all those
that should go up with him to build
Yerushalayim. 48 He wrote letters also to
all the governors that were in the Hollow of
Aram and Phoenicia, and to them in
Levanon, that they should bring cedar
wood from Levanon to Yerushalayim, and
that they should build the city with him.

49 Moreover he wrote for all the Yehudim
that should go out of his realm up into
Yehudah, and concerning their freedom
that no officer, nor governor, nor local
governor, nor treasurer, should forcibly
enter into their doors; 50 and that all the
country which they occupied should be free
to them without tribute; and that the
Edomites should give over the villages of
the Yehudim which then they held, 51 and
that there should be yearly given twenty
talents to the building of the Temple, until
the time of its building was complete;
52 and another ten talents yearly for burnt
offerings to be presented upon the altar
every day, as they had a command to offer
seventeen *offerings*. 53 And that all those
who should come from Bavel to build the
city should have their freedom, as well they
as their descendants, and all the priests that
came. 54 He wrote also to give them their
charges, and the priests' vestments with
which they minister; 55 and for the Levites
he wrote that their charges should be given
to them until the day that the house was
finished, and Yerushalayim built up.
56 And he commanded to give land and
wages to all that kept the city. 57 He also
sent away all the vessels from Bavel, that
Koresh had set apart; and all that Koresh
had given in command, the same he also
charged to be done, and sent to
Yerushalayim.

58 Now when this young man was gone
forth, he lifted up his face to heaven toward
Yerushalayim, and praised the King of
Heaven, 59 and said, "From You comes
victory, from You comes wisdom, and
Yours is the glory, and I am Your servant.
60 Blessed are You, who have given me
wisdom, and to You I give thanks, O
Master of our fathers."

61 And so he took the letters, and went out,
and came to Bavel, and told it to all his
family. 62 And they praised the Elohim of

their fathers, because He had given them
freedom and liberty 63 to go up, and to
build Yerushalayim, and the Temple which
is called by His Name. and they feasted
with instruments of music and gladness for
seven days.

5 1 After this the chiefs of fathers' houses
were chosen to go up according to their
tribes, with their wives and sons and
daughters, with their manservants and
maidservants, and their cattle. 2 And
Daryavesh sent with them a thousand
horsemen, until they had brought them
back to Yerushalayim in peace, and with
musical instruments, timbrels and flutes.
3 And all their brethren played, and he
made them go up together with them.

4 And these are the names of the men
which went up, according to their families
among their tribes, after their several
divisions. 5 The priests, the sons of
Pineḥas, the sons of Aharon: Yehoshua the
son of Yehotsadaq, the son of Serayah, and
Yehoyaqim the son of Zerubbavel, the son
of Shealti'el, of the house of David, of the
lineage of Perets, of the tribe of Yehudah;
6 who spoke wise sentences before
Daryavesh the king of Paras in the second
year of his reign, in the month Nisan,
which is the first month.

7 And these are the Yehudim that came up
from the captivity, where they lived as
strangers, whom Nevukhadnetsar the king
of Bavel had carried away to Bavel. 8 And
they returned to Yerushalayim, and to the
other parts of Yehudah, every man to his
own city, who came with Zerubbavel and
with Yehoshua: Neḥemyah, and Zeraḥyah,
Reelyah[a], Naḥamani[b], Mordekhai, Bilshan,
Mispar, Bigvai[c], Reḥum[d], and Ba'anah,
their leaders. 9 The number of those of the
nation, and their leaders: the children of
Parosh, two thousand one hundred and
seventy-two. The children of Shephatyah,
three[e] hundred and seventy-two. 10 The
children of Araḥ, seven hundred and fifty-
six.[f] 11 The children of Paḥath-Moav, of the
children of Yeshua and Yoav, two thousand
eight hundred and twelve[g]. 12 The children
of Elam, one thousand two hundred and

---

[a] 5:8 This name is given as Reelyah in Ezra 2:2, but is named Ra'amyah in Neḥemyah 7:7. I have chosen Reelyah here, as it is closest to the Greek form that is recorded, which is Resaias.

[b] 5:8 This name is given as Eneneus in Greek, though it is the only other name corresponding to the list of 12 leaders given in Neḥemyah 7:7. Ezra does not list the 12th leader in Ezra 2.

[c] 5:8 This name is given as Reelias in Greek. However, its placement (and lack of other corresponding names) indicates it corresponds to Bigvai. Both Neḥemyah 7:7 and Ezra 2:2 give the name as Bigvai. Most likely, the name is a corrupted form of Reelyah, as mentioned in footnote a. This was probably caused by scribal error, inadvertently copying the wrong name.

[d] 5:8 This name is given as Romias in Greek. This corresponds to the name Reḥum from Ezra 2:2; however, Neḥemyah 7:7 gives this name as Neḥum.

[e] 5:9 Greek texts records this number as four hundred. The Latin text omits this entirely. Neḥemyah 7:9 and Ezra 2:4 both give this number as three hundred, as does the Greek version of Ezra and Neḥemyah. I have restored the reading of three hundred based on these. Likely caused by a scribal error.

[f] 5:10 Greek text records the number as given here. Ezra 2:5 states there were 775 from Araḥ, while Neḥemyah 7:10 reads 652. Latin text reads 757.

[g] 5:11 Greek text records this number as given here. This agrees with Ezra 2:6. However, Neḥemyah 7:11 reads 2,818. Latin text reads 2,302.

fifty-four. The children of Zattu, nine[a]
hundred and forty-five. The children of
Zakkai, seven hundred and five[b]. The
children of Bani, six hundred and forty-
eight.[c] **13** The children of Bevai, six
hundred and twenty-three.[d] The children of
Azgad, one thousand three hundred and
twenty-two.[e] **14** The children of Adoniqam,
six hundred and sixty-seven.[f] The children
of Bigvai, two thousand and sixty-six.[g] The
children of Adin, four hundred and fifty-
four.

15 The children of Ater, of Ḥizqiyah,
ninety-two.[h] The children of Kilan and
Azetas, sixty-seven. The children of Azzur,
four hundred and thirty-two. **16** The
children of Annis, one hundred and one.
The children of Arom, of the children of
Betsai, three hundred and twenty-three.[i]
The children of Arsiphurith, one hundred
and twelve. **17** The children of Baiterus,
three thousand and five. The children of
Beth-leḥem, one hundred and twenty-three.
18 Those from Netophah, fifty-five.[j] Those
from Anathoth, one hundred and fifty-
eight. Those from Beth-azmaveth, forty-
two. **19** Those from Qiryath-Yearim,
twenty-five. Those from Kephirah and
Veeroth, seven hundred and forty-three.[k]
20 Those from Ḥadiasai and Ammidioi,
four hundred and twenty-two. Those from
Ramah and Gava, six hundred and twenty-
one. **21** Those from Mikhmas, one hundred
and twenty-two. Those from Beth-El, fifty-
two. The children of Niphis, one hundred
and fifty-six.

22 The children of Lod, and Ḥadid, and
Ono, seven hundred and twenty-five.[l] The
children of Yeriḥo, three hundred and
forty-five. **23** The children of Sena'ah, three
thousand three hundred[m] and thirty.

24 The priests: the children of Yedayah, the
son of Yeshua, among the children of

---

[a] 5:12 Greek text records this number as given here. This agrees with Ezra 2:8. However, Neḥemyah 7:13 reads 845.

[b] 5:12 Greek text records this number as given here. Both Ezra and Neḥemyah record this as 760. Latin text reads 1,205.

[c] 5:12 Greek text records this number as given here. This agrees with the Latin text as well as with Neḥemyah 7:15. However, Ezra 2:10 records this as 642.

[d] 5:13 Greek text records this number as given here. This agrees with Ezra 2:11. However, Neḥemyah 7:16 records this as 628. Latin text reads 603.

[e] 5:13 Greek text records this number as given here. This agrees with Neḥemyah 7:17. However, Ezra 2:12 records this as 1,222. Latin text reads 427.

[f] 5:14 Greek text records this number as given here. This agrees with Neḥemyah 7:18. However, Ezra 2:13 records this as 666. Latin text reads 37.

[g] 5:14 Greek text records this number as given here. This agrees with the Latin text. However, Ezra 2:14 records this as 2,056; Neḥemyah 7:19 records this as 2,067.

[h] 5:15 Greek text records this number as given here. However, Ezra 2:16 and Neḥemyah 7:20 record this as 98. Latin texts reads 108.

[i] 5:16 Greek text records this number as given here. This agrees with Ezra 2:17. However, Neḥemyah 7:23 records this as 324. Latin text omits.

[j] 5:18 Greek text records this number as given here. This agrees with the Latin text. However, Ezra 2:22 records this as 56.

[k] 5:19 Greek text records this number as given here. However, Ezra 2:15 and Neḥemyah 7:29 record the number 743 as including the 25 from Qiryath-Yearim.

[l] 5:22 Greek text records this number as given here. This agrees with Ezra 2:33; however, Neḥemyah 7:37 records this as 721.

[m] 5:23 Greek text records this number as given here. Ezra 2:35 records this as 3,630, while Neḥemyah 7:38 records this as 3,930.

Elyashiv[a], nine hundred and seventy-two.[b]
The children of Immer, one thousand and
fifty-two. **25** The children of Pashchur, one
thousand two hundred and forty-seven. The
children of Charme, one thousand and
seventeen.

26 The Levites: the sons of Yeshua, of
Qadmi'el, and Bannah, and Sudyah,
seventy-four.[c]

27 The set-apart singers: the children of
Asaph, one hundred and twenty-eight.[d]

28 The gatekeepers: the children of
Shallum, the children of Ater, the children
of Talmon, the children of Aqquv, the
children of Ḥatita, the children of Shovai,
in all one hundred and thirty-nine.[e]

29 The Temple servants: the children of
Tsiḥa, the children of Ḥasupha, the children
of Tabbaoth, the children of Qeros, the
children of Siaha, the children of Padon,
the children of Levanah, the children of
Ḥagavah. **30** The children of Aqquv, the
children of Uta[f], the children of Ketav, the
children of Ḥagav, the children of Shalmai,
the children of Ḥanan, the children of
Giddel, the children of Gaḥar, **31** the
children of Yair, the children of Retsin, the
children of Neqoda, the children of Ḥaseva,
the children of Gazzam, the children of
Uzza, the children of Paseaḥ, the children
of Azara, the children of Besai, the children
of Asnah, the children of Meunim, the
children of Nephisesim, the children of
Vaqbuq, the children of Ḥaqupha, the
children of Ḥarchur, the children of
Paraqim, the children of Batslit, **32** the
children of Meḥida, the children of Koutha,
the children of Ḥarsha, the children of
Varqos, the children of Sisera, the children
of Tamaḥ, the children of Netsiaḥ, the
children of Ḥatipha.

33 The children of the servants of
Shelomoh: the children of Sophereth, the
children of Perida, the children of Ya'alah,
the children of Darqon, the children of
Giddel, the children of Shephatyah, **34** the
children of Ḥattil, the children of
Pokhereth-Tsevayim[g], the children of
Sarothei, the children of Masias, the
children of Ga'ash, the children of Addus,
the children of Subas, the children of
Apherra, the children of Barodis, the
children of Shephatyah, the children of
Allon. **35** All the Temple-servants, and the
children of the servants of Shelomoh, were
three hundred and seventy-two.[h]

---

[a] 5:24 Greek text records this name as Sanasib. This does not correspond to any name from Ezra or Neḥemyah. The Latin text preserves this name as Eliasib, which is a form of the Hebrew name Elyashiv, as it has been rendered here.

[b] 5:24 Greek text records this number as given here. Both Ezra and Neḥemyah record this as 973. Latin text reads 872.

[c] 5:26 In Ezra and Neḥemyah the names Bannah and Sudyah are not listed, but rather one name is given: Hodavyah. The number of descendants, however, is the same.

[d] 5:27 Greek text records this number as given here. This agrees with Ezra 2:41; however, Neḥemyah 7:44 records this as 148.

[e] 5:28 Greek text records this number as given here. This agrees with Ezra 2:42; however, Neḥemyah 7:45 records this as 138. Latin text reads 128.

[f] 5:30 Uta appears to be a corruption of the name name Aqquv, which in Greek is written Akud. This was most likely caused by a scribal error of accidental repetition, known as dittography.

[g] 5:34 Most Greek and Latin texts record two separate names here: Phakareth and Sabie. However, Codex Vaticanus correctly renders it as one name, as is found in Ezra 2:57 and Neḥemyah 7:59.

[h] 5:35 Greek text records this number as given here. Ezra and Neḥemyah both read 392. Latin text reads 482.

36 These came up from Tel-Melaḥ, and Tel-
Ḥarsha, Ḥara'athalan[a] leading them, and
Allar; 37 but they could not show their
father's house, nor *could* their seed, how
they were of Yisra'el. The children of Delayah, the children of Toviyah, the children of Neqoda, six hundred and fifty-two[b].

38 And of the priests, those who usurped the office of the priesthood and were not found: the children of Ḥavayah, the children of Qots, the children of Barzillai, who married Augia one of the daughters of Barzillai, and was called after his name.

39 And when the description of the families of these men was sought in the register, and was not found, they were removed from executing the office of the priesthood.
40 And Neḥemyah and Attharias told them that they would not be partakers of the set-apart things, until a high priest rose up wearing the Urim and Thummim.

41 So all those of Yisra'el, from twelve years old and upward, beside manservants and maidservants, were forty-two thousand
three hundred and sixty. 42 Their
manservants and maidservants were seven thousand three hundred and thirty-seven. The musicians and singers, two hundred
and forty-five.[c] 43 *Along with* four hundred
and thirty-five camels, seven thousand and thirty-six horses,[d] two hundred and forty-five mules, and five thousand five hundred
and twenty-five donkeys.[e] 44 And certain of
the chief men of their families, when they came to the Temple of Elohim that is in Yerushalayim, vowed to set the House up again in its own place according to their
ability, 45 and to give one thousand
drachmas of gold, five thousand *drachmas* of silver, and one hundred priestly garments into the set-apart treasury of the
work. 46 And the priests and the Levites
and those who were of the people lived in Yerushalayim and the country; the set-apart singers also and the gatekeepers and all Yisra'el in their villages.

47 But when the seventh month came, and when the children of Yisra'el were each in their own place, they all came together as one man into the broad place before the first porch which is toward the east.
48 Then Yeshua the son of Yehotsadaq stood up, and his brothers the priests, and Zerubbavel the son of Shealti'el, and his brothers, and they built the altar of the
Elohim of Yisra'el, 49 to offer burnt
offerings on it, as it is written in the Torah
of Mosheh the man of Elohim. 50 And
certain were gathered to them out of the other nations of the land, and they built the altar in its own place, because they were terrified of all the nations of the land, and *the nations* oppressed them; and they offered slaughterings according to the time, and burnt offerings to יהוה both morning and evening.

---

[a] 5:36 Ḥara'athalan – Most likely a Greek corruption of the three Hebrew names Ḥeruv, Addon, and Immer.
[b] 5:37 Greek text records this number as given here. This agrees with Ezra 2:60; however, Neḥemyah 7:62 records this as 642. Latin text records this as 1,052.
[c] 5:42 Greek text records this number as given here. This agrees with Neḥemyah 7:67; however, Ezra 2:65 reads 200. Latin text reads 265.
[d] 5:43 Greek text records this number as given here. This agrees with the Latin text. Ezra 2 and Neḥemyah 7 both record this as 736.
[e] 5:43 Greek text records this number as given here. This agrees with the Latin text. Ezra 2 and Neḥemyah 7 both record this as 6,720.

51 Also they kept the Feast of Tabernacles,
as it is commanded in the Torah, and
offered slaughterings daily, as was wise.
52 And after that, the continual offerings,
and the offerings of the Sabbaths, and of
the new moons, and of all the set apart
Feasts. 53 And all those who had made any
vow to Elohim began to offer slaughterings
to Elohim from the new moon of the
seventh month, although the Temple of
Elohim was not yet built. 54 And they gave
money to the stone-cutters and carpenters;
and meat and drink, 55 and wagons to those
from Tsidon and Tsor, that they should
bring cedar trees from Levanon, and
convey them in floats to the port of Yapho,
according to the command which was
written for them by Koresh king of the
Parasians.

56 And in the second year after his coming
to the Temple of Elohim at Yerushalayim,
in the second month, Zerubbavel the son of
Shealti'el, and Yeshua the son of
Yehotsadaq, and their brothers, and the
priests the Levites, and all those who were
come to Yerushalayim out of the captivity,
57 began to lay the foundation of the
Temple of Elohim on the new moon of the
second month, in the second year after they
came to Yehudah and Yerushalayim.
58 And they appointed the Levites from
twenty years old *and above* over the works
of יהוה. Then Yeshua stood up, and his
sons and brothers with him, and Qadmi'el
his brother, and the sons of Yeshua,
Ḥenadad, and the sons of Ḥodavyah the son
of Ḥenadad, and their sons and brothers, all
the Levites, with one accord, those who
worked business, laboring to advance the
works in the House of Elohim. So the
builders built the Temple of יהוה. 59 And
the priests stood arrayed in their garments
with musical instruments and trumpets, and
the Levites the sons of Asaph with their
cymbals, 60 singing songs of thanksgiving,
and praising יהוה, after the order of David,
king of Yisra'el.

61 And they sang aloud, praising יהוה in
songs of thanksgiving, because His
goodness and His glory are everlasting in
all Yisra'el. 62 And all the people sounded
trumpets, and shouted with a loud voice,
singing songs of thanksgiving to יהוה for
the raising up of the House of יהוה. 63 Also
of the priests the Levites, and of the heads
of their families, the ancients who had seen
the former house, came to the building of
this with lamentation and great weeping.
64 But many with trumpets and joy shouted
with loud voice, 65 so much that the people
could not hear the trumpets for the weeping
of the people; for the multitude sounded
greatly, so that it was heard far away.

66 Therefore when the enemies of the tribe
of Yehudah and Benyamin heard it, they
came to inquire what the noise of the
trumpets meant. 67 And they saw that those
who were of the captivity were building the
Temple of יהוה, the Elohim of Yisra'el.
68 So they went to Zerubbavel and Yeshua,
and to the chief men of the families, and
said to them, "We will build together with
you. 69 For we, like you, obey יהוה, and
slaughter to him from the days of Esar-
Ḥaddon the king of the Ashuwrites, who
brought us here."

70 Then Zerubbavel and Yeshua and the
chief men of the families of Yisra'el said to
them, "It is not for you to build the House
to יהוה our Elohim. 71 We ourselves alone
will build *it* to the Elohim of Yisra'el,

according to the command of Koresh the king of the Parasians."

72 But the heathens of the land laid heavy
upon the inhabitants of Yehudah, and
weakened their hands, and thus hindered
their building. 73 And by their secret plots,
and popular persuasions and commotions,
they hindered the finishing of the building
all the time that King Koresh lived; so they
were hindered from building for two years'
time, until the reign of Daryavesh.

6 1 Now in the second year of the reign of
Daryavesh, Ḥaggai and Zekharyah the son
of Iddo, the prophets,[a] prophesied to the
Yehudim in Yehudah and Yerushalayim; in
the name of יהוה, the Elohim of Yisra'el,
they prophesied to them. 2 Then
Zerubbavel the son of Shealti'el stood up,
and Yeshua the son of Yehotsadaq with
him, and they began to build the House of
Elohim at Yerushalayim; the prophets of
Elohim were with them, and helped them.

3 At the same time Tattenai the governor of
Aram and Phoenicia came to them, with
Shethar-Boznai and his companions, and
said to them, 4 "By whose authority do you
build this house and this roof, and perform
all these other things? And who are the
builders that perform these things?"

5 Nevertheless the elders of the Yehudim
obtained favor, because יהוה had visited
the captivity; 6 and they were not hindered
from building, until such time as
communication was made to Daryavesh
concerning them, and his answer signified.

7 The copy of the letter which Tattenai, governor of Aram and Phoenicia, and Shethar-Boznai, with their companions, the rulers in Aram and Phoenicia, wrote and sent to Daryavesh:

8 "To King Daryavesh, greetings. Let all
things be known to our master the king,
that having come into the country of
Yehudah, and entered into the city of
Yerushalayim, we found in the city of
Yerushalayim the elders of the Yehudim
that were of the captivity 9 building a house
to יהוה, great and renewed, of hewn and
costly stones, with timber laid in the walls.
10 And those works are done with great
speed, and the work goes on successfully in
their hands, and with all glory and
diligence it is accomplished. 11 Then asked
we these elders, saying, 'By whose
command do you build this House, and lay
the foundations of these works?'
12 Therefore, to the intent that we might
give knowledge to you by writing who
were the chief workers, we questioned
them, and we required of them the names in
writing of their principal men. 13 So they
gave us this answer, 'We are the servants of
יהוה, who made heaven and earth. 14 And
as for this House, it was built many years
ago by a great and strong king of Yisra'el,
and was complete. 15 But when our fathers
sinned against the Elohim of Yisra'el who
is in heaven, and provoked Him to wrath,
He gave them over into the hands of
Nevukhadnetsar king of Bavel, king of the
Kaldeans. 16 And the *Kaldeans* pulled
down the house, and burned it, and carried
the people away as captives to Bavel.
17 But in the first year that Koresh reigned

[a] 6:1 Ḥaggai and Zekharyah – The two prophets who also wrote their respective books of the Bible.

over the country of Bavel, king Koresh
wrote to build up this house. 18 And the set-
apart vessels of gold and of silver, that
Nevukhadnetsar had carried away out of
the House at Yerushalayim, and had set up
in his own temple, those Koresh the king
brought forth again out of the temple in
Bavel, and they were delivered to
Zerubbavel and to Sheshbatsar the
governor, 19 with command that he should
carry away all these vessels, and put them
in the Temple at Yerushalayim; and that the
Temple of יהוה should be built in its place.
20 Then Sheshbatsar, having come here,
laid the foundations of the House of יהוה
which is in Yerushalayim; and from that
time to this, still being built, it is not yet
fully complete.'

21 "Now therefore, if it seems good, O
king, search among the royal archives of
our master the king that are in Bavel; 22 and
if it is found that the building of the House
of יהוה which is in Yerushalayim has been
done with the consent of king Koresh, and
it seems good to our master the king, let
him signify this *fact* to us."

23 Then King Daryavesh commanded that
the archives that were laid up at Bavel be
examined; and so at Aḥmetha, at the
palace, which is in the country of Media,
there was found a scroll in which these
things were written: 24 "In the first year of
the reign of Koresh, King Koresh
commanded to build up the House of יהוה
which is in Yerushalayim, where they
slaughter with continual fire, 25 whose
height will be sixty cubits, and the width
sixty cubits, with three rows of hewn
stones, and one row of new wood of that
country; and the expenses of it are to be
given out of the house of King Koresh.
26 And that the set-apart vessels of the
House of יהוה, both gold and silver, that
Nevukhadnetsar took out of the House at
Yerushalayim, and carried away to Bavel,
should be restored to the House at
Yerushalayim, and be set in the place
where they were before."

27 And so he commanded that Tattenai the
governor of Aram and Phoenicia, and
Shethar-Boznai, and their companions, and
those which were appointed rulers in Aram
and Phoenicia, should be careful not to
meddle with the place, but allow
Zerubbavel, the servant of יהוה, and
governor of Yehudah, and the elders of the
Yehudim, to build the House of יהוה in its
place.

28 "And I also command to have it built up
whole again, and that they look diligently
to help those that be of the captivity of
Yehudah, until the House of יהוה be
finished. 29 And out of the tribute of the
Hollow of Aram and Phoenicia a portion
shall be carefully given these men for the
slaughterings to יהוה, that is, *given* to
Zerubbavel the governor, for bulls, and
rams, and lambs; 30 and also grain, salt,
wine, and oil, and that continually every
year without further question, according as
the priests that be in Yerushalayim shall
signify to be daily spent, 31 that drink
offerings may be made to the El Elyon for
the king and for his children, and that they
may pray for their lives. 32 And a command
shall be given that whoever transgresses,
yes, or neglects anything written here, out
of his own house shall a tree be taken, and
he shall be hanged on it, and all his goods
seized for the king.

33 Therefore יהוה, whose Name is there
called upon, shall utterly destroy every king
and nation, that shall stretch out his hand to
hinder or damage that House of יהוה in
Yerushalayim. 34 I Daryavesh the king
have ordained that according to these
things it be done with diligence."

7 1 Then Tattenai the governor of the
Hollow of Aram and Phoenicia, and
Shethar-Boznai, with their companions,
following the commands of king
Daryavesh, 2 very carefully oversaw the
set-apart works, assisting the elders of the
Yehudim and rulers of the Temple. 3 And
so the set-apart works prospered, while
Ḥaggai and Zekharyah the prophets
prophesied.

4 And they finished these things by the
command of יהוה, the Elohim of Yisra'el,
and with the consent of Koresh, Daryavesh,
and Artaḥshasta, kings of the Parasians.
5 And thus was the House finished by the
twenty-third day of the month Adar, in the
sixth year of king Daryavesh. 6 And the
children of Yisra'el, the priests, and the
Levites, and the others that were of the
captivity that were added to them, did
according to the things written in the book
of Mosheh.

7 And for the dedication of the Temple of
יהוה they offered a hundred bulls, two
hundred rams, four hundred lambs, 8 and
twelve he-goats for the sin of all Yisra'el,
according to the number of the twelve
princes of the tribes of Yisra'el. 9 The
priests also and the Levites stood arrayed in
their garments, according to their families,
for the services of יהוה, the Elohim of
Yisra'el, according to the book of Mosheh;
and the gatekeepers at every gate.

10 And the children of Yisra'el that came
out of the captivity kept the Pesaḥ on the
fourteenth day of the first month, when the
priests and the Levites were set apart
together, 11 and all those who were of the
captivity; for they were set apart. For the
Levites were all set apart together, 12 and
they offered the Pesaḥ for all those of the
captivity, and for their brothers the priests,
and for themselves. 13 And the children of
Yisra'el that came out of the captivity ate,
even all those who had separated
themselves from the abominations of the
heathens of the land, and sought יהוה.
14 And they kept the Feast of Unleavened
Bread seven days, being joyful before
יהוה, 15 for He had turned the counsel of
the king of Ashuwr toward them, to
strengthen their hands in the works of
יהוה, the Elohim of Yisra'el.

8 1 And after these things, when
Artaḥshasta the king of the Parasians
reigned, came Ezra the son of Serayah, the
son of Azaryah, the son of Ḥilqiyahu, the
son of Shallum, 2 the son of Tsadoq, the
son of Aḥituv, the son of Amaryah, the son
of Azaryah, the son of Merayoth, the son of
Zeraḥyah, the son of Uzzi, the son of
Buqqi, the son of Avishua, the son of
Pineḥas, the son of Elazar, the son of
Aharon, the chief priest.

3 This Ezra went up from Bavel, being a
ready scribe in the Torah of Mosheh that
was given by the Elohim of Yisra'el. 4 And
the king honored him, for he found favor in
his eyes in all his requests. 5 There went up
with him also certain of the children of
Yisra'el, and of the priests, and Levites, and

set-apart singers, and gatekeepers, and
temple servants, to Yerushalayim, 6 in the
seventh year of the reign of Artaḥshasta, in
the fifth month, being the king's seventh
year. For they went from Bavel on the new
moon of the first month, and came to
Yerushalayim, according to the successful
journey which יהוה gave them for His
sake. 7 For Ezra had very great skill, so that
he omitted nothing of the Torah and
commands of יהוה, but taught all Yisra'el
the statutes and judgments.

8 Now the commission, which was written
from Artaḥshasta the king, came to Ezra the
priest and reader of the Torah of יהוה, and
this that follows is a copy *of that letter*:

9 "King Artaḥshasta to Ezra the priest and
reader of the Torah of יהוה, greetings.
10 Having determined to deal favorably, I
have given order, that such of the nation of
the Yehudim, and of the priests and
Levites, and of those within our realm, as
are willing and who desire, should go with
you to Yerushalayim. 11 As many as have a
mind to do so, let them depart with you, as
it has seemed good both to me and my
seven friends the counselors, 12 that they
may look to the affairs of Yehudah and
Yerushalayim agreeably to that which is in
the Torah of יהוה, 13 and carry the gifts to
the Elohim of Yisra'el to Yerushalayim,
which I and my friends have vowed; and
that all the gold and silver that can be found
in the country of Bavel for יהוה in
Yerushalayim, 14 with that also which is
given from the people for the Temple of
יהוה their Elohim that is at Yerushalayim,
be collected; even the gold and silver for
bulls, rams, and lambs, and things that
pertain to them; 15 to the end that they may
offer slaughterings to יהוה upon the altar
of יהוה their Elohim, which is in
Yerushalayim. 16 And whatever you and
your brothers decide to do with gold and
silver, do so, according to the will of your
Elohim.

17 "And the set-apart vessels of יהוה,
which are given to you for the use of the
Temple of your Elohim, which is in
Yerushalayim, 18 and whatever other thing
you shall remember for the use of the
Temple of your Elohim, you shall give it
out of the king's treasury. 19 And, I King
Artaḥshasta, have also commanded the
keepers of the treasuries in Aram and
Phoenicia, that whatever Ezra the priest and
reader of the Torah of the El Elyon sends
for, they should give it him with all
diligence, 20 to the sum of a hundred talents
of silver, and also of wheat even to a
hundred measures, and a hundred skins of
wine, and salt in abundance. 21 Let all
things be performed according to the Torah
of Elohim diligently to El Elyon, that wrath
may not come upon the kingdom of the
king and his sons.

22 "I command you also, that no tax, nor
any other imposition, shall be laid upon any
of the priests, or Levites, or set-apart
singers, or gatekeepers, or Temple servants,
or any that have employment in this
Temple, and that no man have authority to
impose anything upon them. 23 And you,
Ezra, according to the wisdom of Elohim,
ordain judges and rulers, that they may
judge in all Aram and Phoenicia all those
that know the Torah of your Elohim; and
those that do not know it, you shall teach.
24 And whoever transgresses the Torah of
your Elohim, and of the king, shall be
punished severely, whether it be by death,

or other punishment, by penalty of money,
or by imprisonment."

25 Then Ezra the scribe said, "Blessed be
יהוה, the Elohim of my fathers, who has
put these things into the heart of the king,
to glorify His House that is in
Yerushalayim. 26 And *He* has honored me
in the eyes of the king and his counselors
and all his friends and nobles. 27 Therefore
I was encouraged by the help of יהוה my
Elohim, and gathered men together out of
Yisra'el to go up with me. 28 And these are
the chief according to their families and
their several divisions, that went up with
me from Bavel in the reign of king
Artaḥshasta:

29 Of the sons of Pineḥas, Gershom. Of the
sons of Ithamar, Dani'el. Of the sons of
David, Ḥattush. Of the sons of Shekhanyah,
30 *who was* of the sons of Parosh,
Zekharyah, and with him were counted one
hundred and fifty men. 31 Of the sons of
Paḥath-Moav, Elyehoenai, the son of
Zeraḥyah, and with him two hundred men.
32 Of the sons of Shekhanyah the son of
Yaḥazi'el, and with him three hundred men.
Of the sons of Adin, Eved, the son of
Yonathan, and with him two hundred and
fifty men.[a] 33 Of the sons of Elam,
Yeshayah son of Athalyah, and Gotholyah,
and with him seventy men. 34 of the sons of
Shephatyah, Zevadyah, the son of Mikha'el,
and with him seventy men.[b] 35 Of the sons
of Yoav, Ovadyah the son of Yeḥi'el, and
with him two hundred and twelve men.[c]

36 Of the sons of Benayah, Shelomith son
of Yosiphyah, and with him one hundred
and sixty men. 37 Of the sons of Bevai,
Zekharyah son of Bevai, and with him
twenty-eight men. 38 Of the sons of Azgad,
Yoḥanan son of Haqqatan, and with him
one hundred and ten men. 39 Of the sons of
Adoniqam, the last, and these are their
names, Eliphelet, Yei'el, and Shemayah,
and with them seventy men.[d] 40 Of the sons
of Bigvai, Uthai the son of Zavud, and with
him seventy men.

41 And I gathered them together to the river
called Theras; and there we pitched our
tents three days, and I surveyed them.
42 But when I had not found there any of
the priests and Levites, 43 I sent to Elazar,
and Ari'el, and Shemayah, 44 and Elnathan,
and Yariv, and Elnathan, and Nathan, and
Zekharyah, and Meshullam, leading men,
and men of understanding. 45 And I told
them that they should go to Iddo, the
captain, who was in the place of Kasiphya,
the treasury; 46 and I commanded them that
they should speak to Iddo, and to his
brothers, and to the treasurers in that place,
to send us such men as might execute the
priests' office in the House of יהוה.

47 And by the mighty hand of יהוה they
brought to us men of understanding of the
sons of Maḥli the son of Levi, the son of
Yisra'el, Sherevyah, and his sons, and his
brother, who were eighteen. 48 And
Ḥashavyah, and Annuus, and Yeshayah his
brother, of the sons of Merari, and their
sons were twenty men. 49 And of the
Temple-servants whom David and the
leading men had appointed for the servants
of the Levites, two hundred and twenty
Temple-servants, the catalogue of all their
names was showed.

---

[a] 8:32 Ezra 8:6 records this number as 50.
[b] 8:34 Ezra 8:8 records this number as 80.
[c] 8:35 Ezra 8:9 records this number as 218.
[d] 8:39 Ezra 8:13 records this number as 60.

50 And there I vowed a fast for the young
men before יהוה, to desire a successful
journey from Him, both for us and for our
children and cattle that were with us. 51 For
I was ashamed to ask for soldiers from the
king, and horsemen, and guard for safety
against our adversaries. 52 For we had said
to the king that the power of our Elohim
would be with those who seek Him, to
support them in all ways. 53 And again we
sought יהוה concerning these things, and
found Him favorable to us.

54 Then I separated twelve men of the
chiefs of the priests, Sherevyah, and
Ḥashavyah, and ten of their brothers with
them. 55 And I weighed the silver to them,
and the gold, and the set-apart vessels of
the House of יהוה, which the king and his
counselors and the nobles and all Yisra'el
had given. 56 And when I had weighed it, I
delivered six hundred and fifty talents of
silver to them, and silver vessels of a
hundred talents, and a hundred talents of
gold, 57 and twenty golden vessels, and
twelve vessels of copper, even of fine
copper, glittering like gold.

58 And I said to them, "Both of you are set-
apart to יהוה, and the vessels are set-apart,
and the gold and the silver are a vow to
יהוה, Elohim of our fathers. 59 Therefore
watch, and guard them until you deliver
them to the chief priests and Levites, and to
the leading men of the families of Yisra'el,
in Yerushalayim, in the chambers of the
House of יהוה."

60 So the priests and the Levites, who
received the silver and the gold and the
vessels which were in Yerushalayim,
brought them into the Temple of יהוה.

61 And from the river Theras we departed
the twelfth day of the first month, until we
came to Yerushalayim, by the mighty hand
of יהוה which was upon us, and יהוה
delivered us from assault by the way, from
every enemy, and so we came to
Yerushalayim. 62 And when we had been
there three days, the silver and gold was
weighed and delivered to the House of
יהוה on the fourth day to Meremoth the
priest the son of Uriyah. 63 And with him
was Elazar the son of Pineḥas, and with
them were Yozavad the son of Yeshua and
Noadyah the son of Binnui, the Levite; and
all was delivered to them by number and
weight. 64 And all the weight of them was
written up the same hour. 65 Moreover
those who came out of the captivity offered
slaughterings to יהוה, the Elohim of
Yisra'el, even twelve bulls for all Yisra'el,
and ninety-six rams, 66 seventy-two lambs,[a]
and twelve goats for a peace offering; all of
them a slaughtering to יהוה. 67 And they
delivered the king's commands to the king's
stewards, and to the governors of the
Hollow of Aram and Phoenicia; and they
honored the people and the Temple of
יהוה.

68 Now when these things were done, the
leading men came to me, and said, 69 "The
nation of Yisra'el, and the princes, and the
priests, and the Levites have not put away
from them the strange people of the land,
nor the uncleanness of the nations, that is,
the Kana'anites, Ḥittites, Perizzites,
Yevusites, the Moavites, Mitsrites, and
Edomites. 70 For both they and their sons

[a] 8:66 Ezra 8:35 records this number as 77.

have married with their daughters, and the
set-apart seed is mixed with the strange
people of the land; and from the beginning
of this, the rulers and the nobles have taken
part in this lawlessness."

71 And as soon as I had heard these things,
I tore my clothes, and my set-apart
garment, and plucked the hair from off my
head and beard, and sat down in sadness
and heaviness. 72 So all those who were
moved at the word of יהוה, the Elohim of
Yisra'el, assembled to me, while I mourned
for this lawlessness. But I sat still, full of
heaviness until the evening slaughtering.
73 Then, rising up from the fast with my
clothes and my set-apart garment torn, and
bowing my knees, and stretching forth my
hands to יהוה, 74 I said, "O יהוה, I am
ashamed and confounded before Your face;
75 for our sins are multiplied above our
heads, and our errors have reached up to
heaven, 76 ever since the time of our
fathers. We are in great sin, even to this
day. 77 And for our sins and our fathers'
sins we, with our families and our kings
and our priests, were given up to the kings
of the earth, to the sword, and to captivity,
and for plunder with shame, even to today.

78 "And now in some measure You have
shown favor to us, O יהוה, that there
should a root left to us, and a name in the
place of Your dwelling; 79 and to reveal to
us a light in the House of יהוה our Elohim,
and to give us food in the time of our
servitude. 80 Yes, when we were in
bondage, we were not forsaken by our
Elohim; but He made us favorable before
the kings of Paras, so that they gave us
food, 81 and glorified the Temple of our
Elohim, and raised up the desolate Tsion, to
give us a sure dwelling in Yehudah and
Yerushalayim.

82 "And now, O יהוה, what shall we say,
having these things? For we have
transgressed Your commands, which You
gave by the hand of Your servants the
prophets, saying, 83 'The land which you
enter into to possess as an inheritance, is a
land polluted with the pollutions of the
strangers of the land, and they have filled it
with their uncleanness. 84 Now therefore
you shall not join your daughters to their
sons, neither shall you take their daughters
to your sons. 85 You shall not seek to have
peace with them forever, that you may be
strong, and eat the good things of the land,
and that you may leave it for an inheritance
to your children for evermore.'

86 "And all that has happened has been so
because of our wicked works and great
sins; for You, O יהוה, made our sins as
nothing, 87 and gave us such a root; but we
have turned back again to transgress Your
Torah, in mingling ourselves with the
uncleanness of the heathens of the land.
88 You were not angry with us to destroy
us, until you had left us neither root, seed,
nor name. 89 O Elohim of Yisra'el, You are
true, for we are left a root this day.
90 Behold, now are we before You in our
lawlessness, for we cannot stand before
You anymore because of these things."

91 And as Ezra made his confession in
prayer, with weeping, and lying flat upon
the ground before the Temple, a very great
throng of men and women and children
gathered to him from Yerushalayim, for
there was great weeping among the
multitude. 92 Then Shekhanyah the son of
Yeḥi'el, one of the sons of Yisra'el, called
out, and said, "O Ezra, we have sinned

against יהוה Elohim, we have married strange women of the heathens of the land, yet now Yisra'el has hope. 93 Let us make an oath to יהוה now, that we will put away all our *foreign* wives which we have taken of the strangers, with their children, 94 as it seems good to you and to those who obey the Torah of יהוה. 95 Arise, and do it: for this matter pertains to you, and we will be with you to do valiantly."

96 So Ezra arose, and took an oath of the chief of the priests and Levites of all Yisra'el to do after these things; and so they swore.

9 1 Then Ezra, rising from the court of the Temple, went to the chamber of Yehoḥanan the son of Elyashiv, 2 and stayed there, and did eat no bread nor drink water, mourning for the great lawlessness of the multitude. 3 And a proclamation was made in all Yehudah and Yerushalayim to all those who were of the captivity, that they should be gathered together at Yerushalayim, 4 and that whoever did not meet there within two or three days, according to how the elders that bare rule appointed, their cattle should be seized for the use of the Temple, and the one himself cast out from the multitude of those who were of the captivity.

5 And in three days all those from the tribe of Yehudah and Benyamin gathered together at Yerushalayim. It was the ninth month, on the twentieth day of the month. 6 And all the multitude sat together trembling in the broad place before the Temple because of this matter, and the heavy rain.

7 So Ezra rose up and said to them, "You have transgressed the Torah and married strange wives, thereby increasing the sins of Yisra'el. 8 And now confess, and give glory to יהוה, the Elohim of our fathers, 9 and do His will, and separate yourselves from the heathens of the land, and from the strange women."

10 Then the whole multitude cried, and said with a loud voice, "As you have spoken, so will we do. 11 But because the multitude is great, and the rain is heavy, so that we cannot stand outside, and this is not a work of one or two days – seeing our sin in these things is spread far – 12 let the rulers of the multitude stay, and let all of them of our habitations that have strange wives come at the time appointed, 13 and with them the rulers and judges of every place, until we turn away the wrath of יהוה from us for this matter."

14 Then Yonathan the son of Asahel and Yaḥazyah the son of Tiqvah took the matter upon them; and Meshallum and Shebbethai the Levite assisted them. 15 And those who were of the captivity did according to all these things. 16 And Ezra the priest chose leading men of their families, all by name. And on the new moon of the tenth month they were shut in together to examine the matter. 17 So their cause that held strange wives was brought to an end by the new moon of the first month. 18 And of the priests that came together, and had strange wives, there were found 19 of the sons of Yeshua the son of Yehotsadaq, and his brothers: Ma'aseiyah, and Eliezar, and Yariv, and Gedalyah. 20 And they gave

their hands to put away their wives, and to
offer rams to reconcile them for their error.[a]

21 And of the sons of Immer: Ḥanani, and
Zevadyah, and Ma'aseyah, and Shemayah,
and Yeḥi'el, and Uzziyah. 22 And of the
sons of Pashchur: Eliyoenai, Ma'aseiyah,
Yisma'el, and Nathana'el, and Yozavad,
and Elasah.

23 And of the Levites: Yozavad, and
Shimei, and Qelayah, who was called
Qelita, and Pethaḥyah, and Yehudah, and
Eliezer.

24 Of the set-apart singers: Elyashiv,
Bakḥouros. 25 Of the gatekeepers: Shallum
and Telem.

26 Of Yisra'el, of the sons of Parosh:
Ramyah, and Yeziyah, and Malkiyah, and
Miyamin, and Elazar, and Malkiyah, and
Benayah. 27 Of the sons of Elam:
Mattanyah, Zekharyah, and Yeḥi'el, and
Avdi, and Yeremoth, and Elyah. 28 And of
the sons of Zattu: Eliyoenai, Elyashiv,
Mattanyah, Yeremoth, Zavad, and Aziza.

29 Of the sons of Bevai: Yehoḥanan, and
Ḥananyah, and Zabbai, and Athlai. 30 Of
the sons of Bani: Meshullam, Mallukh,
Adayah, Yashuv, and Sheal, and Ramoth.
31 And of the sons of Paḥath-Moav: Adna,
and Khelal, Benayah, and Ma'aseiyah, and
Mattanyah, and Vetsal'el, Binnui, and
Manasheh.

32 And of the sons of Ḥarim: Eliezer,
Yishyah, and Malkiyah, and Shemayah,
and Shimon, and Benyamin, and Mallukh,
and Shemaryah. 33 And of the sons of
Ḥashum: Mattenai, and Mattathah, and
Zavad, Eliphelet, and Menasheh, and
Shimei. 34 And of the sons of Bani:
Yirmeyah, Momdis, Ismaerus, Yu'el,
Mamdai, and Pedias, and Anos,
Karabasion, and Enasibus, and
Mamnitamenus, Elyashiv, Binnui, Eliali,
Shemayah, Shelemyah, Nathanyah. And of
the sons of Ezora; Shashai, Sharai, Azar'el,
Shelemyah, Shemaryah, Yoseph. 35 And of
the sons of Nevo: Yei'el, Zavad, Zevina,
Yaddai, and Benayah.

36 All these had taken strange wives, and
they put them away with their children.
37 And the priests and Levites, and those
who were of Yisra'el, lived in
Yerushalayim, and in the country, on the
new moon of the seventh month, and the
children of Yisra'el in their habitations.

38 And the whole multitude were gathered
together with one accord into the broad
place before the porch of the Temple
toward the east, 39 and they said to Ezra the
priest and reader, "Bring the Torah of
Mosheh, that was given from יהוה, the
Elohim of Yisra'el."

40 So Ezra the chief priest brought the
Torah to the whole multitude both of men
and women, and to all the priests, to hear
the Torah on the new moon of the seventh
month. 41 And he read in the broad place
before the porch of the Temple from
morning to mid-day, before both men and
women; and all the multitude heard the
Torah. 42 And Ezra the priest and reader of
the Torah stood up upon the pedestal of
wood, which was made for that purpose.
43 And Mattithyah, Shema, Ananyah,
Uriyah, Ḥilqiyah, and Ma'aseiyah, stood up
with him on the right hand. 44 And on his
left hand stood Pedayah, Misha'el,

[a] 9:20 Gave their hands – In the form of raising a hand in an oath.

Malkiyah, Ḥashum, Ḥashbadanah,
Zekharyah [and Meshullam][a].

45 Then Ezra took the book of the Torah
before the multitude, and sat honorably in
the first place before all. 46 And when he
opened the Torah, they all stood straight
up. So Ezra blessed יהוה El Elyon, Elohim
Tsevaot, El Shaddai. 47 And all the people
answered, "Amein." And lifting up their
hands they fell to the ground and worshiped
יהוה.

48 Also Yeshua, Bani, Sherevyah, Yamin,
Aqquv, Shabbethai, Hodiyah, Ma'aseiyah,
and Qelita, Azaryah, and Yozavad, and
Ḥanan, Pelayah, and the Levites taught the
Torah of יהוה, and read the Torah of יהוה
to the multitude, causing them to
understand it.

49 Then Neḥemyah said to Ezra the chief
priest and reader, and to the Levites that
taught the multitude, even to all, 50 "Today
is set-apart to יהוה;" (now they all wept
when they heard the Torah;) 51 "go then,
and eat the fat, and drink the sweet, and
send portions to those who have nothing.
52 For this day is set-apart to יהוה. And do
not weep, for יהוה will bring you to
honor."

53 So the Levites proclaimed all *these*
things to the people, saying, "This day is
set-apart; do not weep."

54 Then they went their way, every one, to
eat and drink, and be joyful, and to give
portions to those who had nothing, and to
make abundant gladness, 55 because they
understood the words which they had been
instructed, and for which they had been
assembled.

---

[a] 9:44 Neḥemyah 8 contains this name, though Greek texts here omit it.

מַקַבִּים א

Maqabiym א
[1 Maccabees]

1 1 It came to pass, after Alexandros the
Makedonian, the son of Philippos, who
came out of the land of Kittim, and struck
Daryavesh king of the Parasians and
Medes, it came to pass, after he had struck
him, that he reigned in his stead, the first
over Greece. 2 And he fought many
battles, and won many strongholds, and
killed the kings of the earth, 3 and went
through to the ends of the earth, and took
spoils of a multitude of nations. And the
earth was quiet before him, and he was
exalted, and his heart was lifted up, 4 and
he gathered together an exceedingly
strong army, and ruled over countries and
nations and principalities, and they
became tributary to him. 5 And after these
things he fell sick, and perceived that he
should die. 6 And he called his servants,
which were honorable, which had been
brought up with him from his youth, and
he divided to them his kingdom, while he
was yet alive. 7 And Alexandros reigned
twelve years, and he died. 8 And his
servants bare rule, each one in his place.
9 And they all put diadems[a] upon
themselves after he was dead, and so did
their sons after them, *for* many years: and
they multiplied evils in the earth.

10 And there came forth out of them a
sinful root, Antioḥos Epiphanes, son of
Antioḥos the king, who had been a
hostage at Rome, and he reigned in the
hundred and thirty-seventh year[b] of the
kingdom of the Greeks.

11 In those days wicked men[c] came forth
out of Yisra'el, and persuaded many,
saying, "Let us go and cut a covenant with
the nations that are around us; for since we
were parted from them many evils have
befallen us." 12 And the saying was good
in their eyes. 13 And certain of the people
went promptly to the king, and he
authorized them to introduce the laws[d] of
the nations. 14 And they built a
gymnasium[e] in Yerushalayim according to
the work of the nations. 15 And they made
their foreskin uncircumcised, and forsook
the set-apart covenant, and joined
themselves to the nations, and sold
themselves to do evil. 16 And the kingdom
was well ordered in the sight of Antioḥos,
and he thought to reign over Mitsrayim,
that he might reign over the two

---

[a] 1:9 Greek word rendered as "diadems" here is διαδημα (*diadema*), the origin for the English word "diadem." The type of diadems mentioned here were blue and white bands that were bound to the turban or tiara by Parasian kings. A symbol of authority much like a crown, though not as extravagant. Used throughout Maqabiym א.

[b] 1:10 Approximately 176 BCE.

[c] 1:11 Syr. reads as it is here. LXX, however, uses the word παρανομοι (*para'nomoi*) which literally means "violators of the Law."

[d] 1:13 Greek reads "ordinances" while the Syriac reads "laws."

[e] 1:14 Gymnasium (from the Greek word of the same spelling). Much like the modern usage of the term, it was considered a chief instrument in Hellenistic culture. A place of exercise, sport, and an intellectual center, the gymnasium was only for men, and all activities were carried out naked. Youths were trained in military skills, and many Yehudim were won by the Greeks on account of the gymnasium. On account of the need to be naked – it is believed by most scholars – some of the Yehudim sought to reverse their circumcision. The Greeks considered circumcision to be offensive.

kingdoms. [17] And he entered into
Mitsrayim with a heavy multitude, with
chariots, and with elephants[a], and with
horsemen, and with a great armament[b];
[18] and he made war against Ptolemy king
of Mitsrayim; and Ptolemy was put to
shame before him, and fled; and many fell
wounded. [19] And they gained possession
of the strong cities in the land of
Mitsrayim; and he took the spoils of
Mitsrayim.

[20] And Antioḥos, after he had struck
Mitsrayim, returned in the hundred and
forty-third year, and went up against
Yisra'el and Yerushalayim with a great
multitude. [21] And *he* entered into the set-
apart place proudly, and took the golden
altar, and the menorah of the light, and all
that pertained to it. [22] And the table of the
bread of the presence, and the cups with
which to pour, and the bowls, and the
golden censers, and the veil, and the
crowns, and the adorning of gold which
was before the Temple, and he scaled it all
off. [23] And he took the silver and the gold
and the precious vessels; and he took the
hidden treasures which he found. [24] And
when he had taken all, he went away into
his own land, and he made a great
slaughter, and spoke very proudly.

[25] And there came great mourning upon
Yisra'el, in every place where they were.
[26] And the rulers and elders groaned, the
virgins and young men were made feeble,
and the beauty of the women was
changed. [27] Every bridegroom took up
lamentation; she that sat in the marriage
chamber was in mourning. [28] And the land
was moved for its inhabitants, and all the
house of Ya'aqov was clothed with shame.

[29] And after two years of days, the king
sent a chief collector of tribute to the cities
of Yehudah, and he came to Yerushalayim
with a strong multitude. [30] And he spoke
deceitful words of peace to them in, and
they gave him credence: and he fell upon
the city suddenly, and struck it very
severely, and destroyed many people out
of Yisra'el. [31] And he took the spoils of
the city, and set it on fire, and pulled down
its houses and its walls on every side.
[32] And they led the women and the
children captive, and they took the cattle
in possession.

[33] And they built the city of David with a
great and strong wall, with strong towers,
and it became to them a fortress. [34] And
they put there a sinful people,
transgressors of the Torah, and they
strengthened themselves in *it*. [35] And they
stored up arms and food, and gathering
together the spoils of Yerushalayim, they
laid them up there, and they became a
great snare. [36] And it became a place to lie
in wait in against the set-apart place, and
an evil adversary[c] to Yisra'el continually.
[37] And they shed innocent blood on every
side of the set-apart place, and defiled the
set-apart place. [38] And the inhabitants of
Yerushalayim fled because of them; and
she became a habitation of foreigners, and
she became foreign to those who were

---

[a] 1:17 Elephants were considered a very important part of the Seleucid army, and their military use was probably learned in Hodu (India).

[b] 1:17 Greek word rendered "armament" here is στολω (*stolow*) meaning "armament," "assignment" or, in many versions, "navy."

[c] 1:36 LXX reads as it is here. Syr. reads ܘܠܡܐܟܠ ܩܪ̈ܨܐ (*wl'm'akal qirt'siyn*) meaning literally "to eat/consume *the* pieces." This is an Aramaic idiom for being a slanderer, or adversary.

born in her, and her children forsook her.
39 Her set-apart place was laid waste like a
wilderness, her Feasts were turned into
mourning, her Sabbaths into shame, her
honor into contempt. 40 According to her
glory, so was her dishonor multiplied, and
her high estate was turned into mourning.

41 And king Antioḥos wrote to his whole
kingdom, that all should be one people,
42 and that each should forsake his own
laws. And all the nations agreed according
to the word of the king; 43 and many of
Yisra'el were well-pleased in his worship,
and slaughtered to the idols, and profaned
the Sabbath. 44 And the king sent letters
by the hand of messengers to
Yerushalayim and the cities of Yehudah,
that they should follow laws foreign to the
land, 45 and should forbid burnt offerings
and slaughterings and drink offerings in
the set-apart place; and should profane the
Sabbaths and Feasts, 46 and pollute the
set-apart place and those who were set-
apart; 47 that they should build altars and
temples and shrines for idols, and should
slaughter swine's flesh and unclean beasts.
48 And that they should leave their sons
uncircumcised, that they should make
their beings abominable with all manner
of uncleanness and profanation; 49 so that
they might forget the Torah, and change
all justice[a]. 50 And whoever shall not do
according to the word of the king, he shall
die. 51 According to all these words wrote
he to his whole kingdom; and he
appointed overseers over all the people,
and he commanded the cities of Yehudah
to slaughter, city by city. 52 And many
from the people were gathered together to
them, every one that had forsaken the
Torah; and they did evil things in the land;
53 and they made Yisra'el to flee to the
hidden places.

54 And on the fifteenth day of Kislev, in
the hundred and forty-fifth year, they built
an abomination of desolation[b] upon the
altar[c], and in the cities of Yehudah on
every side they built idol-altars[d]. 55 And at
the doors of the houses and in the streets
they burned incense. 56 And they tore in
pieces the books of the Torah which they
found, and set them on fire. 57 And
wherever a book of the covenant was
found with anyone, and if any agreed to
the Torah, the king's sentence delivered
him to death. 58 Thus they did in their
might to Yisra'el, to those that were found
month by month in the cities. 59 And on
the twenty-fifth day of the month they
slaughtered upon the idol-altar which was
on the altar. 60 And the women that had
circumcised their children they put to
death according to the command. 61 And
they hanged their infants about their
necks, and destroyed their houses, and
those who had circumcised them. 62 And

---

[a] 1:49 Syr. reads ܢܡܘܣܐ (*n'musa*) meaning "laws" instead of "justice."

[b] 1:54 See also Dani'el 11:31; 12:11; Mattithyahu [Matthew] 24:15; Markos 13:14.

[c] 1:54 Greek word rendered "altar" here is θυσιαστεηριον (*thusiasterion*). This word literally means "altar" and is used throughout the Greek NT for "altar." The Syr. uses ܡܕܒܚܐ (*mad'b'ḥa*) which also means "altar."

[d] 1:54 Greek word rendered "idol-altar" here is not *thusiasterion*, but rather βωμος (*bow'mos*). *Bomos* also means "altar," (or more literally, a "raised stand") but is only used in the Greek NT once, in reference to a pagan altar in Ma'asei [Acts] 17:23. This particular type of altar was used for pagan slaughterings to idols, thus it has been rendered as "idol-altar." The Syr. also distinguishes between the two, as it uses ܦܪܟܐ (*pra'ka*) meaning "idol-shrine." Also in verse 59.

many in Yisra'el were fully resolved and
confirmed in themselves not to eat unclean
things. 63 And they chose to die, that they
might not be defiled with the meats, and
that they might not profane the set-apart
covenant: and they died. 64 And very great
wrath came upon Yisra'el.

2 1 In those days rose up Mattithyah the
son of Yoḥanan[a], the son of Shimon, a
priest of the sons of Yoyariv[b], from
Yerushalayim; and he lived at Modin[c].
2 And he had five sons: Yoḥanan, who
was surnamed Gaddi; 3 Shimon, who was
called Tarsi; 4 Yehudah, who was called
Maqabi; 5 Elazar, who was called Ḥoran;
Yonathan, who was called Ḥephos.

6 And he saw the blasphemies that were
committed in Yehudah and in
Yerushalayim.

7 And he said, "Woe is me! Why was I
born to see the destruction of my people,
and the destruction of the set-apart city,
and to dwell there, when *the city* was
given into the hand of the enemy, the
sanctuary into the hand of foreigners?
8 Her Temple is become as a man that lost
his glory: 9 her vessels of glory are carried
away into captivity, **her infants are slain
in her streets, her young men with the
sword of the enemy**.[d]

10 What nation has not inherited her
palaces, and gained possession of her
spoils? 11 Her adorning is all taken away.
Instead of a free woman she has become a
bondwoman, 12 and, behold, our set-apart
things and our beauty and our glory are
laid waste, and the nations have profaned
them. 13 Why should we live any longer?"

14 And Mattithyah and his sons tore their
clothes, and put on sackcloth, and
mourned exceedingly.

15 And the king's officers, those that were
enforcing the apostasy, came into the city
of Modin to slaughter. 16 And many of
Yisra'el came to them, and Mattithyah and
his sons were gathered together.

17 And the king's officers answered and
spoke to Mattithyah, saying, "You are a
ruler and an honorable and great man in
this city, and strengthened with sons and
brethren. 18 Now therefore, you come
first, and do the command of the king, as
all the nations have done, and the men of
Yehudah, and those who remain in
Yerushalayim; and you and your house
shall be in the number of the king's
beloved[e], and you and your sons shall be

---

[a] 2:1 Yoḥanan was also a descendant of Hasmoneus. This is where the term "Hasmonean" comes from. See Josephus' *Wars of the Jews* Book 5, 1:3.

[b] 2:1 LXX uses the word Ιωαριβ (*Ioarib*), which is the Greek version of the Hebrew name יויריב (*Yoyariv*) as it has been rendered here. However, the Syr. records this name as ܝܘܢܕܒ (*Yonadav*). According to Neḥemyah 11:10, Yoyariv was a priest, though there is no record of a priest named Yonadav in Scripture. See also Divrei Ha'Yamim א [1 Chronicles] 9:10; 24:7. This does not, however, mean there was no priestly line from Yonadav, merely that it is not recorded.

[c] 2:1 Modin. The LXX records the name of the city as "Modin" (seen throughout the book of Maqabiym א). The Syr. records this name as ܡܘܪܝܡ (*Mow'riym*). This discrepancy could be due to a Hebrew original. In the Hebrew block (Ashuri) script, the letter "Dalet" (D: ד) looks very similar to the letter "Resh" (R: ר), and they are commonly mistaken.

[d] 2:9 See Eikhah [Lamentations] 2:11; 2:21.

[e] 2:18 King's Beloved – Phrase referring to an order of nobility in Hellenistic courts. This title was only bestowed upon those that the king

honored with silver and gold and many
gifts."

19 And Mattithyah answered and said with
a loud voice, "If all the nations that are in
the house of the king's dominion listen to
him, to fall away each one from the
worship of his fathers, and have made
choice to follow his commands, 20 I and
my sons and my brethren will still walk in
the covenant of our fathers. 21 Heaven
forbid that we should forsake the Torah
and justice[a]. 22 We will not listen to the
king's words, to go aside from our
worship, on the right hand, or on the left."

23 And when he had left speaking these
words, there came a Yehudite in the sight
of all to slaughter on the altar which was
at Modin, according to the king's
command. 24 And Mattithyah saw it, and
his zeal was kindled, and his kidneys[b]
trembled, and he showed forth his wrath
according to judgment, and ran, and killed
him upon the altar. 25 And he killed at that
time the king's officer, who forced men to
slaughter, and pulled down the altar.
26 And he was zealous for the Torah, even
as Pineḥas did to Zimri the son of Salu.[c]

27 And Mattithyah cried out in the city
with a loud voice, saying, "Whoever is
zealous for the Torah, and establishes the
covenant, let him come forth after me."

28 And he and his sons fled into the
mountains, and forsook all that they had in
the city.[d]

29 Then many that sought after justice and
judgment went down into the wilderness[e],
to dwell there. 30 They, and their sons, and
their wives, and their cattle; because evils
were multiplied upon them. 31 And it was
told to the king's officers, and the forces
that were in Yerushalayim, the city of
David, that certain men, who had broken
the king's command, were gone down into
the secret places in the wilderness. 32 And
many pursued after them, and having
overtaken them, they encamped against
them, and set the battle in array against
them on the Sabbath day.

33 And they said to them, "*That is* far
enough. Come forth, and do according to
the word[f] of the king, and you shall live."

34 And they said, "We will not come forth,
neither will we do the word of the king, to
profane the Sabbath day."

35 And they hurried to give them battle.
36 And they did not answer them, neither
did they cast a stone at them, nor did they
stop up the secret places, 37 saying, "Let
us die all in our innocence: heaven and

---

personally trusted. This phrase is translated from the Greek phrase φιλων του βασιλεως (*Phil'own tou bas'ile'ows*), meaning "friend/beloved of the king." The Syr. uses the phrase ܪܚܡܐ ܕܡܠܟܐ (*raḥ'ma d'malka*) meaning "beloved of the king." Used throughout the books of Maqabiym.

a 2:21 LXX reads "justice" as it is here. Syr. reads "decrees."

b 2:24 Greek and Syriac both read "kidneys" here. In Hebraic thinking, the kidneys are the seat of the emotions, while the heart is the seat of understanding (the mind). This phrase is an idiom meaning Mattithyah was overcome with passion and emotion.

c 2:26 See Bemidbar [Numbers] 25:6-15.

d 2:28 See Maqabiym ב [2 Maccabees] 5:27.

e 2:29 This "wilderness" in Greek (or ܚܘܪܒܐ [*chuw'r'ba*] "wasteland" in Syriac) is believed to be the area around the Qumran caves near the Dead Sea, where the Dead Sea Scrolls were found.

f 2:33 Syr. reads "decrees." LXX reads λογον (*logon*) meaning "words" as it is here.

earth witness over us, that you put us to
death without trial." 38 And they rose up
against them in battle on the Sabbath, and
they died; they and their wives, and their
children, and their cattle, to the number of
a thousand beings of men.[a]

39 And Mattithyah and his friends knew it,
and they mourned over them exceedingly.
40 And one said to another, "If we all do
as our brethren have done, and fight not
against the nations for our lives and our
judgments, they will now quickly destroy
us from off the earth."

41 And they took counsel on that day,
saying, "Whoever shall come against us to
battle on the Sabbath day, let us fight
against him, and we shall in no way all
die, as our brethren died in the secret
places."

42 Then a company was gathered together
to them of Ḥasidim[b], mighty men of
Yisra'el, every one that offered himself
willingly for the Torah. 43 And all those
who fled from the evils were added to
them, and became a stay to them. 44 And
they mustered an army, and struck sinners
in their anger, and lawless men in their
wrath: and the rest fled to the nations for
safety. 45 And Mattithyah and his
companions went around, and pulled
down the altars; 46 and they circumcised
by force the children that were
uncircumcised, as many as they found in
the coasts of Yisra'el. 47 And they pursued
after the sons of pride, and the work
prospered in their hand. 48 And they
rescued the Torah out of the hand of the
nations, and out of the hand of the kings,
neither did they give a horn to the sinner.[c]

49 And the days of Mattithyah drew near
that he should die, and he said to his sons,
"Pride and rebuke have gotten strong, and
a season of overthrow, and wrath of
indignation. 50 And now, my children, be
zealous for the Torah, and give your lives
for the covenant of your fathers. 51 And
call to remembrance the deeds of our
fathers which they did in their generations;
and receive great glory and an everlasting
name. 52 Was not Avraham found faithful
in trial, and it was reckoned to him for
righteousness?[d] 53 Yosef in the time of his
distress kept the command, and became
master of Mitsrayim.[e] 54 Pineḥas our
father, for that he was zealous
exceedingly, obtained the covenant of an
everlasting priesthood. 55 Yehoshua, for
fulfilling the word, became a judge in
Yisra'el. 56 Kalev, for bearing witness in
the assembly, obtained a heritage in the
land.[f] 57 David, for being merciful,
inherited the throne of a kingdom forever
and ever.[g] 58 Eliyahu, for that he was
exceeding zealous for the Torah, was

---

[a] 2:32-38 See Maqabiym ב [2 Maccabees] 6:11
[b] 2:42 Ḥasidim – Greek word άσιδαιοι (*Has'I'dai'oi*). This is the Greek transliteration of the Hebrew word חסידים (*ḥasidim*), which means "kind ones." Related to, but not to be confused with, Hasidic Judaism of modern times, which uses the term for the same reason. These Ḥasidim were, for a time, supportive of the revolt of the Maqabiym, and were considered very valiant warriors.

[c] 2:48 Greek phrase rendered "give a horn to the sinner" is και ουκ έδωκαν κέρας τώ άμαρτωλω (*kai ouk ker'as tow am'ar'to'lo*). This literally means "give a horn to the sinner" but is figuratively believed to mean "give victory to the sinner" as the blowing of a horn signaled victory. The Syriac likewise reads the same.
[d] 2:52 See Bereshiyt [Genesis] 15:6.
[e] 2:53 See Bereshiyt [Genesis] 41:39-43.
[f] 2:56 See Yehoshua [Joshua] 14:14.
[g] 2:57 See Shemu'el ב [2 Samuel] 7:16.

taken up into the heavens.[a] 59 Ḥananyah,
Azaryah, *and* Mishael believed, and were
saved out of the flame.[b] 60 Dani'el for his
innocence was delivered from the mouth
of lions.[c] 61 And thus, consider from
generation to generation, that none that
put their trust in Him shall lack for
strength. 62 And do not be afraid of the
words of a sinful man; for his glory shall
be dung and worms. 63 Today he shall be
lifted up, and tomorrow he shall in no way
be found, because he is returned to his
dust, and his thought is perished.

64 "And you, my children, be strong, and
show yourselves men on behalf of the
Torah; for in it you shall obtain glory.
65 And, behold, Shimon your brother, I
know that he is a man of counsel; give ear
to him always: he shall be a father to you.
66 And Yehudah Maqabi, he has been
strong and mighty from his youth: he shall
be your captain, and shall fight the battle
of the people. 67 And take to you all the
doers of the Torah, and avenge the wrong
of your people. 68 Render a reward to the
nations, and take heed to the commands of
the Torah."

69 And he blessed them, and was gathered
to his fathers. 70 And he died in the
hundred and forty-sixth year, and his sons
buried him in the graves of his fathers at
Modin, and all Yisra'el made great
lamentation for him.

3 1 And his son Yehudah, who was called
Maqabi, rose up in his stead. 2 And all his
brethren helped him, and so did all those
who cleaved to his father, and they fought
the battle of Yisra'el with gladness. 3 And
he got his people great glory, and put on a
breastplate as a giant, and girded his
warlike harness about him, and set battles
in array, protecting the army with his
sword. 4 And he was like a lion in his
deeds, and as a lion's whelp roaring for
prey. 5 And he pursued the lawless,
seeking them out, and he burned up those
that troubled his people. 6 And the lawless
shrunk for fear of him, and all the workers
of lawlessness were severely troubled, and
salvation prospered in his hand.

7 And he angered many kings, and made
Ya'aqov glad with his acts, and his
memorial is blessed forever. 8 And he
went about among the cities of Yehudah,
and destroyed the wicked out of *the land*,
and turned away wrath from Yisra'el.
9 And he was renowned to the utmost part
of the earth, and he gathered together
those that were perishing.

10 And Apollonios gathered the nations
together, and a great army from
Shomeron, to fight against Yisra'el.
11 And Yehudah perceived it, and he went
forth to meet him, and struck him, and
killed him: and many fell wounded, and
the rest fled. 12 And they took their spoils,
and Yehudah took the sword of
Apollonios, and he fought with it all his
days.

13 And Seron, the commander of the army
of Aram, heard that Yehudah had gathered
a gathering and an assembly of faithful
men with him, of those that go out to war.
14 And he said, "I will make myself a
name and get me glory in the kingdom;
and I will fight against Yehudah and those

---

[a] 2:58 See Melakhim א [1 Kings] 19:10; Melakhim ב [2 Kings] 2:11.

[b] 2:59 See Dani'el 3:19-27.

[c] 2:60 See Dani'el 6:19-24.

who are with him, that made the word of the king as nothing."

15 And there went up with him also a mighty army of the wicked to help him, to take vengeance on the children of Yisra'el.
16 And he came near to the going up of Beth-Ḥoron, and Yehudah went forth to meet him with a small company.

17 But when they saw the army coming to meet them, they said to Yehudah, "What? Shall we, being a small company, be able to fight against so great and strong a multitude? And we for our part are faint, having tasted no food this day."

18 And Yehudah said, "It is an easy thing for many to be shut up in the hands of a few; and with Elohim[a] in heaven, it is all the same: to save by many or by few.[b]
19 For victory in battle stands not in the multitude of an army, but in strength from
heaven. 20 They come to us full of pride and lawlessness, to destroy us, and our wives, and our children, *and* to plunder us.
21 But we fight for our beings and our
Torot[c]. 22 And He Himself will overthrow them before our face: but as for you, do not be afraid of them."

23 Now when he had left off speaking, he leapt suddenly upon them, and Seron and his army were overthrown before him.
24 And they pursued them in the going down of Beth-Ḥoron to the plain, and there fell of them about eight hundred men; but the remnant fled into the land of the Philistines.

25 And the fear of Yehudah and his brethren, and the dread of them, began to
fall upon the nations around them. 26 And
his name came near even to the king, and every nation told of the battles of Yehudah.

27 But when king Antioḥos heard these words, he was full of indignation: and he sent and gathered together all the forces of
his realm, a very strong army. 28 And he
opened his treasury, and gave his forces pay for a year, and commanded them to be
ready for every need. 29 And he saw that
the money failed from his treasury, and that the tributes of the country were small, because of the dissension and plague which he had brought upon the land, to the end that he might take away the laws
which had been from the first days; 30 and
he feared that he should not have enough as at other times for the charges and the gifts which he had previously given with a liberal hand, and he abounded above the
kings that were before him. 31 And he was
very perplexed in his mind, and he determined to go into Paras, and to take the tributes of the countries, and to gather
much money. 32 And he left Lysias, an
honorable man, and one of the royal seed, to be over the affairs of the king from the river Euphrates to the borders of
Mitsrayim, 33 and to bring up his son,
Antioḥos, until he came again.

34 And he delivered to him the half of his forces, and the elephants, and gave him charge of all the things that he would have done, and concerning those who lived in

[a] 3:18 LXX reads "Elohim in heaven" and the Syr. reads just "heaven." This is common throughout the book, as the author refrains from using Names or Titles for Elohim, instead utilizing the word "heaven."

[b] 3:18 See also Shemu'el א [1 Samuel] 14:6.

[c] 3:21 Torot – Hebrew word תורת, the plural of "Torah" meaning "Laws" or "instructions." Used throughout Maccabees.

Yehudah and in Yerushalayim, 35 that he
should send an army against them, to root
out and destroy the strength of Yisra'el,
and the remnant of Yerushalayim, and to
take away their memorial from the place;
36 and that he should make foreigners to
dwell on all their coasts, and should divide
their land to them by lot. 37 And the king
took the half that remained of the forces,
and removed from Antioḥ, from his royal
city, *in* the hundred and forty-seventh
year, and he passed over the river
Euphrates, and went through the upper
countries.

38 And Lysias chose Ptolemy the son of
Dorymenes, and Niqanor, and Gorgias,
mighty men of the king's beloved; 39 and
with them he sent forty thousand footmen,
and seven thousand horse, to go into the
land of Yehudah, and to destroy it,
according to the word of the king. 40 And
they removed with all their army, and
came and pitched near to Emmaus in the
plain country. 41 And the merchants of the
country heard the fame of them, and took
great amounts of silver and gold, with
fetters, and came into the camp to take the
children of Yisra'el for servants: and there
were added to them the forces of Aram
and of the land of the Philistine[a].

42 And Yehudah and his brethren saw that
evils were multiplied, and that the forces
were encamping in their borders; and they
took knowledge of the king's words which
he had commanded, to destroy the people
and make an end of them.

43 And they said each man to his neighbor,
"Let us raise up the ruin of our people, and
let us fight for our people and the set-apart
place." 44 And the assembly was gathered
together, that they might be ready for
battle, and that they might pray, and ask
for mercy and compassion. 45 And
Yerushalayim was without inhabitant as a
wilderness, there was none of her
offspring that went in or went out; and the
set-apart place was trodden down, and the
sons of foreigners were in the fortress. The
nations lodged therein; and joy was taken
away from Ya'aqov, and the pipe and the
harp ceased. 46 And they gathered
themselves together, and came to Mitspah,
near Yerushalayim; for in Mitspah there
was previously a place of prayer for
Yisra'el.[b] 47 And they fasted that day, and
put on sackcloth, and put ashes upon their
heads, and tore their clothes, 48 and laid
open the book of the Torah, to learn about
the things for which the nations consulted
the images of their idols.

49 And they brought the priests' garments,
and the first fruits, and the tithes: and they
stirred up the separated ones[c], who had
accomplished their days.

50 And they cried aloud toward heaven,
saying, "What shall we do with these men,
and to where shall we carry them away?
51 And Your set-apart place is trodden

---

[a] 3:41 LXX reads άλλοφυλων (*allophulon*) meaning "foreigners." Syr. reads ܕܦܠܫܬܝܐ (*d'philistiya*) meaning "the Philistine" here. Compare verse 23, where both the Greek and the Syriac read "Philistine."

[b] 3:46 Possible reference to Shemu'el א [1 Samuel] 7:5.

[c] 3:49 Separated one – Greek word ναζιραίους (*nazir'ai'ous*). Syriac word ܢܙܝܪܐ (*na'zira*). Both of these are transliterations of the Hebrew word נזיר (*Nazir*) which is usually rendered as "Nazirite" but literally means "separated one." Thus the reference to having "accomplished" their days means the days they remain in separation. See also Bemidbar [Numbers] 6.

down and profaned, and Your priests are
in murning and brought low. 52 And,
behold, the nations are assembled together
against us to destroy us: You know what
things they imagine against us. 53 How
shall we be able to stand before them,
except You be our help?" 54 And they
sounded with their horns, and cried with a
loud voice.

55 And after this Yehudah appointed
leaders of the people, captains of
thousands, and captains of hundreds, and
captains of fifties, and captains of tens.
56 And he said to those who were building
houses, and were betrothing wives, and
were planting vineyards, and were fearful,
that they should return, each man to his
own house, according to the Torah.[a]
57 And the army removed, and encamped
upon the south side of Emmaus.

58 And Yehudah said, "Gird yourselves,
and be valiant men, and be in readiness
against the morning, that you may fight
with these nations that are assembled
together against us to destroy us, and our
set-apart place. 59 For it is better for us to
die in battle, than to look upon the evils of
our nation and the set-apart place.
60 Nevertheless, as may be the will in
heaven, so shall He do."[b]

4 1 And Gorgias took five thousand
footmen, and a thousand elect horseman,
and the army removed by night, 2 that it
might fall upon the army of the Yehudim
and strike them suddenly; and the men of
the fortress were his guides. 3 And
Yehudah heard about it, and removed
himself, and the valiant men *with him*, that
he might strike the king's army which was
at Emmaus, 4 while as yet the forces were
dispersed from the camp. 5 And Gorgias
came into the camp of Yehudah by night,
and found no man; and he sought them in
the mountains; for he said, "These men
flee from us." 6 And as soon as it was day,
Yehudah appeared in the plain with three
thousand men, who had neither the armor
nor the swords they desired. 7 And they
saw the camp of the nations: strong and
fortified, and horsemen encompassing
around it; and these were experts in war.

8 And Yehudah said to the men that were
with him, "Do not fear their multitude,
neither be afraid of their attack.
9 Remember how our fathers were saved
in the Sea of Reeds, when Pharaoh
pursued them with an army. 10 And now
let us cry to heaven: if He will have us,
and will remember the covenant of our
fathers, and destroy this army before our
face today, 11 then all the nations shall
know that there is one who redeems and
saves Yisra'el."

12 And the foreigners lifted up their eyes,
and saw them coming near them. 13 And
they went out of the camp to battle. And
those who were with Yehudah sounded
their horns, 14 and joined battle, and the
nations were overthrown, and fled into the
plain. 15 But all the hindmost fell by the
sword: and they pursued them to Gezer,
and to the plains of Edom, and Ashdod
and Yavneel, and there fell of them about
three thousand men.

16 And Yehudah and his army returned
from pursuing after them. 17 And he said
to the people, "Do not be greedy with the

---

[a] 3:56 See Devarim [Deuteronomy] 20:5-8.

[b] 3:38-60 See Maqabiym ב [2 Maccabees] 8:9-23.

spoils, for there is a battle before us,
18 and Gorgias and his army are near to us
in the mountain. But stand now against
our enemies, and fight against them, and
afterwards take the spoils with boldness."

19 While Yehudah was yet making an end
of these words, there appeared a part of
them looking out from the mountain.
20 And they saw that their army had been
put to flight, and that the Yehudim were
burning the camp; for the smoke that was
seen declared what was done. 21 But when
they perceived these things, they were
very afraid. And perceiving also the army
of Yehudah in the plain ready for battle,
22 they fled all of them into the land of the
Philistines[a]. 23 And Yehudah returned to
plunder the camp, and they got much gold,
and silver, and blue, and sea-purple, and
great riches. 24 And they returned home,
and sang a song of thanksgiving, and gave
praise to heaven; because His mercy is
good, because His mercy endures to the
age.[b] 25 And Yisra'el had a great
deliverance that day.

26 But the foreigners, as many as had
escaped, came and told Lysias all the
things that had happened. 27 But when he
heard thereof, he was confounded and
discouraged, because neither the things
which he willed to be done, nor the things
the king had commanded him came to
pass.

28 And in the next year he gathered
together sixty thousand elect footmen, and
five thousand horsemen, that he might
subdue them. 29 And they came into
Edom, and encamped at Beth-Tsur; and
Yehudah met them with ten thousand men.

30 And he saw that the army was strong,
and he prayed and said, "Blessed are You,
O Savior of Yisra'el, who overwhelmed
the attack of the mighty man by the hand
of Your servant David, and did deliver the
army of the Philistines into the hands of
Yonathan the son of Sha'ul, and of his
armor bearer: 31 shut up this army in the
hand of Your people Yisra'el, and let them
be ashamed for their army and their
horsemen. 32 Give them faintness of heart,
and cause the boldness of their strength to
melt away, and let them quake at their
destruction. 33 Cast them down with the
sword of those who love You, and let all
that know Your Name praise You with
thanksgiving."

34 And they joined battle; and there fell of
the army of Lysias, about five thousand
men, and they fell down near them. 35 But
when Lysias saw that his array was put to
flight, and the boldness that had come
upon those who were with Yehudah, and
how they were ready either to live or to
die nobly, he removed to Antioḥ, and
gathered together hired soldiers, that he
might come again into Yehudah with an
even greater company.

36 But Yehudah and his brethren said,
"Behold, our enemies are overthrown: let
us go up to cleanse the set-apart place, and
to dedicate it renewed."

37 And all the army was gathered together,
and they went up to Mount Tsion. 38 And
they saw the set-apart place laid desolate,
and the altar profaned, and the gates
burned up, and shrubs growing in the
courts as in a forest or as on one of the
mountains, and the priests' chambers

---

[a] 422 See footnote at 3:41.

[b] 424 See also Tehillim [Psalms] 118:1-4.

pulled down[a]. 39 And they tore their
clothes, and made great lamentation, and
put ashes upon their heads, 40 and fell on
their faces to the ground, and blew with
the shofars, and cried toward heaven.
41 Then Yehudah appointed certain men to
fight against those that were in the
fortress, until he should have cleansed the
set-apart place.

42 And he chose blameless priests, such as
had pleasure in the Torah, 43 and they
cleansed the set-apart place, and removed
the stones of defilement into an unclean
place. 44 And they took counsel
concerning the altar of burnt offerings,
which had been profaned, what they
should do with it. 45 And they thought it
best that they should pull it down, lest it
should be a reproach to them, because the
nations had defiled it. And they pulled
down the altar, 46 and laid up the stones in
the mountain of the house in a convenient
place, until there should come a prophet to
give an answer concerning them. 47 And
they took whole stones according to the
Torah, and built a new altar after the
fashion of the former;[b] 48 and they built
the set-apart place, and the inner parts of
the house; and they set apart the courts.
49 And they renewed the set-apart vessels,
and they brought the menorah, and the
altar of burnt offerings and of incense, and
the table, into the Temple. 50 And they
burned incense upon the altar, and they lit
the lamps that were upon the menorah,
and they gave light in the Temple. 51 And
they set loaves upon the table, and spread
out the veils, and finished all the works
which they made.

52 And they rose up early in the morning,
on the twenty-fifth day of the ninth month,
which is the month Kislev, in the hundred
and forty-eighth year, 53 and offered
slaughterings according to the Torah upon
the renewed altar of burnt offerings which
they had made. 54 At what time and on
what day the nations had profaned it, even
on that day was it dedicated renewed, with
songs and harps and lutes, and with
cymbals. 55 And all the people fell upon
their faces, and worshipped, and gave
praise to heaven, which had given them
good success. 56 And they kept the
dedication of the altar eight days, and
offered burned offerings with gladness,
and slaughtered a slaughtering of salvation
and praise. 57 And they decked the
forefront of the Temple with crowns of
gold and small shields, and dedicated the
gates and the priests' chambers renewed,
and made doors for them. 58 And there
was exceedingly great gladness among the
people, and the reproach of the nations
was turned away. 59 And Yehudah and his
brethren and the whole assembly of
Yisra'el decreed, that the days of the
dedication of the altar should be kept in
their seasons from year to year by the
space of eight days, from the twenty-fifth
day of the month Kislev, with gladness
and joy.[c] 60 And at that season they built
up the Mount Tsion with high walls and
strong towers round about, so that the
nations could not easily come and trample
it as they had previously. 61 And he set a
force there to guard it, and they fortified

---

[a] 4:37-38 Compare Tehillim [Psalms 74].
[b] 4:47 See Shemoth [Exodus] 20:25.
[c] 4:59 This is the institution of the festival today known by its Hebrew name, Ḥanukkah, which means "dedication." See also Yoḥanan [John] 10:22.

Beth-Tsur to guard it; that the people
might have a stronghold near Edom.

5 1 And it came to pass, when the
surrounding nations heard that the altar
was built, and the set-apart place
dedicated as before, they were very angry.
2 And they took counsel to destroy the
race of Ya'aqov that was in the midst of
them, and they began to kill and destroy
among the people. 3 And Yehudah fought
against the children of Esav in Edom at
Akrabattine, because they besieged
Yisra'el. And he struck them with a great
slaughter, and brought down their pride,
and took their plunder. 4 And he
remembered the wickedness of the
children of Baean, who were a snare to the
people and a stumbling block, lying in
wait for them in the ways. 5 And they
were shut up by him in the towers; and he
encamped against them, and destroyed
them completely, and burned with fire the
towers of the place, with all that were in
them.[a] 6 And he passed over to the
children of Ammon, and found a mighty
band, and many people, with Timotheos
for their leader. 7 And he fought many
battles with them, and they were
overthrown before his face; and he struck
them,[b] 8 and gained possession of Yazer,
and its villages, and returned again into
Yehudah.

9 And the nations that were in Gilad
gathered themselves together against the
Yisra'elites that were on their borders, to
destroy them. And they fled to the
stronghold of Dathema[c]. 10 And *they* sent
letters to Yehudah and his brethren,
saying, "The nations that are around us are
gathered together against us to destroy us,
11 and they are preparing to come and get
possession of the stronghold to which
have fled for refuge, and Timotheos is the
leader of their army. 12 Now therefore,
come and deliver us from their hand, for
many of us have fallen. 13 And all our
brethren that were in the land of Tov have
been put to death; and they have carried
their wives and their children and their
possessions into captivity; and they
destroyed there about a thousand men."

14 While the letters were being read,
behold, there came other messengers from
Galilee with their clothes torn, bringing a
report after this way, 15 saying, "There
were gathered together against them those
of Akko, and of Tsor, and of Tsidon, and
all Galilee of the nations[d] to consume
them."

16 Now when Yehudah and the people
heard these words, a great assembly
assembled together, to consult what they
should do for their brethren that were in
tribulation, and were attacked by them.

17 And Yehudah said to Shimon his
brother, "Choose men, and go and deliver
your brethren that are in Galilee, but I and
Yonathan my brother will go into the land
of Gilad."

---

[a] 5:3-5 See also Maqabiym ב [2 Maccabees] 10:15-23.

[b] 5:6-7 See also Maqabiym ב [2 Maccabees] 8:30-33.

[c] 5:9 Syr. reads "stronghold of Ramta" instead of "Dathema." This is believed by some to be referring to Ramoth Gilad, and thus representing a possible misreading of the Dalet/Resh issue by the Greek translator. For reference, see footnote at 2:1.

[d] 5:15 Syr. reads "Philistines" instead of "nations" here.

18 And he left Yosef the son of Zekaryah,
and Azaryah, as leaders of the people,
with the remnant of the army, in Yehudah,
to guard it. 19 And he gave command to
them, saying, "Take charge of this people,
and fight no battle with the nations until
we return." 20 And to Shimon were
divided three thousand men to go into
Galilee, but to Yehudah eight thousand
men to go into the land of Gilad.

21 And Shimon went into Galilee, and
fought many battles with the nations, and
the nations were overthrown before him.
22 And he pursued them to the gate of
Akko; and there fell of the nations about
three thousand men, and he took their
spoils. 23 And they took to them those that
were in Galilee, and in Arbatta, with their
wives and their children, and all that they
had, and brought them into Yehudah with
great gladness. 24 And Yehudah Maqabi
and his brother Yonathan passed over
Yarden, and went three days' journey in
the wilderness; 25 and they met with the
Nabathites[a], and these met them in a
peaceful manner, and told them all things
that had befallen their brethren in the land
of Gilad, 26 and how that many of them
were shut up in Bosora, and Beor, and
Alema, Kasphor, Maked, and Qarnayim;
all these cities are strong and great: 27 and
how that they were shut up in the rest of
the cities of the land of Gilead, and that
the following day they had appointed to
encamp against the strongholds, and to
take them, and to destroy all these men in
one day.

28 And Yehudah and his army turned
suddenly by the way of the wilderness to
Bosora; and he took the city, and killed all
the males with the edge of the sword, and
took all their spoils, and burned the city
with fire. 29 And he removed from there
by night, and went until he came to the
stronghold. 30 And the morning came, and
they lifted up their eyes, and behold, many
people who could not be counted, bearing
ladders and engines of war, to take the
stronghold; and they were fighting against
them. 31 And Yehudah saw that the battle
had begun, and that the cry of the city
went up to heaven, with shofars and a
great sound, 32 and he said to the men of
his army, "Fight this day for your
brethren."

33 And he went forth behind them in three
companies, and they sounded with their
shofars, and cried out in prayer. 34 And
the army of Timotheos perceived that it
was Maqabi, and they fled from before
him: and he struck them with a great
slaughter; and about eight thousand men
of them fell that day. 35 And he turned
away to Mitspah and fought against it, and
took it, and killed all the males thereof,
and took its spoils, and burned it with fire.
36 From there he removed, and took
Kasphor, Maked, Beor, and the other
cities of the land of Gilad.

37 Now after these things Timotheos
gathered another army, and encamped
near Raphon beyond the brook. 38 And
Yehudah sent men to spy out the army;
and they brought him word, saying, "All
the nations that are around us are gathered
together to them, a very great army.
39 And they have hired Aravians to help
them, and are encamping beyond the

---

[a] 5:25 Nabathites, also called Nabataeans, were inhabitants of Aravia and Aram.

brook, ready to come against you to
battle." And Yehudah went to meet them.

40 And Timotheos said to the captains of
his army, when Yehudah and his army
drew near to the brook of water, "If he
passes over first to us, we shall not be able
to withstand him; for he will mightily
prevail against us. 41 But if he is afraid,
and encamps beyond the river, we will
cross over to him, and prevail against
him."

42 Now when Yehudah came near to the
brook of water, he caused the scribes of
the people to remain by the brook, and
gave command to them, saying, "Do not
allow any man to encamp, but let all come
to the battle."

43 And he crossed over the first against
them, and all the people after him: and all
the nations were overthrown before his
face, and cast away their arms, and fled to
the temple at Qarnayim. 44 And they took
the city, and burned the temple with fire,
together with all that were therein. And
Qarnayim was subdued, and they could
not stand any longer before the face of
Yehudah.[a]

45 And Yehudah gathered together all
Yisra'el, those who were in the land of
Gilad, from the least to the greatest, and
their wives, and their children, and their
possessions, a very great army, that they
might come into the land of Yehudah.
46 And they came as far as Ephron, and
this same city was great, and it was in the
way as they should go, very strong. They
could not turn away from it on the right
hand or on the left, but had to pass through
the midst of it. 47 And those of the city
shut them out, and stopped up the gates
with stones.

48 And Yehudah sent to them with words
of peace, saying, "We will pass through
your land to go into our own land, and
none shall do you any harm: we will only
pass by on our feet." And they would not
open to him. 49 And Yehudah commanded
proclamations to be made in the army, that
each man should encamp in the place
where he was. 50 And the men of the army
encamped, and fought against the city all
that day and all that night, and the city
was delivered into his hands. 51 And he
destroyed all the males with the edge of
the sword, and razed the city, and took its
spoils, and passed through the city over
those who were slain. 52 And they went
over Yarden into the great plain near
Beth-Shan. 53 And Yehudah gathered
together those that lagged behind, and
encouraged the people all the way
through, until he came into the land of
Yehudah. 54 And they went up to Mount
Tsion with gladness and joy, and offered
burnt offerings, because not so much as
one of them was slain until they returned
in peace.

55 And in the days when Yehudah and
Yonathan were in the land of Gilad, and
Shimon his brother in Galilee before
Akko, 56 Yosef the son of Zekaryah, and
Azaryah, rulers of the army, heard of their
exploits and of the war, what things they
had done; 57 and they said, "Let us also
get us a name, and let us go fight against
the nations that are around us."

---

[a] 5:37-44 See also Maqabiym ב [2 Maccabees] 12:17-25.

58 And they gave charge to the men of the
army that was with them, and went toward
Yavneel. 59 And Gorgias and his men
came out of the city to meet them in battle.
60 And Yosef and Azaryah were put to
flight, and were pursued to the borders of
Yehudah; and there fell on that day of the
people of Yisra'el about two thousand
men. 61 And there was a great overthrow
among the people, because they did not
listen to Yehudah and his brethren,
thinking to do some exploit. 62 But they
were not of the seed of those men, by
whose hand deliverance was given to
Yisra'el.

63 And the man Yehudah and his brethren
were greatly glorified in the sight of all
Yisra'el, and of all the nations, wherever
their name was heard of; 64 and men
gathered together to them, acclaiming
them.

65 And Yehudah and his brethren went
forth, and fought against the children of
Esav in the land toward the south; and he
struck Ḥevron and its villages, and pulled
down its strongholds, and burned its
towers round about. 66 And he removed to
go into the land of the Philistines, and he
went through Shomeron. 67 In that day
certain priests, desiring to do exploits
there, were slain in battle, as they went out
to battle unadvisedly. 68 And Yehudah
turned toward Ashdod, to the land of the
Philistines, and pulled down their idol-
altars, and burned the carved images with
fire, and took the plunder of their cities,
and returned into the land of Yehudah.

6 1 And king Antioḥos was journeying
through the upper countries; and he
received word that in Elam in Paras there
was a city renowned for riches, for silver
and gold; 2 and that the temple which was
in it was very rich, and that there were
golden shields, and breastplates, and arms
in it, which Alexandros, son of Philippos,
the Makedonian king, who reigned first
among the Greeks, left behind there.
3 And he came and sought to take the city,
and to pillage it; and he was not able,
because the thing was known to them of
the city, 4 and they rose up against him to
battle: and he fled, and removed *from*
there with great heaviness, to return to
Bavel.

5 And there came one bringing him tidings
into Paras, that the armies, which went
against the land of Yehudah, had been put
to flight; 6 and that Lysias went first with
a strong army, and was put to shame
before them; and that they had grown
strong by reason of arms and power, and
with store of spoils, which they took from
the armies that they had cut off; 7 and that
they had pulled down the abomination
which he had built upon the altar that was
in Yerushalayim; and that they had
encompassed about the set-apart place
with high walls, as before, and Beth-Tsur,
his city. 8 And it came to pass, when the
king heard these words, he was astonished
and greatly moved: and he laid him down
upon his bed, and fell sick for grief,
because things did not befall him that he
expected. 9 And he was there many days,
because great grief was renewed upon
him, and he made account that he should
die.

10 And he called for all his beloved, and
said to them, "Sleep departs from my eyes,
and my heart fails for care. 11 And I said
in my heart, 'To what tribulation have I
come, and how great of a flood is it, that I

am in now!' For I was gracious and
beloved in my power. 12 But now I
remember the evils which I did at
Yerushalayim, and that I took all the
vessels of silver and gold that were there,
and sent forth to destroy the inhabitants of
Yehudah without a cause. 13 I perceive
that on this account these evils are come
upon me, and, behold, I perish through
great grief in a strange land."[a]

14 And he called for Philippos, one of his
beloved, and set him over all his kingdom,
15 and gave him his crown, and his robe,
and his signet ring, to the end he should
bring Antioḥos his son, and raise him up
that he might be king. 16 And king
Antioḥos died there in the hundred and
forty-ninth year. 17 And Lysias knew that
the king was dead, and he set up Antioḥos
his son to reign, whom he had raised up
being young, and he called his name
Eupator.[b]

18 And those who were in the fortress shut
up Yisra'el around the set-apart place, and
always sought their hurt, and the
strengthening of the nations. 19 And
Yehudah thought to destroy them, and
called all the people together to besiege
them. 20 And they were gathered together,
and besieged them in the hundred and
fiftieth year, and he made mounds to shoot
from, and engines of war. 21 And there
came forth some of those who were shut
up, and there were joined to them certain
wicked men of Yisra'el.

22 And they went to the king, and said,
"How long will you not execute judgment,
and avenge our brethren? 23 We were
willing to serve your father, and to walk
after his words, and to follow his
commands, 24 and for this cause the
children of our people besieged the
fortress, and were alienated from us. But
as many of us as they could find, they
killed, and plundered our inheritances.
25 And they did not stretch out their hand
against us only, but also against all their
borders. 26 And behold, they are
encamped this day against the fortress at
Yerushalayim, to take it: and the set-apart
place and Beth-Tsur have they fortified.
27 And if you do not deal with them
quickly, they will do greater things than
these, and you shall not be able to control
them."

28 And when the king heard this, he was
angry, and gathered together all his
emissaries, even the rulers of his army,
and those who were over the horsemen.
29 And there came to him from other
kingdoms, and from isles of the sea, bands
of hired soldiers. 30 And the number of his
forces was a hundred thousand footmen,
and twenty thousand horsemen, and thirty-
two elephants trained for war. 31 And they
went through Edom, and encamped
against Beth-Tsur, and fought against it
many days, and made engines of war; and
those of Beth-Tsur came out, and burned
them with fire, and fought valiantly.
32 And Yehudah removed from the
fortress, and encamped at Beth-Zekaryah,
near the king's camp. 33 And the king rose
early in the morning, and removed his
army at full speed along the road to Beth-
Zekaryah, and his forces made them ready
to battle, and sounded with the shofars.
34 And they showed the elephants the
blood of grapes and mulberries, that they

[a] 6:1-13 See also Maqabiym ב [2 Maccabees] 1:13-17; 9:1-29; Dani'el 11:40-45.

[b] 6:17 See also Maqabiym ב [2 Maccabees] 10:10-11.

might prepare them for the battle.[a] 35 And
they divided the beasts among the
formations, and they set by each elephant
a thousand men armed with coats of mail,
and helmets of brass on their heads. And
for each beast were appointed five
hundred elect horsemen. 36 These were
ready beforehand, wherever the beast was;
and wherever the beast went, they went
with him; they did not depart from him.

37 And towers of wood were upon them,
strong and covered, one upon each beast,
girded fast upon him with cunning
devices; and upon each beast were thirty-
two valiant men that fought upon them,
beside his Indian 38 (and the remnant of
the horsemen he set on this side and that
side at the two parts of the army), striking
terror into the enemy, and protected by the
formations. 39 Now when the sun shone
upon the shields of gold and brass, the
mountains shone with them, and blazed
like torches of fire. 40 And a part of the
king's army was spread upon the high
mountains, and some on the low ground,
and they went on faithfully and in order.

41 And all that heard the noise of their
multitude, and the marching of the
multitude, and the rattling of the arms, did
tremble: for the army was very great and
strong. 42 And Yehudah and his army
drew near for battle, and six hundred men
of the king's army fell there. 43 And
Elazar, who was called Avaran, saw one
of the beasts armed with royal
breastplates, and he was higher than all the
beasts, and the king seemed to be upon
him; 44 and he gave himself to deliver his
people, and to get him an everlasting
name; 45 and he ran upon him
courageously into the midst of the
formation, and killed on the right hand and
on the left, and they parted in half from
him on this side and on that. 46 And he
crept under the elephant, and thrust him
from beneath, and killed him; and the
elephant fell to the earth upon him, and he
died there. 47 And they saw the strength of
the kingdom, and the fierce attack of the
army, and turned away from them.

48 But they of the king's army went up to
Yerushalayim to meet them, and the king
encamped toward Yehudah, and toward
Mount Tsion. 49 And he made peace with
those of Beth-Tsur; and he came out of the
city, because they had no food there to
endure the siege, because it was a Sabbath
to the land.[b] 50 And the king took Beth-
Tsur, and appointed a garrison there to
keep it. 51 And he encamped against the
sanctuary many days; and set mounds
there to shoot from, and engines of war,
and instruments for casting fire and
stones, and pieces to cast darts, and slings.
52 And they also made engines against
their engines, and fought for many days.
53 But there were no food in the set-apart
place, because it was the seventh year, and
those who fled for safety into Yehudah

---

[a] 6:34 "And they showed them the blood of grapes and mulberries" – that is, wine made from these fruits. It was discovered during this time period that giving alcohol to elephants would cause them to become especially enraged, and therefore more likely to stomp and kill anything that aggravated it. This is mentioned specifically in the Pseudepigraphal book of 3 Maccabees as a form of "execution by elephant" practiced by Ptolemy in Mitsrayim. Similarly, historian Flavius Josephus also mentions the intoxication of elephants for the purpose of "execution by elephant" in his writing *Against Apion* II:5.

[b] 6:49 Sabbath to the land – Every seven years the land is to rest from reaping and sowing, and thus have a "Sabbath." See Vayyiqra [Leviticus] 25.

from among the nations had eaten up the
remnant of the store. 54 And there were
but a few left in the set-apart place,
because the famine prevailed against
them, and they were scattered, each man
to his own place.

55 And Lysias received word that
Philippos, whom Antioḥos the king, while
he was yet alive, appointed to raise up his
son Antioḥos, that he might be king,
56 was returned from Paras and Media,
and with him the forces that went with the
king, and that he was seeking to take to
him the reign.

57 And he made haste, and gave consent to
depart; and he said to the king and the
leaders of the army and to the men, "We
decay daily, and our food is scarce, and
the place where we encamp is strong, and
the affairs of the kingdom lie upon us:
58 now therefore let us give the right hand
to these men, and make peace with them
and with all their nation, 59 and covenant
with them, that they shall walk after their
own laws, as *they* previously *did*: for
because of their laws which we abolished
they were angered, and did all these
things."

60 And the saying pleased the king and the
princes, and he sent to them to make
peace; and they accepted it. 61 And the
king and the princes swore to them, so
they came forth from the stronghold.
62 And the king entered into Mount Tsion;
and he saw the strength of the place, and
reneged on the oath which he had sworn,
and gave command to pull down the wall
round about. 63 And he removed in haste,
and returned to Antioḥ, and found
Philippos master of the city; and he fought
against him, and took the city by force.

7 1 In the hundred and fifty-first year,
Demetrios the son of Seleukos came forth
from Rome, and went up with a few men
to a city by the sea, and reigned there.
2 And it came to pass, when he would go
into the house of the kingdom of his
fathers, that the army laid hands on
Antioḥos and Lysias, to bring them to
him. 3 And the thing was known to him,
and he said, "Do not show their faces to
me."

4 And the army killed them. And
Demetrios sat upon the throne of his
kingdom. 5 And there came to him all the
lawless and wicked men of Yisra'el; and
Elyaqum was their leader, desiring to be
high priest; 6 and they accused the people
to the king, saying, "Yehudah and his
brethren have destroyed all your friends,
and have scattered us from our own land.
7 Now therefore send a man whom you
trust, and let him go and see all the havoc
which he has made of us, and of the king's
country, and how he has punished them
and all that helped them."[a]

8 And the king chose Bacchides, one of
the king's emissaries, who was ruler in the
country beyond the river, and was a great
man in the kingdom, and faithful to the
king. 9 And he sent him, and that wicked
Elyaqum, and promised to him the high
priesthood, and he commanded him to
take vengeance upon the children of
Yisra'el.

---

[a] 7:1-7 See also Maqabiym ב [2 Maccabees] 14:1-11.

10 And they removed, and came with a great army into the land of Yehudah, and he sent messengers to Yehudah and his brethren with words of peace deceitfully. 11 And they gave no heed to their words; for they saw that they were come with a great army. 12 And there were gathered together to Elyaqum and Bacchides a company of scribes, to seek for justice. 13 And the Ḥasidim were the first among the children of Yisra'el that sought peace of them; 14 for they said, "One that is a priest of the seed of Aharon is come with the forces, and he will do us no wrong."

15 And he spoke with them words of peace, and swore to them, saying, "We will not seek to hurt you, nor your friends." 16 And they gave him credence: and he laid hands on sixty of them, and killed them in one day, according to the word which the psalmist wrote, 17 "**The flesh of your set-apart ones did they cast out, and their blood did they shed around Yerushalayim; and there was no man to bury them**.[a]"

18 And the fear and the dread of them fell upon all the people, for they said, "There is neither truth nor judgment in them; for they have broken the covenant and the oath which they swore."

19 And Bacchides removed from Yerushalayim, and encamped in Bezeth. And he sent and took away many of the deserters that were with him, and certain of the people, and he killed them, and cast them into the great well. 20 And he promised the country to Elyaqum, and left with him a force to aid him; and Bacchides went away to the king.

21 And Elyaqum strove for his high priesthood. 22 And there were gathered to him all those who troubled their people, and they gained control of the land of Yehudah, and did great harm in Yisra'el. 23 And Yehudah saw all the mischief that Elyaqum and his company had done among the children of Yisra'el, even above the nations, 24 and he went out into all the coasts of Yehudah round about, and took vengeance on the men that had deserted from him, and they were restrained from going forth into the country. 25 But when Elyaqum saw that Yehudah and his company grew strong, and knew that he was not able to withstand them, he returned to the king, and brought evil accusations against them.

26 And the king sent Niqanor, one of his honorable princes, a man that hated Yisra'el and was their enemy, and commanded him to destroy the people. 27 And Niqanor came to Yerushalayim with a great army; and he sent to Yehudah and his brethren deceitfully with words of peace, saying, 28 "Let there be no battle between me and you; I will come with a few men, that I may see your faces in peace."[b]

29 And he came to Yehudah, and they saluted one another peaceably. And the enemies were ready to take away Yehudah by violence. 30 And the thing was known to Yehudah, so that he came to him with deceit, and he was very afraid of him, and would see his face no more. 31 And Niqanor knew that his counsel was

[a] 7:17 See Tehillim [Psalms] 79:1-3.

[b] 7:26-28 See also Maqabiym ב [2 Maccabees] 8:9; 14:12-13.

discovered; and he went out to meet
Yehudah in battle beside Kaphar-
Shalama;[a] 32 and there fell of Niqanor's
side about five thousand men, and they
fled into the city of David.

33 And after these things Niqanor went up
to Mount Tsion: and there came some of
the priests out of the set-apart place, and
some of the elders of the people, to salute
him peaceably, and to show him the burnt
offering that was being offered for the
king. 34 And he mocked them, and
laughed at them, and defiled them,[b] and
spoke haughtily, 35 and swore in a rage,
saying, "Unless Yehudah and his army be
now delivered into my hands, it shall be
that, if I come again in peace, I will burn
up this house." And he went out in a great
rage. 36 And the priests entered in, and
stood before the altar and the Temple; and
they wept, and said, 37 "You did choose
this House to be called by Your Name, to
be a house of prayer and petition for Your
people. 38 Take vengeance on this man
and his army, and let them fall by the
sword: remember their blasphemies, and
do not allow them to live any longer."

39 And Niqanor went forth from
Yerushalayim, and encamped in Beth-
Ḥoron, and there he met the army of
Aram. 40 And Yehudah encamped in
Adasa with three thousand men: and
Yehudah prayed and said, 41 "When those
who came from the king blasphemed,
Your messenger went out, and struck a
hundred and eighty-five thousand of
them.[c] 42 Even so, overthrow this army
before us today, and let all the rest know
that he has spoken wickedly against Your
set-apart place, and judge him according
to his wickedness."[d]

43 And on the thirteenth day of the month
of Adar, the armies joined battle: and
Niqanor's army was overthrown, and he
himself was the first to fall in the battle.
44 Now when his army saw that Niqanor
was fallen, they cast away their arms, and
fled. 45 And they pursued after them a
day's journey from Adasa until you come
to Gezer, and they sounded an alarm after
them with shofars. 46 And they came forth
out of all the villages of Yehudah around
there, and closed them in; and these turned
them back on those, and they all fell by
the sword, and there was not one of them
left. 47 And they took the spoils, and the
plunder, and they struck off Niqanor's
head, and his right hand, which he
stretched out so haughtily, and brought
them, and hanged them up beside
Yerushalayim.[e] 48 And the people were
very glad, and they kept that day as a day
of great gladness. 49 And they decreed to
keep this day year by year, the thirteenth
day of Adar. 50 And the land of Yehudah
had rest *a* few days.

8 1 And Yehudah heard of the fame of the
Romans, that they were men of valor, and
had pleasure in all that joined themselves
to them, and made beloved *friends* with all

---

[a] 7:31 Kaphar-Shalama – Believed to be formed from the Hebrew words כפר (*kaphar*) and שלום (*shalom*): "Cover of Peace" or possibly "Smearing of Peace." Exact location is disputed.

[b] 7:34 It is believed by most that he defiled the priests by spitting on them, rendering them unclean by Temple standards of the time. Compare Vayyiqra [Leviticus] 15:8.

[c] 7:41 See Melakhim ב [2 Kings] 19:35-36.

[d] 7:39-42 See also Maqabiym ב [2 Maccabees] 15:22-24.

[e] 7:47 See also Maqabiym ב [2 Maccabees] 15:30-35.

such as come to them. 2 And that they were men of valor. And they told him of their wars and exploits which they do among the Galatians, and how that they conquered them, and brought them under tribute. 3 And what things they did in the land of Spain, that they might become masters of the mines of silver and gold which were there, 4 and how they, by their policy and persistence, conquered all the place (and the place was very far from them), and the kings that came against them from the uttermost part of the earth, until they had overthrown them, and struck them very severely; and how the rest gave them tribute year by year. 5 And they overthrew in battle and conquered Philippos, and Perseus, king of Kittim, and those who lifted up themselves against them. 6 Antioḥos[a] also, the great king of Asia, who came against them to battle, having a hundred and twenty elephants, with horsemen, and chariots, and a very great army; and he was overthrown by them. 7 And they took him alive, and appointed that both he and those that reigned after him should give them a great tribute, and should give hostages, and a parcel of land, namely, 8 the country of Hodu[b], and Media, and Lydia, and the best of their countries. And they took them from him, and gave them to king Eumenes.[c] 9 And *they also told* how they of Greece took counsel to come and destroy them; 10 and the thing was known to them, and they sent against them a captain, and fought against them, and many of them fell wounded, and they made their wives and their children captive, and plundered them, and conquered their land, and pulled down their strongholds, and plundered them, and brought them into bondage to this day. 11 And the remnant of the kingdoms and of the isles, as many as rose up against them at any time, they destroyed and made them to be their servants. 12 But they kept friendship with their beloved, and those that relied upon them; and they conquered the kingdoms that were near and those that were far off, and all that heard of their fame were afraid of them.

13 Moreover, whoever they desire to support and to make kings, they make kings; and whoever they desire *to remove,* they remove; and they are greatly exalted. 14 And for all this, none of them ever put on a crown, neither did they clothe themselves with purple, to be magnified by it. 15 And how they had made for themselves a senate house, and day by day three hundred and twenty men sat in council, consulting always for the people, to the end they might be well ordered. 16 And *they also told* how they commit their government to one man year by year, that he should rule over them, and be master over all their country, and all are obedient to that one, and there is neither envy nor rivalry among them.

17 And Yehudah chose Eupolemus the son of Yoḥanan, the son of Haqots, and Iason the son of Elazar, and sent them to Rome, to make an alliance of friendship and alliance with them, 18 and that they should

---

[a] 8:6 This refers to Antioḥos the III, whereas Antioḥos Epiphanes – who is mentioned throughout the early chapters of Maqabiym א [1 Maccabees] – is Antioḥos the IV.

[b] 8:8 LXX reads Ινδικην (*Indi'keyn*) which is the equivalent of the Hebrew הדו (*Hodu*) meaning "India." Syr., however, reads ܟܘܫ (*Kush*) which is Ethiopia.

[c] 8:8 Eumenes: most likely Eumenes the II, king of Pergamum, who gained much after the overthrow of Antioḥos the III.

take the yoke from them; for they saw that
the kingdom of the Greeks did keep
Yisra'el in bondage. 19 And they went to
Rome (and the way was very long), and
they entered into the senate house, and
answered and said, 20 "Yehudah, who is
also called Maqabi, and his brethren, and
the people of the Yehudim, have sent us to
you, to make a alliance and peace with
you, and that we might be registered as
your allies and beloved."

21 And the thing was well-pleasing in their
sight. 22 And this is the copy of the
writing which they wrote back again on
tables of brass, and sent to Yerushalayim,
that it might be with them there for a
memorial of peace and alliance:

23 "Good success be to the Romans, and to
the nation of the Yehudim, by sea and by
land forever: the sword also and the
enemy be far from them. 24 But if war
arise for Rome first, or any of their allies
in all their dominion, 25 the nation of the
Yehudim shall help them as allies with all
their heart, as the occasion shall prescribe
to them. 26 And to those who make war
upon them they shall not give, neither
supply, food, arms, money, or ships, as it
has seemed good to Rome, and they shall
keep their judgments without taking
anything therefore. 27 In the same manner,
moreover, if war comes first upon the
nation of the Yehudim, the Romans shall
help them as allies with all their being, as
the occasion shall prescribe to them.
28 And there shall not be given food, arms,
money, or ships to those who are allies
with the enemies *of the Yehudim*, as it has
seemed good to Rome. And they shall
keep these observances without deceit.
29 According to these words have the
Romans cut a covenant with the people of
the Yehudim. 30 But if, after this, the one
party and the other shall take counsel to
add or diminish anything together, they
shall do it at their pleasure, and whatever
they shall add or take away shall be
established. 31 And as touching the evils
which king Demetrios does to them, we
have written to him, saying, 'Why have
you made your yoke heavy upon our
beloved *friends* and allies the Yehudim?'
32 If therefore they plead any more against
you, we will execute judgment, and fight
with you by sea and by land."

9 1 And Demetrios heard that Niqanor
was fallen with his forces in battle, and he
sent Bacchides and Elyaqum again into
the land of Yehudah a second time, and
the right wing of his army with them.
2 And they went by the way that leads to
Gilgal, and encamped against Mesaloth,
which is in Arbela, and got possession of
it, and destroyed many beings of men.
3 And in the first month of the hundred
and fifty-second year they encamped
against Yerushalayim. 4 And they
removed, and went to Berea, with twenty
thousand footmen and two thousand
horsemen. 5 And Yehudah was encamped
at Elasa, and three thousand elect men
with him. 6 And they saw the multitude of
the forces, for they were many; and they
feared greatly. And many slipped away
out of the army; there were not left of
them more than eight hundred men. 7 And
Yehudah saw that his army slipped away,
and that the battle pressed upon him, and
he was very troubled in heart, for that he
had no time to gather them together, and
he grew faint.

8 And he said to those who were left, "Let
us arise and go up against our adversaries,

if perhaps we may be able to fight with
them."

9 And they would have dissuaded him,
saying, "We shall in no way be able. But
rather, let us save our lives now. Let us
return again, us and our brethren, and fight
against them *later*. But *today* we are few."

10 And Yehudah said, "Let it not be so that
I should do this thing, to flee from them:
and if our time is come, let us die bravely
for the sake of our brethren, and not leave
a cause of reproach against our glory."

11 And the army removed from the camp,
and stood to encounter them, and the
horsemen was parted into two companies,
and the slingers and the archers went
before the army, along with all the mighty
men that fought in the front of the battle.
12 But Bacchides was in the right wing;
and the formation drew near on the two
parts, and they blew with their horns.
13 And the men of Yehudah's side, even
they sounded with their horns, and the
earth shook with the shout of the armies,
and the battle was joined, and continued
from morning until evening. 14 And
Yehudah saw that Bacchides and the
strength of his army were on the right
side, and all the brave in heart went with
him. 15 And they overthrew the right
wing, and he pursued after them to the
mount of Ashdod. 16 And those who were
on the left wing saw that the right wing
was overthrown, and they turned and
followed upon the footsteps of Yehudah
and of those that were with him. 17 And
the battle grew intense, and many on both
sides fell wounded. 18 And Yehudah fell,
and the rest fled. 19 And Yonathan and
Shimon took Yehudah their brother, and
buried him in the grave of his fathers at
Modin. 20 And they bewailed him, and all
Yisra'el made great lamentation for him,
and mourned many days, and said,
21 "How is the mighty fallen, the savior of
Yisra'el!"[a]

22 And the rest of the acts of Yehudah,
and his wars, and the valiant deeds which
he did, and his greatness, they are not
written; for they were far too many.

23 And it came to pass after the death of
Yehudah, that the lawless put forth their
heads in all the coasts of Yisra'el, and all
those who committed iniquity rose up,
24 and the country went over with them.
(In those days there was a very great
famine). 25 And Bacchides elected the
wicked men, and made them masters of
the country. 26 And they sought out and
searched for the brethren of Yehudah, and
brought them to Bacchides, and he took
vengeance on them, and used them
spitefully. 27 And there was great
tribulation in Yisra'el, such as was not
since the time that no prophet appeared to
them.

28 And all the brethren of Yehudah were
gathered together, and they said to
Yonathan, 29 "Since your brother Yehudah
has died, we have no man like him to go
forth against our enemies and Bacchides,
and among them of our nation that hate us.
30 Now therefore we have chosen you this
day to be our prince and leader in his
stead, that you may fight our battles."

31 And Yonathan took the governance
upon himself at that time, and rose up in
the stead of his brother Yehudah.

---

[a] 9:21 Compare Shemu'el ב [2 Samuel] 1:19-27.

32 And Bacchides knew it, and he sought
to kill him. 33 And Yonathan, and Shimon
his brother, and all that were with him,
knew it; and they fled into the wilderness
of Teqoa, and encamped by the water of
the pool Asphar. 34 And Bacchides knew
it on the Sabbath day, and came, he and all
his army, over Yarden. 35 And Yonathan
sent his brother, a leader of the multitude,
and implored his friends the Nabathites,
that they might leave with them their
baggage, which was much. 36 And the
children of Iambri came out of Madaba,
and took Yoḥanan, and all that he had, and
went their way with it.

37 But after these things they brought
word to Yonathan and Shimon his brother,
that the children of Iambri were making a
great wedding *feast*, and were bringing the
bride from Nadabath with a great train, a
daughter of one of the great nobles of
Kana'an. 38 And they remembered
Yoḥanan their brother, and went up, and
hid themselves under the cover of the
mountain, 39 and they lifted up their eyes,
and saw, and behold, a great commotion
and much baggage. And the bridegroom
came forth, and his friends and his
brethren, to meet them with timbrels, and
minstrels, and many weapons. 40 And they
rose up against them from their ambush,
and killed them, and many fell wounded,
and the remnant fled into the mountain,
and they took all their spoils. 41 And the
marriage was turned into mourning, and
the voice of their minstrels into
lamentation. 42 And they avenged fully the
blood of their brother, and turned back to
the marsh of Yarden

43 And Bacchides heard it, and he came on
the Sabbath day to the banks of Yarden
with a great army. 44 And Yonathan said
to his company, "Let us stand up now and
fight for our lives, for today it is not like it
once was, as yesterday and the day before.
45 For behold, the battle is before us and
behind us; moreover the water of the
Yarden is on this side and on that side, and
marsh and wood; and there is no place to
escape. 46 Now therefore cry to heaven,
that you may be delivered out of the hand
of your enemies."

47 And the battle was joined, and
Yonathan stretched forth his hand to strike
Bacchides, and he turned away back from
him. 48 And Yonathan and those who were
with him leapt into the Yarden, and swam
over to the other side: and they did not
pass over Yarden against them. 49 And
about three thousand of Bacchides'
company fell that day. 50 And he returned
to Yerushalayim. And they built strong
cities in Yehudah; *and* the stronghold that
was in Yeriḥo, and Emmaus, and Beth-
Ḥoron, and Beth-El, and Timnath,
Pharathon, and Tephon, with high walls
and gates and bars. 51 And in them he set a
garrison, to aggravate Yisra'el. 52 And he
fortified the city Beth-Tsur, and Gezer,
and the fortress, and put forces in them,
and store of food. 53 And he took the sons
of the chief men of the country for
hostages, and put them in prison in the
fortress at Yerushalayim.

54 And in the hundred and fifty-third year,
in the second month, Elyaqum
commanded to pull down the wall of the
inner court of the set-apart place. He also

pulled down the works of the prophets.[a]
55 And he began to pull down. At that
time Elyaqum was stricken, and his works
were hindered, and his mouth was
stopped, and he was taken with a palsy,
and he could no more speak anything and
give order concerning his house. 56 And
Elyaqum died at that time with great
torment. 57 And Bacchides saw that
Elyaqum was dead, and he returned to the
king: and the land of Yehudah had rest
two years.

58 And all the lawless men took counsel,
saying, "Behold, Yonathan and those with
him are dwelling in peace and security:
now therefore we will bring Bacchides,
and he shall lay hands on them all in one
night."

59 And they went and consulted with him.
60 And he removed, and came with a great
army, and sent letters secretly to all his
allies that were in Yehudah, that they
should lay hands on Yonathan and those
that were with him. And they could not,
because their counsel was known to them.
61 And those who were with Yonathan
laid hands on about fifty of the men of the
country, that were authors of the
wickedness, and he killed them. 62 And
Yonathan, and Shimon, and those who
were with him, got them away to Beth-
Basi, which is in the wilderness, and he
built up that which had been pulled down,
and they made it strong. 63 And Bacchides
knew it, and he gathered together all his
multitude, and sent word to those who
were of Yehudah. 64 And he went and
encamped against Beth-Basi, and fought
against it many days, and made engines of
war. 65 And Yonathan left his brother
Shimon in the city, and went forth into the
country, and he went with a few men.
66 And he struck Odomera and his
brethren, and the children of Phasiron in
their tent. 67 And they began to strike
them, and to go up with their forces. And
Shimon and those who were with him
went out of the city, and set the engines of
war on fire, 68 and fought against
Bacchides, and he was overthrown by
them, and they afflicted him severely; for
his counsel and work was in vain.

69 And they were very angry with the
lawless men that gave him counsel to
come into the country, and they killed
many of them. And he took counsel to
depart into his own land. 70 And Yonathan
had knowledge of this, and sent emissaries
to him, to the end that they should make
peace with him, and that he should restore
to them the captives. 71 And he accepted
the thing, and did according to his words,
and swore to him that he would not seek
his hurt all the days of his life.

72 And he restored to him the captives
which he had previously taken out of the
land of Yehudah, and he returned and
departed into his own land, and no longer
came into their borders. 73 And the sword
ceased from Yisra'el. And Yonathan lived
at Mikmash[b]; and Yonathan began to
judge the people; and he destroyed the
wicked out of Yisra'el.

10 1 And in the hundred and sixtieth year,

---

[a] 9:54 The phrase "works of the prophets" could be a reference to Ḥaggai and Zekaryah, as they both prophesied about the rebuilding of the Temple.

[b] 9:73 Mikmash – Famous for the exploits of Yonathan, the son of Sha'ul. Compare Shemu'el א [1 Samuel] 14.

Alexandros Epiphanes, the son of
Antioḥos, went up and took possession of
Akko: and they received him, and he
reigned there. 2 And king Demetrios heard
of this, and he gathered together very great
forces, and went forth to meet him in
battle. 3 And Demetrios sent letters to
Yonathan with words of peace, so as to
magnify him.

4 For he said, "Let us make peace with
them in advance, or else he will make
peace with Alexandros against us: 5 for he
will remember all the evils that we have
done against him, and to his brethren and
to his nation."

6 And he gave him authority to gather
together forces, and to provide arms, and
that he should be his ally: and he
commanded that they should deliver up to
him the hostages that were in the fortress.

7 And Yonathan came to Yerushalayim,
and read the letters in the audience of all
the people, and of those who were in the
fortress, 8 and they were very afraid when
they heard that the king had given him
authority to gather together an army.
9 And they of the fortress delivered up the
hostages to Yonathan, and he restored
them to their parents. 10 And Yonathan
lived in Yerushalayim, and began to build
and renew the city. 11 And he commanded
those who did the work to build the walls,
and Mount Tsion round about with square
stones[a] for defense; and they did so.
12 And the foreigners that were in the
strongholds which Bacchides had built
fled away. 13 And each man left his place,
and departed into his own land. 14 Only at
Beth-Tsur were there left certain of those
that had forsaken the Torah and the
commands; for it was a place of refuge to
them.

15 And king Alexandros heard all the
promises which Demetrios had sent to
Yonathan: and they told him of the battles
and the valiant deeds which he and his
brethren had done, and of the toils which
they had endured.

16 And he said, "Shall we find such
another man? And now we will make him
our friend and ally."

17 And he wrote letters, and sent them to
him, according to these words, saying,
18 "King Alexandros to his brother
Yonathan, greetings: 19 We have heard of
you, that you are a mighty man of valor,
and meet to be our friend. 20 And now we
have appointed you this day to be high
priest of your nation, and to be called the
king's friend." And he sent to him a purple
robe and a crown of gold, "and to take our
part, and to keep friendship with us."

21 And Yonathan put on the set-apart
garments in the seventh month of the
hundred and sixtieth year, at the Feast of
Tabernacles, and he gathered together
forces, and provided arms in abundance.[b]

22 And Demetrios heard these things, and
he was grieved, and said, 23 "What is this
that we have done, that Alexandros has

---

[a] 10:11 Some LXX and most Syriac manuscripts read as it is here. Other Greek manuscripts read "four-foot stones" rather than "square stones." It is possible that the difference is due to a misunderstanding of "four" meaning "four-sided" (square) rather than the actual length.

[b] 10:21 "Put on the set-apart garments": meaning Yonathan began to act as high priest. After the death of Alqimos, there was no high priest for a number years. Thus Yonathan began to fill in the vacant position.

gone before us in establishing friendship
with the Yehudim, to strengthen himself?
24 I also will write to them words of
encouragement and of honor and of gifts,
that they may be with me to aid me."

25 And he sent to them according to these
words: "King Demetrios to the nation of
the Yehudim, greetings: 26 Since you have
kept your covenants with us, and
continued in our friendship, and have not
joined yourselves to our enemies, we have
heard of this, and are glad. 27 And now,
continue to keep faith with us, and we will
repay to you good things in return for your
dealings with us, 28 and will grant you
many immunities, and give you gifts.
29 And now I free you, and release all the
Yehudim from the tributes, and from the
customs of salt, and from the crowns.
30 And instead of the third part of the
seed, and instead of the half of the fruit of
the trees, which falls to me to receive, I
release it from this day forward, so that I
will not take it from the land of Yehudah,
and from the three governments which are
added to it from the country of Shomeron
and Galilee, from this day forth and for all
time.

31 "And let Yerushalayim be set-apart and
free, and her borders; the tenths and the
tolls also. 32 I yield up also my authority
over the fortress which is at
Yerushalayim, and give it to the high
priest, that he may appoint in it such men
as he shall choose to keep it. 33 And every
being of the Yehudim that has been
carried captive from the land of Yehudah
into any part of my kingdom, I set at
liberty without price; and let all remit the
tributes of their cattle also. 34 And all the
Feasts, and the Sabbaths, and new moons,
and appointed times, and three days before
a Feast, and three days after a Feast, let
them all be days of immunity and release
for all the Yehudim that are in my
kingdom.[a] 35 And no man shall have
authority to exact from any of them, or to
trouble them concerning any matter.

36 "And let there be about thirty thousand
men of the Yehudim enrolled among the
king's forces, and pay shall be given to
them, as belongs to all the king's forces.
37 And of them some shall be placed in the
king's great strongholds, and some of them
shall be placed over the affairs of the
kingdom, which are of trust: and let those
that are over them, and their rulers, be of
themselves, and let them walk after their
own Torot, even as the king has
commanded in the land of Yehudah.

38 "And the three governments that have
been added to Yehudah from the country
of Shomeron, let them be added to
Yehudah, that they may be reckoned to be
under one, that they may not obey *any*
other authority besides that of the high
priest. 39 As for Akko, and the land
pertaining to it, I have given it as a gift to
the set-apart place that is at Yerushalayim,
for the expenses that suit the set-apart
place. 40 And I give every year fifteen
thousand shekels of silver from the king's
revenues from the places that are
convenient. 41 And all the interest, which
those who manage the king's affairs did
not pay in the first years, they shall give
from now on toward the works of the
house. 42 And beside this, the five

---

[a] 10:34 "Immunity and release": meaning all Yehudim would be allowed to cease from work on these days.

thousand shekels of silver, which they
received from the uses of the set-apart
place from the revenue year by year, this
also is released, because it belongs to the
priests that minister.

43 "And whoever shall flee to the Temple
that is at Yerushalayim, and be found
within any of its borders, whether one owe
moneys to the king, or any other matter,
let them go free, and all that they have in
my kingdom. 44 And for the building and
renewing of the works of the set-apart
place the expense shall be given also out
of the king's revenue. 45 And the expense
for the building of the walls of
Yerushalayim, and for the fortifying of it
be given also out of the king's revenue,
and for the building of the walls in
Yehudah."

46 Now when Yonathan and the people
heard these words, they gave no credence
to them, nor did they receive them,
because they remembered the great evil
which he had done in Yisra'el, and that he
had afflicted them very severely. 47 And
they were well pleased with Alexandros,
because he was the first that spoke words
of peace to them, and they were allied
with him always. 48 And king Alexandros
gathered together great forces, and
encamped near Demetrios. 49 And the two
kings joined battle, and the army of
Alexandros fled; and Demetrios followed
after him, and prevailed against them.
50 And he strengthened the battle greatly
until the sun went down, and Demetrios
fell that day.

[51 And Alexandros sent emissaries to
Ptolemy king of Mitsrayim according to
these words, saying, 52 "Since I have
returned to my kingdom, and I am set on
the throne of my fathers, and have gotten
the dominion, and have overthrown
Demetrios, and have gotten possession of
our country 53 (yes, I joined battle with
him, and he and his army were overthrown
by us, and we sat upon the throne of his
kingdom): 54 now also let us establish
friendship one with the other, and give me
now your daughter to wife: and I will be
your son-in-law, and will give both you
and her gifts worthy of you."

55 And Ptolemy the king answered,
saying, "Happy is the day when you
returned into the land of your fathers, and
sat on the throne of their kingdom. 56 And
now will I do to you, as you have written:
but meet me at Akko, that we may see one
another; and I will become your father-in-
law, even as you have said."

57 And Ptolemy went out of Mitsrayim,
himself and Kleopatra[a] his daughter, and
came to Akko in the hundred and sixty-
second year. 58 And king Alexandros met
him, and he bestowed on him his daughter
Kleopatra, and celebrated her marriage at
Akko with great splendor, in the manner
of kings.[b]

59 And king Alexandros wrote to
Yonathan, that he should come to meet
him. 60 And he went with splendor to
Akko, and met the two kings, and gave
them and their friends silver and gold, and

[a] 10:57 Kleopatra Thea, at the time, was about 15-years-old.

[b] 10:58 Akko was a neutral territory. Here Ptolemy gave Kleopatra to Alexandros as wife, in hopes of forming an alliance. Later (in Maqabiym א [1 Maccabees] 11:9,-0) she is given to Demetrios II as wife, and later still to his brother Antioḥos VII.

many gifts, and *he* found favor in their
sight.

61 And there were gathered together
against him certain pestilent men out of
Yisra'el – men that were transgressors of
the Torah – to complain against him, and
the king gave no heed to them. 62 And the
king commanded, and they took off
Yonathan's garments, and clothed him in
purple: and thus they did. 63 And the king
made him sit with him, and said to his
princes, "Go forth with him into the midst
of the city, and make proclamation, that
no man complain against him for any
matter, and let no man trouble him for any
manner of cause."

64 And it came to pass, when those who
complained against him saw his glory
according to the herald that made
proclamation, and saw him clothed in
purple, they all fled away. 65 And the king
gave him honor, and wrote him among his
chief friends, and made him a captain, and
governor of a province. 66 And Yonathan
returned to Yerushalayim with peace and
gladness.][a]

67 And in the hundred and sixty-fifth year
came Demetrios, son of Demetrios, out of
Kaphtor into the land of his fathers, 68 and
king Alexandros heard about it, and he
grieved greatly, and returned to Antioḥ.
69 And Demetrios appointed Apollonios,
who was over Koele-Aram, and he
gathered together a great army, and
encamped in Yavneel, and sent to
Yonathan the high priest, saying,

70 "You alone lift up yourself against us,
but I am had in contempt and in reproach
because of you. And why do you flaunt
your power against us in the mountains?
71 Now therefore, if you trust in your
forces, come down to us into the plain,
and there let us try the matter together; for
with me is the power of the cities. 72 Ask
and learn who I am, and the rest that help
us; and they say, 'Your foot cannot stand
before our face; for your fathers have been
twice put to flight in their own land.'
73 And now you shall not be able to abide
the horsemen and such an army as this in
the plain, where is neither stone nor flint,
nor a place to which you may flee."

74 Now when Yonathan heard the words
of Apollonios, he was moved in his mind,
and he elected ten thousand men, and went
forth from Yerushalayim, and Shimon his
brother met him to help him. 75 And he
encamped against Yapho: and those of the
city shut him out, because Apollonios had
a garrison in Yapho: 76 and they fought
against it. And those of the city were
afraid, and opened to him: and Yonathan
became master of Yapho. 77 And
Apollonios heard, and he gathered an
army of three thousand horsemen, and a
great army, and went to Ashdod as though
he were on a journey, and there he drew
onward into the plain, because he had a
multitude of horsemen, and trusted in
them. 78 And he pursued after him to
Ashdod, and the armies joined battle.

79 And Apollonios had left a thousand
horsemen behind them secretly. 80 And
Yonathan knew that there was an ambush
behind him. And they encompassed
around his army, and cast their darts at the
people, from morning until evening: 81 but
the people stood still, as Yonathan

[a] 10:51-66 Most Syriac manuscripts, including Codex Ambrosianus, do not contain verses 51-66, thus omitting the story of Kleopatra completely. The reason for this is unknown.

commanded them: and their horses were
wearied. 82 And Shimon drew forth his
army, and joined battle with the formation
(for the horsemen were spent), and they
were overthrown by him, and fled. 83 And
the horsemen were scattered in the plain,
and they fled to Ashdod, and entered into
Beth-Dagon, the temple of their idol, to
save themselves.

84 And Yonathan burned Ashdod, and the
cities round about it, and took their spoils.
And the temple of Dagon, and those who
fled into it, he burned with fire. 85 And
those who had fallen by the sword, with
those who were burned, were about eight
thousand men. 86 And from there
Yonathan removed, and encamped against
Ashqelon, and they of the city came forth
to meet him with great splendor. 87 And
Yonathan, with those who were on his
side, returned to Yerushalayim with many
spoils. 88 And it came to pass, when king
Alexandros heard these things, he honored
Yonathan yet more; 89 and he sent to him
a buckle of gold, like the ones given to the
brethren of the kings: and he gave him
Eqron and all its coasts for a possession.

11 1 And the king of Mitsrayim gathered
together great forces, as the sand which is
by the sea shore, and many ships, and
sought to make himself master of
Alexandros' kingdom by deceit, and to add
it to his own kingdom. 2 And he went
forth into Aram with words of peace, and
they of the cities opened to him, and met
him. For king Alexandros's command was
that they should meet him, because he was
his father-in-law. 3 Now as he entered into
the cities of Akko, he set his forces for a
garrison in each city. 4 But when he came
near to Ashdod, they showed him the
temple of Dagon burned with fire, and
Ashdod and its pasture-lands pulled down,
and the bodies cast abroad, and those who
had been burned, whom he burned in the
war, for they had made heaps of them in
his way. 5 And they told the king what
things Yonathan had done, that they might
cast blame on him: and the king held his
peace. 6 And Yonathan met the king with
splendor at Yapho, and they saluted one
another, and they slept there. 7 And
Yonathan went with the king as far as the
river that is called Eleutherus, and
returned to Yerushalayim. 8 But king
Ptolemy became master of the cities upon
the sea coast, to Seleukia which is by the
sea,[a] and he devised evil plans concerning
Alexandros.

9 And he sent emissaries to king
Demetrios, saying, "Come, let us cut a
covenant with one another, and I will give
you my daughter whom Alexandros has,
and you shall reign over your father's
kingdom; 10 for I have regret that I gave
my daughter to him, for he sought to kill
me."[b]

11 And he cast blame on him, because he
coveted his kingdom. 12 And taking his
daughter from him, he gave her to
Demetrios, and was estranged from
Alexandros, and their enmity was openly
seen. 13 And Ptolemy entered into Antioḥ,

---

[a] 11:8 Seleukia which is by the sea – A port city of Antioḥ.

[b] 11:10 According to Flavius Josephus' *Antiquities of the Jews* Book XIII, Ch. 4, § 6, Alexandros' friend Ammonios had attempted to kill Ptolemy. When Ptolemy found out, he sent to Alexandros, demanding that Amonnios be delivered to him for punishment. When Alexandros did not comply, Ptolemy blamed him for the assassination attempt.

and put the diadem of Asia on himself;
and he put two diadems upon his head, the
diadem of Mitsrayim and that of Asia.
14 But king Alexandros was in Kilikia at
that season, because the people in those
parts were in revolt. 15 And Alexandros
heard of it, and he came against him in
war: and Ptolemy led forth his army, and
met him with a strong force, and put him
to flight. 16 And Alexandros fled into
Aravia, that he might be sheltered there;
but king Ptolemy was exalted. 17 And
Zavdiel the Aravian took off Alexandros'
head, and sent it to Ptolemy. 18 And king
Ptolemy died the third day after, and his
people who were in the strongholds were
slain by those who were in the
strongholds. 19 And Demetrios reigned in
the hundred and sixty-seventh year.

20 In those days Yonathan gathered
together those of Yehudah, to take the
fortress that was at Yerushalayim: and he
made many engines of war against it.
21 And certain *men* that hated their own
nation, men that transgressed the Torah,
went to the king, and reported to him that
Yonathan was besieging the fortress.
22 And he heard, and was angered; but
when he heard it, he set forth immediately,
and came to Akko, and wrote to Yonathan
that he should not besiege it, and that he
should meet him and speak with him at
Akko with all speed.

23 But when Yonathan heard this, he
commanded to besiege it still: and he
elected certain of the elders of Yisra'el and
of the priests, and put himself in peril,
24 and taking silver and gold and raiment
and various presents besides, went to
Akko to the king. And he found favor in
his sight. 25 And certain lawless men of
those who were of the nation made
complaints against him, 26 and the king
did to him even as his predecessors had
done to him, and exalted him in the sight
of all his beloved, 27 and confirmed to him
the high priesthood, and all the other
honors that he had before, and gave him
preeminence among his chief beloved.
28 And Yonathan requested of the king,
that he would make Yehudah free from
tribute, and the three provinces, and the
country of Shomeron; and promised him
three hundred talents. 29 And the king
consented, and wrote letters to Yonathan
concerning all these things after this
manner:

30 "King Demetrios to his brother
Yonathan, and to the nation of the
Yehudim, greetings: 31 The copy of the
letter which we wrote to Lasthenes our
kinsman concerning you, we have written
also to you, that you may see it.

32 'King Demetrios to Lasthenes his father,
greetings: 33 We have determined to do
good to the nation of the Yehudim, who
are our friends, and observe what is just
toward us, because of their good will
toward us. 34 We have confirmed
therefore to them the borders of Yehudah,
and also the three governments of
Aphaerema and Lod and Ramathaim
(these were added to Yehudah from the
country of Shomeron), and all things
belonging to them, for all such as do
slaughtering in Yerushalayim, instead of
the king's dues which the king previously
received of them yearly from the produce
of the earth and the fruits of trees. 35 And
as for the other things that pertain to us
from here on, of the tenths and the tolls
that pertain to us, and the salt pits, and the
crowns that pertain to us, all these we will
bestow upon them. 36 And not one of

these things shall be annulled from this time forth and forever.'

37 "Now therefore be careful to make a copy of these things, and let it be given to Yonathan, and let it be set up on the set-apart mount in a light and obvious place."

38 And king Demetrios saw that the land was quiet before him, and that no resistance was made to him, and he sent away all his forces, each man to his own place, except the foreign forces, which he had raised from the isles of the nations: and all the forces of his fathers hated him. 39 Now Tryphon was of those who had previously been of Alexandros' part, and he saw that all the forces grumbled against Demetrios, and he went to Yimalk the Aravian, who was raising up Antioḥos the young child of Alexandros, 40 and pressed severely upon him that he should deliver him to him, that he might reign in his father's stead: and he told him all that Demetrios had done, and the hatred with which his forces hated him; and he stayed there many days.

41 And Yonathan sent to king Demetrios, that he should cast out of Yerushalayim them of the fortress, and those who were in the strongholds; for they fought against Yisra'el continually. 42 And Demetrios sent to Yonathan, saying, "I will not only do this for you and your nation, but I will greatly honor you and your nation, if I find fair occasion. 43 Now therefore you shall do well, if you send me men who shall fight for me; for all my forces have revolted."

44 And Yonathan sent him three thousand valiant men to Antioḥ: and they came to the king, and the king was glad at their coming. 45 And those of the city gathered themselves together into the midst of the city, to the number of a hundred and twenty thousand men, and they purposed to kill the king. 46 And the king fled into the court of the palace, and those of the city seized the passages of the city, and began to fight. 47 And the king called the Yehudim to help him, and they were gathered together to him all at once, and they dispersed themselves in the city, and killed that day to the number of a hundred thousand. 48 And they set the city on fire, and got many spoils that day, and saved the king. 49 And those of the city saw that the Yehudim had made themselves masters of the city as they would, and they grew faint in their hearts, and they cried out to the king with petitions, saying, 50 "Give us your right hand, and let the Yehudim cease from fighting against us and the city."

51 And they cast away their arms, and made peace; and the Yehudim were glorified in the sight of the king, and before all that were in his kingdom; and they returned to Yerushalayim, having many spoils. 52 And king Demetrios sat on the throne of his kingdom, and the land was quiet before him. 53 And he lied in all that he spoke, and estranged himself from Yonathan, and did not repay him according to the benefits with which he had repaid him, and afflicted him greatly.

54 Now after this Tryphon returned, and with him the young child Antioḥos; and he reigned, and put on a crown. 55 And all the forces which Demetrios had sent away with disgrace were gathered to him, and they fought against him, and he fled and was put to flight. 56 And Tryphon took the elephants and became master of Antioḥ.

57 And the young Antioḥos wrote to
Yonathan, saying, "I confirm to you the
high priesthood, and appoint you over the
four governments, and to be one of the
king's friends."

58 And he sent to him golden vessels and
furniture for the table, and gave him leave
to drink in golden vessels, and to be
clothed in purple, and to have a golden
buckle. **59** And he made his brother
Shimon captain from the Ladder of Tsor to
the borders of Mitsrayim.[a] **60** And
Yonathan went forth, and took his journey
beyond the river and through the cities;
and all the forces of Aram gathered
themselves to him for to be his allies. And
he came to Ashqelon, and they of the city
met him honorably. **61** And he departed
from there to Gaza, and those of Gaza shut
him out; and he laid siege to it, and burned
its pasture-lands with fire, and plundered
them. **62** And those of Gaza made request
to Yonathan, and he gave them his right
hand, and took the sons of their princes for
hostages, and sent them away to
Yerushalayim; and he passed through the
country as far as Dammeseq.

63 And Yonathan heard that Demetrios'
princes had come to Qadesh, which is in
Galilee, with a great army, purposing to
remove him from his office; **64** and he
went to meet them, but he left Shimon his
brother in the country.

65 And Shimon encamped against Beth-
Tsur, and fought against it many days, and
shut it up: **66** and they made request to him
that he would give them his right hand,
and he gave it to them; and he put them
out from there, and took possession of the
city, and set a garrison over it. **67** And
Yonathan and his army encamped at the
water of Kinnereth, and early in the
morning they got them to the plain of
Ḥatsor. **68** And, behold, an army of
foreigners met him in the plain, and they
laid an ambush for him in the mountains,
but they themselves met him face to face.
69 But those who lay in ambush rose out
of their places, and joined battle; and all
those who were of Yonathan's side fled:
70 not one of them was left, except
Mattithyah the son of Avshalom, and
Yehudah the son of Kalphi, captains of the
forces. **71** And Yonathan tore his clothes,
and put earth upon his head, and prayed.
72 And he turned again to them in battle,
and put them to the flight, and they fled.
73 And those of his side that fled saw it,
and returned to him, and pursued with him
to Qadesh to their camp, and they
encamped there. **74** And about three
thousand men of the foreigners fell on that
day: and Yonathan returned to
Yerushalayim.

12 **1** And Yonathan saw that the time
served him, and he elected men, and sent
them to Rome, to confirm and renew the
friendship that they had with them. **2** And
to the Spartans, and to other places, he
sent letters after the same manner. **3** And
they went to Rome, and entered into the
senate house, and said, "Yonathan the high
priest, and the nation of the Yehudim,
have sent us, to renew for them the

[a] 11:59 From the Ladder of Tsor to the borders of Mitsrayim – Phrase indicating that the Hasmoneans controlled the coastlines from Aram (Syria) to Mitsrayim (Egypt). The "Ladder of Tsor" refers to the mountains of Tsor, which reached the edge of the sea, where a coastal road ascended up a series of steps.

friendship and the alliance, as in former
time."

4 And they gave them letters to the men in
every place, that they should bring them
on their way to the land of Yehudah in
peace. 5 And this is the copy of the letters
which Yonathan wrote to the Spartans:

6 "Yonathan the high priest, and the senate
of the nation, and the priests, and the rest
of the people of the Yehudim, to their
brethren the Spartans, greetings: 7 Even
before this time were letters sent to
Ḥoniyo the high priest from Darios, who
was reigning among you, to signify that
you are our brethren, as the copy here
attached shows. 8 And Ḥoniyo entreated
honorably the man that was sent, and
received the letters, wherein declaration
was made of alliance and friendship.
9 Therefore we also, albeit we need none
of these things, having for our
encouragement the set-apart books[a] which
are in our hands,[b] 10 have decided to send
that we might renew our brotherhood and
friendship with you, to the end that we
should not become estranged from you
altogether: for long time is passed since
you sent to us.

11 "We, therefore, at all times without
ceasing, both in our Feasts, and on the
other convenient days, do remember you
in the slaughterings which we offer, and in
our prayers, as it is right and proper to be
mindful of brethren: 12 and moreover are
glad for your glory. 13 But as for
ourselves, many afflictions and many wars
have encompassed us, and the kings that
are around us have fought against us.
14 We were not minded therefore to be
troublesome to you, and to the rest of our
allies and friends, in these wars; 15 for we
have the help which is from heaven to
help us, and we have been delivered from
our enemies, and our enemies have been
brought low. 16 We chose therefore
Numenios the son of Antioḥos, and
Antipater the son of Iason, and have sent
them to the Romans, to renew the
friendship that we had with them, and the
former alliance. 17 We commanded them
therefore to go also to you, and to salute
you, and to deliver you our letters
concerning the renewing of friendship and
our brotherhood. 18 And now you shall do
well if you give us an answer in return."

19 And this is the copy of the letters which
they sent to Ḥoniyo:

20 "Darios king of the Spartans to Ḥoniyo
the chief priest, greetings: 21 It has been
found in writing, concerning the Spartans
and the Yehudim, that they are brethren,
and that they are of the stock of Avraham.
22 And now, since this has come to our
knowledge, you shall do well to write to
us of your peace. 23 And we moreover do
write on our part to you, that your cattle
and goods are ours, and ours are yours.
We do command therefore that they make
report to you on this way."

24 And Yonathan heard that Demetrios'
princes were returned to fight against him
with a greater army than before, 25 and he
removed from Yerushalayim, and met
them in the country of Ḥamath; for he
gave them no respite to set foot in his
country. 26 And he sent spies into his

---

[a] 12:9 Set-apart books – Most likely a reference to the Tanakh, ('Old Testament'). See also Ben Sira 50.

[b] 12:9 See also Maqabiym ב [2 Maccabees] 2:14.

camp, and they came again, and reported
to him that they were appointed in such
and such a way to fall upon them in the
night season. **27** But as soon as the sun
was down, Yonathan commanded his men
to watch, and to be in arms, that all the
night long they might be ready for battle:
and he put forth sentinels around the
camp. **28** And the adversaries heard that
Yonathan and his men were ready for
battle, and they feared, and trembled in
their hearts, and they kindled fires in their
camp. **29** But Yonathan and his men did
not know until the morning, for they saw
the lights burning. **30** And Yonathan
pursued after them, and did not overtake
them, for they had passed over the river
Eleutherus. **31** And Yonathan turned
toward the Aravians, who are called
Zevadites, and struck them, and took their
spoils. **32** And he came out from there, and
came to Dammeseq, and took his journey
through all the country.

33 And Shimon went forth, and took his
journey as far as Ashqelon, and the
strongholds that were near to it. And he
turned toward Yapho, and took possession
of it; **34** for he had heard that they
purposed to deliver the stronghold to the
men of Demetrios; and he set a garrison
there to keep it.

35 And Yonathan returned, and called the
elders of the people together; and he took
counsel with them to build strongholds in
Yehudah, **36** and to make the walls of
Yerushalayim higher, and to raise a great
mound between the fortress and the city,
to separate it from the city, that so it might
be all alone, that men might neither buy
nor sell. **37** And they were gathered
together to build the city, and part of the
wall of the brook that is on the east side
fell down, and he repaired that which is
called Kaphenatha. **38** And Shimon also
built Adida in the plain country, and made
it strong, and set up gates and bars.

39 And Tryphon sought to reign over Asia
and to put the crown on himself, and to
stretch forth his hand against Antioḥos the
king. **40** And he was afraid that Yonathan
would not permit him, and that he might
fight against him. And he sought a way to
take him, that he might destroy him. And
he removed, and came to Beth-Shan.
41 And Yonathan came forth to meet him
with forty thousand elect men for battle,
and came to Beth-Shan. **42** And Tryphon
saw that he came with a great army, and
he was afraid to stretch forth his hand
against him.

43 And he received him honorably, and
commended him to all his friends, and
gave him gifts, and commanded his forces
to be obedient to him, as to himself.
44 And he said to Yonathan, "Why have
you put all this people to trouble, seeing
there is no war between us? **45** And now
send them away to their homes, but
choose for yourself a few men who shall
be with you, and come you with me to
Akko, and I will give it up to you, and the
rest of the strongholds and the rest of the
forces, and all the king's officers: and I
will return and depart; for this is the cause
of my coming."

46 And he put his trust in him, and did
even as he said, and sent away his forces,
and they departed into the land of
Yehudah. **47** But he reserved to himself
three thousand men, of whom he left two
thousand in Galilee, but one thousand
went with him. **48** Now as soon as
Yonathan entered into Akko, those of
Akko shut the gates, and laid hands on

him; and they killed all those who came in
with him with the sword. 49 And Tryphon
sent forces and horsemen into Galilee, and
into the great plain, to destroy all
Yonathan's men. 50 And they perceived
that he was taken and had perished, and
those who were with him; and they
encouraged one another, and went on their
way close together, prepared to fight.
51 And those who followed upon them saw
that they were ready to fight for their
lives, and turned back again. 52 And they
all came in peace into the land of
Yehudah, and they mourned for Yonathan,
and those who were with him, and they
were very afraid; and all Yisra'el mourned
with a great mourning. 53 And all the
nations that were around them sought to
destroy them utterly: for they said, "They
have no ruler, nor any to help them: now
therefore let us fight against them, and
take away their memory from among
men."

13 1 And Shimon heard that Tryphon had
gathered together a mighty army to come
into the land of Yehudah, and destroy it
utterly. 2 And he saw that the people
trembled and was in great fear; and he
went up to Yerushalayim, and gathered the
people together; 3 and he encouraged
them, and said to them, "You yourselves
know all the things that I and my brethren,
and my father's house, have done for the
Torah and the set-apart place, and the
battles and the distresses which we have
seen, 4 by reason that all my brethren have
perished for Yisra'el's sake, and I alone am
left. 5 And now, be it far from me that I
should spare my own life in any time of
affliction; for I am not better than my
brethren. 6 But I will take vengeance for
my nation, and for the set-apart, and for
our wives and children; because all the
nations are gathered to destroy us out of
great hatred."

7 And the spirit of the people revived, as
soon as they heard these words. 8 And
they answered with a loud voice, saying,
"You are our leader instead of Yehudah
and Yonathan your brother. 9 Fight our
battles, and all that you shall say to us,
that will we do."

10 And he gathered all the men of war
together, and made haste to finish the
walls of Yerushalayim, and he fortified it
round about. 11 And he sent Yonathan the
son of Avshalom, and with him a great
army, to Yapho: and he cast out those who
were there, and stayed there in it

12 And Tryphon removed from Akko with
a mighty army to enter into the land of
Yehudah, and Yonathan was with him in
prison. 13 But Shimon encamped at Adida,
near the plain. 14 And Tryphon knew that
Shimon had risen up instead of his brother
Yonathan, and meant to join battle with
him, and he sent emissaries to him, saying,
15 "It is for money which Yonathan your
brother owed to the king's treasure, by
reason of the offices which he had, that we
hold him fast. 16 And now send a hundred
talents of silver, and two of his sons for
hostages, that when he is set at liberty he
may not revolt from us, and we will set
him at liberty."

17 And Shimon knew that they spoke to
him deceitfully, but he sent the money and
the sons, lest perhaps he should procure to
himself great hatred of the people, 18 and
they should say, "Because I did not send
him the money and the children, he
perished."

19 And he sent the children and the
hundred talents. And he dealt falsely, and
did not set Yonathan at liberty. 20 And
after this Tryphon came to invade the
land, and destroy it, and he went around
by the way that leads to Adora[a]: and
Shimon and his army marched near him to
every place, wherever he went. 21 Now
those of the fortress sent emissaries to
Tryphon, asking him to come to them
through the wilderness, and to send them
food. 22 And Tryphon made ready all his
horsemen to come. And on that night a
great snowfall fell, and he did not go
because of the snow. And he removed, and
came into the country of Gilad. 23 But
when he came near to Baskama, he killed
Yonathan, and he was buried there. 24 And
Tryphon returned, and went away into his
own land.

25 And Shimon sent, and took the bones of
Yonathan his brother, and buried him at
Modin, the city of his fathers. 26 And all
Yisra'el made great lamentation over him,
and mourned for him many days. 27 And
Shimon built a monument upon the grave
of his father and his brethren, and raised it
high to be seen, with polished stone in the
front and the back. 28 And he set up seven
pyramids, one near another, for his father,
and his mother, and his four brothers.
29 And for these he made cunning devices,
setting about them great pillars, and upon
the pillars he fashioned all manner of arms
for a perpetual memory, and beside the
arms, carved ships, that they should be
seen of all that sail on the sea. 30 This is
the grave which he made at Modin, and it
is there to this day.

31 Now Tryphon dealt deceitfully with the
young king Antioḥos, and killed him,
32 and reigned in his stead, and put the
diadem of Asia on himself, and brought a
great calamity upon the land. 33 And
Shimon built the strongholds of Yehudah,
and fenced them about with high towers,
and great walls, and gates, and bars; and
he laid up food in the strongholds. 34 And
Shimon elected men, and sent to king
Demetrios, to the end he should give the
country an immunity, because all that
Tryphon did was to plunder. 35 And king
Demetrios sent to him according to these
words, and answered him, and wrote a
letter to him, after this manner:

36 "King Demetrios to Shimon the high
priest and friend of kings, and to the elders
and nation of the Yehudim, greetings:
37 The golden crown, and the palm branch
which you sent, we have received: and we
are ready to make a lasting peace with
you, yes, and to write to our officers to
grant immunities to you. 38 And whatever
things we confirmed to you, they are
confirmed; and the strongholds, which you
have built, let them be your own. 39 As for
any oversights and faults committed to
this day, we forgive them, and the crown
which you owed us: and if there were any
other toll exacted in Yerushalayim, let it
be exacted no longer. 40 And if there be
any among you pleased to be enrolled in
our court, let them be enrolled, and let
there be peace between us."

41 In the hundred and seventieth year the
yoke of the nations was taken away from
Yisra'el.

---

[a] 13:20 LXX reads "Adora" as above. Syr. reads ܐܕܘܡ (*Adowm*).

42 And the people began to write in their
instruments and contracts, "In the first
year of Shimon, the great high priest and
captain and leader of the Yehudim."

43 In those days he encamped against
Gezer[a], and encompassed around it with
armies; and he made a siege engine, and
brought it up to the city, and struck a
tower, and took it. 44 And those who were
in the engine leaped forth into the city;
and there was a great uproar in the city.
45 And those of the city tore their clothes,
and went up on the walls with their wives
and children, and cried with a loud voice,
making request to Shimon to give them his
right hand.

46 And they said, "Do not deal with us
according to our evils, but according to
your mercy."

47 And Shimon was reconciled to them,
and did not fight against them. And he put
them out of the city, and cleansed the
houses that had idols in them, and entered
into the city with singing and giving
praise. 48 And he put all uncleanness out
of it, and placed in it such men as would
keep the Torah, and made it stronger than
it was before, and built a dwelling place
for himself in it.

49 But those of the fortress in
Yerushalayim were hindered from going
forth, and from going into the country, and
from buying and selling; and they
hungered greatly, and a great number of
them perished through famine. 50 And
they cried out to Shimon, that he should
give them his right hand; and he gave it to
them. And he put them out from there, and
he cleansed the fortress from its
pollutions. 51 And he entered into it on the
twenty-third day of the second month, in
the hundred and seventy-first year, with
praise and palm branches, and with harps,
and with cymbals, and with viols, and
with hymns, and with songs: because a
great enemy was destroyed out of Yisra'el.

52 And he decreed that they should keep
that day every year with gladness. And he
made the hill of the Temple that was by
the fortress stronger than before, and he
lived there, himself and his men. 53 And
Shimon saw that Yoḥanan his son was a
man of valor, and he made him leader of
all his forces; and he lived in Gezer.

14 1 And in the hundred and seventy-
second year king Demetrios gathered his
forces together, and went into Media, to
get help, that he might fight against
Tryphon. 2 And Arsak, the king of Paras
and Media, heard that Demetrios was
come into his borders, and he sent one of
his princes to take him alive: 3 and he
went and struck the army of Demetrios,
and took him, and brought him to Arsak;
and he put him in prison.

4 And the land had rest all the days of
Shimon: and he sought the good of his
nation, and his authority and his glory was
well-pleasing to them all his days. 5 And
amid all his glory he took Yapho for a
haven, and made it an entrance for the
isles of the sea. 6 And he enlarged the
borders of his nation, and gained
possession of the country. 7 And he

---

[a] 13:43 Some manuscripts differ in this reading, and it is debated whether it should be "Gezer" or "Gaza."

gathered together a great number of captives, and gained the dominion of Gezer, and Beth-Tsur, and the fortress, and he took away from it its uncleanness; and there was none that resisted him.

8 And they tilled their land in peace, and the land gave her increase, and the trees of
the plains their fruit.[a] 9 The old men sat in
the streets, they communed all of them together of good things, and the young men put on glorious and warlike apparel.[b]
10 He provided food for the cities, and furnished them with all implements of defense, until the name of his glory was
named to the end of the earth. 11 He made
peace in the land, and Yisra'el rejoiced
with great joy. 12 And they sat each man
under his vine and his fig tree, and there
was none to make them afraid.[c] 13 And
there ceased in the land any that fought against them: and the kings were
overthrown in those days. 14 And he
strengthened all those of his people that were brought low. He was zealous for the Torah, and every lawless and wicked
person he took away. 15 He glorified the
set-apart place, and he multiplied the vessels of the Temple.

16 And it was heard at Rome that Yonathan was dead, and even to Sparta,
and they were deeply grieved. 17 But as
soon as they heard that his brother Shimon was made high priest in his stead, and ruled the country, and the cities therein,
18 they wrote to him on tables of brass, to renew with him the friendship and the alliance which they had confirmed with Yehudah and Yonathan his brethren;
19 and they were read before the assembly
at Yerushalayim. 20 And this is the copy
of the letters which the Spartans sent: "The rulers of the Spartans, and the city, to Shimon the high priest, and to the elders, and the priests, and the remnant of the people of the Yehudim, our brethren,
greetings: 21 The emissaries that were sent
to our people made report to us of your glory and honor: and we were glad for
their coming. 22 And we registered the
things that were spoken by them in the public records after this manner: Numenios son of Antioḥos, and Antipater son of Iason, the emissaries of the Yehudim, came to us to renew the friendship they had with us."

23 And it pleased the people to entertain the men honorably, and to put the copy of their words in the public records, to the end that the people of the Spartans might have a memorial of them: moreover they wrote a copy of these things to Shimon the high priest.

24 After this Shimon sent Numenios to Rome with a great shield of gold of a thousand minas weight, in order to confirm the alliance with them.

25 But when the people heard these things, they said, "What thanks shall we give to
Shimon and his sons? 26 For he and his
brethren and the house of his father have made themselves strong, and have chased away in fight the enemies of Yisra'el from them, and confirmed liberty to Yisra'el."

27 And they wrote on tables of brass, and set them upon pillars in Mount Tsion: and this is the copy of the writing: "On the eighteenth day of Elul, in the hundred and seventy-second year, and this is the third

[a] 14:8 Compare Vayyiqra [Leviticus] 26:3-4.
[b] 14:9 Compare Zekharyah 8:4-12.
[c] 14:12 Compare Mikhah 4:4; Zekharyah 3:10.

year of Shimon the high priest, 28 in
Asaramel[a], in a great assembly of priests
and people and princes of the nation, and
of the elders of the country, was it notified
to us. 29 Since of often times there have
been wars in the country, but Shimon the
son of Mattithyah, the son of the sons of
Yoyariv, and his brethren, put themselves
in danger, and withstood the enemies of
their nation, that their set-apart place and
the Torah might be established, and
glorified their nation with great glory.
30 And Yonathan assembled their nation
together, and became their high priest, and
was gathered to his people.

31 And their enemies planned to invade
their country, that they might destroy their
country completely, and stretch forth their
hands against their set-apart place. 32 Then
Shimon rose up, and fought for his nation,
and spent much of his own substance, and
armed the men of valor of his nation, and
gave them wages. 33 And he fortified the
cities of Yehudah, and Beth-Tsur that lies
upon the borders of Yehudah, where the
arms of the enemies had previously been,
and set a garrison there of Yehudim.

34 "And he fortified Yapho which is upon
the sea, and Gezer which is upon the
borders of Ashdod, where the enemies had
previously lived, and placed Yehudim
there, and set there all things convenient
for the compensation for it. 35 And the
people saw the faith[b] of Shimon, and the
glory which he thought to bring to his
nation, and they made him their leader and
high priest, because he had done all these
things, and for the judgment and the faith
which he kept to his nation, and because
he sought by all means to exalt his people.
36 And in his days things prospered in his
hands, so that the nations were taken away
out of their country, and also those that
were in the city of David, those who were
in Yerushalayim, who had made
themselves a fortress, out of which they
issued, and polluted all things around the
set-apart place, and did great harm to its
purity. 37 And he placed Yehudim in it,
and fortified it for the safety of the
country and the city, and made the walls
of Yerushalayim high.

38 "And king Demetrios confirmed to him
the high priesthood according to these
things, 39 and made him one of his friends,
and honored him with great honor; 40 for
he had been told that the Yehudim had
been called by the Romans 'friends' and
'allies' and 'brethren,' and that they had
met the emissaries of Shimon honorably,
41 and that the Yehudim and the priests
were well pleased that Shimon should be
their leader and high priest forever, until
there should arise a faithful prophet.
42 And that he should be captain over
them, and should take charge of the set-
apart place, to set them over their works,
and over the country, and over the arms,
and over the strongholds; and that he
should take charge of the set-apart place.

---

[a] 14:28 The exact meaning of this word is uncertain. It is possibly derived from the Hebrew words חצר (*chat'ser*) עם (*ahm*) and אל (*el*) meaning "court," "people" and "El," respectively. Thus, it could be a title, such as "One who stands in the court of the people of El." Given the context of Shimon standing in the assembly of all the leaders and priests, this makes the most sense, though the meaning is still debated.

[b] 14:35 LXX reads "faith" as it is here. Syr. reads ܥܒܕܘܗ (*Abodeh*), meaning literally "labor." However it is also used idiomatically to indicate service and acts of worship.

43 "And that he should be obeyed by all,
and that all instruments in the country
should be written in his name, and that he
should be clothed in purple, and wear
gold; 44 and that it should not be lawful
for any of the people or of the priests to
renege any of these things, or to oppose
the words that he should speak, or to
gather an assembly in the country without
him, or to be clothed in purple, or wear a
buckle of gold. 45 But whoever should do
otherwise, or renege any of these things,
he should be liable to punishment."

46 All the people consented to decree for
Shimon that he should do according to
these words. 47 And Shimon accepted this,
and consented to be high priest, and to be
captain and governor of the Yehudim and
of the priests, and to be protector of all.

48 And they commanded to put this
writing on tables of brass, and to set them
up within the precinct of the set-apart
place, in an obvious place. 49 And
moreover to put the copies of it in the
treasury, to the end that Shimon and his
sons might have them.

15 1 And Antioḥos son of Demetrios the
king sent letters from the isles of the sea to
Shimon the priest and governor of the
Yehudim, and to all the nation; 2 and the
contents thereof were after this manner:
"King Antioḥos to Shimon the chief priest
and governor, and to the nation of the
Yehudim, greetings: 3 Since as certain
pestilent men have made themselves
masters of the kingdom of our fathers –
but my purpose is to claim the kingdom,
that I may restore it as it was before –
moreover I have raised a multitude of
foreign soldiers, and have prepared ships
of war. 4 Moreover I have decided to land
in the country, that I may punish those
who have destroyed our country, and those
who have made many cities in the
kingdom desolate. 5 Now therefore I
confirm to you all the exactions which the
kings that were before me promised to
you, and whatever gifts besides they
promised to you.

6 "And I give you leave to coin money for
your country with your own stamp, 7 but
that Yerushalayim and the set-apart place
should be free. And all the arms that you
have prepared, and the strongholds that
you have built, which you have in your
possession, let them remain to you. 8 And
everything owing to the king, and the
things that shall be owing to the king from
now and forever more, let them be paid to
you. 9 Moreover, when we have
established our kingdom, we will glorify
you and your nation and the Temple with
great glory, so that your glory shall be
made manifest in all the earth."

10 In the hundred and seventy-fourth year
Antioḥos went forth into the land of his
fathers; and all the forces came together to
him, so that there were few men with
Tryphon. 11 And king Antioḥos pursued
him, and he came, as he fled to Dor, which
is by the sea. 12 For he knew that troubles
had come upon him all at once, and that
his forces had forsaken him. 13 And
Antioḥos encamped against Dor with a
hundred and twenty thousand men of war,
and eight thousand horsemen. 14 And he
encompassed the city, and the ships joined
in the attack from the sea; and he
aggravated the city by land and sea, and
suffered no man to go out or in.

15 And Numenios and his company came
from Rome, having letters to the kings and

to the countries, wherein were written
these things:

16 "Lucius, consul of the Romans, to king
Ptolemy, greetings: 17 The emissaries of
the Yehudim came to us as our friends and
allies, to renew the old friendship and
alliance, being sent from Shimon the high
priest, and from the people of the
Yehudim. 18 Moreover they brought a
shield of gold of a thousand mina. 19 It
pleased us therefore to write to the kings
and to the countries, that they should not
seek their harm, nor fight against them,
and their cities, and their country, nor be
allies with any that fight against them.

20 "Moreover it seemed good to us to
receive the shield from them. 21 If
therefore any pestilent men have fled from
their country to you, deliver them to
Shimon the high priest, that he may take
vengeance on them according to their
Torah."

22 And the same things wrote he to
Demetrios the king, and to Attalus, and to
Arathes, and to Arsak, 23 and to all the
countries, and to Sampsames, and to
Sparta, and to Delos, and to Myndos, and
to Sikyon, and to Karia, and to Samos, and
to Pamphylia, and to Lycia, and to
Halicarnassus, and to Rhodes, and to
Phaselis, and to Kos, and to Side, and to
Aradus, and Gortyna, and Knidos, and
Kupros, and Kurene. 24 But they wrote a
copy of it to Shimon the high priest.

25 But Antioḥos the king encamped
against Dor the second day, bringing his
forces up to it continually, and making
engines of war, and he shut up Tryphon
from going in or out. 26 And Shimon sent
him two thousand elect men to fight on his
side; and silver, and gold, and instruments
of war in abundance. 27 And he would not
receive them, but reneged all the
covenants which he had previously cut
with him, and was estranged from him.
28 And he sent to him Athenobios, one of
his friends, to commune with him, saying,
"You hold possession of Yapho and
Gezer, and the fortress that is in
Yerushalayim, cities of my kingdom.
29 You have wasted its borders, and done
great harm in the land, and gained the
dominion of many places in my kingdom.
30 Now therefore deliver up the cities
which you have taken, and the tributes of
the places where you have gained
dominion outside the borders of Yehudah.
31 Or else give me five hundred talents of
silver for them. And for the harm that you
have done, and the tributes of the cities,
another five hundred talents: or else we
will come and subdue you."

32 And Athenobios the king's beloved
came to Yerushalayim; and he saw the
glory of Shimon, and the cupboard of gold
and silver vessels, and his great
attendance, and he was amazed; and he
reported to him the king's words.

33 And Shimon answered, and said to him,
"We have neither taken other men's land,
nor have we possession of that which
belongs to others, but of the inheritance of
our fathers. For it was had in possession of
our enemies wrongfully for a certain time.
34 But we, having opportunity, hold fast
the inheritance of our fathers. 35 But as
touching Yapho and Gezer, which you
demand, they did great harm among the
people throughout our country: *so* we will
give a hundred talents for them." And he
answered him not a word, 36 but returned
in a rage to the king, and reported to him
these words, and the glory of Shimon, and

all that he had seen: and the king was very
angry.

37 But Tryphon embarked on board a ship,
and fled to Orthosia. 38 And the king
appointed Qendebiyos chief captain of the
sea coast, and gave him foot soldiers and
horsemen. 39 And he commanded him to
camp before Yehudah, and he commanded
him to build up Qidron, and to fortify the
gates, and that he should fight against the
people: but the king pursued Tryphon.
40 And Qendebiyos came to Yavneel, and
began to provoke the people, and to
invade Yehudah, and to take the people
captive, and to kill them. 41 And he built
Qidron, and set horsemen there, and foot
soldiers, so that they could patrol the ways
of Yehudah, as the king commanded him.

16 1 And Yoḥanan went up from Gezer,
and told Shimon his father what
Qendebiyos was doing. 2 And Shimon
called his two oldest sons, Yehudah and
Yoḥanan, and said to them, "I and my
brethren and my father's house have
fought the battles of Yisra'el from our
youth, even to this day, and matters have
prospered in our hands, that we should
deliver Yisra'el numerous times. 3 But
now I am old, and you moreover, by His
mercy, are of a sufficient age: be instead
of me and my brother, and go forth and
fight for our nation; but let the help which
is from heaven be with you."

4 And he elected out of the country twenty
thousand men of war and horsemen, and
they went against Qendebiyos, and slept at
Modin. 5 And rising up in the morning,
they went into the plain, and behold, a
great army came to meet them, of foot
soldiers and horsemen: and there was a
brook between them. 6 And he camped
near them, he and his people: and he saw
that the people were afraid to pass over the
brook, so he passed over first. And *when*
the men saw him, they passed over after
him. 7 And he divided the people, and set
the horsemen in the midst of the foot
soldiers: but the enemies' horsemen were
very numerous. 8 And they sounded with
the shofars; and Qendebiyos and his army
were put to flight, and many of them fell
wounded, but those who were left fled to
the stronghold. 9 At that time Yehudah,
Yoḥanan's brother, was wounded: but
Yoḥanan pursued after them, until he
came to Qidron, which Qendebiyos had
built. 10 And they fled to the towers that
are in the fields of Ashdod, and he burned
it with fire; and about two thousand men
of them fell. And he returned into
Yehudah in peace. 11 And Ptolemy the son
of Abubus[a] had been appointed captain for
the plain of Yeriḥo, and he had great
amounts of silver and gold,

12 for he was the high priest's son-in-law.

13 And his heart was lifted up, and he
thought to make himself master of the
country, and he took counsel deceitfully
against Shimon and his sons, to take them
away.

14 Now Shimon was visiting the cities that
were in the country, and carefully
governing them in good; and he went
down to Yeriḥo, himself and Mattithyah
and Yehudah his sons, in the hundred and
seventy-seventh year, in the eleventh

---

[a] 11 LXX reads as it is here. Syr. reads ܚܒܘܒܐ (*cha'buw'ba*): "Ḥabuba."

month, the same is the month Shevat.
15 And the son of Abubus received them
deceitfully into the little stronghold that is
called Doq, which he had built, and made
them a great banquet, and hid men there.
16 And when Shimon and his sons had
drunk freely, Ptolemy and his men rose
up, and took their arms, and came in upon
Shimon into the banquet hall, and killed
him, and his two sons, and certain of his
servants. 17 And he committed a great
iniquity, and repaid evil for good.

18 And Ptolemy wrote these things, and
sent to the king, that he should send him
forces to aid him, and should deliver him
their country and the cities. 19 And he sent
others to Gezer to take Yoḥanan away:
and to the captains of thousands he sent
letters to come to him, that he might give
them silver and gold and gifts. 20 And
others he sent to take possession of
Yerushalayim, and the Temple Mount.
21 And one ran before to Gezer, and told
Yoḥanan that his father and brethren were
dead, "and he has sent to kill you also."
22 And when he heard, he was greatly
amazed; and he laid hands on the men that
came to destroy him, and killed them; for
he perceived that they were seeking to
destroy him.

23 And the rest of the acts of Yoḥanan,
and of his wars, and of his valiant deeds
which he did, and of the building of the
walls which he built, and of his doings,
24 behold, they are written in the
chronicles of his high priesthood, from the
time that he was made high priest after his
father.

[*The* whole *of* Book One of the Maqabiym][a]

[a] 16:24 Bracketed section indicates reading present in Syriac texts but absent from Greek.

מַקַּבִּים ב

Maqabiym ב
[2 Maccabees]

1 1 [a]The brethren, the Yehudim that are in
Yerushalayim, and those who are in the
country of Yehudah, send greetings to the
brethren, the Yehudim that are throughout
Mitsrayim, and wish them good peace.
2 May Elohim do good to you, and
remember His covenant with Avraham and
Yitschaq and Ya'aqov, His faithful
servants; 3 and give you all a heart to
worship Him and do His wills with a great
heart and a willing being; 4 and open your
heart in His Torah and in His commands,
and make peace. 5 And *may He* listen to
your petitions, and be reconciled with you,
and not forsake you in an evil time. 6 And
now we here are praying for you. 7 In the
reign of Demetrios, in the hundred sixty-
ninth year, we the Yehudim have already
written to you in the tribulation and in the
extremity that has come upon us in these
years, from the time that Iason and his
company revolted from the set-apart land
and the kingdom, 8 and set the gate on fire,
and shed innocent blood: and we implored
יהוה, and were heard. And we offered
slaughtering and meal offering, and we
lighted the lamps, and we set forth the
bread of the presence.[b] 9 And now see that
you keep the Days of the Feast of
Tabernacles of the month Kislev.[c]
10 Written in the hundred sixty-eighth year.
Those that are in Yerushalayim and those
who are in Yehudah and the senate and
Yehudah, to Aristobulos, king Ptolemy's
teacher, who is also of the stock of the
anointed priests, and to the Yehudim that
are in Mitsrayim, send greeting and health.

11 Having been saved by Elohim out of
great perils, as men arrayed against a king,
we thank Him greatly. 12 For *He* Himself
cast forth those who arrayed themselves
against us in the set-apart city into Paras.
13 For when the prince was come there, and
the army with him that seemed unbeatable,
they were cut to pieces in the temple of
Nanaea[d] by the treachery of Nanaea's
priests. 14 For Antioḥos, on the pretense
that he would marry her, came into the
place, he and his friends that were with
him, that they might take a great part of the
treasures in name of a dowry. 15 And when
the priests of Nanaea's temple had set the
treasures forth, and he had come there with
a small company within the wall of the

---

[a] 1:1 The LXX begins as it is here. The Syr., however, contains an introduction prior to verse 1. This introduction reads ܣܦܪܐ ܕܬܪܝܢ ܕܡܩܒܝܐ ܐܚܐ (*sepra d'tareyn d'maqa'biya aḥa*) meaning "The second book of brother Maqabi." This introduction was likely added at a later date, as is commonly found in Syriac literature.

[b] 1:8 See also Maqabiym א [1 Maccabees] 4:50-51.

[c] 1:9 This refers not to Sukkot, the Feast of Tabernacles, but to Ḥanukkah, the Feast of Dedication. As with Sukkot, which is celebrated for 8 days (including the Festival of the Eighth Day), Ḥanukkah is also celebrated 8 days. It is believed that the reason the Maqabiym instituted Ḥanukkah as an 8 day celebration is because they considered it a time of joy, and wanted it to mirror Sukkot, which was already considered the most joyful time of year. Thus, references to the Feast of Tabernacles in the month of Kislev refer to Ḥanukkah, which begins on the 25th day of Kislev, also referred to as the "day of the purification of the Temple." Compare Maqabiym ב [2 Maccabees] 10:6.

[d] 1:13 Nanaea was a Persian goddess, comparable to Artemis of the Greeks.

precincts, they shut the temple when Antioḥos was come in. 16 And opening the secret door of the paneled ceiling, they threw stones and struck down the prince as a thunderbolt, and they hewed him and his company in pieces, and struck off their heads, and cast them to those that were outside. 17 Blessed be our Elohim in all things, who gave for plunder those who had committed wickedness.[a]

18 Whereas we are now about to keep the purification of the Temple in the month Kislev, on the twenty-fifth day, we thought it necessary to certify you, that you also may keep a Feast of Tabernacles, and a memorial of the fire which was given when Neḥemyah offered slaughterings,[b] after he had built both the Temple and the altar.
19 For indeed when our fathers were about to be led into the land of Paras, the devout priests of that time took of the fire of the altar, and hid it secretly in the hollow of a well that was without water, wherein they made it sure, so that the place was unknown to all men. 20 Now after many years, when it pleased Elohim, Neḥemyah, having received a charge from the king of Paras, sent to search for the fire that the descendants of the priests hid. When they declared to us that they had found no fire, but *rather* thick water, 21 he commanded them to draw it out and bring to him: and when the slaughterings had been offered on the altar, Neḥemyah commanded the priests to sprinkle both the wood and the things laid on it with the water. 22 And when it was done, and some time had passed, and the sun shone out, which before was hid with clouds, there was kindled a great blaze, so that all men marveled. 23 And the priests made a prayer while the slaughtering was consuming, both the priests and all others, *with* Yonathan leading and the rest answering, as Neḥemyah did. 24 And the prayer was after this manner: "O יהוה, יהוה Elohim, the Creator of all things, who is awesome and strong and righteous and merciful, who alone is King; and gracious, 25 who alone supplies every need, who alone is righteous and Almighty and eternal, You that save Yisra'el out of all evil, who made the fathers Your elect, and did set them apart:
26 accept the slaughtering for all Your people Yisra'el, and guard Your own portion, and set it apart. 27 Gather together our Dispersion, set at liberty those who are in bondage among the heathen, look upon those who are despised and abhorred, and let the heathen know that You are our Elohim. 28 Torment those who oppress us and in arrogance shamefully entreat us.
29 Plant Your people in Your set-apart place, even as Mosheh said.[c]"

30 And there the priests sang the hymns.
31 And as soon as the slaughtering was consumed, then Neḥemyah commanded to pour on great stones the water that was left.
32 And when this was done, a flame was kindled; but when the light from the altar shone near it, all was consumed. 33 And when the matter became known, and it was told the king of the Parasians, that, in the

---

[a] 1:12-17 See also Dani'el 11:40-45; Maqabiym א [1 Maccabees] 6:1-13.
[b] 1:18 The writer here refers to Neḥemyah son of Ḥakalyah, who went back to Yerushalayim to rebuild the city and Temple (Neḥemyah / Nehemiah 2). The story mentioned regarding Neḥemyah and the fire, however, is not mentioned in Scripture at all.
[c] 1:29 Compare Shemoth [Exodus] 15:17.

place where the priests that were led away
had hid the fire, there appeared the water,
with which Neḥemyah and those who were
with him purified the slaughtering. **34** Then
the king, inclosing the place, made it
sacred, after he had proved the matter.
35 And when the king would show favor to
any, he would take from them many
presents and give them some of this water.
36 And Neḥemyah and those who were with
him called this thing Nephthar, which is by
translation, 'Cleansing,' but most men call it
Nephthai.[a]

2 **1** It is also found in the records, that
Yirmeyahu the prophet commanded those
who were carried away to take of the fire,
as has been signified above: **2** and how the
prophet charged those who were carried
away, having given them the Torah, that
they should not forget the statutes of יהוה,
neither be led astray in their minds, when
they saw images of gold and silver, and its
adornment.[b] **3** And with other such words
exhorted he them, that the Torah should not
depart from their heart.

4 And it was contained in the writing, that
the prophet, being warned from Elohim,
commanded that the Tabernacle and the ark
should follow with him, when he went
forth into the mountain where Mosheh
went up and saw the heritage of Elohim.[c]
5 And Yirmeyahu came and found a
chamber in the rock, and there he brought
in the Tabernacle, and the ark, and the altar
of incense; and he made fast the door.
6 And some of those that followed with him
came there that they might mark the way,
and could not find it. **7** But when
Yirmeyahu perceived it, he blamed them,
saying, "Yes, and the place shall be
unknown until Elohim gathers the people
again together, and mercy comes; **8** and
then shall יהוה disclose these things, and
the glory of יהוה shall be seen, and the
cloud." As also it was showed with
Mosheh; as also Shelomoh implored that
the place[d] might be set apart greatly, **9** and
it was also declared that he, having
wisdom, offered a slaughtering of
dedication, and of the finishing of the
Temple; so we would have it now. **10** As
Mosheh prayed to יהוה, and fire came
down out of heaven and consumed the
slaughtering,[e] even so prayed Shelomoh
also, and the fire came down and consumed
the burnt offerings; **11** (and Mosheh said,
"**Because the sin offering had not been
eaten, it was consumed in like manner
with the rest**;")[f]

12 and Shelomoh kept the eight days *for
dedicating the Temple*.[g]

---

[a] 1:36 What is described here as "water" and called "Nepthai" is most likely Naphtha, commonly known as "Greek fire." It is a petroleum product similar to what is today known as "white gas" such as camping fuel. Here is it stated the men called it "Nephthar" but most call it "Nephthai." This shows a Hebrew word play, as the Hebrew word נתר (*na'thar*) means "to spring up" or "to loosen/shake off" such as a cleansing fire.

[b] 2:2 Most likely a reference to Barukh 6.

[c] 2:4 See also Devarim [Deuteronomy] 32:49; 34:1.

[d] 2:8 the place – namely, the Temple.

[e] 2:10 See Vayyiqra [Leviticus] 9:23,24.

[f] 2:11 See Vayyiqra [Leviticus] 10:16-20.

[g] 2:12 Shelomoh did not celebrate the dedication of the Temple for eight days only, but rather for fourteen. However, according to Divrei Ha'Yamim ב [2 Chronicles] 7:9, he did have a

13 And the same things were related both in the public archives and in the records that concern Neḥemyah; and how he, founding a library, gathered together the books about the kings and prophets, and the books of David, and letters of kings about sacred gifts. 14 And in like manner Yehudah also gathered together for us all those writings that had been scattered by reason of the war, and they are still with us.[a] 15 If, therefore, you have need of them, send some to fetch them to you. 16 Seeing then that we are about to keep the purification, we write to you; you will therefore do well if you keep the days.

17 Now Elohim, who saved all His people, and restored the heritage to all, and the kingdom, and the priesthood, and the setting-apart, 18 even as He promised through the Torah; in Elohim we have hope, that He will quickly have mercy upon us, and **gather us together out of *all* the earth under the heavens**[b] to the set-apart place: for He delivered us out of great evils, and purified the place.

19 Now the things concerning Yehudah Maqabi and his brethren, and the purification of the great Temple, and the dedication of the altar, 20 and further the wars against Antioḥos Epiphanes, and Eupator his son, 21 and the manifestations that came from heaven to those that strove with one another in brave deeds for the religion of the Yehudim; so that, being but a few, they rescued the whole country, and took the barbarous multitudes for prey. 22 And *they* recovered again the Temple *that is* renowned all the world over, and freed the city, and restored the Torot which were about to be overthrown, seeing יהוה became kind to them with all forbearance. 23 These things, I say, which have been declared by Iason the Kurene in five books, we will evaluate to abridge in one work.

24 For having in view the confused mass of the numbers, and the difficulty which awaits those who would enter into the narratives of the history, by reason of the abundance of the matter, 25 we were careful that they who choose to read may be attracted, and that they who desire good for our cause may find it easy to recall what we have written, and that all readers may have profit.

26 And although to us, who have taken upon us the painful labor of the abridgement, the task is not easy, but a matter of sweat and watching 27 (even as it is no light thing to him that prepares a banquet, and seeks the benefit of others); yet for the sake of the gratitude of the many we will gladly endure the painful labor, 28 leaving to the historian the exact handling of every detail, and again having no strength to fill in the outlines of our abridgement. 29 For as the master-builder of a new house must care for the whole structure, and again he that undertakes to decorate and paint it must seek out the things fit for its adorning; even so I think it is also with us. 30 To occupy the ground, and to indulge in long discussions, and to be curious of particulars, becomes the first author of the history: 31 but to strive after briefness of expression, and to avoid a

special assembly on the eighth day, so this may be what the writer is referring to.

[a] 2:14 See also Maqabiym א [1 Maccabees] 1:57.

[b] 2:18 See Devarim [Deuteronomy] 30:3-5.

labored fullness in the treatment, is to be granted to him that would bring a writing into a new form. **32** Here then let us begin the narration, only adding thus much to that which has been already said; for it is a foolish thing to make a long prologue to the history, and to abridge the history itself.

3 1 When the set-apart city was inhabited with all peace, and the Torot were guarded very well, because of the righteousness of Ḥoniyo[a] the high priest, and his hatred of wickedness, **2** it came to pass that even the kings themselves honored the place, and glorified the Temple with most noble presents. **3** So much so, that even Seleukus the king of Asia of his own revenues bore all the costs belonging to the services of the slaughterings. **4** But one Shimon of the tribe of Benyamin, having been made guardian of the Temple, fell out with the high priest about the ruling of the market in the city. 5 And when he could not overcome Ḥoniyo, he gave him to Apollonios the son of Thrasaeus, who at that time was governor of Koele-Aram and Phoenicia. 6 And he brought him word how that the treasury in Yerushalayim was full of untold sums of money, so that the multitude of the funds was innumerable, and that they did not pertain to the account of the slaughterings, but that it was possible that these should fall under the king's power.

7 And when Apollonios met the king, he informed him of the money of which he had been told; and the king appointed Heliodoros, who was his chancellor, and sent him with a command to accomplish the removal of the money. **8** So Heliodoros immediately took his journey, under a guise of visiting the cities of Koele-Aram and Phoenicia, but in fact to execute the king's purpose.

9 And when he came to Yerushalayim, and had been courteously received by the high priest of the city, he laid before them an account of the information which had been given him, and declared what he came for; and he inquired if in truth these things were so. **10** And the high priest explained to him that there were in the treasury deposits of widows and orphans,[b] **11** and moreover some money belonging to Hyrqanos the son of Toviyah, a man in very high place, and that the case was not as that wicked Shimon falsely alleged; and that in all there were four hundred talents of silver and two hundred of gold. **12** And that it was altogether impossible that wrong should be done to them that had put trust in the set-apartness of the place, and in the majesty and sacredness of the Temple, honored

---

[a] 3:1 Ḥoniyo – Typically referred to by his Greek name, Onias, Ḥoniyo is believed to be the son of Simeon the Just. According to many historical sources, Simeon the Just was a high priest during the time of the Second Temple who was greatly renowned for his love of his nation, and for his benevolence toward his people. According to Ben Sira 50:1-14, he rebuilt the walls of Yerushalayim. According to Flavius Josephus, Alexandros the Great even bowed to him when he came to Yerushalayim, noting that the Elohim of Simeon had appeared to him in a dream. (*Antiquities of the Jews,* Book XI, Ch. 8, § 5). Simeon is also mentioned numerous times in the Babylonian Talmud (Avot 1, Yoma 9, Nazir 4, etc.) as well as other Jewish sources such as the Midrash and Tosefta. Ḥoniyo, his son, was high priest right up to the time when Antioḥos defiled to Temple, having died in about 175 BCE.

[b] 3:10 See also Devarim [Deuteronomy] 26:12.

over all the world. 13 But Heliodoros,
because of the king's commands given to
him, said that in any case this money must
be confiscated for the king's treasury.

14 So having appointed a day, he entered in
to direct the inquiry concerning these
matters; and there was no small distress
throughout the whole city. 15 And the
priests, prostrating themselves before the
altar in their priestly garments, and looking
toward heaven, called upon Him that gave
the Torah concerning deposits, that He
should preserve these treasures safe for
those that had deposited them.[a]

16 And whoever saw the expression of the
high priest was wounded in mind; for his
countenance and the change of his
countenance betrayed the distress of his
being. 17 For a terror and a shuddering of
the body had come over the man, whereby
the pain that was in his heart was plainly
shown to those who looked upon him.
18 And those who were in the houses
rushed flocking out to make a universal
petition, because the place was like to come
into contempt. 19 And the women, girded
with sackcloth under their breasts, thronged
the streets, and the maidens that were kept
inside ran together, some to the gates,
others to the walls, and some looked out
through the windows. 20 And all, stretching
forth their hands toward heaven, made their
solemn petition. 21 Then it would have
pitied a man to see the multitude
prostrating themselves all mingled together,
and the expectation of the high priest in his
severe distress.

22 While they called upon the Almighty
Elohim to keep the things entrusted to them
safe and secure for those that had entrusted
them, 23 Heliodoros went on to execute that
which had been decreed. 24 But when he
was already present there with his guards
near the treasury, the Master of spirits and
of all authority caused a great apparition, so
that all that had presumed to come in with
him, were struck with dismay at the power
of Elohim, *and* fainted and were severely
afraid. 25 For there was seen by them a
horse with a terrible rider upon him, and
adorned with beautiful trappings, and he
rushed fiercely and struck at Heliodoros
with his front feet, and it seemed that he
that sat upon the horse had complete armor
of gold. 26 Two others also appeared to
him, young men notable in their strength,
and beautiful in their glory, and splendid in
their apparel, who stood by him on either
side, and scourged him unceasingly,
inflicting on him many severe stripes.

27 And when he had fallen suddenly to the
ground, and great darkness had come over
him, his guards caught him up and put him
into a stretcher, 28 and carried him, him that
had just now entered with a great train and
all his guard into the aforesaid treasury,
himself now brought to utter helplessness,
manifestly made to recognize the
sovereignty of Elohim. 29 And so, while he,
through the working of Elohim, speechless
and bereft of all hope and deliverance, lay
prostrate, 30 they blessed יהוה, that made
His own place marvelous; and the Temple,
which a little before was full of terror and
alarm, was filled with joy and gladness
after יהוה Almighty appeared.

31 But quickly certain of Heliodoros's
familiar friends implored Ḥoniyo to call

---

[a] 3:15 See also Shemoth [Exodus] 22:6-14.

upon Elyon, and grant life to him who was
at his last breath. 32 And the high priest,
secretly fearing lest the king might come to
think that some treachery toward
Heliodoros had been perpetrated by the
Yehudim, brought a slaughtering for the
deliverance of the man.

33 But as the high priest was making the
atoning slaughtering, the same young men
appeared again to Heliodoros, arrayed in
the same garments; and they stood and
said, "Give Ḥoniyo the high priest great
thanks, for because of him, יהוה has
granted you life. 34 And *make sure* you,
since you have been scourged from heaven,
proclaim to all men the sovereign majesty
of Elohim. And when they had spoken
these words, they vanished out of sight.
35 So Heliodoros, having offered a
slaughtering to Elohim[a] and vowed great
vows to Him that had saved his life, and
having graciously received Ḥoniyo,
returned with his army to the king. 36 And
he witnessed to all men the works of the
great Elohim which he had seen with his
eyes.

37 And when the king asked Heliodoros,
what manner of man was fit to be sent yet
once again to Yerushalayim, he said, 38 "If
you have any enemy or conspirator against
the state, send him there, and you shall
receive him back well scourged, if he even
escape with his life; because of a truth there
is a power of Elohim about the place. 39 For
He that has His dwelling in the heavenly
Himself has His eyes upon that place, and
helps it; and those who come to hurt it He
strikes and destroys."

40 And such was the history of Heliodoros
and the keeping of the treasury.[b]

4 1 But Shimon (who was previously
mentioned), he who had given information
of the money, and had betrayed his country,
slandered Ḥoniyo, saying that it was he
who had incited Heliodoros, and made
himself the author of these evils. 2 And him
that was the benefactor of the city, and the
guardian of his fellow countrymen, and a
zealot for the Torot, he dared to call a
conspirator against the state. 3 But when the
growing enmity between them grew so
great, that even murders were perpetrated
through one of those approved by Shimon,
4 Ḥoniyo, (seeing the danger of the
contention, and that Apollonios the son of
Menestheus, the governor of Koele-Aram
and Phoenicia, was increasing Shimon's
malice) 5 went himself to the king, not to be
an accuser of his fellow-citizens, but
looking to the good of all the people, both
public and private. 6 For he saw that
without the king's wisdom it was
impossible for the state to obtain peace any
more, and that Shimon would not cease
from his madness.

7 But when Seleukus was dead, and
Antioḥos, who was called Epiphanes,
succeeded to the kingdom, Iason[c] the

---

[a] 3:35 Syr. reads ܐܠܗܐ (*Alaha*) meaning "Elohim" as it is here. LXX reads Κυριω (*Kurio*) meaning "Master" here.

[b] 3:1-40 The writer relates the story of Heliodoros here showing the inviolability of the Temple. This is contrasted with 5:17,18, when it is stated that what took place was allowed because of the sins of the people.

[c] 4:7 Iason – Greek name of the brother of Ḥoniyo (Onias) III, son of Shimon (Simeon) the II. According to Flavius Josephus in *Antiquities of the Jews Book XII, chapter 5, section 1,*

brother of Ḥoniyo supplanted his brother in the high priesthood, 8 having promised to the king three hundred and sixty talents of silver, (and out of another fund eighty talents) at an audience. 9 And besides this, he undertook to assign a hundred and fifty more, if it might be allowed him through the king's authority to set up a Greek gymnasium and youth center, and to register the inhabitants of Yerushalayim as citizens of Antioḥ.[a]

10 And when the king had given permission, and he had gotten possession of the office *of high priest*, he immediately brought them of his own race over to the Greek fashion. 11 And setting aside the royal ordinances of special favor to the Yehudim, granted by the means of Yoḥanan the father of Eupolemus, who went to the Romans for friendship and alliance, and seeking to overthrow the lawful modes of life, he brought in new customs forbidden by the Torah. 12 For he eagerly established a Greek gymnasium under the fortress itself[b]; and caused the noblest of the young men to wear the Greek cap.[c] 13 And thus there was an extreme of Greek fashions, and an advance of an foreign religion, by reason of the exceeding profaneness of Iason, that wicked man, and no high priest; 14 so that the priests had no more any zeal for the services of the altar: but despising the set-apart place, and neglecting the slaughterings, they hastened to enjoy that which was unlawfully provided in the arena, after the summons of the discus[d]; 15 making the honors of their fathers of no account, and thinking the glories of the Greeks best of all. 16 For this reason severe calamity came on them; and the men whose ways of living they earnestly followed, and to whom they desired to be made like in all things, these they had to be their enemies and to punish them. 17 For it is not a light thing to do wickedly against the Torot of Elohim: but the time following shall declare these things.

18 Now when certain games that came every fifth year were kept at Tsor, and the king was present. 19 The vile Iason sent representatives of the Antioḥians of Yerushalayim, bearing three hundred drachmas of silver to the slaughtering to Hercules, which even its bearers thought not right to use for any slaughtering, because it was not fit, but to expend on another charge. 20 And though in the purpose of the sender this money was for slaughtering to Hercules, on account of present circumstances it went to the equipment of the galleys[e].

21 Now when Apollonios the son of Menestheus was sent into Mitsrayim for the

---

Iason's name was actually Yehoshua. However, due to his love of Hellenistic culture, he changed his name, and adopted the Greek name "Iason." Compare also verse 10.

[a] 4:9 Youth Center – Refers to an educational institution where youths were taught in the Greek language about intellectual culture and physical fitness.

[b] 4:12 "Under the fortress" would mean the gymnasium would be built directly next to the Temple on its eastern side. The eastern side of the Temple faced the Mount of Olives.

[c] 4:12 The "Greek cap" mentioned here is most likely the wide-brimmed hat traditionally depicted being worn by Hermes, the patron deity of athletic contests. It was part of the traditional uniform worn by those of the youth center.

[d] 4:14 Summons of the discus – Phrase referring to the sport of throwing the discus, common among Greek youths.

[e] 4:20 Naval ships with three banks of oars.

coronation of Ptolemy Philometor as king,
Antioḥos (learning that Ptolemy had shown
himself opposed toward the state) took
thought for the security of his realm;
wherefore, going by sea to Yapho, he
travelled on to Yerushalayim. 22 And being
magnificently received by Iason and the
city, he was brought in with torches and
shouting. After this was done, he led his
army down into Phoenicia.

23 Now after a space of three years Iason
sent Menelaus, the previously mentioned
brother of Shimon, to bear the money to the
king, and to make reports concerning some
necessary matters. 24 But he, being
commended to the king and having
glorified himself by the flattering of his
authority, got the high priesthood for
himself, outbidding Iason by three hundred
talents of silver. 25 And having received the
royal mandates he came to Yerushalayim,
bringing nothing worthy the high
priesthood, but having the passion of a
cruel tyrant, and the rage of a savage beast.
26 And whereas Iason, who had supplanted
his own brother, was supplanted by another
and driven as a fugitive into the country of
the Ammonites, 27 Menelaus had
possession of the office: but of the money
that had been promised to the king nothing
was duly paid, even though Sostratus the
governor of the fortress demanded it.
28 (For the gathering of the revenues
belonged to him); for which cause they
were both called by the king to his
presence. 29 And Menelaus left his own
brother Lusimaḥus for his successor in the
high priesthood; and Sostratus left Krates,
who was over those of Kupros.

30 Now while such was the state of things,
it came to pass that they of Tarsus and
Mallus rebelled, because they were to be
given as a present to Antioḥos, the king's
concubine. 31 The king therefore came to
Kilikia quickly to settle matters, leaving for
his successor Andronikos, a man of high
rank. 32 And Menelaus, supposing that he
had gotten a favorable opportunity,
presented to Andronikos certain vessels of
gold belonging to the Temple, which he
had stolen: he had already sold into Tsor
and the cities around other vessels. 33 And
when Ḥoniyo had sure knowledge of this,
he sharply reproved him, having withdrawn
himself into a place at Daphne, which is
near Antioḥ. 34 Wherefore Menelaus,
taking Andronikos apart, asked him to kill
Ḥoniyo. And coming to Ḥoniyo, (and being
persuaded to use treachery, and being
received *by him* as a friend), Andronikos
gave him his right hand with oaths of
fidelity, and, though he was suspected by
him, so persuaded him to come out of the
set-apart place; and he immediately killed
him without regard of justice.

35 For *this* reason not only Yehudim, but
many also of the other nations, had
indignation and displeasure at the unjust
murder of the man. 36 And when the king
had come back again from the places in
Kilikia, the Yehudim that were in the city[a]
pleaded before him against Andronikos (the
Greeks also joining with them in hatred of
the wickedness), urging that Ḥoniyo had
been wrongfully slain. 37 Antioḥos
therefore was greatly sorry, and was moved
to pity, and wept, because of the sober and
well-ordered life of him that was dead.
38 And being inflamed with passion, he

---

[a] 4:36 the city – namely, Antioḥ.

immediately stripped off Andronikos' purple robe, and tore off his under garments, and when he had led him through the whole city to that very place where he had committed wickedness against Ḥoniyo, there he put the murderer out of the way, יהוה rendering to him the punishment he had deserved.

39 Now when many profane things had been committed in the city[a] by Lusimaḥus with the consent of Menelaus, and when its fruit was spread abroad outside, the people gathered themselves together against Lusimaḥus, after many vessels of gold had been already dispersed. 40 And when the multitudes were rising against him, and were filled with anger, Lusimaḥus armed about three thousand men, and with unrighteous violence began the conflict, one Ḥavran, a man far gone in years and no less also in madness, leading the attack. 41 But when they perceived the assault of Lusimaḥus, some caught up stones, others logs of wood, and some took handfuls of the ashes that lay near, and they threw them all together upon Lusimaḥus and those who were with him; 42 because of this many of them were wounded, and some they struck to the ground, and all of them they forced to flee, but the author of the profanation himself they killed beside the treasury.

43 But touching these matters there was an accusation laid against Menelaus. 44 And when the king came to Tsor, the three men that were sent by the senate pleaded the cause before him. 45 But Menelaus, seeing himself now defeated, promised much money to Ptolemy the son of Dorymenes, that he might win over the king. 46 Then Ptolemy took the king aside into a cloister, as it were to take in some air, and changed his mind: 47 and he that was the cause of all the evil, Menelaus, he discharged from the accusations; but these unfortunate men, who, if they had pleaded even before Scythians[b], would have been discharged uncondemned, them he sentenced to death. 48 Soon after that, those who were spokesmen for the city and the families of Yisra'el and the set-apart vessels suffered that unrighteous penalty. 49 For which cause even certain Tsorites, moved with hatred of the wickedness, provided magnificently for their burial. 50 But Menelaus through the covetous dealings of those who were in power remained still in his office, cleaving to wickedness, *and* established as a great conspirator against his fellow-citizens.

5 1 Now about this time Antioḥos made his
second trip into Mitsrayim. 2 And it so happened that throughout all the city, for the space of almost forty days, there appeared in the midst of the sky horsemen in swift motion, wearing robes made with gold and carrying spears, equipped in troops for battle; 3 and drawing of swords; and on the other side squadrons of horsemen in array; and encounters and charges of both armies; and shaking of shields, and multitudes of lances, and casting of darts, and flashing of golden trappings, and girding on of all sorts of armor. 4 Wherefore all men implored that

---

[a] 4:39 the city – namely, Yerushalayim.
[b] 4:47 Scythians – Term applied to a wide number of people groups throughout the East, from parts of Paras (modern Iran) to the Black Sea. Scythians were considered by the Greeks to be barbaric and uncivilized.

the manifestation might have been given
for good.

5 But when a false rumor had arisen that
Antioḥos was dead, Iason took not less than
a thousand men, and suddenly perpetrated
an assault upon the city; and those who
were upon the wall were put to flight, and
the city was then at length nearly taken,
Menelaus took refuge in the fortress. 6 But
Iason killed his own citizens without
mercy, not considering that good success
against kinsmen is the greatest ill-success,
but supposing himself to be setting up
trophies over enemies, and not over fellow-
countrymen. 7 However he did not get the
office, but, receiving shame as the end of
his conspiracy, he passed again a fugitive
into the country of the Ammonites.
8 Finally he met with a miserable end:
having been shut up at the court of Aretas
the prince of the Aravians, fleeing from city
to city, pursued by all men, hated as an
apostate from the Torot, and held in
abomination as the butcher of his country
and his fellow-citizens, he was cast forth
into Mitsrayim. 9 And he that had driven
many from their own country into foreign
lands perished himself in a foreign land,
having crossed the sea to the Laodikeans,
as thinking to find shelter there because
they were near of kin; 10 and he that had
cast out a multitude unburied had none to
mourn for him, nor had he any funeral at
all, or place in the grave of his fathers.

11 Now when news came to the king
concerning that which was done, he
thought that Yehudah was in revolt. So
setting out from Mitsrayim in a furious
mind, he took the city by force of arms,
12 and commanded his soldiers to cut down
without mercy any that stood in the way,
and to kill any that went up upon the
houses. 13 And there was killing of young
and old. Taking away of boys, women, and
children, slaying of maidens and infants.
14 And in all the three days of the slaughter
there were destroyed eighty thousand, of
which forty thousand were slain in close
combat, and no fewer were sold than slain.

15 But not content with this he presumed to
enter into the most set-apart Temple of all
the earth, having Menelaus for his guide
(him that had proved himself a traitor both
to the Torot and to his country), 16 even
taking the sacred vessels with his profane
hands, and dragging down with his profane
hands the offerings that had been dedicated
by other kings to the augmentation and
glory and honor of the place. 17 And
Antioḥos was lifted up in mind, not seeing
that because of the sins of those who lived
in the city the Sovereign Master had been
provoked to anger a little while, and
therefore His eye was then turned away
from the place. 18 But had it not so been
that they were already held by many sins,
this man, even as Heliodoros who was sent
by Seleukus the king to view the treasury,
would, so soon as he pressed forward, have
been scourged and turned back from his
daring deed.

19 However, יהוה did not choose the
nation for the place's sake, but the place for
the nation's sake. 20 Wherefore also the
place itself, having partaken in the
calamities that happened to the nation, did
afterward share in its benefits; and the
place which was forsaken in the wrath of
the Almighty was, at the reconciliation of
the great Sovereign, restored again with all
glory. 21 As for Antioḥos, when he had
carried away out of the Temple a thousand

and eight hundred talents, he departed
quickly to Antioḥ, thinking in his arrogance
to make the land navigable and the sea
passable by foot, because his heart was
lifted up. **22** And moreover he left
governors to afflict the race: at
Yerushalayim, Philippos, by race a
Phrygian, and in character more barbarous
than him that set him there. **23** And at
Gerizim, Andronikos; and besides these,
Menelaus, who worse than all the rest
exalted himself against his fellow-citizens.
And having a malicious mind toward the
Yehudim whom he had made his citizens,
24 he sent that chief[a] of profanation
Apollonios with an army of twenty-two
thousand, commanding him to kill all those
that were of full age, and to sell the women
and the male youths.

25 And he came to Yerushalayim, and
played the man of peace, waiting until the
set-apart day of the Sabbath, and finding
the Yehudim at rest from work, he
commanded his men to parade in arms.
26 And he put to the sword all those who
came forth to the spectacle; and running
into the city with the armed men he killed
great multitudes. **27** But Yehudah, who is
also called Maqabi, with about nine others,
withdrew himself, and with his company
kept himself alive in the mountains after
the manner of wild beasts; and they
continued feeding on such poor herbs as
grew there, that they might not be partakers
of the threatened profanation.

6 **1** And not long after this the king sent an
elder of Athens to compel the Yehudim to
depart from the Torot of their fathers, and
not to live after the Torot of Elohim; **2** and
also to profane the set-apart place in
Yerushalayim, and to call it by the name of
'Zeus Olympius'[b], and to call the place in
Gerizim by the name of 'Zeus the Protector
of Foreigners', even as those that lived in
the place. **3** But severe and utterly grievous
was the visitation of this evil. **4** For the
Temple was filled with riot and reveling by
the heathen, who amused themselves with
whores, and had relations with women
within the sacred courts. And moreover
they brought inside things that were not fit.
5 And the place of slaughtering was filled
with those abominable things which had
been prohibited by the Torah. **6** And a man
could neither guard the Sabbath, nor
observe the Feasts of the fathers, nor so
much as confess himself to be a Yehudite.

7 And on the day of the king's birth every
month they were led along with bitter
constraint to eat of the slaughterings; and
when the feast of Bacchus came, they were
compelled to go in procession in honor of
Bacchus, wearing wreaths of ivy.[c] **8** And

---

[a] 5:24 LXX uses the word μυσαρχ (*musarḥ*), while the Syr. reads ܪܝܫ (*Riysh*). *Mysarḥ* is believed to mean literally "ruler of the Mysians." Meanwhile, the Aramaic word *Riysh* means "chief" or "head" and as such it has been rendered here, as it makes the most sense given the context.

[b] 6:2 Zeus Olympius – In Aramaic, this term is "Ba'al Shamen" meaning "lord/owner of the heavens." To the Hebrews, this would be the equivalent of שקוץ משומם (*shi'quts m'shomem*). Rendered literally, this is "abomination of desolation" though *m'shomem* is a wordplay on שמים (*sham'ayim*) meaning "heavens." Thus the connection between the Hebrew phrase and the Aramaic title "lord of the heavens."

[c] 6:7 Feast of Bacchus – Bacchus, also known as Dionysus, was the el of grape harvest and wine. His so-called "feast" was celebrated with wine, cult prostitution, and the decoration of ivy.

there went out a decree to the neighboring
Greek cities, by the suggestion of Ptolemy
that they should observe the same conduct
against the Yehudim, and should make
them eat of the slaughterings; 9 and that
they should kill those that did not choose to
go over to the Greek rituals. So the present
misery was for all to see: 10 for two women
were brought up for having circumcised
their children; and these, when they had led
them publicly around the city, with the
infants hung from their breasts, they threw
down headfirst from the wall. 11 And
others, that had run together into the caves
nearby to keep the seventh day secretly,
being betrayed to Philippos, were all
burned together, because they refrained
from defending themselves, having decided
to honor that most solemn day.

12 I beg, therefore, those that read this
book: that they not be discouraged because
of the calamities, but account that these
punishments were not for the destruction,
but for the discipline of our race. 13 For
indeed that those who act wickedly are not
left alone for long, but are quickly met with
retribution, is a sign of great kindness.
14 For in the case of the other nations the
Sovereign Master waits patiently, until He
punishes them when they have reached the
full measure of their sins; but not so when
He judges us, 15 that He may not take
vengeance on us afterward, when we reach
the height of our sins. 16 Wherefore He
never withdraws His mercy from us; but
though He chastises with calamity, yet He
does not forsake His own people. 17 Let
these words suffice for recalling this truth.
Without further ado, we must go on with
our story.

18 Elazar, one of the principal scribes, a
man already well stricken in years, and of a
noble countenance, was forced to open his
mouth to eat swine's flesh. 19 But he,
welcoming death with renown rather than
life with profanation, advanced of his own
accord to the instrument of torture, but first
spat forth the flesh, 20 coming forward as
men ought to come that are resolute to repel
such things as not even for the natural love
of life is it lawful to taste.

21 But those who had the charge of that
forbidden feast took the man aside, for they
were acquaintances of old times with him,
and privately implored him to bring flesh of
his own providing, such as was fit for him
to use, and to make as if he did eat of the
flesh from the slaughtering, as had been
commanded by the king; 22 that by so
doing he might be delivered from death,
and for his old friendship with them might
be treated kindly.

23 But he made up his mind in a noble
manner, worthy of his years, the dignity of
his advanced age, the merited distinction of
his gray hair, and of the admirable life he
had lived from childhood. Above all, loyal
to the set-apart Torot given by Elohim, he
swiftly declared, "Send me to Sheol! 24 For
it is not fitting for our years to mislead,"
said he, "that through this many of the
young should suppose that Elazar, the man
of ninety years, had gone over to a foreign
religion; 25 and so they, by reason of my
disguise, and for the sake of this brief and
momentary life, should be led astray
because of me, and thus I get to myself a
profanation and a stain of my old age.
26 For even if for the present time I shall
remove from me the punishment of men,
yet shall I not escape the hands of the

Almighty, either living or dead.
27 Wherefore, by bravely parting with my
life now, I will show myself worthy of my
old age, 28 and leave behind a noble
example to the young, to die willingly and
nobly a glorious death for the revered and
set-apart Torot." And when he had said
these words, he went directly to the
instrument of torture.

29 And those who had previously been kind
to him, now became hostile, because these
words of his were, as they thought, sheer
madness. 30 And when he was at the point
of death with the stripes, he groaned aloud
and said, "To יהוה, that has the set-apart
knowledge, it is manifest that, whereas I
might have been delivered from death, I
endure severe pains in my body by being
scourged; but in being I gladly suffer these
things for my fear of Him."

31 So this man also died after this manner,
leaving his death for an example of
nobleness and a memorial of virtue, not
only to the young but also to the great body
of his nation.

7 1 And it came to pass that seven brethren
– along with their mother – were taken at
the king's command and shamefully
handled with scourges and cords, to force
them to taste of the abominable swine's
flesh.[a] 2 But one of them made himself the
spokesman and said, "What would you ask
and learn of us? For we are ready to die
rather than transgress the Torot of our
fathers."

3 And the king fell into a rage, and
commanded to heat pans and caldrons:
4 and when these were heated, he
commanded to cut out the tongue of him
that had been their spokesman, and to scalp
him, and to cut off his extremities, the rest
of his brethren and his mother looking on.
5 And when he was completely maimed,
the king commanded to bring him to the
fire, being yet alive, and to fry him in the
pan. And as the vapor of the pan spread far,
they and their mother also exhorted one
another to die nobly, saying thus:

6 "יהוה Elohim sees, and in truth is
entreated for us, as Mosheh declared in his
song, which witnesses against the people to
their faces, saying, '**And He shall have
compassion on His servants**.'"[b]

7 And when the first had died after this
manner, they brought the second to the
mocking; and they pulled off the skin of his
head with the hair and asked him, "Will
you eat, before your body be punished in
every limb?" 8 But he answered in the
language of his fathers and said to them,
"No." Then he also underwent the next
torture in succession, as the first had done.
9 And when he was at his last breath, he
said, "You, miscreant, do release us out of
this present life, but the King of the world
shall raise up us, who have died for his
Torot, to an eternal renewal of life."

10 And after him was the third made into a
mocking. And when he was required, he
quickly put out his tongue, and stretched
forth his hands courageously, 11 and nobly
said, "From heaven I possess these; and for
the sake of His Torot I disregard these; and

---

[a] 7:1 Compare Yirmeyahu [Jeremiah] 15:9.

[b] 7:6 See Devarim [Deuteronomy] 31:21; 32:36-38.

from Him I hope to receive these back
again." 12 Even the king himself and those
who were with him were astonished at the
young man's being, for he regarded the
suffering as nothing. 13 And when he, too,
was dead, they shamefully handled and
tortured the fourth in like manner.

14 And being come near to death he said:
"It is good to die at the hands of men and
look for the hopes which are given by
Elohim, that we shall be raised up again by
Him. But as for you, you shall have no
resurrection to life."

15 And next after him they brought the
fifth, and shamefully handled him. 16 But
he looked toward the king and said,
"Because you have authority among men,
though you are yourself corruptible, you do
what you will; yet do not think that our race
has been forsaken by Elohim; 17 but hold
your way, and behold His sovereign
majesty, how it will torture you and your
seed."

18 And after him they brought the sixth.
And when he was at the point to die he
said, "Do not be vainly deceived, for we
suffer these things for our own doings, as
sinning against our own Elohim: marvelous
things are come to pass; 19 but do not think
that you shall be unpunished, having
thought to fight against Elohim."

20 But above all was the mother marvelous
and worthy of honorable memory; for when
she looked on seven sons perishing within
the space of one day, she bore the sight
with a good courage for the hopes that she
had set on יהוה. 21 And she exhorted each
one of them in the language of their fathers,
filled with a noble temper and stirring up
her womanish thought with manly passion,
saying to them, 22 "I do not know how you
came into my womb, neither was it I that
bestowed on you your spirit and your life,
and it was not I that brought into order the
first elements of each one of you.
23 Therefore the Creator of the world, who
fashioned the generation of man and
devised the generation of all things, in
mercy gives back to you again both your
spirit and your life, as you now disregard
your own selves for the sake of His Torot."[a]

24 But Antioḥos, thinking himself to be
despised, and suspecting the reproachful
voice, while the youngest was yet alive did
not only make his appeal to him by words,
but also at the same time promised with
oaths that he would enrich him and raise
him to high estate, if he would turn from
the customs of his fathers, and that he
would take him for his friend and entrust
him with affairs. 25 But when the young
man would in no way give heed, the king
called to him his mother, and exhorted her
that she would counsel the young man to
save himself.

26 And when he had exhorted her with
many words, she undertook to persuade her
son. 27 But bending toward him, in defiance
to the cruel tyrant, she spoke thus in the
language of her fathers: "My son, have pity
upon me that carried you nine months in
my womb, and nursed you three years, and
nourished and brought you up to this age,
and sustained you. 28 I implore you, my
child, to lift your eyes to the heavens and
the earth, and to see all things that are in
them, and thus to recognize that Elohim

---

[a] 7:22-23 See also Qoheleth [Ecclesiastes] 11:5.

made them not of things that were, and that the race of men in this way came into being. 29 Do not be afraid of this tormentor, but, proving yourself worthy of your brethren, accept your death, that in the mercy of Elohim I may receive you again with your brethren."

30 But before she had yet ended speaking, the young man said, "Whom do you wait for? I do not obey the command of the king, but I listen to the command of the Torah that was given to our fathers through Mosheh. 31 But you, that have devised all manner of evil against the Hebrews, shall in no way escape the hands of Elohim. 32 For we are suffering because of our own sins; 33 and if for rebuke and chastening יהוה Elohim has been angered a little while, yet shall He again be reconciled with His own servants. 34 But you, O profane man and of all most vile, do not be vainly lifted up in your wild pride with uncertain hopes, raising your hand against the servants of Elohim. 35 For you have not yet escaped the judgment of the Almighty Elohim that sees all things. 36 For these our brethren, having endured a short pain that brings everlasting life, have now died under the covenant of Elohim. But you, through the judgment of Elohim, shall receive in just measure the penalties of your arrogance.

37 "But I, as my brethren, give up both body and being for the Torot of our fathers, calling upon Elohim that He may speedily become gracious to the nation; and that you may confess that He alone is Elohim amidst trials and plagues; 38 and that in me and my brethren you may stay the wrath of the Almighty, which has been justly brought upon our whole race."

39 But the king, falling into a rage, handled him worse than all the rest, being exasperated at his mocking. 40 So he also died pure from profanation, putting his whole trust in יהוה.

41 And last of all, after her sons, the mother died. 42 Let it then suffice to have said this much concerning the enforcement of feasts and the king's exceeding barbarities.

8 1 But Yehudah, who is also called Maqabi, and those who were with him, making their way secretly into the villages, called to them their kinsfolk; and taking to them those that continued in the religion of the Yehudim, gathered together as many as six thousand. 2 And they called upon יהוה, asking Him to look upon the people that was oppressed by all; and to have compassion on the set-apart place also that had been profaned by the wicked men, 3 and to have pity on the city that was suffering ruin and ready to be leveled to the ground; and to listen to the blood that cried to Him; 4 and to remember also the lawless slaughter of the innocent infants, and the blasphemies that had been committed against His Name; and to show His hatred of wickedness.

5 And when Maqabi had trained his men for service, the heathen at once found him unbeatable, for the wrath of יהוה was turned into pity. 6 And coming unnoticed he set fire to cities and villages. And in winning back the most important positions, putting to flight no small number of the enemies, 7 he especially took advantage of the nights for such assaults. And his courage was loudly spoken of everywhere.

8 But when Philippos saw the man gaining ground little by little, and increasing more and more in his prosperity, he wrote to Ptolemy, the governor of Koele-Aram and Phoenicia, that he should support the king's cause. **9** And Ptolemy quickly appointed Niqanor the son of Patroclus, one of the king's Chief Friends, and sent him, in command of no fewer than twenty thousand of all nations, to destroy the whole race of Yehudah; and with him he joined Gorgias also, a captain and one that had experience in matters of war. **10** And Niqanor undertook by the sale of the captive Yehudim to make up for the king the tribute of two thousand talents which he was to pay to the Romans.[a] **11** And immediately he sent to the cities upon the sea coast, inviting them to buy Yehudite slaves, promising to allow ninety slaves for a talent, not expecting the judgment that was to follow upon him from the Almighty.[b]

12 But when word came to Yehudah concerning the coming of Niqanor; and when he communicated to those who were with him the presence of the army, **13** those who were cowardly and distrustful of the judgment of Elohim ran away and left the country. **14** And others sold all that was left over to them, and with it implored יהוה to deliver those who had been sold as slaves by the wicked Niqanor before he met them. **15** And this, if not for their own sakes, yet for the covenants cut with their fathers, and because He had called them by His revered and glorious Name. **16** And Maqabi gathered his men together, six thousand in number, and exhorted them not to be stricken with dismay at the enemy, nor to fear the great multitude of the heathen who came wrongfully against them; but to contend nobly, **17** setting before their eyes the outrage that had been lawlessly perpetrated upon the set-apart place, and the shameful handling of the city that had been turned to mockery, and further the overthrow of the mode of life received from their ancestors.

18 "For they," said he, "trust in arms, and their deeds of daring; but we trust in the Almighty Elohim, since He is able with a nod to cast down those who are coming against us, and even the whole world."

19 And he recounted to them the help given from time to time in the days of their ancestors, both the help given in the days of Sancheriv, how that a hundred and eighty-five thousand perished,[c] **20** and the help given in the land of Bavel, even the battle that was fought against the Galatians[d], how that they came to the engagement eight[e]

---

[a] 8:10 During the Treaty of Apamea in 188 BCE, a number of restrictions were placed on Antioḥos. He had to abandon all of Europe and all of Asia west of Taurus (mountains in modern day Turkey). He had to surrender all elephants, and could only maintain a fleet of twelve warships, solely for the purpose of keeping his subjects under control. He was forced to give twenty men, chosen by the Romans, as hostages, including his own son. He was also required to pay large taxes, which is what is mentioned here.

[b] 8:11 The fact that they were only seeking one talent for ninety slaves expressed their extreme contempt for the Yehudim, as this was well below the normal rate for so many slaves.

[c] 8:19 See also Melakhim ב [2 Kings] 19.

[d] 8:20 Galatians – Most likely a mercenary force of the Gauls, natives of Galatia.

[e] 8:20 Syr. records this number as "eighty" instead of "eight."

thousand in all, with four[a] thousand
Makedonians, and how that, the
Makedonians being hard pressed, the six
thousand destroyed the hundred and twenty
thousand, because of the assistance which
they had from heaven, and took great
plunder. **21** And when he had with these
words made them of good courage, and
ready to die for the Torot and their country,
he divided his army into four parts.
22 Appointing his brethren to be with
himself leaders of the several bands,
namely, Shimon and Yosef[b] and Yonathan,
giving each the command of fifteen
hundred men, **23** and moreover Elazar[c] also:
then, having read aloud the sacred book,
and having given as watchword[d], "the help
of Elohim," leading the first band himself,
Yehudah joined battle with Niqanor.

24 And, since the Almighty fought on their
side, they killed of the enemy above nine
thousand, and wounded and disabled the
greater part of Niqanor's army, and
compelled all to flee. **25** And they took the
money of those that had come there to buy
them. And after they had pursued them for
some distance, they returned, being
constrained by the time of the day; **26** for it
was the day before the Sabbath, and for this
cause they made no effort to chase them
far. **27** And when they had gathered the
arms of the enemy together, and had
stripped off their spoils, they occupied
themselves about the Sabbath, blessing and
thanking יהוה exceedingly, who had saved
them to this day, for that He had caused a
beginning of mercy to distil upon them.
28 And after the Sabbath, when they had
given of the spoils to the maimed, and to
the widows and orphans, they distributed
what was left over among themselves and
their children.[e] **29** And when they had
accomplished these things, and had made a
common petition, they implored the
merciful Master to be wholly reconciled
with His servants.

30 And having had an encounter with the
forces of Timotheos and Bacchides, they
killed above twenty thousand of them, and
made themselves masters of strongholds
exceedingly high, and divided very much
plunder, giving the maimed and orphans
and widows, and moreover the aged also,
an equal share with themselves. **31** And
when they had gathered the arms of the
enemy together, they stored them all up
carefully in the most important positions,
and the remnant of the spoils they carried
to Yerushalayim. **32** And they killed the
commander of Timotheos' forces, a most
profane man, and one who had done the
Yehudim much harm. **33** And as they kept
the feast of victory in the land of their
fathers, they burned those that had set the
sacred gates on fire, and among them
Qalesteniys, who had fled into a solitary

---

[a] 8:20 Syr. records this number as "forty" instead of "four."
[b] 8:22 Yosef – Most likely the same as the Yoḥanan mentioned in Maqabiym א [1 Maccabees] 2:2.
[c] 8:23 Elazar – This phrase reads awkwardly in both Greek and Aramaic. It is most commonly believed to be a parenthetical reference to the fifth Maqabi brother named Elazar. See Maqabiym א [1 Maccabees] 2:5.
[d] 8:23 "Watchword" - In Greek, this is συνθημα (*sun'thema*) meaning "motto" or "slogan." In the Syr., however, this is actually two words: ܐܬܐ ܕܦܘܪܩܢܐ (*at'a d'pur'qana*) which means "sign" and "salvation" respectively: "the sign of salvation."
[e] 8:28 See also Devarim [Deuteronomy] 26:12-13; Shemu'el א [1 Samuel] 30:21-26.

hut; and so they received the chance reward
of their profanation.

34 And the thrice-accursed Niqanor, who
had brought the thousand merchants to buy
the Yehudim for slaves, 35 being humbled
by them who in his eyes were held to be of
least account [with the help of the Master][a],
put off his glorious apparel, and passing
through the midland, shunning all company
like a fugitive slave, arrived at Antioḥ,
having, as he thought, had the greatest
possible good fortune, though his army was
destroyed. 36 And he that had taken upon
him to make tribute sure for the Romans by
the captivity of the men of Yerushalayim
proclaimed abroad that the Yehudim had
One who fought for them, and that on
account of this the Yehudim were
invulnerable, because they followed the
Torot ordained by Him.[b]

9

1 Now about that time it happened that
Antioḥos [the king][c] had returned in
dishonor from the region of Paras. 2 For he
had entered into the city called Persepolis,
and he thought to rob a temple[d] and to hold
down the city. While *he was* there, there
was an attack of the multitudes, and
Antioḥos and his men turned to make
defense with arms; and it came to pass that
Antioḥos was put to flight by the people of
the country and broke up his camp with
disgrace. 3 And while he was at Aḥmetha,
they brought him news about what had
happened to Niqanor and the forces of
Timotheos. 4 And being lifted up by his
passion, he thought to make the Yehudim
suffer even for the evil-doing of those that
had put him to flight. Accordingly, the
judgment from heaven also accompanying
him, he gave order to his charioteer to drive
without ceasing and dispatch the journey;
for thus he arrogantly spoke: "I will make
Yerushalayim a common graveyard of
Yehudim, when I come there."

5 But the All-seeing יהוה, the Elohim of
Yisra'el, struck him with a fatal and
invisible stroke; and as soon as he had
ceased speaking this word, an incurable
pain of the bowels seized him, and bitter
torments of the inner parts.[e] 6 And that
most justly, for he had tormented other
men's bowels with many and strange
sufferings. 7 But he in no way ceased from
his rude insolence; no, still more was he
filled with arrogance, breathing fire in his
passion against the Yehudim, and
commanding to haste the journey. But it
came to pass moreover that he fell from his
chariot as it rushed along, and having a
grievous fall was racked in all the members
of his body. 8 And he that until now had
supposed himself to have the waves of the
sea at his bidding, so arrogant was he
beyond the condition of a man, and that
thought to weigh the heights of the
mountains in a balance, was now brought
to the ground and carried in a stretcher,
showing to all that the power belonged to
Elohim. 9 Then out of the body of the
wicked man worms swarmed, and while he

---

[a] 8:35 Syr. omits the bracketed section here, LXX includes it.
[b] 8:36 LXX reads, "they followed the Torot (laws)" as it is here. Syr., however, reads ܕܡܗܠܟܝܢ ܒܦܘܩܕܢܘܗܝ (*d'm'halakh b'puqdanuwh*) meaning "they walked in the commands."
[c] 9:1 LXX omits the bracketed section here, Syr. includes it.
[d] 9:2 LXX reads "temple" as it is here. Syr. reads ܒܝܬ ܦܬܟܪܐ (*beyt patkra*) meaning "idol house" here.
[e] 9:5 Compare Ma'asei [Acts] 12:20-23.

was still living in anguish and pains, his
flesh fell off, and by reason of the stench all
the army turned with loathing from his
corruption.[a] 10 And the man that a little
before supposed himself to touch the stars
of heaven, no one could endure to carry for
his intolerable stench. 11 After this,
therefore, he began in great part to cease
from his arrogance, being broken in spirit,
and to come to knowledge under the
scourge of Elohim, his pains increasing
every moment.

12 And when he himself could not abide his
own smell, he said these words: "It is right
to be subject to Elohim, and that one who is
mortal should not be minded arrogantly."[b]
13 And the vile man vowed to the
Sovereign Master, who now no more would
have pity upon him, saying on this way:
14 that the set-apart city, to the which he
was going in haste, to level it to the ground
and to make it a common graveyard, he
would declare free; 15 and as touching the
Yehudim, whom he had decided not even
to count worthy of burial, but to cast them
out to the beasts with their infants, for the
birds to devour, he would make them all
equal to citizens of Athens; 16 and the set-
apart place, which before he had plundered,
he would adorn with the best offerings, and
would restore all the sacred vessels many
times multiplied, and out of his own
revenues would pay the charges that were
required for the slaughterings.

17 And besides all this, that he would
become a Yehudite, and would visit every
inhabited place, proclaiming abroad the
might of Elohim. 18 But when his
sufferings did not cease, for the judgment
of Elohim had come upon him in
righteousness, having given up all hope of
himself, he wrote to the Yehudim the letter
written below, having the nature of a
petition, to this effect:

19 "To the worthy Yehudim, his fellow-
citizens, Antioḥos, king and general,
wishes much joy and health and prosperity.
20 May you and your children fare well;
and your affairs shall be to your mind.
Having my hope in heaven, 21 I
remembered with affection your honor and
good-will toward me. Returning out of the
region of Paras, and being taken with a
repulsive sickness, I deemed it necessary to
take thought for the common safety of all,
22 not despairing of myself, but having
great hope to escape from the sickness.
23 But considering that my father also, at
what time he led an army into the upper
country, appointed his successor, 24 to the
end that, if anything fell out contrary to
expectation, or if any unwelcome tidings
were brought, they that remained in the
country, knowing to whom the state had
been left, might not be troubled.

25 "And, besides all this, observing how
that the princes that are borderers and
neighbors to my kingdom watch
opportunities, and look for the future event,
I have appointed my son Antioḥos to be
king, whom I often committed and
commended to most of you, when I was
hastening to the upper provinces; and I
have written to him what is written below.
26 I exhort you, therefore, and beg you,
remembering the good things done to you
as a whole and individually, to preserve
each of you your present good-will toward

---

[a] 9:9 Possible reference to the Yehudith 16:17.

[b] 9:12 Compare Dani'el 4:31-34.

me and my son. 27 For I am persuaded that
he, in gentleness and kindness, will follow
my purpose and treat you with indulgence."

28 So the murderer and blasphemer, having
endured the most severe sufferings, even as
he had dealt to other men, ended his life
among the mountains by a most piteous
fate in a foreign land. 29 And Philippos his
foster-brother[a] conveyed the body home;
and then, fearing the son of Antioḥos, he
went to Ptolemy Philometor in Mitsrayim.[b]

10 1 And Maqabi and those who were
with him, יהוה leading them on, recovered
the Temple and the city; 2 and they pulled
down the altars that had been built in the
marketplace by the foreigners, and also the
walls of sacred enclosures. 3 And having
cleansed the set-apart place, they made
another altar of slaughtering; and striking[c]
stones and taking fire out of them, they
offered slaughterings, after they had ceased
for two years, and burned incense, and
lighted menorahs, and set forth the bread of
the presence. 4 And when they had done
these things, they fell prostrate and
implored יהוה that they might fall no more
into such evils; but that, if ever they should
sin, they might be disciplined by Him with
patience, and not be delivered to
blaspheming and barbarous heathens.

5 Now on the same day that the set-apart
place was profaned by foreigners, upon that
very day it came to pass that the cleansing
of the set-apart place was made, even on
the twenty-fifth day of the same month,
which is Kislev. 6 And they kept eight days
with gladness in the manner of the Feast of
Tabernacles, remembering how that not
long before, during the Feast of
Tabernacles, they were wandering in the
mountains and in the caves after the
manner of wild beasts.

7 Then bearing wands wreathed with
leaves, and fair boughs, and palms also,
they offered up hymns of thanksgiving to
Him that had prosperously brought to pass
the cleansing of His own place.[d] 8 They
ordained also with a common statute and
decree, for all the nation of the Yehudim,
that they should keep these days every year.
9 And such was the end of Antioḥos, who
was called Epiphanes.

10 But now we will declare what came to
pass under Antioḥos named Eupator, who
proved himself a true son of that wicked
man, and will briefly gather up the many
evils of the wars. 11 For this man, when he

---

[a] 9:29 "Foster-brother" – Greek word συντροφος (*suwn'troph'os*) is translated literally as "playmate" or "comrade" though was used in Greek writings as an honorary title to someone close to them, whether they were raised together or not. Syr. uses the phrase ܒܪ ܡܪܒܝܢܘܗ (*bar m'r'beynuwh*) meaning "son, one being raised." This expression is used in Targum Neofiti Marginalia in Bereshiyt [Genesis] 17:23, where we read that Avraham took "all that were born in his house." Thus we find the phrase "foster-brother" a suitable fit for both the Greek as well as the Syriac, which implies individuals having been raised together.

[b] 9:29 Philippos tried to seize control of Antioḥ from the young Antioḥos V, and fled to Mitsrayim when he failed. Compare also verses 1-29 to Dani'el 11:40-45.

[c] 10:3 In both the Greek and Syriac this reads literally as "firing." That is, they were creating fire with stones.

[d] 10:7 Similar to the act of waving branches commanded during Sukkot, the Feast of Tabernacles. See also Vayyiqra [Leviticus] 23:40.

succeeded to the kingdom, appointed one Lysias to be chancellor, and supreme governor of Koele-Aram and Phoenicia.

12 For Ptolemy that was called Makron, setting an example of observing justice toward the Yehudim because of the wrong that had been done to them, endeavored to conduct his dealings with them on peaceful terms. 13 Consequently being accused by the king's beloved before Eupator, and hearing himself called 'traitor' at every turn, because he had abandoned Kupros which Philometor had entrusted to him, and had withdrawn himself to Antioḥos called Epiphanes, and failing to uphold the honor of his office, he took poison and took away his being.[a]

14 But Gorgias, when he was made governor of the district, maintained a force of mercenaries, and at every turn kept up war with the Yehudim. 15 And together with him the Edomites also, being masters of important strongholds, harassed the Yehudim; and receiving to them those that had taken refuge there from Yerushalayim, they decided to keep up war. 16 But Maqabi and his men, having made solemn petition and implored Elohim to fight on their side, rushed upon the strongholds of the Edomites. 17 And assaulting them vigorously they made themselves masters of the positions, and kept off all that fought upon the wall, and killed those that fell in their way, and killed no fewer than twenty thousand. 18 And because no less than nine thousand were fled into two towers exceedingly strong and having all things needed for a siege, 19 Maqabi (having left Shimon and Yosef, and Zakkai besides and those who were with him, a force sufficient to besiege them), departed to places where he was most needed. 20 But Shimon and those who were with him, loving money, were bribed by certain of those that were in the towers, and receiving seventy[b] thousand drachmas let some of them slip away.
21 But when word was brought to Maqabi of what was done, he gathered the leaders of the people together, and accused those men of having sold their brethren for money, by setting their enemies free to fight against them. 22 So he killed these men for having become traitors, and immediately took possession of the two towers. 23 And prospering with his arms in all things he took in hand, he destroyed in the two strongholds more than twenty thousand.

24 Now Timotheos, who had been before defeated by the Yehudim, gathered together foreign forces in great multitudes, and collected the horsemen which belonged to Asia, not a few, *and* came as though he would take Yehudah by force of arms.
25 But as he drew near, Maqabi and his men sprinkled earth upon their heads and girded their loins with sackcloth, in petition to Elohim, 26 and falling down upon the step in front of the altar, asked Him to become gracious to them, and be an enemy to their enemies and an adversary to their adversaries, as the Torah declares.[c] 27 And rising from their prayer they took up their arms, and advanced some distance from the city; and when they had come near to their enemies they halted.

[a] 10:13 That is, he killed himself.
[b] 10:20 Syr. reads "seven" instead of "seventy" here.
[c] 10:26 See Shemoth [Exodus] 23:22.

28 And when the dawn was spreading, the
two armies joined battle; the one part
having this, besides their virtue, for a
pledge of success and victory, that they had
fled to יהוה for refuge, the others made
their passion their leader in the strife.
29 But when the battle grew strong, there
appeared out of heaven to their adversaries
five men on horses with bridles of gold, in
splendid array; and two of them, leading on
the Yehudim, 30 and taking Maqabi in the
midst of them, and covering him with their
own armor, guarded him from wounds,
while on the adversaries they shot forth
arrows and thunderbolts; by which they
were blinded and thrown into confusion,
and were cut to pieces, filled with
confusion. 31 And there were slain twenty
thousand and five hundred, besides six
hundred horsemen.

32 But Timotheos himself fled into a
stronghold called Gezer, a fortress of great
strength, Ḥaereas being in command there.
33 But Maqabi and his men were glad and
laid siege to the fortress twenty-four days.
34 And those who were within, trusting to
the strength of the place, blasphemed
exceedingly, and hurled wicked words.
35 But at dawn of the twenty-fifth day,
certain young men of the company of
Maqabi, inflamed with passion because of
the blasphemies, assaulted the wall with
masculine force and with furious passion,
and cut down whoever came in their way.
36 And others climbing up in like manner,
while the besieged were distracted with
them that had made their way within, set
fire to the towers, and kindling fires burned
the blasphemers alive; while others broke
open the gates, and, having given entrance
to the rest of the band, occupied the city.
37 And they killed Timotheos, who was
hidden in a cistern, and his brother Ḥaereas,
and Apollophanes. 38 And when they had
accomplished these things, they blessed
יהוה with hymns and thanksgivings, Him
who gives great assistance to Yisra'el, and
gives them the victory.

11 1 Now after a very little time Lysias,
the king's guardian and kinsman and
chancellor, being severely displeased for
the things that had come to pass, 2 collected
about eighty thousand footmen and all his
horsemen and came against the Yehudim,
thinking to make the city a place for
Greeks[a] to dwell in, 3 and to levy tribute on
the Temple, as on the other sacred places of
the nations, and to put up the high
priesthood for sale every year. 4 Holding in
no account the might of Elohim, he was
puffed up with his [ten thousands of]
footmen, and his [thousands of] horsemen,
and his [eighty] elephants.[b] 5 And coming
into Yehudah and drawing near to Beth-
Tsur, which was a strong place and distant
from Yerushalayim about five stadia[c], he
pressed it hard.

6 But when Maqabi and his men learned
that he was besieging the strongholds, they

[a] 11:2 LXX reads "for Greeks" as it is here. Syr., however, reads ܠܥܡܐ (*l'amma*) meaning "for people."

[b] 11:4 Bracketed sections indicate readings present in LXX but absent from Syr.

[c] 11:5 Five stadia – approximately 3/5 of a mile. This verse's text is believed to be corrupted, as the actual distance between Beth-Tsur and Yerushalayim is about 20 miles. Though it could possibly be referring to the distance he was from Yerushalayim as he headed towards Beth-Tsur.

and all the people with lamentations and
tears made petition to יהוה to send a good
messenger to save Yisra'el. 7 And Maqabi
himself took up arms first, and exhorted the
others to join themselves together with him
and aid their brethren; and they charged
forth with him willingly. 8 And as they
were there, close to Yerushalayim, there
appeared at their head one on horseback in
white apparel, brandishing weapons of
gold. 9 And they all together praised the
merciful Elohim, and were yet more
strengthened in heart. They, being ready to
attack not men only but the wildest beasts,
and walls of iron, 10 advanced in array,
having Him that is in heaven to fight on
their side, for Elohim[a] had mercy on them.
11 And hurling themselves like lions upon
the enemy, they killed of them eleven
thousand footmen and one thousand six
hundred horsemen, and forced all the rest to
flee.

12 But the greater part of them escaped
wounded and naked; and Lysias also
himself escaped by shameful flight. 13 But
as he was a man not void of understanding,
weighing with himself the defeat which had
befallen him, and considering that the
Hebrews could not be overcome, because
the Almighty Elohim fought on their side,
he sent again to them, 14 and persuaded
them to come to terms on condition that all
their rights were acknowledged, and
promised that he would also persuade the
king to become their friend. 15 And Maqabi
gave consent upon all the conditions which
Lysias proposed to him, being careful of
the common good; for whatever requests
Maqabi delivered in writing to Lysias
concerning the Yehudim the king allowed.
16 For the letters written to the Yehudim
from Lysias were to this effect: "Lysias to
the people of the Yehudim, greetings.
17 Yoḥanan and Avshalom, who were sent
from you, having delivered the petition
written below, made request concerning the
things signified therein. 18 Whatever things,
therefore, had needed to be brought before
the king I declared to him, and what things
were possible he allowed. 19 If then you
will preserve your good-will toward the
state, from here on I also will endeavor to
contribute to your good. 20 And on this
behalf I have given order in detail, both to
these men and to those that are sent from
me, to confer with you. 21 Farewell."
Written in the hundred and forty-eighth
year, on the twenty-fourth day of the month
Tishri[b].

22 And the king's letter was in these words:
"King Antioḥos to his brother Lysias,
greetings. 23 Seeing that our father passed
to the elohim having the wish that the
subjects of his kingdom should be
undisturbed and give themselves to the care
of their own affairs, 24 we, having heard
that the Yehudim do not consent to our
father's purpose to turn them to the customs
of the Greeks, but choose rather their own
manner of living, and make request that the
customs of their Torah be allowed to
them,— 25 choosing therefore that this
nation also should be free from disturbance,

---

[a] 11:10 Syr. reads ܐܠܗܐ (*Alaha*) meaning "Elohim" as it is here. LXX, however, reads του Κυριου (*tou Kuriou*) meaning "the Master."

[b] 11:21 LXX calls the month "Dioscorinthius." However, this name is not found anywhere else in the book, and is thought to be corrupt. The Syr. records this month as "Tishri", the seventh month according to the Hebrew calendar, after it took the names of the Babylonian calendar.

we determine that their Temple be restored
to them, and that they walk according to the
customs and the Torot of their fathers.
26 You will therefore do well to send
messengers to them and give them the right
hand of friendship, that they, knowing our
mind, may be of good heart, and gladly
occupy themselves with the conduct of
their own affairs."

27 And to the nation the king's letter was
after this manner: "King Antioḥos to the
senate of the Yehudim and to the other
Yehudim, greetings. 28 If you fare well, we
have our desire: we ourselves also are in
good health. 29 Menelaus informed us that
your desire was to return home and follow
your own business. 30 They therefore that
depart home up to the thirtieth day of
Nisan[a] shall have our right hand *of*
friendship, with full permission 31 that the
Yehudim use their own proper meats and
observe their own Torot, even as up to this
time; and not one of them shall be in any
way wronged for the things that have been
ignorantly done. 32 Moreover I have sent
Menelaus also, that he may encourage you.
33 Farewell." Written in the hundred forty-
eighth year, on the fifteenth day of Nisan.[b]

34 And the Romans also sent to them a
letter in these words: "Quintus Memmius
and Titus Manius, emissaries of the
Romans, to the people of the Yehudim,
greetings. 35 In regard to the things which
Lysias the king's kinsman granted you, we
also give consent. 36 But as for the things
which he judged should be referred to the
king, send one immediately, after you have
advised, that we may proclaim such decrees
as fit your case; for we are on our way to
Antioḥ. 37 Send some with speed
accordingly, that we also may learn what is
in your mind. 38 Farewell." Written in the
hundred forty-eighth year, on the fifteenth
day of Nisan.

12 1 So when these covenants had been
cut, Lysias departed to the king, and the
Yehudim went about their farming. 2 But
certain of the governors of districts,
Timotheos and Apollonios the son of
Gennaeus, and Hieronymus also and
Demophon, and beside them Niqanor the
governor of Kupros, would not allow them
to enjoy tranquility and live in peace. 3 And
men of Yapho committed this great
transgression: they invited the Yehudim
that lived among them to go with their
wives and children into the boats which
they had provided, as though they had no
ill-will towards them; 4 and when the
Yehudim, relying on the common decree of
the city, accepted the invitation, as men
desiring to live in peace and suspecting
nothing, they took them out to sea and
drowned them, in number not less than two
hundred.

5 But when Yehudah heard of the cruelty
done to his fellow-countrymen, giving
command to the men that were with him
6 and calling upon Elohim the righteous
Judge, he came against the murderers of his
brethren, and set the haven on fire by night,

---

[a] 11:30 LXX calls the month "Xanthicus." The Syr., however, records this month as Nisan, the first month according to the Hebrew calendar, after it took the names of the Babylonians calendar. Also in verses 33 & 38.

[b] 11:33 The fifteenth day of the first month (here called Nisan) is the first day of the Feast of Unleavened Bread. See Shemoth [Exodus] 12; Vayyiqra [Leviticus] 23; Devarim [Deuteronomy] 16.

and burned the boats, and put to the sword
those that had fled there. 7 But when the
town was closed against him, he withdrew,
intending to come again to root out the
whole community of the men of Yapho.
8 But learning that the men of Yavneel
were minded to do in like manner to the
Yehudim that sojourned among them, 9 he
fell upon the Yavneelites also by night, and
set fire to the haven together with the fleet,
so that the glare of the light was seen at
Yerushalayim, two hundred and forty
furlongs away.

10 Now when they had drawn off nine
furlongs from there, as they marched
against Timotheos, an army of Aravians
attacked him, no fewer than five thousand
footmen and five hundred horsemen.
11 And when a severe battle had been
fought, and Yehudah and his company by
the help of Elohim had good success, the
nomads being overcome asked Yehudah to
grant them friendship, promising to give
him cattle, and to help his people in all
other ways. 12 So Yehudah, thinking that
they would indeed be profitable in many
things, agreed to live in peace with them;
and receiving pledges of friendship they
departed to their tents.

13 And he also fell upon a certain city
Gephyrun, strong and fenced about with
walls, and inhabited by a mixed multitude
of various nations; and it was named
Kaspin. 14 But those who were within,
trusting to the strength of the walls and to
their store of provisions, behaved
themselves rudely toward Yehudah and
those who were with him, railing, and also
blaspheming and speaking wicked words.
15 But Yehudah and his company, calling
upon the great King of the world, who
without rams and cunning engines of war
hurled down Yeriḥo in the times of
Yehoshua, rushed wildly against the wall.
16 And having taken the city by the will of
Elohim, they made unspeakable slaughter,
so much that the adjoining lake, which was
two furlongs broad, appeared to be filled
with a flood of blood.

17 And when they had drawn off seven
hundred and fifty furlongs from there, they
made their way to Ḥaraka[a], to the Yehudim
that are called Tubieni[b]. 18 And they did not
find Timotheos occupying that district, for
he had then departed from the district
without accomplishing anything, but had
left behind a garrison, and that a very
strong one, in a certain post. 19 But
Dositheus and Sosipater, who were of
Maqabi's captains, sallied forth and
destroyed those that had been left by
Timotheos in the stronghold, above ten
thousand men. 20 And Maqabi, ranging his
own army by bands, set these two over the
bands, and marched in haste against
Timotheos, who had with him a hundred
and twenty thousand footmen and two
thousand and five hundred horsemen.

21 But when Timotheos heard of the
coming of Yehudah, he sent away the

---

[a] 12:17 LXX records the word Χαρακα (*Ḥa'raka*) as a proper noun, that is, the name of a city. However, the Syr. records this as ܟܪܟܐ (*karka*) which means "walled or enclosed city" and thus may refer to a walled city, rather than a city named "Karka."

[b] 12:17 Tovieni – A group of Yehudim from the land of Tov. See also Maqabiym א [1 Maccabees] 5:13. In Hebrew and Aramaic, tov (תוב) means "good."

women and the children and also the
baggage at once into the fortress called
Karnion; for the place was hard to besiege
and difficult of access by reason of the
narrowness of the approaches on all sides.
22 But when the band of Yehudah, who led
the caravan, appeared in sight, and when
terror came upon the enemy and fear,
because the manifestation of Him who sees
all things came upon them, they fled away,
carried this way and that, so that they were
often hurt by their own men, and pierced
with the points of their swords. 23 And
Yehudah continued the pursuit even more,
putting the wicked wretches to the sword,
and he destroyed as many as thirty
thousand men. 24 But Timotheos himself,
falling in with the company of Dositheus
and Sosipater, asked them with much crafty
words to let him go with his life, because
he had in his power the parents of many of
them and the brethren of some:
"otherwise," said he, "little regard will be
shown to these." 25 So when he had with
many words confirmed the agreement to
restore them without hurt, they let him go
that they might save their brethren.
26 And Yehudah, marching against Karnion
and the temple of Ataratheh[a], killed twenty-
five thousand [bodies][b]. 27 And after he had
put these to flight and destroyed them, he
marched against Ephron also, a strong city,
where multitudes of people of all nations
were; and determined young men placed on
the walls made a vigorous defense; and
there were great stores of engines and darts
there. 28 But calling upon the Sovereign
who with might breaks in pieces the
strength of the enemy, they got the city into
their hands, and killed as many as twenty-
five thousand of those who were within.
29 And setting out from there they marched
in haste against Beth-Shan, which is six
hundred furlongs from Yerushalayim.
30 But when the Yehudim that were settled
there testified of the good-will that those of
Beth-Shan had shown them, and of their
kindly bearing toward them in the times of
their misfortune, 31 they gave thanks, and
further exhorted them to remain well-
affected toward the race for the future; and
they went up to Yerushalayim, the Feast of
Weeks[c] being close at hand.

32 But after the Feast called Pentecost[d] they
marched in haste against Gorgias the

---

[a] 12:26 Ataratheh – chief goddess of northern Aram, she was the ba'alat ("mistress") of the Aramean people. She was primarily seen as a goddess of fertility. Ataratheh is usually identified with Ashtoreth, Astarte, Ishtar, Eostre, Easter, and others of similar name. According to one legend, Ataratheh was the mother of Semiramis, the wife-mother of Tammuz.

[b] 12:26 LXX reads the plural of σωμα (*so'ma*) meaning "body" here. Syr. omits.

[c] 12:31 LXX reads της των εβδομαδων εορτης (*tes tow'n eb'dom'adown eor'tes*) meaning "the feast of weeks" here. The Feast of Weeks is called שבועות (*Shavuot*) in Hebrew, and Πεντηκοντε (*Pentekonte / Pentecost*) in Greek. However, here it is given a generic name as "feast of weeks." Although this is what the name means, it is not what the individual day is called. The Syr., however, states that this day was ܥܕܥܐܕܐ ܕܦܛܝܪܐ (*ad'eda d'patiyra*) meaning "Feast of Unleavened *Bread*." This is a much more specific name, and is written the same way in the Syriac version of both the Tanakh as well as the Gospels (see Syriac version of Vayyiqra [Leviticus] 23:6 & Loukas [Luke] 22:1). The major difference here, however, is that the Feast of Weeks is in the third Hebrew month, while the Feast of Unleavened Bread is in the first Hebrew month.

[d] 12:32 While verse 31 in Greek gives a general description for the day (that is, 'Feast of Weeks'), here it uses the word Πεντηκοστην

governor of Edom. **33** And he came out
with three thousand footmen and four
hundred horsemen. **34** And when they had
set themselves in array, it came to pass that
a few of the Yehudim fell. **35** And a certain
Dositheus, one of Bakenor's company, who
was on horseback and a strong man,
pressed hard on Gorgias, and taking hold of
his cloak drew him along by force; and
while he thought to take the accursed man
alive, one of the Thrakian horsemen bore
down upon him and disabled his shoulder,
and so Gorgias escaped to Marisa. **36** And
when those who were with Esdris had been
fighting long and were wearied out,
Yehudah called upon יהוה to show
Himself, fighting on their side and leading
the caravan of the battle. **37** And then in the
language of his fathers he raised the battle-
cry joined with hymns, and rushing
unawares upon the troops of Gorgias put
them to flight.

38 And Yehudah, gathering his army, came
to the city of Adullam; and as the seventh
day was coming on, they purified
themselves according to the custom, and
kept the Sabbath there. **39** And on the
following day, at which time it had become
necessary, Yehudah and his company came
to take up the bodies of those who had
fallen, and in company with their kinsmen
to bring them back to the graves of their
fathers. **40** But under the garments of each
one of the dead they found set-apart tokens
of the idols of Yavneel, which the Torah
forbids the Yehudim to have anything to do
with; and it became clear to all that it was
for this cause that they had fallen. **41** All
therefore, blessing the works of Elohim, the
righteous Judge, who makes manifest the
things that are hidden, **42** made petitions,
asking that the sin committed might be
wholly blotted out. And the noble Yehudah
exhorted the multitude to keep themselves
from sin, even as they had seen before their
eyes what things had come to pass because
of the sin of those who had fallen. **43** And
when he had made a collection man by man
to the sum of two thousand drachmas of
silver, he sent to Yerushalayim to offer a
slaughtering for sin, doing righteously and
honorably, in that he took thought for a
resurrection. **44** For if he were not expecting
that those who had fallen would rise again,
it were superfluous and foolish to pray for
the dead. **45** (And if he did it looking to an
honorable memorial of gratitude laid up for
those who die in devoutness, set-apart and
devout was the thought.) Then he made the
atoning slaughtering for those who had
died, that they might be released from their
sin.[a]

13 **1** In the hundred forty-ninth year news
was brought to Yehudah and his company
that Antioḥos Eupator was coming with

(*Pente'kosten*) which is undoubtedly Shavuot [Penetcost]. Syr. reads ܦܢܛܝܩܘܣܛܐ (*Pentiy'qosta*) or "Pentecost" also.

[a] 12:38-45 Early reference to praying for the dead. This was a common Pharisaic practice, and is believed to be connected with the Mourner's Kaddish, a hymn of praise to Elohim recited after the death of a loved one in Judaism. It should be noted that while typical Roman Catholic prayers for the dead are recited to help the "afterlife experiences" of the deceased, both the traditional Jewish prayers and the one mentioned here are stated to be for the deceased "on that day." With "that day" being the day of resurrection and judgment, as implied in verse 43.

great multitudes against Yehudah, 2 and with him Lysias his guardian and chancellor, each having a Greek force, a hundred and ten thousand footmen, and five thousand and three hundred horsemen, and twenty-two elephants, and three hundred chariots armed with scythes.

3 And Menelaus also joined himself with them, and with great disguise encouraged Antioḥos, not for the saving of his country, but because he thought that he would be set over the government. 4 But the King of kings stirred up the passion of Antioḥos against the wicked wretch; and when Lysias informed him that this man was the cause of all the evils, the king commanded to bring him to Berea, and to put him to death after the manner of that place. 5 Now there is in that place a tower of fifty cubits high, full of ashes[a], and it had all round it a gallery descending sheer on every side into the ashes. 6 Here him that is guilty of profanation, or that has attained a preeminence in any other evil deeds, they all push forward into destruction. 7 By such a fate it happened to the breaker of the Torah, Menelaus, to die, without obtaining so much as a grave in the earth, and rightfully so. 8 For just as he had perpetrated many sins against the altar, whose fire and whose ashes were set-apart, in ashes did he receive his death.

9 Now the king, infuriated in spirit, was coming with the intention of inflicting on the Yehudim sufferings that were severe as the worst they had seen in the time of his father. 10 But when Yehudah heard of these things, he gave charge to the multitude to call upon יהוה day and night, seeking Him, if ever at any other time, so now to aid those who were at the point to be deprived of the Torah and their country and the set-apart Temple, 11 and not to allow the people that had been but now a little while revived, to fall into the hands of those profane heathens.

12 So when they had all done the same thing together, seeking the merciful Master with weeping and fastings and prostration for three days without ceasing, Yehudah exhorted them and commanded they should join him for service. 13 And having gone apart with the elders he resolved that, before the king's army should enter into Yehudah and make themselves masters of the city, they should go forth and try the matter in fight by the help of Elohim.
14 And committing the decision to the Master of the world, and exhorting those who were with him to contend nobly even to death for Torah, Temple, city, country, and commonwealth, he pitched his camp by Modin. 15 And given out to his men the watchword, 'victory belongs to Elohim,' with a chosen body of the bravest young men, he fell upon the camp by night and penetrated to the king's tent, and killed of the army as many as two thousand men, and brought down the chief elephant with him that was in the tower upon him.

16 And at last they filled the army with terror and alarm, and departed with good success. 17 And this had been accomplished when the day was but now dawning,

[a] 13:5 Ashes – Most likely this building was similar to the Persian fire towers, which are believed to be the early forms of Dahkma. These were towers where dead bodies were kept to be disposed of, usually by being eaten by various carrion birds. The remains were burned, and thus the tower was filled with ash.

because of the protection of יהוה that gave
Yehudah help.

18 But the king, having had a taste of the
great boldness of the Yehudim, made
attempts by scheme upon their positions,
19 and upon a strong fortress of the
Yehudim at Beth-Tsur; he advanced, was
turned back, failed, was defeated, 20 And
Yehudah conveyed such things as were
necessary to those who were within. 21 But
Rowdoqos, from the Yehudite ranks, made
known to the enemy the secrets[a] of his
countrymen. He was sought out, and taken,
and shut up in prison. 22 The king treated
with them in Beth-Tsur the second time,
gave his hand, took theirs, departed,
attacked the forces of Yehudah, was put to
flight. 23 He heard that Philippos, who had
been left as chancellor in Antioḥ, had
become reckless, *and* was confounded, *and*
made to the Yehudim an overture of peace,
submitting himself and swearing to
acknowledge all their rights. *And he* came
to terms with them and offered
slaughtering, honored the set-apart place,
24 showed kindness, and graciously
received Maqabi. *He* left Hegemonides
governor from Akko even to the
Gerrenians[b], 25 *and he* came to Akko. The
men of Akko were displeased at the treaty,
for they had exceedingly great indignation
against the Yehudim: they desired to annul
the articles of the agreement. 26 Lysias
came forward to speak, *and* made the best
defense that was possible; *he* persuaded,
pacified, made them well affected, *and*
departed to Antioḥ. This was the issue of
the coming and going of the king.

14 1 Now after a span of three years, news
was brought to Yehudah and his company
that Demetrios the son of Seleukus, having
sailed into the haven of Tripolis with a
mighty army and a fleet, 2 had gained
possession of the country, having made
away with Antioḥos and Lysias his
guardian.

3 But one Elyaqum (who had formerly been
high priest, and had willfully profaned
himself in the times when there was no
mingling with the nations, considering that
there was no deliverance for him in any
way, nor any more access to the set-apart
altar) 4 came to king Demetrios in about the
hundred and fifty-first year, presenting to
him a chaplet of gold and a palm, and
beside these some of the festal olive boughs
of the Temple. And for that day he held his
peace; 5 but having gotten opportunity to
further his own madness, being called by
Demetrios into a meeting of his council,
and asked how the Yehudim stood affected
and what they purposed, he answered thus:

6 "Those of the Yehudim that he called
Ḥasdim[c], whose leader is Yehudah Maqabi,
keep up war, and are rebellious, not
allowing the kingdom to find tranquility.
7 Wherefore, having laid aside my ancestral
glory, I mean the high priesthood, I have
come here; 8 first for the sincere care I have
for the things that concern the king, and

[a] 13:21 Most likely these "secrets" were about the lack of provisions within the city. Compare Maqabiym א [1 Maccabees] 6:49.

[b] 13:24 Gerrenians – Most likely inhabitants of Gerar, though the Syr. records this as ܓܙܪ (*Gezer*).

[c] 14:6 See footnote at Maqabiym א [1 Maccabees] 2:42.

secondly because I have regard also to my
own fellow-citizens: for, through the
unadvised dealing of those of whom I
spoke before, our whole race is in great
misfortune. 9 But do you, O king, having
informed yourself of these things
individually, take thought both for our
country and for our race, which is
surrounded by foes, according to the
gracious kindness with which you receive
all. 10 For as long as Yehudah remains
alive, it is impossible that the state should
find peace."

11 And when he had spoken such words as
these, at once the rest of the king's beloved,
having ill-will against Yehudah, inflamed
Demetrios yet more. 12 And immediately
appointing Niqanor, who had been master
of the elephants, and making him governor
of Yehudah, he sent him forth, 13 giving
him written instructions to make away with
Yehudah himself and to scatter those who
were with him, and to set up Elyaqum as
high priest of the great Temple. 14 And
those in Yehudah that had before driven
Yehudah into exile thronged to Niqanor in
flocks, supposing that the misfortunes and
calamities of the Yehudim would be
successes to themselves.

15 But when the Yehudim heard of
Niqanor's coming and the assault of the
heathen, they sprinkled earth upon their
heads and made solemn petition to Him
who had established His own people
forevermore, and who always, making
manifest His presence, upholds those who
are His own portion. 16 And when the
leader had given his commands, he
immediately set out from there, and joined
battle with them at a village called Lessau.
17 But Shimon, the brother of Yehudah, had
encountered Niqanor, yet not until recently,
having been set back because of the sudden
dismay caused by his adversaries.

18 Nevertheless Niqanor, hearing of the
manliness of those who were with
Yehudah, and their courage in fighting for
their country, shrank from bringing the
matter to the decision of the sword. 19 So
he sent Posidonios and Theodotos and
Mattithyah to give and receive pledges of
friendship. 20 So when these proposals had
been long considered, and the leader had
made the troops acquainted with them, and
it appeared that they were all of like mind,
they consented to the covenants. 21 And
they appointed a day on which to meet
together by themselves. And a stretcher
was brought forward from each army; they
set chairs of state; 22 Yehudah stationed
armed men ready in convenient places, in
the event that there should suddenly be
treachery on the part of the enemy. They
held such conference as was chance.
23 Niqanor tarried in Yerushalayim, and did
nothing to cause disturbance, but dismissed
the flocks of people that had gathered
together. 24 And he kept Yehudah always in
his presence; he had gained a hearty
affection for the man; 25 he urged him to
marry and beget children; he married,
settled quietly, took part in common life.

26 But Elyaqum, perceiving the good-will
that was between them, and having gained
possession of the covenants that had been
cut, came to Demetrios and told him that
Niqanor had contempt for the state, for he
had appointed that conspirator against his
kingdom, Yehudah, to be his successor.
27 And the king, falling into a rage, and
being exasperated by the slanders of that
most wicked man, wrote to Niqanor,

signifying that he was displeased at the
covenants, and commanding him to send
Maqabi prisoner to Antioḥ immediately.
28 And when this message came to
Niqanor, he was confounded, and was
severely troubled at the thought of
annulling the articles that had been agreed
upon, the man having done no wrong.
29 But because there was no dealing against
the king, he watched his time to execute
this purpose by scheme. **30** But Maqabi,
noticing that Niqanor was harsher in his
dealings with him, and acting with
unaccustomed rudeness when they met,
concluded that this harshness was not a
good sign. So he gathered together not a
few of his men, and went into hiding from
Niqanor. **31** But the other, when he became
aware that he had been bravely defeated by
the scheme of Yehudah, came to the great
and set-apart Temple, while the priests
were offering the usual slaughterings, and
commanded them to deliver up the man.
32 And when they declared with oaths that
they had no knowledge where the man was
whom he sought, **33** he stretched forth his
right hand toward the set-apart place, and
swore this oath: "If you will not deliver up
to me Yehudah as a prisoner, I will level
this Temple of Elohim to the ground, and
will break down the altar, and I will erect
here a temple to Bacchus for all to see."

34 And having said this, he departed. But
the priests, stretching forth their hands
toward heaven, called upon Him that fights
for our nation forever, in these words:
35 "You, O יהוה, of all things, who in
Yourself have need of nothing, were well
pleased that a dwelling place of Your
habitation should be set among us; **36** so
now, O set-apart יהוה of all, keep this
house undefiled forever that has been
recently cleansed."

37 Now information was given to Niqanor
against one Razis[a], an elder of
Yerushalayim, as being a lover of his
countrymen and a man of very good report,
and one called 'Father of the Yehudim' for
his good-will toward them. **38** For in the
former times when there was no mingling
with the nations he had been accused of
cleaving to the religion of the Yehudim,
and had jeopardized body and life with all
earnestness for the religion of the Yehudim.
39 And Niqanor, wishing to make evident
the ill-will that he bore to the Yehudim,
sent more than five hundred soldiers to take
him; **40** for he thought by taking him to
inflict a calamity upon them. **41** But when
the troops were on the point of taking the
tower, and were forcing the door of the
court, and called to bring fire and burn the
doors, he – being surrounded on every side
– fell upon his sword, **42** choosing rather to
die nobly than to fall into the hands of the
wicked wretches, and suffer outrage
unworthy of his own nobleness. **43** But he
missed his stroke through the excitement of
the struggle, and the crowds rushed within
the door, *and* he ran bravely up to the wall
and cast himself down bravely among the
crowds. **44** But as they quickly gave back, a
space was made, and he fell on the middle
of his side.

---

[a] 14:37 LXX calls this man Ραζις (*Razis*). This word is possibly a Hellenized (and masculine) form of the female name *Razia*, which is an Arabic word meaning "contended." The Syr. calls him ܪܓܫ (*Ragash*). *Ragash* means "rage" or "to tremble with anger." It is also used to describe thunder.

45 And having yet breath within him, and
being inflamed with passion, he rose up,
and though his blood gushed out in streams
and his wounds were grievous, he ran
through the crowds, and standing upon a
steep rock, 46 when as his blood was now
nearly all spent, he drew forth his bowels
through the wound, and taking them in both
his hands he shook them at the crowds; and
calling upon Him who is Ruler of the life
and the spirit to restore these to him again,
and then he died.

15 1 But Niqanor, hearing that Yehudah
and his company were in the region of
Shomeron, resolved to set upon them on
the day of rest[a], *since he felt* he would be
safe. 2 And when the Yehudim that were
forced to follow him said, "O do not
destroy so savagely and barbarously, but
give due glory to the day which He who
sees all things has honored and set apart
above other days;" 3 then the thrice-
accursed wretch asked if there were a
Sovereign in heaven that had commanded
to keep the Sabbath day. 4 And when they
declared, "There is יהוה, Himself the living
Sovereign in heaven, who commanded us
to guard the Sabbath day." 5 Then said the
other, "I also am a sovereign upon the
earth, who now commands to take up arms
and execute the king's business."
Nevertheless he did prevail to execute his
cruel purpose.

6 And Niqanor, in exceeding pride and
haughtiness, had determined to set up a
monument of complete victory[b] over
Yehudah and all those who were with him.
7 But Maqabi still trusted unceasingly, with
all hope that he would obtain help from
Elohim. 8 And he exhorted his company not
to be fearful at the coming of the heathen,
but, keeping in mind the help which of old
they had often received from heaven, so
now also to look for the victory which
would come to them from the Almighty.
9 And comforting them out of the Torah
and the prophets, and likewise putting them
in mind of the conflicts that they had
maintained, he made them more eager for
the battle.

10 And when he had roused their minds, he
gave them his commands, at the same time
pointing out the treachery of the heathen
and their breach of their oaths. 11 And
arming each one of them, not so much with
the sure defense of shields and spears as
with the encouragement that lies in good
words, and moreover relating to them a
dream worthy to be believed, he made them
all exceedingly glad.

12 And the vision of that dream was this:
He saw Ḥoniyo, the one who had been high
priest, a noble and good man, revered in
bearing, yet gentle in manner and well-
spoken, and exercised from a child in all
points of virtue, with outstretched hands
invoking blessings on the whole body of
the Yehudim. 13 Then he saw a man appear,
of venerable age and exceeding glory, and
wonderful and most majestic was the
dignity around him, 14 And Ḥoniyo
answered and said, "This is the lover of the
brethren, he who prays much for the people
and the set-apart city, Yirmeyahu the

[a] 15:1 LXX reads "the day of rest" as it is here. Syr., however, reads "the day of the Sabbath."

[b] 15:6 Monument of complete victory – A heap of stones covered with the weapons and armor of the fallen enemy.

prophet of Elohim. 15 And Yirmeyahu, stretching forth his right hand, delivered to Yehudah a sword of gold, and in giving it to him, he addressed him this way: 16 'Take the set-apart sword, a gift from Elohim, with which you shall strike down the adversaries.'"

17 And being encouraged by the words of Yehudah, which were of a lofty strain, and able to incite to virtue and to stir the beings of the young to manly courage, they determined not to carry on a campaign, but nobly to bear down upon the enemy, and fighting hand to hand with all courage bring the matter to an issue, because the city and the set-apart place and the Temple were in danger. 18 For their fear for wives and children, and furthermore for brethren and kinsfolk, was the lesser of their concern; but greatest and first was their fear for the set apart sanctuary. 19 And they also that were shut up in the city were in no light distress, being troubled because of the encounter in the open ground. 20 And when all were now waiting for the decision of the issue, and the enemy had already joined battle, and the army had been set in array, and the elephants brought back to a convenient post, and the horsemen drawn up on the flank, 21 Maqabi, (perceiving the presence of the troops, and the various arms with which they were equipped, and the savageness of the elephants) held up his hands to heaven and called upon יהוה who works wonders, recognizing that success comes not by arms, but that, according as יהוה shall judge, he gained the victory for those who are worthy.

22 And calling upon Elohim he said after this manner: "You, O Sovereign Master, did send Your messenger in the time of Ḥizqiyahu king of Yehudah, and he killed of the army of Sancheriv as many as a hundred and eighty-five thousand. 23 So now also, O Sovereign of the heavens, send a good messenger before us, to bring terror and trembling: 24 through the greatness of Your arm, let them be stricken with dismay, those that (with blasphemy) have come here against Your set-apart people." And as he ended with these words, 25 Niqanor and his company advanced with shofars and paeans; 26 but Yehudah and his company joined battle with the enemy with invocation and prayers. 27 And contending with their hands, and praying to Elohim with their hearts, they killed no less than thirty-five thousand men, being made exceedingly glad by the manifestation of Elohim.

28 And when the engagement was over, and they were returning again with joy, they recognized Niqanor lying dead in full armor, 29 and a shout and tumult arose, and then they blessed the Sovereign Master in the language of their fathers. 30 And he that in all things was in body and being the foremost champion of his fellow-citizens, he that kept through life the good-will of his youth toward his countrymen, commanded to cut off Niqanor's head, and his hand with the shoulder, and bring them to Yerushalayim. 31 And when he had arrived there, and had called his countrymen together and set the priests before the altar, he sent for those who were in the fortress; 32 and showing the head of the vile Niqanor, and the hand of that profane man, who had stretched out against the set-apart house of the Almighty in prideful statements, 33 and cutting out the tongue of the wicked Niqanor, he said that he would give it by pieces to the birds, and

hang up the rewards of his madness near
the set-apart place. 34 And they all, looking
up to heaven, blessed יהוה who had
manifested Himself, saying, "Blessed be He
that has preserved His own place
undefiled." 35 And he hanged Niqanor's
head and shoulder from the fortress, a sign,
evident to all and manifest, of the salvation
of Elohim. 36 And they all ordained with a
common decree in no way to let this day
pass undistinguished, but to mark with
honor the thirteenth day of the twelfth
month (it is called Adar in the Aramean
tongue), the day before the day of
Mordekai[a].

37 This, then, having been the issue of the
attempt of Niqanor, and the city having
from those times been held by the
Hebrews, I also will here make an end of
my book. 38 And if I have written well and
to the point in my story, this is what I
myself desired. But if meanly and
indifferently, this is all I could attain to.
39 For as it is distasteful to drink wine alone
and in like manner again to drink water
alone, while the mingling of wine with
water at once gives full pleasantness to the
flavor; so also the fashioning of the
language delights the ears of those who
read the story. And here shall be the end.

[*The* whole *of* Book Two of the Maqabiym].[b]

---

[a] 15:36 The day of Mordekhai – Known in Hebrew as פורים (*Purim*). See Hadassah [Esther] 3:7; 9:20-23. This takes place on the fourteenth and fifteenth days of the month Adar.

[b] This phrase is found at the end of the Syriac text, though not in the Greek.

תְּפִילַּת אֲזַרְיָה

T'fillat Azaryah [Prayer of Azarias]

1 1 They walked in the midst of the fire,
praising Elohim, and blessing יהוה. 2 Then
Azaryah stood, and prayed on this manner;
and opening his mouth in the midst of the
fire said,

3 "Blessed are You, O יהוה, Elohim of our
fathers, who is worthy to be praised; and
Your Name is glorified forevermore. 4 For
You are righteous in all the things that You
have done: yes, true are all Your works,
and Your ways are right, and all Your
judgments are true. 5 In all the things that
You have brought upon us, and upon the
set-apart city of our fathers, even
Yerushalayim, You have executed true
judgments. For according to truth and
justice You have brought all these things
upon us because of our sins. 6 For we have
sinned and committed lawlessness in
departing from You. 7 We have trespassed
in all things, and have not obeyed Your
commands, nor guarded them, neither done
as You have commanded us, that it might
go well with us. 8 So all that You have
brought upon us, and everything that You
have done to us, You have done in true
judgment. 9 And You delivered us into the
hands of lawless enemies, and most hateful
forsakers of Elohim, and to an unjust king,
and the most wicked in all the world.

10 "And now we cannot open our mouth.
Shame and reproach have fallen on Your
servants, and those who worship You.
11 Do not deliver us up completely, for
Your Name's sake, neither nullify Your
covenant. 12 And do not cause Your
kindness to depart from us, for the sake of
Avraham whom You love, and for the sake
of Yitschaq Your servant, and Yisra'el
Your set-apart one, 13 to whom You
promised that You would multiply their
seed as the stars of heaven, and as the sand
that is upon the sea shore. 14 For we, O
יהוה, have become smaller than any other
nation, and have been kept under all the
world today because of our sins. 15 Neither
is there any longer a prince, or prophet, or
leader, or burnt offering, or slaughtering, or
drink offering, or incense, or place to offer
before You, and to find kindness.

16 "Nevertheless in a contrite heart and a
humble spirit let us be accepted. 17 As in
the burnt offerings of rams and bulls, and
as in ten thousands of fat lambs; so let our
offering be before Your eyes today, and
grant that we may wholly go after You, for
they shall not be ashamed that put their
trust in You. 18 And now we follow You
with all our heart, we fear You, and seek
Your face. 19 Do not put us to shame, but
deal with us after Your kindness, and
according to the multitude of Your
compassion. 20 Deliver us also according to
Your marvelous works, and give glory to
Your Name, O יהוה: and let all those who
harm Your servants be confounded. 21 Let
them be ashamed of all their power and
might, and let their strength be broken.
22 Let them know that You are יהוה, the
only Elohim, and glorious over the whole
world."

23 And the king's servants that put them in,
did not stop making the furnace hot with
naphtha, pitch, tow, and kindling, 24 so that
the flame streamed forth above the furnace

forty-nine cubits. 25 And it spread, and burned those Kaldeans whom it found about the furnace. 26 But the messenger of יהוה came down into the furnace together with Azaryah and his fellows, and he struck the flame of the fire out of the furnace; 27 and made the midst of the furnace as if it had been a moist whistling wind, so that the fire did not touch them at all, neither did it harm them or troubled them.

28 Then the three, as out of one mouth, praised, and glorified, and blessed Elohim in the furnace, saying, 29 "Blessed are You, O יהוה, Elohim of our fathers: be praised and exalted above all forever. 30 And blessed is Your glorious and Set-Apart Name: be praised and exalted above all forever. 31 Blessed are You in the Temple of Your Set-Apart glory: be praised and glorified above all forever. 32 Blessed are You that behold the depths, and sit upon the kerubim: be praised and exalted above all forever. 33 Blessed are You on the throne of Your kingdom: be praised and extolled above all forever. 34 Blessed are You in the expanse of heaven: be praised and glorified forever.

35 O all you works of יהוה, bless יהוה. Praise and exalt Him above all forever. 36 O you heavens, bless יהוה. Praise and exalt Him above all forever. 37 O you messengers of יהוה, bless יהוה. Praise and exalt Him above all forever. 38 O all you waters that are above the heaven, bless יהוה. Praise and exalt Him above all forever. 39 O all you powers of יהוה, bless יהוה. Praise and exalt Him above all forever. 40 O you sun and moon, bless יהוה. Praise and exalt Him above all forever. 41 O you stars of heaven, bless יהוה. Praise and exalt Him above all forever. 42 O every shower and dew, bless you יהוה. Praise and exalt Him above all forever. 43 O all you winds, bless יהוה. Praise and exalt Him above all forever. 44 O you fire and heat, bless יהוה. Praise and exalt Him above all forever. 45 [O you winter and summer, bless יהוה. Praise and exalt Him above all forever. 46 [O you dews and storms of snow, bless יהוה. Praise and exalt Him above all forever.][a] 47 O you nights and days, bless יהוה. Praise and exalt him above all forever. 48 O you light and darkness, bless יהוה. Praise and exalt Him above all forever. 49 O you cold and heat, bless יהוה. Praise and exalt Him above all forever. 50 O you frost and snow, bless יהוה. Praise and exalt Him above all forever. 51 O you lightnings and clouds, bless יהוה. Praise and exalt Him above all forever. 52 O let the earth bless יהוה: let it praise and exalt him above all forever. 53 O you mountains and hills, bless יהוה. Praise and exalt Him above all forever. 54 O all you things that grow on the earth, bless יהוה. Praise and exalt Him above all forever. 55 O sea and rivers, bless יהוה. Praise and exalt Him above all forever. 56 O you springs, bless יהוה. Praise and exalt Him above all forever.

---

[a] 1:45-46 Bracketed section indicates reading present in some Greek and Latin texts, but absent from others.

57 O you whales, and all that move in the
waters, bless יהוה. Praise and exalt Him
above all forever. 58 O all you fowls of the
air, bless יהוה. Praise and exalt Him above
all forever. 59 O all you beasts and cattle,
bless יהוה. Praise and exalt Him above all
forever. 60 O you children of men, bless
יהוה. Praise and exalt Him above all
forever. 61 O let Yisra'el bless יהוה. Praise
and exalt Him above all forever. 62 O you
priests of יהוה, bless יהוה. Praise and exalt
Him above all forever. 63 O you servants of
יהוה, bless יהוה. Praise and exalt Him
above all forever. 64 O you spirits and
beings of the righteous, bless יהוה. Praise
and exalt Him above all forever. 65 O you
that are set-apart and humble of heart, bless
יהוה. Praise and exalt Him above all
forever. 66 O Ḥananyah, Azaryah, and
Misha'el, bless יהוה. Praise and exalt Him
above all forever; for He has rescued us
from Sheol, and saved us from the hand of
death. He has delivered us out of the midst
of the furnace and burning flame, even out
of the midst of the fire has He delivered us.
67 O give thanks to יהוה, for He is good,
and His kindness endures forever. 68 O all
you that worship יהוה, bless the Elohim of
elohim, praise Him, and give Him thanks,
for His kindness endures forever."

שׁוֹשַׁנָּה

Shoshanah [Susanna]

1 1 A man lived in Bavel, and his name
was Yehoyaqim: 2 and he took a wife,
whose name was Shoshannah, the daughter
of Ḥilqiyahu, a very beautiful woman, and
one that feared יהוה. 3 Her parents were
also righteous, and taught their daughter
according to the Torah of Mosheh.

4 Now Yohoyaqim was a great rich man,
and had a beautiful garden joining to his
house, and the Yehudim turned to him for
help, because he was more honorable than
all others. 5 The same year, two of the
elders of the people were appointed to be
judges, such ones as יהוה spoke of,
"Wickedness came from Bavel, from
ancient judges, who seemed to govern the
people."

6 These spent much time at Yehoyaqim's
house, and all those who had any lawsuits
came to them. 7 Now when the people
departed away at noon, Shoshannah went
into her husband's garden to walk. 8 And
the two elders saw her going in every day
and walking, so that their lust was inflamed
toward her. 9 And they perverted their own
mind and turned away their eyes, so that
they would not look to heaven, nor
remember just judgments. 10 And although
they both were wounded with her love, still
each dared not show the other his grief.
11 For they were ashamed to declare their
lust, that they desired to have to do with
her. 12 Yet they watched diligently from
day to day to see her.

13 And the one said to the other, "Let us go
home now, for it is dinner time."

14 So when they had gone out, they each
parted from the other, and turning back
again they came to the same place; and
after they had asked each another the
reason, they acknowledged their lust, then
they both appointed themselves a time
when they might find her alone. 15 And it
happened, as they watched for a fitting
time, that she went in as before, just her
and her two handmaids, and she intended to
bathe herself in the garden, for it was hot.
16 And there was none there except the two
elders, who had hidden themselves and
watched her.

17 Then she said to her handmaids, "Bring
me oil and washcloths and shut the garden
doors, so that I may wash myself."

18 And they did as she asked them, and shut
the garden doors, and went out through
private doors to fetch the things that she
had commanded them; but they did not see
the elders, because they were hidden.
19 Now when the handmaids were gone, the
two elders rose up and ran to her, saying,

20 "Behold, the garden doors are shut, so
that no man can see us, and we are in love
with you; therefore consent to us, and lie
with us. 21 If you will not, we will bear
witness against you that a young man was
with you, and therefore you sent your
handmaids away from you."

22Then Shoshannah sighed and said, "I am
hemmed in on every side; for if I do this
thing, it is death to me; and if I do not do it,
I cannot escape your hands. 23 It is better
for me to fall into your hands and not do it,
than to sin in the eyes of יהוה."

24 With that, Shoshannah cried with a loud
voice, and the two elders cried out against
her. 25 Then the one ran and opened the
garden door. 26 So when the servants of the
house heard the cry in the garden, they
rushed in through the private door to see
what had happened to her. 27 But when the
elders declared their story, the servants
were greatly ashamed, for there was never
such a report made of Shoshannah. 28 And
it happened the next day, when the people
were assembled before her husband
Yehoyaqim, that the two elders also came,
full of mischievous thoughts against
Shoshannah to put her to death.

29 And they said before the people, "Send
for Shoshannah, the daughter of Ḥilqiyahu,
Yehoyaqim's wife." And so they sent for
her. 30 So she came with her father and
mother, her children, and all her family.
31 Now, Shoshannah was a very delicate
woman and beautiful to behold. 32 And
these wicked men commanded her to
uncover her face, (for she was covered,)
that they might be filled with her beauty.
33 Therefore, her friends and all that saw
her wept. 34 Then the two elders stood up
in the midst of the people and laid their
hands upon her head. 35 And she looked up
toward heaven weeping, for her heart
trusted in יהוה.

36 And the elders said, "As we walked in
the garden alone, this woman came in with
two handmaids and shut the garden doors
and sent the handmaids away. 37 Then a
young man, who was hidden there, came to
her and lay with her. 38 Then, standing in a
corner of the garden, we saw this
wickedness and ran towards them. 39 And
when we saw them together, we could not
lay hold on the man, for he was stronger
than us, and he opened the door and leaped
out. 40 But having taken this woman, we
asked her who the young man was, but she
would not tell us. These are the things to
which we witness."

41 Then the assembly believed them
because they were the elders and judges of
the people; so they condemned her to
death.

42Then Shoshannah cried out with a loud
voice and said, "O everlasting Elohim, who
knows the secrets and knows all things
before they occur. 43 You know that they
have borne false witness against me, and
behold I must die, though I never did such
things as these men have maliciously
invented against me."

44 And יהוה heard her voice. 45 Therefore,
when she was led to be put to death, יהוה
raised up the set-apart spirit of a youth
whose name was Dani'el, 46 who cried with
a loud voice, "I am free of the blood of this
woman!"

47 Then all the people turned toward him
and said, "What do these words you have
spoken mean?"

48 So, standing in the midst of them, he
said, "Are you such fools, you sons of
Yisra'el, that you have condemned a
daughter of Yisra'el without examination or
knowledge of the truth? 49 Return again to
the place of judgment, for they have borne
false witness against her."

50 Therefore all the people returned again
in haste, and the elders said to him, "Come,
sit down among us and teach us, since
Elohim has given you the honor of an
elder."

51 Then Dani'el said to them, "Separate these two, one from another, and I will examine them."

52 So when they were put apart one from another, he called one of them and said to him, "O you who has grown old in wickedness, now your sins which you have committed before this time have come to
light. 53 For you have pronounced false judgment and have condemned the innocent and have let the guilty go free; even though יהוה says, 'The innocent and
righteous you shall not kill.' 54 Now then, if you saw her, tell me, under what *type of* tree did you see them consorting together?" He answered, "Under a mastic tree."

55 And Dani'el said, "Very well; you have lied against your own head; for even now the messenger of Elohim has received the sentence of Elohim to cut you in two."[a]

56 So he put him aside and commanded them to bring the other, and he said to him, "O you, offspring of Kana'an and not of Yehudah, beauty has deceived you and lust
has perverted your heart. 57 Thus have you dealt with the daughters of Yisra'el, and they consorted with you out of fear; but this daughter of Yehudah would not tolerate
your wickedness. 58 Now therefore, tell me: under what *type of* tree did you find them consorting together?" He answered, "Under a holm tree."

59 Then Dani'el said to him, "Well, you also have lied against your own head; for the messenger of Elohim waits with the sword to saw you in two, that he may destroy you."[b]

60 With that all the assembly cried out with a loud voice and praised Elohim, who saves
those who trust in Him. 61 And they arose against the two elders, for Dani'el had convicted them of false witness by their
own mouth. 62 And, according to the Torah of Mosheh, they did to them in the same way as they maliciously intended to do to their neighbor; and they put them to death. Thus innocent blood was saved that same day.

63 Therefore Ḥilqiyahu and his wife praised Elohim for their daughter Shoshannah, with Yehoyaqim her husband and all their family, because there was no dishonesty found in her.

64 And from that day forth, Dani'el had a great reputation in the eyes of the people.

---

[a] 1:55 This is a pun in Greek. The Greek term for "mastic tree" is σχινον (*sḥinon*), while the word for "cut" is σχισει (*sḥisei*).

[b] 1:59 This is a pun in Greek. The Greek term for "holm tree" is πρινον (*prinon*), while the word for "saw" is πρισαι (*prisai*).

ΒΕΛ ΚΑΙ ΤΟΝ ΔΡΑΚΟ

Bel kai ton Drako [Bel and the Dragon]

1 1 And king Astyages was gathered to his fathers, and Koresh of Paras received his kingdom. 2 And Dani'el conversed with the king and was honored above all his friends.

3 Now the Bavelians had an idol, called Bel, and every day twelve great measures of fine flour and forty sheep and six vessels of wine were spent upon it. 4 And the king worshipped it and went daily to adore it; but Dani'el worshipped his own El. And the king said to him, "Why do you not worship Bel?"

5 He answered and said, "Because I may not worship idols made with hands, but only the living El, who has created the heavens and the earth and [has sovereignty][a] over all flesh, [to whom *I* bow down][b]."

6 Then the king said to him, "Do you not think that Bel is a living el? Do you not see how much he eats and drinks every day?"

7 Then Dani'el smiled and said, "O king, do not be deceived; for this is only clay on the inside and copper on the outside; it has never eaten or drank anything."

8 So the king was angry and called for his priests, and said to them, "If you do not tell me who it is that consume these offerings, you shall die! 9 But, if you can prove to me that Bel consumes them, then Dani'el shall die, for he has spoken blasphemy against Bel." And Dani'el said to the king, "Let it be according to your word."

10 Now there were seventy priests of Bel, besides their wives and children. And the king went with Dani'el into the temple of Bel.

11 So Bel's priests said, "Behold, we go out; but you, O king, set out the meat and prepare the wine, and shut the door fast and seal it with your own signet. 12 And tomorrow when you come in, if you do not find that Bel has eaten all, we will suffer death, or else Dani'el, who speaks falsely against us."

13 And they had little concern about it because under the table they had made a private entrance, whereby they entered in continually and consumed those things. 14So when they had gone, the king set out the meats before Bel. Now Dani'el had commanded his servants to bring ashes, and those they strewed throughout the entire temple in the presence of the king alone; then they went out and shut the door, and sealed it with the king's signet, and so departed. 15 Now in the night the priests with their wives and children came, as they were accustomed to do, and they ate and drank it all. 16 In the early morning the king arose, and Dani'el with him.

17 And the king said, "Dani'el, are the seals whole?" And he said, "Yes, O king, they are whole." 18 And as soon as he had opened the door, the king looked upon the table and cried with a loud voice, "How great you are, O Bel, and there is no deceit with you at all!" 19 Then Dani'el laughed, and held the king back so that he would not

[a] 1:5 Bracketed section indicates reading present in Greek text. Latin text reads, "has power."

[b] 1:5 Bracketed section indicates reading present in Syriac text but absent from Greek and Latin texts.

go in, and he said, "Behold now the
pavement, and mark well whose footsteps
these are."

20 And the king said, "I see the footsteps of
men, women, and children." And then the
king was angry, 21 and he took the priests
with their wives and children, who showed
him the private doors where they came in
and consumed such things as were on the
table. 22 Therefore the king king them, and
delivered Bel into Dani'el's power, who
destroyed him and his temple.

23 And in that same place there was a great
dragon, which they of Bavel worshipped.
24 And the king said to Dani'el, "Will you
also say that this is mere copper? Behold,
he lives, he eats, and he drinks; you cannot
say that he is no living el; therefore,
worship him." 25 Then Dani'el said to the
king, "I will worship יהוה my Elohim; for
He is the living El. 26 But give me
permission, O king, and I shall kill this
dragon without sword or staff." The king
said, "I give you permission."

27 Then Dani'el took pitch and fat and hair,
and boiled them together, and made them
into cakes; he placed them in the dragon's
mouth, and the dragon burst open; and
Dani'el said, "Behold, these are the elohim
you worship." 28 When those of Bavel
heard this, they took great offense and
conspired against the king, saying, "The
king has become a Yehudite and he has
destroyed Bel; he has killed the dragon and
put the priests to death." 29 So they came to
the king and said, "Deliver Dani'el to us or
else we will destroy you and your house."

30 Now when the king saw that they
pressed him severely, being constrained, he
delivered Dani'el to them. 31 They cast him
into the lions' den, where he was for six
days. 32 And in the den there were seven
lions, and they had given them two
carcasses and two sheep every day; *but* this
time they had not been given to them, so
that they might devour Dani'el.

33 Now there was among the Yehudim a
prophet, called Ḥavaqquq, who had made
pottage and had broken bread in a bowl,
and was going into the field, to bring it to
the reapers. 34 But the messenger of יהוה
said to Ḥavaqquq, "Go, carry the meal that
you have into Bavel to Dani'el, who is in
the lions' den." 35 And Ḥavaqquq said,
"Master, I never saw Bavel; neither do I
know where the den is." 36 Then the
messenger of יהוה took him by the crown
of his head, and carried him by his hair, and
through the power of his spirit set him in
Bavel over the den.

37 And Ḥavaqquq cried, saying, "O Dani'el,
Dani'el, take the meal which Elohim has
sent you." 38And Dani'el said, "You have
remembered me, O Elohim; and You have
not forsaken those who seek You and love
You."

39 So Dani'el arose and ate; and the
messenger of יהוה set Ḥavaqquq in his
own place again immediately. 40 On the
seventh day the king went to bewail
Dani'el; and when he came to the den, he
looked in, and behold, Dani'el was sitting.
41 Then the king cried with a loud voice,
saying, "Great are You, יהוה, Elohim of
Dani'el: there is no other beside You!"

42 And he drew him out, and cast those
who were the cause of his destruction into
the den; and they were devoured in a
moment before his face.

הֲדַסָּה

Hadassah [Esther]

*[Editor's note: The entire book of
Hadassah [Esther] is included here for the
benefit of the reader. The translation is
taken from the Shem Qadosh Version of
Scripture. Bracketed sections in the text
will mark where the Greek contains
additions that are not present in Hebrew.
These sections contain their own verse
numbering system to separate them from
the rest of the text.]*

1 [1 In the second year of the reign of
Aḥashverosh the great king, on the first day
of Nisan, Mordekhai the son of Yair, the
son of Shimi, the son of Qish, of the tribe
of Benyamin, a Yehudite dwelling in the
city Shoshan, a great man, serving in the
king's palace, saw a vision. 2 Now he was
of the captivity which Nevukhadnetstsar
king of Bavel had carried captive from
Yerushalayim, with Yokonyah the king of
Yehudah. 3 This was his dream: Behold,
voices and a noise, thunders and
earthquakes, tumult upon the earth. 4 And,
behold, two great serpents came out, both
ready for conflict. A great voice came from
them. 5 Every nation was prepared for
battle by their voice, even to fight against
the nation of the just. 6 Behold, a day of
darkness and blackness, affliction and
anguish, affection and tumult upon the
earth. 7 And all the righteous nation was
troubled, fearing their own afflictions. They
prepared to die, and cried to Elohim.
8 Something like a great river from a little
spring with much water, came from their
cry. 9 Light and the sun arose, and the
lowly were exalted, and devoured the
honorable.

10 Mordekhai, who had seen this vision and
what Elohim desired to do, arose, and kept
it in his heart, and desired by all means to
interpret it, even until night.

11 Mordekhai rested quietly in the palace
with Bigtha and Tharrha the king's two
chamberlains, eunuchs who guarded the
palace. 12 He heard their conversation and
searched out their plans. He learned that
they were preparing to lay hands on king
Aḥashverosh, and he informed the king
concerning them. 13 The king examined the
two chamberlains, and they confessed, and
were led away and executed. 14 The king
wrote these things for a record.
15 Mordekhai also wrote concerning these
matters. 16 The king commanded
Mordekhai to serve in the palace, and gave
gifts for this service. 17 But Haman the son
of Hammedatha the Agagite was honored
in the eyes of the king, and he endeavored
to harm Mordekhai and his people, because
of the king's two chamberlains.][a]

1 Now in the days of Aḥashverosh (this is
Aḥashverosh who reigned from Hodu even
to Kush, over one hundred twenty-seven
provinces), 2 in those days, when the King
Aḥashverosh sat on the throne of his
kingdom, which was in Shushan the palace,
3 in the third year of his reign, he made a
banquet for all his princes and his servants;
the power of Paras and Media, the nobles
and princes of the provinces, being before

---

[a] 1:1-17 Bracketed section indicates reading present in Greek texts but absent from Hebrew. These represent what are called "Additions to Esther."

him. 4 He displayed the riches of his
glorious kingdom and the honor of his
excellent majesty many days, even one
hundred eighty days. 5 When these days
were fulfilled, the king made a seven day
banquet for all the people who were present
in Shushan the palace, both great and small,
in the court of the garden of the king's
palace. 6 There were hangings of white,
green, and blue material, fastened with
cords of fine linen and purple to silver rings
and marble pillars. The couches were of
gold and silver, on a pavement of red,
white, yellow, and black marble. 7 They
gave them drinks in golden vessels of
various kinds, including royal wine in
abundance, according to the bounty of the
king. 8 In accordance with the decree, the
drinking was not compulsory; for so the
king had instructed all the officials of his
house, that they should do according to
every man's pleasure.

9 Also Vashti the queen made a banquet for
the women in the royal house which
belonged to King Aḥashverosh.

10 On the seventh day, when the heart of
the king was merry with wine, he
commanded Mehuman, Biztha, Ḥarvonah,
Bigtha, and Avagtha, Zethar, and Karkas,
the seven eunuchs who served in the
presence of Aḥashverosh the king, 11 to
bring Vashti the queen before the king with
the royal crown, to show the people and the
princes her beauty; for she was beautiful.
12 But the queen Vashti refused to come at
the king's command by the eunuchs.
Therefore the king was very angry, and his
anger burned in him.

13 Then the king said to the wise men, who
knew the times (for it was the king's
custom to consult those who knew decree
and judgment; 14 and the next to him were
Karshena, Shethar, Admatha, Tarshish,
Meres, Marsena, and Memukan, the seven
princes of Paras and Media, who saw the
king's face, and sat first in the kingdom),
15 "What shall we do to the queen Vashti
according to decree, because she has not
done the bidding of the King Aḥashverosh
by the eunuchs?"

16 Memukan answered before the king and
the princes, "Vashti the queen has not done
wrong to just the king, but also to all the
princes, and to all the people who are in all
the provinces of the King Aḥashverosh.
17 For this deed of the queen will become
known to all women, causing them to show
contempt for their husbands, when it is
reported, 'King Aḥashverosh commanded
Vashti the queen to be brought in before
him, but she did not come.' 18 Today, the
princesses of Paras and Media who have
heard of the queen's deed will tell all the
king's princes. This will cause much
contempt and wrath.

19 "If it please the king, let a royal
command go from him, and let it be written
among the decrees of the Parasians and the
Medes, so that it cannot be altered, that
Vashti may never again come before King
Aḥashverosh; and let the king give her
royal estate to another who is better than
she. 20 When the king's edict which he shall
make is published throughout all his
kingdom (for it is great), all the wives will
give their husbands honor, both great and
small."

21 This advice pleased the king and the
princes, and the king did according to the
word of Memukan: 22 for he sent letters
into all the king's provinces, into every
province according to its writing, and to

every people in their language, that every
man should rule his own house, speaking in
the language of his own people.

2 1 After these things, when the wrath of
King Aḥashverosh was pacified, he
remembered Vashti, and what she had
done, and what was decreed against her.
2 Then the king's servants who served him
said, "Let beautiful young virgins be sought
for the king. 3 Let the king appoint officers
in all the provinces of his kingdom, that
they may gather together all the beautiful
young virgins to the citadel of Shushan, to
the women's house, to the custody of Hegai
the king's eunuch, guard of the women. Let
cosmetics be given them; 4 and let the
maiden who pleases the king be queen
instead of Vashti." The thing pleased the
king, and he did so.

5 There was a certain Yehudite in the
citadel of Shushan, whose name was
Mordekhai, the son of Yair, the son of
Shimi, the son of Qish, a Benyamite, 6 who
had been carried away from Yerushalayim
with the captives who had been carried
away with Yekonyah king of Yehudah,
whom Nevukhadnetstsar the king of Bavel
had carried away. 7 He was the faithful
nurturing father of Hadassah, that is,
Esther, his uncle's daughter; for she had
neither father nor mother. The maiden was
fair and beautiful; and when her father and
mother were dead, Mordekhai took her for
his own daughter.

8 So, when the king's word and his decree
was heard, and when many maidens were
gathered together to the citadel of Shushan,
to the custody of Hegai, Esther was taken
into the king's house, to the custody of
Hegai, guard of the women. 9 The maiden
pleased him, and she obtained kindness
from him. He quickly gave her cosmetics
and her portions of food, and the seven
choice maidens who were to be given her
out of the king's house. He moved her and
her maidens to the best place in the
women's house. 10 Esther had not made
known her people nor her relatives, because
Mordekhai had instructed her that she
should not make it known. 11 Mordekhai
walked every day in front of the court of
the women's house, to find out how Esther
was doing, and what would become of her.

12 Each young woman's turn came to go in
to King Aḥashverosh after her purification
for twelve new moons (for so were the days
of their purification accomplished, six new
moons with oil of myrrh, and six new
moons with sweet fragrances and with
preparations for beautifying women).
13 The young woman then came to the king
like this: whatever she desired was given
her to go with her out of the women's house
to the king's house. 14 In the evening she
went, and on the next day she returned into
the second women's house, to the custody
of Sha'ashgaz, the king's eunuch, who
guarded the concubines. She came in to the
king no more, unless the king delighted in
her, and she was called by name. 15 Now
when the turn of Esther, the daughter of
Aviḥayil the uncle of Mordekhai, who had
taken her for his daughter, came to go in to
the king, she required nothing but what
Hegai the king's eunuch, the guard of the
women, advised. Esther obtained favor in
the sight of all those who looked at her.

16 So Esther was taken to King
Aḥashverosh into his royal house in the
tenth new moon, which is the new moon
Tevet, in the seventh year of his reign.

17 The king loved Esther more than all the
women, and she obtained favor and
kindness in his eyes more than all the
virgins; so that he set the royal crown on
her head, and made her queen instead of
Vashti. 18 Then the king made a great
banquet for all his princes and his servants,
even Esther's banquet; and he proclaimed a
rest in the provinces, and gave gifts
according to the king's bounty.

19 When the virgins were gathered together
the second time, Mordekhai was sitting in
the king's gate. 20 Esther had not yet made
known her relatives nor her people, as
Mordekhai had commanded her; for Esther
obeyed Mordekhai, like she did when she
was brought up by him. 21 In those days,
while Mordekhai was sitting in the king's
gate, two of the king's eunuchs, Bigthan
and Teresh, who were doorkeepers, were
angry, and sought to lay hands on the King
Aḥashverosh. 22 This thing became known
to Mordekhai, who informed Esther the
queen; and Esther informed the king in
Mordekhai's name. 23 When this matter
was investigated, and it was found to be so,
they were both hanged on a tree; and it was
written in the book of the chronicles in the
king's presence.

3 1 After these things King Aḥashverosh
promoted Haman the son of Hammedatha
the Agagite, and advanced him, and set his
seat above all the princes who were with
him. 2 All the king's servants who were in
the king's gate bowed down, and paid
homage to Haman; for the king had so
commanded concerning him. But
Mordekhai did not bow down or pay him
homage. 3 Then the king's servants, who
were in the king's gate, said to Mordekhai,
"Why do you disobey the king's
command?" 4 Now it came to pass, when
they spoke daily to him, and he did not
listen to them, that they told Haman, to see
whether Mordekhai's reason would stand;
for he had told them that he was a
Yehudite. 5 When Haman saw that
Mordekhai did not bow down, nor pay him
homage, Haman was full of wrath. 6 But he
scorned the thought of laying hands on
Mordekhai alone, for they had made known
to him Mordekhai's people. Therefore
Haman sought to destroy all the Yehudim
who were throughout the whole kingdom
of Aḥashverosh, even Mordekhai's people.

7 In the first new moon, which is the new
moon Nisan, in the twelfth year of King
Aḥashverosh, they cast Pur, that is, the lot,
before Haman from day to day, and from
new moon to new moon, and chose the
twelfth new moon, which is the new moon
Adar. 8 Haman said to King Aḥashverosh,
"There is a certain people scattered abroad
and dispersed among the peoples in all the
provinces of your kingdom, and their
decrees are different than other people's.
They do not keep the king's decrees.
Therefore it is not for the king's profit to
allow them to remain. 9 If it pleases the
king, let it be written that they be
destroyed; and I will pay ten thousand
talents of silver into the hands of those who
are in charge of the king's business, to bring
it into the king's treasuries."

10 The king took his ring from his hand,
and gave it to Haman the son of
Hammedatha the Agagite, the enemy of the
Yehudim. 11 The king said to Haman, "The
silver is given to you, the people also, to do
with them as it seems good in your eyes."

12 Then the king's scribes were called in on
the first new moon, on the thirteenth day;

and all that Haman commanded was
written to the king's satraps, and to the
governors who were over every province,
and to the princes of every people, to every
province according to its writing, and to
every people in their language. It was
written in the name of King Aḥashverosh,
and it was sealed with the king's ring.
13 Letters were sent by couriers into all the
king's provinces, to destroy, to kill, and to
cause to perish, all Yehudim, both young
and old, little children and women, in one
day, even on the thirteenth day of the
twelfth new moon, which is the new moon
Adar, and to plunder their spoils.

[1 This is the copy of the letter. 2 "From the
great king Aḥashverosh to the rulers and
the governors under them of one hundred
twenty-seven provinces, from Hodu even to
Kush, who hold authority under him:

3 'Ruling over many nations and having
obtained dominion over the whole world, I
was determined – not elated by the
confidence of power, but ever conducting
myself with great moderation and
gentleness – to make the lives of my
subjects continually tranquil, desiring both
to maintain the kingdom quiet and orderly
to its utmost limits, and to restore the peace
desired by all men. 4 When I had asked my
counselors how this should be brought to
pass, Haman – who excels in sound
judgment among us, and has been
manifestly well inclined without wavering
and with unshaken fidelity, and had
obtained the second post in the kingdom –
informed us that a certain ill-disposed
people is mixed up with all the tribes
throughout the world, opposed in their law
to every other nation, and continually
neglecting the commands of the king, so
that the united government blamelessly
administered by us is not quietly
established. 5 Having then conceived that
this nation is continually set in opposition
to every man, introducing as a change a
foreign code of laws, and injuriously
plotting to accomplish the worst of evils
against our interests, and against the happy
establishment of the kingdom, we instruct
you in the letter written by Haman, who is
set over the public affairs and is our
second-in-post, to destroy them all utterly
with their wives and children by the swords
of the enemies, without pitying or sparing
any, on the fourteenth day of the twelfth
month, the month of Adar, of this present
year; 6 that the people aforetime and now
ill-disposed to us having been violently
consigned to death in one day, may
hereafter secure to us continually a well
constituted and quiet state of affairs."][a]

14 A copy of the letter, that the decree
should be given out in every province, was
published to all the peoples, that they
should be ready against that day. 15 The
couriers went out in haste by the king's
command, and the decree was given out in
the citadel of Shushan. The king and
Haman sat down to drink; but the city of
Shushan was perplexed.

4 1 Now when Mordekhai found out all
that was done, Mordekhai tore his clothes,
and put on sackcloth with ashes, and went
out into the middle of the city, and wailed
loudly and bitterly. 2 He came even before
the king's gate, for no one is allowed inside

---

[a] 3:1-6 Bracketed section indicates reading present in Greek texts but absent from Hebrew. These represent what are called "Additions to Esther."

the king's gate clothed with sackcloth. 3 In
every province, wherever the king's word
and his decree came, there was great
mourning among the Yehudim, and fasting,
and weeping, and wailing; and many lay in
sackcloth and ashes.

4 Esther's maidens and her eunuchs came
and told her this, and the queen was
exceedingly grieved. She sent clothing to
Mordekhai, to replace his sackcloth; but he
did not receive it. 5 Then Esther called for
Hathakhh, one of the king's eunuchs, whom
he had appointed to attend her, and
commanded him to go to Mordekhai, to
find out what this was, and why it was. 6 So
Hathakh went out to Mordekhai, to city
square which was before the king's gate.
7 Mordekhai told him of all that had
happened to him, and the exact sum of the
money that Haman had promised to pay to
the king's treasuries for the destruction of
the Yehudim. 8 He also gave him the copy
of the writing of the decree that was given
out in Shushan to destroy them, to show it
to Esther, and to declare it to her, and to
urge her to go in to the king, to seek *favor
from* him, and to make request before him,
for her people.

9 Hathakh came and told Esther the words
of Mordekhai. 10 Then Esther spoke to
Hathakh, and gave him a message to
Mordekhai: 11 "All the king's servants, and
the people of the king's provinces, know,
that whoever, whether man or woman,
comes to the king into the inner court
without being called, there is one decree for
him, that he be put to death, except those to
whom the king might hold out the golden
scepter, that he may live. I have not been
called to come in to the king these thirty
days."

12 They told Esther's words to Mordekhai.
13 Then Mordekhai asked them to return
this answer to Esther: "Do not think to
yourself that you will escape in the king's
house any more than all the Yehudim.
14 For if you remain silent now, then relief
and deliverance will come to the Yehudim
from another place, but you and your
father's house will perish. Who knows if
you have not come to the kingdom for such
a time as this?"

15 Then Esther asked them to answer
Mordekhai, 16 "Go, gather together all the
Yehudim who are present in Shushan, and
fast for me, and neither eat nor drink three
days, night or day. I and my maidens will
also fast the same way. Then I will go in to
the king, which is against the decree; and if
I perish, I perish." 17 So Mordekhai went
his way, and did according to all that Esther
had commanded him.

[18 He prayed to יהוה, making mention of
all the works of יהוה. 19 He said, "יהוה
Elohim, You are king ruling over all, for all
things are in Your power, and there is no
one who can oppose You in Your purpose
to save Yisra'el. 20 For You have made the
heavens and the earth and every wonderful
thing under the heavens. 21 You are Master
of all, and there is no one who can resist
You, יהוה. 22 You know all things. You
know, יהוה, that it is not in insolence, nor
arrogance, nor love of glory, that I have
done this, to refuse to bow down to the
arrogant Haman.

23 "For I would gladly have kissed the soles
of his feet for the safety of Yisra'el. 24 But I
have done this that I might not set the glory
of man above the glory of Elohim. I will
not worship anyone except You, my

Master, and I will not do these things in
arrogance. 25 And now, O יהוה Elohim, the
King, the Elohim of Avraham, spare Your
people, for our enemies are planning our
destruction, and they have desired to
destroy Your ancient inheritance. 26 Do not
overlook Your people, whom You have
redeemed for Yourself out of the land of
Mitsrayim. 27 Listen to my prayer. Have
kindness on Your inheritance and turn our
mourning into gladness, that we may live
and sing praise to Your Name, O יהוה. Do
not utterly destroy the mouth of those who
praise You, O יהוה."

28 All Yisra'el cried with all their might, for
death was before their eyes. 29 And queen
Esther took refuge in יהוה, being taken as
it were in the agony of death. 30 Having
taken off her glorious apparel, she put on
garments of distress and mourning. Instead
of grand perfumes she place on her head
ashes and dung. She greatly brought down
her body, and she filled every place of her
head with tangled hair.

31 She implored יהוה Elohim of Yisra'el,
and said, "O my Master, You alone are our
king. Help me. I am destitute, and have no
helper but You, 32 for my destruction is
near at hand. 33 I have heard from my birth,
in the tribe of my family, that You, יהוה,
took Yisra'el out of all the nations, and our
fathers out of all their families for a
perpetual inheritance, and have done for
them all that You have said. 34 And now
we have sinned before You, and You have
delivered us into the hands of our enemies,
35 because we honored their elohim. You
are righteous, O יהוה. 36 But now they
have not been contented with the bitterness
of our slavery, but have laid their hands on
the hands of their idols, 37 to abolish the
decree of Your mouth, and utterly to
destroy Your inheritance, and to stop the
mouth of those who praise You, and to
extinguish the glory of Your house and
Your altar, 38 and to open the mouth of the
nations to speak the praises of
worthlessness, and that a mortal king
should be admired forever. 39 O יהוה, do
not resign Your scepter to them that are not
Your people, and do not let them laugh at
our fall, but turn their counsel against
themselves, and make an example of him
who has begun to injure us.

40 "Remember us, O יהוה, manifest
Yourself in the time of our affliction.
Encourage me, O King of elohim, and ruler
of all dominion! 41 Put harmonious speech
into my mouth before the lion, and turn his
heart to hate him who fights against us, to
the utter destruction of him who agrees
with him. 42 But deliver us by Your hand,
and help me, who is destitute, and have
none but You, O יהוה. 43 You know all
things, and know that I hate the glory of
transgressors, and that I abhor the couch of
the uncircumcised, and of every stranger.
44 You know my necessity, for I abhor the
symbol of my proud station, which is upon
my head in the days of my splendor. I
abhor it as a menstruous cloth, and I do not
wear it in the days of my tranquility.

45 Your handmaid has not eaten at Haman's
table, and I have not honored the banquet
of the king, neither have I drunk wine of
drink offerings. 46 Neither has your
handmaid rejoiced since the day of my
promotion until now, except in You, O
יהוה, Elohim of Avraham. 47 O Elohim,
who has power over all, listen to the voice
of the desperate, and deliver us from the

hand of those who devise mischief. Deliver
me from my fear.][a]

5 1 Now on the third day, Esther put on her
royal clothing, and stood in the inner court
of the king's house, next to the king's
house. The king sat on his royal throne in
the royal house, next to the entrance of the
house. 2 When the king saw Esther the
queen standing in the court, she obtained
favor in his eyes; and the king held out to
Esther the golden scepter that was in his
hand. So Esther came near, and touched the
top of the scepter. 3 Then the king asked
her, "What would you like, queen Esther?
What is your request? It shall be given you
even to the half of the kingdom."

4 Esther said, "If it seems good to the king,
let the king and Haman come today to the
banquet that I have prepared for him."

5 Then the king said, "Bring Haman
quickly, so that it may be done as Esther
has said." So the king and Haman came to
the banquet that Esther had prepared.

6 The king said to Esther at the banquet of
wine, "What is your petition? It shall be
granted you. What is your request? Even to
the half of the kingdom it shall be
performed."

7 Then Esther answered and said, "My
petition and my request is this. 8 If I have
found favor in the sight of the king, and if it
please the king to grant my petition and to
perform my request, let the king and
Haman come to the banquet that I will
prepare for them, and I will do tomorrow as
the king has said."

9 Then Haman went out that day joyful and
glad of heart, but when Haman saw
Mordekhai in the king's gate, that he did
not stand up nor move for him, he was
filled with wrath against Mordekhai.
10 Nevertheless Haman restrained himself,
and went home. There, he sent and called
for his friends and Zeresh his wife.
11 Haman recounted to them the glory of
his riches, the multitude of his children, all
the things in which the king had promoted
him, and how he had advanced him above
the princes and servants of the king.
12 Haman also said, "Yes, Esther the queen
let no man come in with the king to the
banquet that she had prepared but myself;
and tomorrow I am also invited by her
together with the king. 13 Yet all this avails
me nothing, so long as I see Mordekhai the
Yehudite sitting at the king's gate."

14 Then Zeresh his wife and all his friends
said to him, "Let a gallows be made fifty
cubits high, and in the morning speak to the
king about hanging Mordekhai on it. Then
go in merrily with the king to the banquet."
This pleased Haman, so he had the gallows
made.

6 1 On that night, the king could not sleep.
He commanded the book of records of the
chronicles to be brought, and they were
read to the king. 2 It was found written that
Mordekhai had told of Bigthana and
Teresh, two of the king's eunuchs, who
were doorkeepers, who had tried to lay
hands on the King Aḥashverosh. 3 The king
said, "What honor and dignity has been
given to Mordekhai for this?" Then the

---

[a] 4:18-47 Bracketed section indicates reading present in Greek texts but absent from Hebrew. These represent what are called "Additions to Esther."

king's servants who attended him said,
"Nothing has been done for him."

4 The king said, "Who is in the court?"
Now Haman had come into the outer court
of the king's house, to speak to the king
about hanging Mordekhai on the gallows
that he had prepared for him.

5 The king's servants said to him, "Behold,
Haman stands in the court." The king said,
"Let him come in." 6 So Haman came in.
The king said to him, "What shall be done
to the man whom the king delights to
honor?" Now Haman said in his heart,
"Who would the king delight to honor more
than myself?" 7 Haman said to the king,
"For the man whom the king delights to
honor, 8 let royal clothing be brought which
the king uses to wear, and the horse that the
king rides on, and on the head of which a
crown royal is set. 9 Let the clothing and
the horse be delivered to the hand of one of
the king's most noble princes, that they may
array the man whom the king delights to
honor with them, and have him ride on
horseback through the city square, and
proclaim before him, 'Thus shall it be done
to the man whom the king delights to
honor!'"

10 Then the king said to Haman, "Hurry
and take the clothing and the horse, as you
have said, and do this for Mordekhai the
Yehudite, who sits at the king's gate. Let
nothing fail of all that you have spoken."

11 Then Haman took the clothing and the
horse, and arrayed Mordekhai, and had him
ride through the city square, and
proclaimed before him, "Thus shall it be
done to the man whom the king delights to
honor!"

12 Mordekhai came back to the king's gate,
but Haman hurried to his house, mourning
and having his head covered. 13 Haman
recounted to Zeresh his wife and all his
friends everything that had happened to
him. Then his wise men and Zeresh his
wife said to him, "If Mordekhai, before
whom you have begun to fall, is of
Yehudite seed, you will not prevail against
him, but you will surely fall before him."
14 While they were yet talking with him,
the king's eunuchs came, and hurried to
bring Haman to the banquet that Esther had
prepared.

7 1 So the king and Haman came to
banquet with Esther the queen. 2 The king
said again to Esther on the second day at
the banquet of wine, "What is your petition,
queen Esther? It shall be granted you. What
is your request? Even to the half of the
kingdom it shall be performed."

3 Then Esther the queen answered, "If I
have found favor in your eyes, O king, and
if it please the king, let my being be given
me at my petition, and my people at my
request. 4 For we are sold, I and my people,
to be destroyed, to be slain, and to perish.
But if we had been sold for male and
female slaves, I would have held my peace,
although the adversary could not have
compensated for the king's loss."

5 Then King Aḥashverosh said to Esther the
queen, "Who is he, and where is he who
dared presume in his heart to do so?"

6 Esther said, "An adversary and an enemy,
even this wicked Haman!" Then Haman
was afraid before the king and the queen.
7 The king arose in his wrath from the
banquet of wine and went into the palace
garden. Haman stood up to make request

for his being to Esther the queen; for he
saw that there was evil determined against
him by the king. 8 Then the king returned
out of the palace garden into the place of
the banquet of wine; and Haman had fallen
on the couch where Esther was. Then the
king said, "Will he even subdue the queen
in front of me in the house?" As the word
went out of the king's mouth, they covered
Haman's face.

9 Then Ḥarvonah, one of the eunuchs who
were with the king said, "Behold, the
gallows fifty cubits high, which Haman has
made for Mordekhai, who spoke good for
the king, is standing at Haman's house."
The king said, "Hang him on it!"

10 So they hanged Haman on the gallows
that he had prepared for Mordekhai. Then
was the king's wrath pacified.

8 1 On that day, King Aḥashverosh gave
the house of Haman, the enemy of the
Yehudim, to Esther the queen. Mordekhai
came before the king; for Esther had told
what he was to her. 2 The king took off his
ring, which he had taken from Haman, and
gave it to Mordekhai. Esther set Mordekhai
over the house of Haman.

3 Esther spoke yet again before the king,
and fell down at his feet, and begged him
with tears to put away the mischief of
Haman the Agagite, and his device that he
had devised against the Yehudim. 4 Then
the king held out to Esther the golden
scepter. So Esther arose, and stood before
the king. 5 She said, "If it pleases the king,
and if I have found favor in his eyes, and
the thing seem right to the king, and I am
pleasing in his eyes, let it be written to
reverse the letters devised by Haman, the
son of Hammedatha the Agagite, which he
wrote to destroy the Yehudim who are in
all the king's provinces. 6 For how can I
endure to see the evil that would come to
my people? How can I endure to see the
destruction of my relatives?"

7 Then King Aḥashverosh said to Esther the
queen and to Mordekhai the Yehudite,
"See, I have given Esther the house of
Haman, and him they have hanged on the
gallows, because he laid his hand on the
Yehudim. 8 Write also to the Yehudim, as
it pleases you, in the king's name, and seal
it with the king's ring; for the writing which
is written in the king's name, and sealed
with the king's ring, may not be reversed by
any man."

9 Then the king's scribes were called at that
time, in the third new moon, which is the
new moon Sivan, on the twenty-third day;
and it was written according to all that
Mordekhai commanded to the Yehudim,
and to the satraps, and the governors and
princes of the provinces which are from
Hodu to Kush, one hundred twenty-seven
provinces, to every province according to
its writing, and to every people in their
language, and to the Yehudim in their
writing, and in their language. 10 He wrote
in the name of King Aḥashverosh, and
sealed it with the king's ring, and sent
letters by courier on horseback, riding on
royal horses that were bred from swift
steeds. 11 In those letters, the king granted
the Yehudim who were in every city to
gather themselves together, and to defend
their being, to destroy, to kill, and to cause
to perish, all the power of the people and
province that would assault them, their
little ones and women, and to plunder their
spoils, 12 on one day in all the provinces of
King Aḥashverosh, on the thirteenth day of

the twelfth new moon, which is the new
moon Adar.

[1 "The great king Aḥashverosh sends
greetings to the rulers of provinces in one
hundred twenty-seven local governance
regions, from Hodu to Kush, even to those
who are faithful to our interests. Many who
have been frequently honored by the most
abundant kindness of their benefactors have
conceived ambitious designs, and not only
endeavor to hurt our subjects, but
moreover, not being able to bear prosperity,
they also endeavor to plot against their own
benefactors. 2 They not only would utterly
abolish gratitude from among men, but
also, elated by the boastings of men who
are strangers to all that is good, they
supposed that they would escape the sin-
hating vengeance of the ever-seeing
Elohim. 3 And oftentimes evil exhortation
has made partakers of the guilt of shedding
innocent blood, and has involved in
incurable calamities, many of those who
had been appointed to offices of authority,
who had been entrusted with the
management of their friends' affairs;
4 while men, by the false illogicality of an
evil disposition, have deceived the simple
candor of the ruling powers.

5 "And it is possible to see this – not so
much from more ancient traditional
accounts – as it is immediately in your
power to see it by examining what things
have been wickedly perpetrated by the
baseness of men unworthily holding power.
6 It is right to take heed with regard to the
future, that we may maintain the
government in undisturbed peace for all
men, adopting necessary changes, and
always judging those cases which come
under our notice with truly equitable
decisions.

7 "For whereas Haman, a Makedonian, the
son of Hammedatha – in reality an alien
from the blood of the Parasians, and
differing widely from our mild course of
government – having been hospitably
entertained by us, obtained so large a share
of our universal kindness as to be called
our father, and to continue the person next
to the royal throne, reverenced of all. 8 He
however, overcome by pride, endeavored to
deprive us of our dominion, and our life;
having by various and subtle artifices
demanded for the destruction of both
Mordekhai our deliverer and perpetual
benefactor, and Esther the blameless
consort of our kingdom, along with their
whole nation. 9 For by these methods he
thought – having surprised us in a
defenseless state – to transfer the dominion
of the Parasians to the Makedonians.

10 "But we find that the Yehudim, who
have been consigned to destruction by the
most abominable of men, are not
malefactors, but living according to the
most just laws, and being the sons of the
living El Elyon, *the* Almighty, who
maintains the kingdom, to us as well as to
our forefathers, in the most excellent order.
11 You will therefore do well in refusing to
obey the letter sent by Haman the son of
Hammedatha, because he who has done
these things has been hanged with his
whole family at the gates of Shoshan, El
Shaddai having swiftly returned to him a
worthy punishment.

12 "We enjoin you then, having openly
published a copy of this letter in every
place, to give the Yehudim permission to
use their own lawful customs, and to
strengthen them, that on the thirteenth of
the twelfth month Adar, on the same day,
they may defend themselves against those

who attack them in a time of affliction.
13 For in the place of the destruction of the
chosen race, El Shaddai has granted them
this time of gladness. 14 Therefore you also,
among your notable feasts, must keep a
distinct day with all festivity, that both now
and hereafter it may be a day of deliverance
to us and who are well disposed toward the
Parasians, but to those that plotted against
us a memorial of destruction. 15 And every
city and province collectively, which shall
not do accordingly, shall be consumed with
vengeance by spear and fire. 16 It shall be
made not only inaccessible to men, but
most hateful to wild beasts and birds
forever.][a]

13 A copy of the letter, that the decree
should be given out in every province, was
published to all the peoples, that the
Yehudim should be ready for that day to
avenge themselves on their enemies. 14 So
the couriers who rode on royal horses went
out, hastened and pressed on by the king's
command. The decree was given out in the
citadel of Shushan.

15 Mordekhai went out of the presence of
the king in royal clothing of blue and white,
and with a great crown of gold, and with a
robe of fine linen and purple; and the city
of Shushan shouted and was glad. 16 The
Yehudim had light, gladness, joy, and
honor. 17 In every province, and in every
city, wherever the king's command and his
decree came, the Yehudim had gladness,
joy, a banquet, and a good day. Many from
among the peoples of the land became
Yehudim; for the fear of the Yehudim was
fallen on them.

9 1 Now in the twelfth new moon, which is
the new moon Adar, on the thirteenth day,
when the king's command and his decree
came near to be put in execution, on the
day that the enemies of the Yehudim hoped
to conquer them, (but it was turned out the
opposite happened, that the Yehudim
conquered those who hated them), 2 the
Yehudim gathered themselves together in
their cities throughout all the provinces of
the King Aḥashverosh, to lay hands on
those who wanted to harm them. No one
could withstand them, because the fear of
them had fallen on all the people. 3 All the
princes of the provinces, the satraps, the
governors, and those who did the king's
business helped the Yehudim, because the
fear of Mordekhai had fallen on them. 4 For
Mordekhai was great in the king's house,
and his fame went out throughout all the
provinces; for the man Mordekhai grew
greater and greater. 5 The Yehudim struck
all their enemies with the stroke of the
sword, and with slaughter and destruction,
and did what they wanted to those who
hated them. 6 In the citadel of Shushan, the
Yehudim killed and destroyed five hundred
men. 7 They killed Parshandatha, Dalphon,
Aspatha, 8 Poratha, Adalia, Aridatha,
9 Parmashta, Arisai, Aridai, and Vaizatha,
10 the ten sons of Haman the son of
Hammedatha, the enemy of the Yehudim,
but they did not lay their hand on the
plunder.

11 On that day, the number of those who
were slain in the citadel of Shushan was
brought before the king. 12 The king said to
Esther the queen, "The Yehudim have slain
and destroyed five hundred men in the

---

[a] 8:1-16 Bracketed section indicates reading present in Greek texts but absent from Hebrew. These represent what are called "Additions to Esther."

citadel of Shushan, including the ten sons
of Haman; what then have they done in the
rest of the king's provinces! Now what is
your petition? It shall be granted you. What
is your further request? It shall be done."

13 Then Esther said, "If it pleases the king,
let it be granted to the Yehudim who are in
Shushan to do tomorrow also according to
today's decree, and let Haman's ten sons be
hanged on the gallows."

14 The king commanded this to be done. A
decree was given out in Shushan; and they
hanged Haman's ten sons. 15 The Yehudim
who were in Shushan gathered themselves
together on the fourteenth day also of the
new moon Adar, and killed three hundred
men in Shushan; but they did not lay their
hand on the plunder. 16 The other Yehudim
who were in the king's provinces gathered
themselves together, defended their beings,
had rest from their enemies, and killed
seventy-five thousand of those who hated
them; but they did not lay their hand on the
plunder.

17 This was done on the thirteenth day of
the new moon Adar; and on the fourteenth
day they rested and made it a day of
banquets and gladness. 18 But the Yehudim
who were in Shushan assembled together
on the thirteenth and on the fourteenth
days; and on the fifteenth they rested, and
made it a day of banquets and gladness.
19 Therefore the Yehudim of the villages,
who live in the unwalled towns, make the
fourteenth day of the new moon Adar a day
of gladness and banquets, a good day, and a
day of sending presents of food to one
another.

20 Mordekhai wrote these things, and sent
letters to all the Yehudim who were in all
the provinces of the King Aḥashverosh,
both near and far, 21 to enjoin them that
they should keep the fourteenth and
fifteenth days of the new moon Adar
yearly, 22 as the days in which the Yehudim
had rest from their enemies, and the new
moon which was turned to them from
sorrow to gladness, and from mourning into
a good day; that they should make them
days of banquets and gladness, and of
sending presents of food to one another,
and gifts to the needy. 23 The Yehudim
accepted the custom that they had begun, as
Mordekhai had written to them; 24 because
Haman the son of Hammedatha, the
Agagite, the enemy of all the Yehudim, had
plotted against the Yehudim to destroy
them, and had cast "Pur", that is the lot, to
consume them, and to destroy them; 25 but
when this became known to the king, he
commanded by letters that his wicked
device, which he had devised against the
Yehudim, should return on his own head,
and that he and his sons should be hanged
on the gallows.

26 Therefore they called these days
"Purim," from the word "Pur." Therefore
because of all the words of this letter, and
of that which they had seen concerning this
matter, and that which had come to them,
27 the Yehudim established, and imposed
on themselves, and on their seed, and on all
those who joined themselves to them, so
that it should not fail, that they would keep
these two days according to what was
written, and according to its appointed
time, every year; 28 and that these days
should be remembered and kept throughout
every generation, every family, every
province, and every city; and that these
days of Purim should not fail from among

the Yehudim, nor their memory perish from
their seed.

29 Then Esther the queen, the daughter of
Aviḥayil, and Mordekhai the Yehudite,
wrote with all authority to confirm this
second letter of Purim. 30 He sent letters to
all the Yehudim, to the hundred twenty-
seven provinces of the kingdom of
Aḥashverosh, with words of peace and
truth, 31 to confirm these days of Purim in
their appointed times, as Mordekhai the
Yehudite and Esther the queen had decreed,
and as they had imposed upon themselves
and their seed, in the matter of the fastings
and their cry. 32 The command of Esther
confirmed these matters of Purim; and it
was written in the book.

10 1 King Aḥashverosh laid a tribute on
the land, and on the islands of the sea. 2 All
the acts of his power and of his might, and
the full account of the greatness of
Mordekhai, to which the king advanced
him, are they not written in the book of the
chronicles of the kings of Media and Paras?
3 For Mordekhai the Yehudite was next to
King Aḥashverosh, and great among the
Yehudim, and accepted by the multitude of
his brothers, seeking the good of his
people, and speaking peace to all his seed.

[4 Mordekhai said, "These things have
come from Elohim. 5 For I remember the
dream which I had concerning these
matters; for not one detail of them has
failed. 6 There was the little spring which
became a river, and there was light, and the
sun and much water. The river is Esther,
who the king married, and was made
queen. 7 The two serpents are Haman and
me. 8 The nations are those nations who
combined to destroy the name of the
Yehudim. 9 But as for my nation, this is
Yisra'el, even those who cried to Elohim
and were delivered; for יהוה delivered His
people. יהוה rescued us out of all these
calamities; and Elohim worked such signs
and great wonders as have not been done
among the nations.

10 "Therefore He ordained two lots. One for
the people of Elohim, and one for all the
other nations. 11 And these two lots came
for an appointed season, and for a day of
judgment, before Elohim, and for all the
nations. 12 Elohim remembered His people
and vindicated His inheritance. 13 They
shall observe these days in the month of
Adar, on the fourteenth *day* and on the
fifteenth day of the month, with an
assembly, joy, and gladness before Elohim,
throughout the generations forever among
His people Yisra'el."

14 In the fourth year of the reign of Ptolemy
and Kleopatra, Dositheus, who said he was
a priest and Levite, and Ptolemy his son,
brought this letter of Purim, which they
said was the same, and that Lysimaḥos the
son of Ptolemy, who was in Yerushalayim,
had translated.][a]

---

[a] 10:4-14 Bracketed section indicates reading present in Greek texts but absent from Hebrew. These represent what are called "Additions to Esther."

תְּהִלִּים קנא - קנה
Tehillim [Psalms] 151-155

151 *This Psalm is a genuine one of David, though extra*[a]*, composed when he fought in single combat with Goliath. [Editor's note: Psalm 151 is found in the LXX as well as the Syriac Peshitta, and even in a fragmentary form in Hebrew among the Dead Sea Scrolls. The form found in the DSS also includes additional text in 151 that is not found in the other versions. It is generally referred to as Psalm 151b. I have included the additional text here in the bracketed sections.]*

1 I was small among my brothers, and youngest in my father's house. I tended my father's sheep.
2 My hands formed a musical instrument, and my fingers tuned a lute.
3 Whom shall tell, my Master? יהוה Himself, He Himself hears.
4 He sent forth His messenger and took me from my father's sheep, and He anointed me with His anointing oil.
5 My brothers were handsome and tall; but יהוה did not take pleasure in them.
6 [*Though* they were of great stature with handsome hair, יהוה Elohim did not choose them.]
7 I went out to meet the Philistine, and he cursed me by his idols.
8 [In the strength of יהוה I threw three stones at him. I struck him between the eyes, and dropped him to the ground.]
9 But I drew his own sword and beheaded him, and removed reproach from the children of Yisra'el.

152 *Spoken by David when he fought with a lion and a wolf which had taken a sheep from his flock.*

1 O help, O help, assist me; help me and save me; deliver my being from the murderer.
2 Shall I descend to Sheol by the mouth of a lion? Or shall the wolf confuse me?
3 Was it not enough for them that they lay in wait for my father's flock, to tear sheep from his flock to pieces? But *now* they even desire to destroy my being.
4 Have pity, O יהוה, on Your chosen one. Save Your set-apart one from destruction, that he might make known Your glory all his days, and may praise Your great Name;
5 when You deliver him from the hands of the destroying lion and the ravaging wolf, and when You turn back my captivity from the mouths of beasts.
6 Quickly, O Adonai[b], send a savior from before You to draw me up out of the gaping abyss which desires to wrap me in its depth.

153 *Spoken by David when he gave thanks to Elohim, when He had delivered*

---

[a] 151 The word for "extra" literally means "supernumerary" or "out side of numbering." The preface here states that although the Psalm is a genuine one written by David, it stands "outside" the traditional number of Psalms.

[b] 152:6 While Adonai is a Hebrew word, it actually appears transliterated here in the Syriac. This could indicate a Hebrew origin of this Psalm.

him from the lion and the wolf, and killed them both.

1 Praise יהוה, all you people, glorify Him and bless His Name;
2 Who rescued the being of His elect from the hands of death, and delivered his set-apart one from destruction;
3 and *who* saved me from the snare of Sheol, and brought out my being from the abyss that cannot be touched.
4 Before my deliverance could go forth from Him, I was almost torn in two by two wild beasts.
5 But He sent His messenger, and closed the gaping mouths from me, and rescued my life from destruction.
6 My being will glorify and exalt Him, because of all His kindnesses which He has shown and will show to me.

154 *The prayer of Ḥizqiyahu, when his enemies surrounded him.*

1 Glorify Elohim with a loud voice; speak His praise in the assembly of many.
2 Glorify His Name in the multitude of the upright, and celebrate His majesty with the faithful.
3 Unite your beings with the good and perfect, to praise the Most High.
4 Assemble together to make His salvation known, and do not hesitate to make known His might and majesty to all the children.
5 For wisdom has been given to make known the glory of יהוה;
6 and she has been revealed to men for the recounting of His many works;
7 to make His power known to children, to explain His greatness to those who lack understanding,
8 those who are far from her gates, those who have strayed from her entrances.
9 For the Most High is the Master of Ya'aqov, and His glory is on all His works.
10 The man who glorifies the Most High is accepted by Him like one who brings an offering,
11 like one who offers rams and calves, like one who fattens the altar with many burnt offerings; as a pleasing aroma from the hand of the righteous.
12 Her voice is heard from the gates of the righteous, and her song *is heard* from the assembly of the reverent.
13 When they eat until they are satisfied, she is mentioned, *as* also when they drink together in community.
14 Their meditation is on the Torah of the Most High, and their words are for making His power known.
15 Her speech is distant from the wicked, as is her knowledge from the immature.
16 Behold the eyes of יהוה have pity on the good.
17 He increases His kindness on those who glorify Him, and He will deliver their being from the time of evil.
18 Bless יהוה who redeems the humble from the hand of foreigners, and delivers the pure from the hand of the wicked;
19 who establishes a horn out of Ya'aqov and a judge of the people out of Yisra'el.
20 He will spread His Tabernacle out in Tsion, and will live forever in Yerushalayim.

155 *When the people were granted permission to return home by Koresh.*

1 O יהוה, I have called to You, listen to me.
2 I spread forth my palms to Your set-apart dwelling;

3 give ear to me, and grant me my petition;
4 do not withhold my request from me.
5 Build up my being and do not cast it
down;
6 do not abandon us in the presence of the
wicked.
7 May the Judge of Truth turn the payment
of the wicked away from me.
8 O יהוה, do not judge me according to my
sin; for no living man is righteous in before
You.
9 Give me discernment, יהוה. Teach me the
judgments of Your Torah;
10 so that the multitudes may hear of Your
works, and the people may praise Your
glory.
11 Remember me and do not forget me, and
do not lead me into unbearable destitution.
12 Cast the sin of my youth away from me,
and no more remember my sins against me.
13 O יהוה, cleanse me of the evil disease,
and do not let it return to me.
14 Dry up its root within me, and do not let
its leaves sprout in me.
15 You are glory, יהוה, therefore my
request is fulfilled before You.
16 To whom can I cry, that he would
answer my request? As for the sons of men,
what more can strength do *for them*?
17 My trust is before You, יהוה. I cried out,
"O יהוה" and He answered me, and healed
the brokenness of my heart.
18 I slumbered and slept. I dreamed and
indeed awoke.
19 You supported me, יהוה, and I called on
יהוה my deliverer.
20 Now I will behold their shame. I have
trusted in You, and I will not be ashamed.
21 Give glory forever and ever. Redeem
Yisra'el, O יהוה, Your elect one, and the
house of Ya'aqov, Your chosen.

בָּרוּךְ א

Barukh א [1 Baruch]

1 1 These are the words of the book, which
Barukh the son of Neriyah, the son of
Maḥseyah, the son of Tsidqiyahu, the son
of Asadyah, the son of Ḥilqiyahu, wrote in
Bavel, 2 in the fifth year, and in the seventh
day of the month, what time as the
Kaldeans took Yerushalayim, and burned it
with fire.

3 And Barukh read the words of this book
in the hearing of Yekonyah the son of
Yehoyaqim king of Yehudah, and in the
hearing of all the people that came to hear
the book, 4 and in the hearing of the mighty
men, and of the kings' sons, and in the
hearing of the elders, and in the hearing of
all the people, from the least to the greatest,
even of all those who lived at Bavel by the
river Sud.

5 And they wept, and fasted, and prayed
before יהוה; 6 they made also a collection
of money according to every man's power;
7 and they sent it to Yerushalayim to
Yehoyaqim the high priest, the son of
Ḥilqiyahu, the son of Shallum, and to the
priests, and to all the people which were
found with him at Yerushalayim, 8 at the
same time when he took the vessels of the
House of יהוה, that had been carried out of
the Temple, to return them to the land of
Yehudah, the tenth day of the month Sivan,
namely, silver vessels, which Tsidqiyahu
the son of Yoshiyahu king of Yehudah had
made, 9 after Nevukhadnetstsar king of
Bavel had carried away Yekonyah, and the
princes, and the captives, and the mighty
men, and the people of the land, from
Yerushalayim, and brought them to Bavel.

10 And they said, "Behold, we have sent
you money; therefore buy burnt offerings
with the money, and sin offerings, and
incense, and prepare an offering, and offer
it upon the altar of יהוה our Elohim.
11 Pray for the life of Nevukhadnetstsar
king of Bavel, and for the life of Belshatsar
his son, that their days may be as the days
of the heavens above the earth, 12 and יהוה
will give us strength, and lighten our eyes,
and we shall live under the shadow of
Nevukhadnetstsar king of Bavel, and under
the shadow of Belshatsar his son, and we
shall serve them many days, and find favor
in their eyes.

13 "Pray for us also to יהוה our Elohim, for
we have sinned against יהוה our Elohim;
and to this day the wrath of יהוה and His
indignation is not turned from us. 14 And
you shall read this book which we have
sent to you, to make confession in the
House of יהוה, on the day of the Feast and
on the days of the solemn assembly. 15 And
you shall say, 'Righteousness belongs to
יהוה our Elohim, but to us *belongs*
confusion of face, as it is today, to the men
of Yehudah, and to the inhabitants of
Yerushalayim, 16 and to our kings, and to
our princes, and to our priests, and to our
prophets, and to our fathers. 17 For we have
sinned before יהוה, 18 and disobeyed Him,
and have not listened to the voice of יהוה
our Elohim, to walk in the commands of
יהוה that He has set before us.'

19 "*And this* since the day that יהוה
brought our fathers out of the land of

Mitsrayim, even to today, we have been
disobedient to יהוה our Elohim, and we
have dealt unadvisedly in not listening to
His voice. 20 So the plagues clung to us,
and the curse, which יהוה commanded
Mosheh His servant to pronounce in the
day that He brought our fathers out of the
land of Mitsrayim, to give us a land that
flows with milk and honey, as it is today.
21 Nevertheless we did not listen to the
voice of יהוה our Elohim, according to all
the words of the prophets whom He sent to
us. 22 Rather, we walked, every man, in the
imagination of his own wicked heart, to
serve strange elohim, and to do that which
is evil in the eyes of יהוה our Elohim."

2 1 "Therefore יהוה has kept His word,
which He pronounced against us, and
against our judges that judged Yisra'el, and
against our kings, and against our princes,
and against the men of Yisra'el and
Yehudah, 2 to bring great plagues upon us,
such as never happened under all the
heavens, as it happened in Yerushalayim,
according to the things that are written in
the Torah of Mosheh. 3 *They happened* that
we should each eat the flesh of his own
son, and every man the flesh of his own
daughter. 4 Moreover He has given them to
be in subjection to all the kingdoms that are
around us, to be a reproach and a desolation
among all the people around, where יהוה
has scattered them. 5 Thus were they cast
down, and not exalted, because we sinned
against יהוה our Elohim, in not listening to
His voice. 6 Righteousness belongs to יהוה
our Elohim; but to us and to our fathers
belongs confusion of face, as it is today.
7 For all these plagues have come upon us,
which יהוה has pronounced against us.
8 Yet have we not sought the favor of יהוה,
in turning every one from the thoughts of
his wicked heart. 9 Therefore יהוה has kept
watch over the plagues, and יהוה has
brought them upon us; for יהוה is righteous
in all His works which He has commanded
us. 10 Yet we have not listened to His
voice, to walk in the commands of יהוה
that He has set before us.

11 "And now, O יהוה, Elohim of Yisra'el,
who has brought Your people out of the
land of Mitsrayim with a mighty hand, and
with signs, and with wonders, and with
great power, and with an outstretched arm,
and have gained a Name for Yourself, as it
is today; 12 יהוה our Elohim, we have
sinned, we have acted profanely, we have
dealt unrighteously in all Your judgments.
13 Let Your wrath turn from us, for we are
but a few left among the heathens, where
You have scattered us.

14 "Hear our prayer, יהוה, and our petition,
and deliver us for Your own sake, and give
us favor in the eyes of those who have led
us away captive, 15 that all the earth may
know that You are יהוה our Elohim,
because Yisra'el and his posterity is called
by Your Name. 16 יהוה, look down from
your set-apart dwelling, and consider us;
give ear, יהוה, and hear; 17 open Your
eyes, and behold: for the dead that are in
Sheol, whose breath is taken from their
bodies, will not give glory to יהוה, nor
righteousness. 18 But the being that is
greatly vexed, which goes stooping and
weak, and the eyes that fail, and the hungry
being, will give You glory and

righteousness, יהוה. 19 For we do not
present our petition before You, יהוה our
Elohim, for the righteousness of our
fathers, and of our kings.

20 "For You have sent Your wrath and
Your indignation upon us, as You have
spoken by Your servants the prophets,
saying, 21 'Thus says יהוה, "Bow your
shoulders to serve the king of Bavel, and
remain in the land that I gave to your
fathers. 22 But if you will not hear the voice
of יהוה, to serve the king of Bavel, 23 I will
cause the voice of joy and the voice of
gladness and the voice of bride and
bridegroom to cease out of the cities of
Yehudah, and from outside Yerushalayim;
and the whole land will be desolate, *and*
without inhabitant."'

24 "But we would not listen to Your voice,
to serve the king of Bavel; therefore You
kept Your words that You spoke by Your
servants the prophets, namely, that the
bones of our kings, and the bones of our
fathers, should be taken out of their places.
25 And behold, they are cast out to the heat
by day, and to the frost by night, and they
died in great miseries by famine, by sword,
and by pestilence. 26 And You have laid
waste the House which is called by Your
Name, as it is today, for the wickedness of
the house of Yisra'el and the house of
Yehudah.

27 "Yet, יהוה our Elohim, You have dealt
with us after all Your kindness, and
according to all Your great compassion,
28 as You spoke by Your servant Mosheh
in the day when You commanded him to
write Your Torah before the children of
Yisra'el, saying, 29 'If you will not hear My
voice, surely this very great multitude shall
be turned into a small number among the
nations, where I will scatter them. 30 For I
know that they will not hear Me, because
they are a stiff-necked people; but in the
land of their captivity they shall take it to
heart, 31 and shall know that I am יהוה
their Elohim. I will give them a heart, and
ears to hear, 32 and they shall praise Me in
the land of their captivity, and think upon
My Name, 33 and shall return from their
stiff-necked ways, and from their wicked
deeds. For they shall remember the way of
their fathers, which sinned before יהוה.
34 And I will bring them again into the land
which I swore to their fathers, to Avraham,
to Yitschaq, and to Ya'aqov, and they shall
be owners of it, and I will increase them,
and they shall not be diminished. 35 And I
will cut an everlasting covenant with them
to be their Elohim, and they shall be My
people. *Then* I will not remove My people
of Yisra'el any more out of the land that I
have given them."'

3 1 "יהוה Almighty, Elohim of Yisra'el,
the being in anguish, the troubled spirit,
cries to You. 2 Hear, יהוה, and be kind; for
You are a kind Elohim. Yes, be kind to us,
because we have sinned before you. 3 For
You sit as king forever, and we perish
evermore.

4 "יהוה Almighty, Elohim of Yisra'el, hear
the prayer of the dead Yisra'elites, and of
the children of those who were sinners
before You, that did not listen to Your
voice, their Elohim; for those who cause
these plagues clung to us. 5 Do not
remember the lawlessness of our fathers,
but remember Your power and Your Name
now at this time. 6 For You are יהוה our

Elohim, and we will praise You, יהוה.
7 Because of this You have put the fear of
You in our hearts, to the intent that we
should call upon Your Name. And we will
praise You in our captivity, for we have
called to mind all the lawlessness of our
fathers who sinned before You. 8 Behold,
we are in our captivity even today, where
You have scattered us, as a reproach and a
curse, and to be subject to penalty,
according to all the lawlessnesses of our
fathers, who departed from יהוה our
Elohim.

9 "Hear, O Yisra'el, the commands of life.
Give ear to understand wisdom. 10 How is
it, O Yisra'el, that you are in your enemies'
land, that you have become old in a strange
country, that you are defiled with the dead,
11 that you are counted with those who go
down into Sheol? 12 You have forsaken the
fountain of wisdom. 13 For if you had
walked in the way of Elohim, you would
have dwelled in peace forever. 14 Learn
where wisdom is, where strength is, where
understanding is; that you may know also
where length of days is, and life; where the
light of the eyes is, and peace. 15 Who has
found out her place? And who has come
into her treasuries? 16 Where are the
princes of the heathen, and those who ruled
the beasts upon the earth? 17 Those whose
hobby was with the fowls of the air, and
those who hoarded up silver and gold, in
which men trust; and of whose getting there
is no end?

18 "For those who worked in silver, and
were so careful, and whose works are past
finding out, 19 they are vanished and gone
down to Sheol, and others have come up in
their places. 20 Younger men have seen the
light, and lived upon the earth, but they
have not known the way of knowledge,
21 neither have they understood its paths.
Neither have their children laid hold of it;
they are far off from their way.

22 "It has not been heard of in Kana'an,
neither has it been seen in Teman. 23 The
sons also of Agar that seek understanding,
which are in the land, the merchants of
Merran and Teman, and the authors of
fables, and the searchers out of
understanding; none of these have known
the way of wisdom, or remembered her
paths. 24 O Yisra'el, how great is the House
of Elohim! And how large is the place of
His possession! 25 *It is* great and it has no
end. *It is* high and unmeasurable. 26 There
were the giants born that were famous of
old, great of stature, and experts in war.
27 Elohim did not choose these, nor did He
give the way of knowledge to them; 28 so
they died, because they had no wisdom.
They died through their own foolishness.
29 Who has gone up into the heavens, and
taken her, and brought her down from the
clouds? 30 Who has gone over the sea, and
found her, and will bring her for choice
gold? 31 There is none that knows her way,
nor any that comprehends her path.

32 "But he that knows all things knows her,
he found her with his understanding. He
that prepared the earth forevermore has
filled it with four-footed beasts. 33 He that
sends forth the light, and it goes; He called
it, and it obeyed Him with fear. 34 The stars
shined in their watches, and were glad;
when He called them, they said, 'Here we
are;' they shined with gladness to Him that
made them. 35 This is our Elohim, and
there is no other like Him. 36 He has found
out all the way of knowledge, and has
given it to Ya'aqov His servant, and to

Yisra'el His beloved. 37 Afterward she
appeared upon earth, and talked with men."

4 1 This is the book of the commands of
Elohim, and the Torah that endures forever:
all those who hold fast to it are appointed to
life; but those that leave it shall die. 2 Turn,
O Ya'aqov, and take hold of it. Walk
towards her, shining in the presence of her
light. 3 Do not give your glory to another,
nor the things that are profitable to you to a
strange nation. 4 O Yisra'el, happy are we,
for the things that are pleasing to Elohim
are made known to us. 5 Be of good cheer,
my people, the memorial of Yisra'el.

6 You were sold to the nations, but not for
destruction. Because you moved Elohim to
wrath, you were delivered to your
adversaries. 7 For you provoked Him that
made you by slaughtering to demons, and
not to Elohim. 8 You forgot the everlasting
Elohim, who brought you up. You also
grieved Yerushalayim, who nursed you.

9 For she saw the wrath that has come upon
you from Elohim, and said, "Listen, you
women that dwell about Tsion, for Elohim
has brought great mourning upon me; 10 for
I have seen the captivity of my sons and
daughters, which the Eternal has brought
upon them. 11 For I nourished them with
joy; but sent them away with weeping and
mourning. 12 Let no man rejoice over me, a
widow, and forsaken of many. I am left
desolate for the sins of my children.
Because they turned away from the Torah
of Elohim, 13 and had no regard for His
statutes, neither did they walk in the ways
of the commands of Elohim, nor trod in the
paths of discipline in His righteousness.
14 Let those who dwell about Tsion come,
and remember the captivity of my sons and
daughters, which the Eternal has brought
upon them.

15 "For he has brought a nation upon them
from afar, a shameless nation, and of a
strange language, who neither respected old
man, nor pitied small child. 16 And they
have carried away the dear beloved sons of
the widow, and left her that was alone
desolate of her daughters. 17 But I, how can
I help you? 18 For He that brought these
plagues upon you will deliver you from the
hand of your enemies. 19 Go your way, O
my children, go your way: for I am left
desolate. 20 I have put off the garment of
peace, and put on the sackcloth of my
petition: I will cry to the Eternal as long as
I live.

21 "Be of good cheer, O my children, cry to
Elohim, and He will deliver you from the
power and hand of the enemies. 22 For I
have trusted in the Eternal, that He will
save you; and joy has come to me from the
Set-Apart One, because of the kindness
which will soon come to you from the
Eternal your Savior. 23 For I sent you out
with mourning and weeping, but Elohim
will give you to me again with joy and
gladness forever. 24 For as now those who
dwell about Tsion have seen your captivity,
so shall they soon see your salvation from
our Elohim, which will come upon you
with great glory, and brightness of the
Eternal. 25 My children, patiently endure
the wrath that has come upon you from
Elohim, for your enemy has persecuted
you; but shortly you shall see his
destruction, and shall tread upon their
necks. 26 My delicate ones have gone rough
ways; they were taken away as a flock
carried off by their enemies.

27 "Be of good cheer, O my children, and
cry to Elohim, for you will be remembered
by Him that has brought these things upon
you. 28 For as it was your desire to stray
from Elohim, so now return and seek Him
ten times more. 29 For He who brought
these plagues upon you will bring you
everlasting joy again with your salvation."

30 Be of good cheer, O Yerushalayim, for
He that called you by name will comfort
you. 31 Those who afflicted you are
miserable, and rejoiced at your fall. 32 The
cities which your children served are
miserable; she that received your sons is
miserable. 33 For as she rejoiced at your
fall, and was glad *at the sight* of your ruin,
so shall she be grieved for her own
desolation. 34 And I will take away her
exultation in her great multitude, and her
boasting shall be turned into mourning.
35 For fire shall come upon her from the
Eternal, *and it will* endure a long time; and
she will be inhabited by demons for a long
time.

36 O Yerushalayim, look around you
toward the east, and behold the joy that
comes to you from Elohim. 37 Behold, your
sons come, whom you sent away; they
come gathered together from the east to the
west at the word of the Set-Apart One,
rejoicing in the glory of Elohim.

5 1 Put off the garment of your mourning
and affliction, O Yerushalayim, and put on
the beauty of the glory that comes from
Elohim forever. 2 Wrap around you the
robe of the righteousness which comes
from Elohim; set a diadem on your head of
the glory of the Eternal. 3 For Elohim will
show your brightness to every region under
the heavens. 4 For Elohim shall forever call
your name, 'The Peace of Righteousness,'
and 'The Glory of the Reverence of
Elohim.' 5 Arise, O Yerushalayim, and
stand upon the height, and look around you
toward the east, and see your children
gathered from the going down of the sun to
its rising at the word of the Set-Apart One,
rejoicing that Elohim has remembered
them. 6 For they went from you on foot,
being led away of their enemies: but
Elohim brings them in to you borne on high
with glory, * as on a royal throne. 7 For
Elohim has appointed that every high
mountain, and the everlasting hills, should
be made low, and the valleys filled up, to
make plain the ground, that Yisra'el may go
safely in the glory of Elohim. 8 Moreover
the woods and every sweet smelling tree
have overshadowed Yisra'el by the
commandment of Elohim. 9 For Elohim
shall lead Yisra'el with joy in the light of
his glory with the mercy and righteousness
that comes from him.

Another letter of Yirmeyahu [a]

[Editor's note: Barukh chapter 6 is actually considered its own writing in some manuscripts, though others include it as a sixth chapter. It is found extant in both Greek and Syriac.]

6 1 A copy of a letter, which Yirmeyahu
sent to them which were to be led captives
into Bavel by the king of the Bavelians, to

---

[a] 6:6 This title "Another letter of Yirmeyahu" is found in the section heading of the Syriac version.

certify them, as he was commanded by
יהוה.

2 Because of the sins which you have
committed before יהוה, you shall be led
away captives to Bavel by Nevuchadnetsar
king of the Bavelians. 3 So when you come
to Bavel, you shall remain there many
years, and for a long season, even for seven
generations, and after that I will bring you
out peaceably from there. 4 But now shall
you see in Bavel elohim of silver, and of
gold, and of wood, carried upon shoulders,
which cause the nations to fear. 5 Beware
therefore that you do not, in any way,
become like the strangers, neither let fear
take hold upon you because of them, when
you see the multitude before them and
behind them, worshipping them. 6 But say
in your hearts, "O יהוה, we must bow
down to You."

7 For my messenger is with you, and I
myself do care for your beings. 8 For their
tongue is polished by the workman, and
they themselves are overlaid with gold and
with silver; yet are they but false, and
cannot speak. 9 And taking gold, as it were
for a maiden that loves to make merry, they
make crowns for the heads of their elohim.
10 And sometimes also the priests convey
from their elohim gold and silver, and
bestow it upon themselves. 11 And they
will even give of it to the common whores:
and they deck them as men with garments,
even the elohim of silver, and elohim of
gold, and of wood.

12 Yet these elohim cannot save themselves
from rust and moths, though they be
covered with purple raiment. 13 They wipe
their faces because of the dust of the
temple, which is thick upon them. 14 And
he that cannot put to death one that offends
against him by holding a scepter, as though
he were judge of a country. 15 He has also a
dagger in his right hand, and an axe, but
cannot deliver himself from war and
robbers.

16 Whereby they are known not to be
elohim: therefore do not fear them. 17 For
like as a vessel that a man uses is worth
nothing when it is broken; even so it is with
their elohim: when they be set up in the
temples their eyes be full of dust through
the feet of those who come in. 18 And as
the courts are made sure on every side upon
him that offends the king, as being
committed to suffer death; even so the
priests make fast their temples with doors,
with locks, and bars, lest they be carried off
by robbers.

19 They light candles for them; yes, more
than for themselves, of which they cannot
see one. 20 They are as one of the beams of
the temple; and men say their hearts are
eaten out, when things creeping out of the
earth devour both them and their raiment.
They do not feel it 21 when their faces are
blackened through the smoke that comes
out of the temple. 22 Bats, swallows, and
birds alight upon the tops of their heads;
and in like manner the weasels also.
23 Whereby you may know that they are no
elohim; therefore do not fear them.

24 Notwithstanding the gold with which
they are beset to make them beautiful,
except one wipe off the rust, they will not
shine: for not even when they were molten
did they feel it. 25 Things in which there is
no breath are bought at any cost. 26 Having
no feet, they are carried upon shoulders,
whereby they declare to men that they be
nothing worth. 27 They also that serve them

are ashamed: for if they fall to the ground
at any time, they cannot rise up again of
themselves; neither can they make
themselves straight if they are set off-
center. But the offerings are set before
them, as if they were dead men. 28 And the
things that are slaughtered to them, their
priests sell and spend; and in like manner
their wives also salt and preserve part of it;
but they give none to the poor and to the
powerless.

29 The menstruous woman and the woman
in childbed touch their slaughterings,
knowing therefore by these things that they
are no elohim: do not fear them. 30 For how
can they be called elohim? Because women
set meat before the elohim of silver, gold,
and wood. 31 And in their temples the
priests sit on seats, having their torn
clothes, and their heads and beards shaved,
and nothing upon their heads. 32 They roar
and cry before their elohim, as men do at
the feast when one is dead. 33 The priests
also take garments off of them and clothe
their wives and children with them.

34 Whether it be evil that one does to them,
or good, they are not able to repay it; they
can neither set up a king, nor put him
down. 35 In the same way, they can neither
give riches nor money. Though a man
make a vow to them, if he does not keep it,
they will never exact it. 36 They cannot
save man from death, neither can they
deliver the weak from the mighty. 37 They
cannot restore sight to a blind man, nor
deliver any that is in distress. 38 They
cannot show kindness to the widow, nor do
good to the orphan. 39 They are like the
stones that are hewn out of the mountain,
these elohim of wood, and that are overlaid
with gold and with silver: those who
minister to them shall be confounded.

40 Why then should a man then think or say
that they are elohim, when even the
Kaldeans themselves dishonor them?
41 Who, if they shall see one dumb that
cannot speak, they bring him, and entreat
him to call upon Bel, as though he were
able to understand. 42 Yet they cannot
perceive this themselves, and forsake them,
for they have no understanding. 43 The
women also sit in the ways, with cords
around them, burning bran for incense. But
if any of them, drawn by some that passes
by, lie with him, she reproaches her fellow,
that she was not thought as worthy as
herself, nor her cord broken. 44 Whatever is
done among them is false. Why would a
man then think or say that they are elohim?
45 They are fashioned by carpenters and
goldsmiths; they can be nothing other than
what the workmen want them to be.
46 Those who fashioned them can never
continue long; how then should the things
that are fashioned by them *continue*? 47 For
they have left lies and reproaches to those
who come after. 48 For when there comes
any war or plague upon them, the priests
consult with themselves, where they may
be hidden with them.

49 How then can men not understand that
they are no elohim, which can neither save
themselves from war, nor from plague?
50 For seeing that they are nothing but
wood, and overlaid with gold and with
silver, it shall be known soon after that they
are false. 51 And it shall be manifest to all
nations and kings that they are no elohim,

but the works of men's hands, and [that
there is no work of Elohim in them][a].

52 Who then may not know that they are no
elohim? 53 For they can neither set up a
king in a land, nor give rain to men.
54 They can neither judge their own cause,
nor repay a wrong, for they are not capable;
for they are as crows between the heavens
and earth. 55 For even when fire falls upon
the house of the elohim of wood, or
overlaid with gold or with silver, their
priests will flee away, and escape, but they
themselves shall be burned up like *wooden*
beams.

56 Moreover they cannot withstand any
king or enemies; why should a man then
allow, or think that they are elohim?
57 Neither are those elohim of wood, and
overlaid with silver or with gold, able to
escape either from thieves or robbers.
58 Whose gold, and silver, and garments
with which they are clothed, they that are
strong will take from them, and go away
with them: neither shall they be able to help
themselves.

59 Therefore it is better to be a king that
shows his manhood, or else a vessel in a
house profitable for that of which the
owner shall have need, than such false
elohim; or even a door in a house, to keep
the things safe that are in it, than such false
elohim; or a pillar of wood in a palace, than
such false elohim.

60 For sun, and moon, and stars, being
bright and sent to do their offices, are
obedient. 61 Likewise also the lightning,
when it glitters, is fair to see; and after the
same manner the wind also blows in every
country. 62 And when Elohim commands
the clouds to go over the whole world, they
do as they are told.

63 And the fire sent from above to consume
mountains and woods does as it is
commanded; but these are to be likened to
them neither in show nor power. 64 Why
then should a man think or say that they are
elohim, seeing they are not able to judge
causes, nor to do good to men?

65 Knowing therefore that they are no
elohim, do not fear them. 66 For they can
neither curse nor bless kings. 67 Neither can
they show signs in the heavens among the
nations, nor shine as the sun, nor give light
as the moon. 68 The beasts are better than
they, for they can get under a covert, and
help themselves.

69 In no way then is it manifest to us that
they are elohim. Therefore, do not fear
them. 70 For as a scarecrow in a garden of
cucumbers that keeps nothing, so are their
elohim of wood, and overlaid with gold and
with silver. 71 Likewise also their elohim of
wood, and overlaid with gold and with
silver, are like to a white thorn in an
orchard, that every bird sits upon; as also to
a dead body, that is cast forth into the dark.

72 And you shall know them to be no
elohim by the bright purple that rots upon
them. And they themselves afterward shall
be consumed, and shall be a reproach in the
country. 73 Better therefore is the just man
that does not have idols: for he shall be far
from reproach.

---

[a] 6:51 Bracketed section indicates reading present in Greek texts. Syr. reads, "all of their latter end is falsehood."

טוֹבִי

Tovi [Tobit]

1 1 The book of the words of Tovi, the son of Tovi'el, the son of Anani'el, the son of Adu'el, the son of Gava'el, of the seed of Asi'el, of the tribe of Naphtali; 2 who in the days of Shalmaneser king of the Ashuwrites was carried away captive out of Thisbe[a], which is on the right hand of Qedesh Naphtali in the Galil above Asher.

3 I, Tovi, walked in the ways of truth and righteousness all the days of my life, and I gave much tsedaqqah to my kindred and my nation, who went with me into the land of the Ashuwrites, to Nineveh. 4 When I was in my own country, in the land of Yisra'el, while I was yet young, all the tribe of Naphtali my father fell away from the house of Yerushalayim, which was chosen out of all the tribes of Yisra'el, that all the tribes should slaughter there, and the Temple of the dwelling-place of Elyon was set apart, and built there for all ages. 5 All the tribes which fell away together sacrificed to the heifer Ba'al, and so did the house of Naphtali my father. 6 I alone went often to Yerushalayim at the Feasts, as it has been ordained to all Yisra'el by an everlasting decree, having the first-fruits and the tithes of my increase, and that which was first shorn; and I gave them at the altar to the priests the sons of Aharon. 7 I gave a tenth part of all my increase to the sons of Levi, who ministered at Yerushalayim. A second tenth part I sold away, and went, and spent it each year at Yerushalayim. 8 A third tenth I gave to them to whom it was appropriate, as Devorah my father's mother had commanded me, because I was left an orphan by my father. 9 When I became a man, I took as wife Ḥannah of the seed of our own family. With her, I became the father of Toviyah. 10 When I was carried away captive to Nineveh, all my kindred and my relatives ate of the bread of the nations; 11 but I kept myself from eating, 12 because I remembered Elohim with all my soul. 13 So Elyon gave me kindness and favor in the sight of Shalmaneser, and I was his spokesman. 14 And I went into Media, and left ten talents of silver in trust with Gava'el, the brother of Gaviyah, at Ragesh of Media.

15 And when Shalmaneser was dead, Sancheriv his son reigned in his place. In his time, the highways were troubled, and I could no longer go into Media. 16 In the days of Shalmaneser, I gave much tsedaqqah to my brethren, and I gave my bread to the hungry, 17 and my garments to the naked. If I saw any of my race dead, and thrown out on the wall of Ninevah, I buried him. 18 If Sancheriv the king killed any, when he came fleeing from Yehudah, I buried them privately; for in his wrath he killed many; and the bodies were sought for by the king, and were not found. 19 But one of the sons of the Ninevites went and informed the king concerning me, that I buried them, and hid myself; and when I knew that I was sought for to be put to death, I withdrew myself for fear. 20 And all my goods were forcibly taken away, and there was nothing left to me except my

[a] 1:2 Thisbe – Name of unknown city. Possibly related to Tishbeh, the city which Eliyahu the Tishbite was from.

wife Ḥannah and my son Toviyah. 21 No more than forty[a] days passed before two of his sons killed him, and they fled into the mountains of Ararat. And Esar-ḥaddon his son reigned in his place; and he appointed Aḥiqar my brother Anan'el's son over all the accounts of his kingdom, and over all his affairs. 22 Aḥiqar requested me, and I came to Nineveh. Now Aḥiqar was cupbearer, keeper of the signet, steward, and overseer of the accounts. Esar-ḥaddon appointed him next to himself, but he was my brother's son.

2 1 Now when I had come home again, and my wife Ḥannah was restored to me, and my son Toviyah, in the Feast of Shavuot, which is the set-apart Feast of the seven weeks, there was a good meal prepared for me, and I sat down to eat. 2 I saw abundance of meat, and I said to my son, "[My son][b], go and bring whatever poor man you find of our brethren, who is mindful of יהוה. Behold, I wait for you."

3 Then he came, and said, "Father, one of our race has been strangled, and cast out in the marketplace."

4 Before I had tasted anything, I sprang up, and took him up into a chamber until the sun had set. 5 Then I returned, washed myself, ate my bread in heaviness, 6 and remembered the prophecy of Amos, as he said, **"Your feasts will be turned into mourning, and all your songs into lamentation."**

7 So I wept: and when the sun had set, I went and dug a grave, and buried him. 8 My neighbors mocked me, and said, "He is no longer afraid to be put to death for this matter; and yet he fled away. Behold, he buries the dead again." 9 The same night I returned from burying him, and slept by the wall of my courtyard, being unclean; and my face was uncovered. 10 I did not know that there were sparrows in the wall. My eyes were open and the sparrows dropped warm dung into my eyes, and white films came over my eyes. I went to the physicians, and they did not help me; but Aḥiqar nourished me, until I went into Elam.

11 My wife Ḥannah wove cloth in the women's chambers, 12 and sent the work back to the owners. They paid her wages on her part, and also gave her a kid *of the goats*. 13 But when it came to my house, it began to cry, and I said to her, "Where did this kid come from? Is it stolen? Give it back to the owners; it is not lawful to eat anything that is stolen."

14 But she said, "It has been given to me for a gift more than the wages." I did not believe her, and I asked her to return it to the owners; and I was ashamed of her. But she answered and said to me, "Where is your tsedaqqah and your righteous deeds? Behold, you and all your works are known."

3 1 I was grieved and wept, and prayed in sorrow, saying, 2 "O יהוה, You are righteous, and all Your works and all Your

---

[a] 1:21 Greek texts read "fifty-five" while the Latin reads "forty-five." Rendering here of forty is from the Aramaic fragments.

[b] 2:2 Bracketed section indicates reading present in Aramaic fragment, but absent from Greek texts.

ways are kindness and truth, and You judge
true and righteous judgment forever.
3 Remember me, and look at me. Do not
take vengeance on me for my sins and my
ignorance, and the sins of my fathers who
sinned before You. 4 For they disobeyed
your commands. You gave us as plunder,
for exile, for death, and for a proverb of
reproach to all the nations among whom we
are dispersed. 5 Now Your judgments are
many and true; that You should deal with
me according to my sins and the sins of my
fathers; because we did not keep Your
commands, for we did not walk in truth
before you. 6 Now deal with me according
to that which is pleasing in Your eyes.
Command my spirit to be taken from me,
that I may be released, and become earth.
For it is more profitable for me to die rather
than to live, because I have heard false
reproaches, and there is much sorrow in
me. Command that I be released from my
distress, now, and go to the everlasting
place. Do not turn Your face away from
me."

7 The same day, this happened to Sarah the
daughter of Ragu'el in Aḥmetha of Media;
she was shamed by her father's
maidservants, 8 because she had been given
to seven husbands, and Asmodaeus the evil
spirit killed them, before they had lain with
her. And they said to her, "Do you not
know that you strangle your husbands?
You have had already seven husbands, and
you have not borne the name of any one of
them. 9 Why do you chastise us? If they are
dead, go along with them. Let us never see
either son or daughter from you."
10 When she heard these things, she was
grieved exceedingly, so that she considered
hanging herself. Then she said, "I am the
only daughter of my father. If I do this, it
will be shame to him, and I will bring down
his old age with sorrow to Sheol." 11 Then
she prayed by the window, and said,
"Blessed are You, O יהוה my Elohim, and
blessed is Your set-apart and honorable
Name forever! Let all Your works praise
You forever! 12 And now, יהוה, I have set
my eyes and my face toward You.
13 Command that I be released from the
earth, and that I no longer hear reproach.
14 You know, יהוה, that I am pure [in my
bones][a] from all sin with man, 15 and that I
have never polluted my name or the name
of my father, in the land of my exile. I am
the only daughter of my father, and he has
no child that will be his heir, nor brother
near him, nor son belonging to him, that I
should keep myself for a wife to him.
Seven husbands have perished on me
already. Why should I live? If it does not
please You to kill me, command that
attention be paid to me, and pity taken of
me, and that I hear no more reproach."

16 The prayer of both was heard before the
glory of the great Elohim. 17 Rapha'el was
sent to heal them both, to scale away the
white films from Tovi's eyes, and to give
Sarah the daughter of Ragu'el for a wife to
Toviyah the son of Tovi; and to bind
Asmodaeus the evil spirit; because it
belonged to Toviyah that he should inherit
her. At that very time, Tovi returned and
entered into his house, and Sarah the

[a] 3:14 Bracketed section indicates reading present in Hebrew fragment but absent from Greek and Latin texts. The Latin includes a rough paraphrase that reads anima meaning "soul" here instead.

daughter of Ragu'el came down from her
upper chamber.

4 1 In that day Tovi remembered the
money which he had left in trust with
Gava'el in Ragesh of Media, 2 and he said
to himself, "I have asked for death; why do
I not call my son Toviyah, that I may
explain to him about the money before I
die?"

3 And he called him, and said, "My son, if I
die, bury me. Do not despise your mother.
Honor her all the days of your life, and do
that which is pleasing to her, and do not
grieve her. 4 Remember, my son, that she
has seen many dangers for you, when you
were in her womb. When she is dead, bury
her by me in one grave. 5 My son, be
mindful of יהוה our Elohim all your days,
and do not let your will be set to sin and to
turn aside from His commands; do
righteousness all the days of your life, and
do not follow the ways of unrighteousness.
6 For if you do what is true, your deeds will
prosperously succeed for you, and for all
those who do righteousness. 7 Give
tsedaqqah from your possessions. When
you give tsedaqqah, do not let your eye be
envious. Do not turn away your face from
any poor man, and the face of Elohim will
not be turned away from you. 8 As your
possessions are, so give tsedaqqah
according to your abundance. If you have
little, do not be afraid to give tsedaqqah
according to that little; 9 for you lay up a
good treasure for yourself against the day
of necessity; 10 because giving tsedaqqah
delivers from death, and does not allow you
to come into darkness. 11 Tsedaqqah is a
good gift in the sight of Elyon for all that
give it.

12 "Beware, my son, of all whoring, and
take a wife of the seed of your fathers. Do
not take a strange wife, who is not of your
father's tribe; for we are the descendants of
the prophets. Remember, my son, that
Noaḥ, Avraham, Yitschaq, and Ya'aqov,
our fathers of old time, all took wives of
their brethren, and were blessed in their
children, and their seed will inherit the
land.

13 "And now, my son, love your brethren,
and do not scorn your brethren and the sons
and the daughters of your people in your
heart, to take a wife of them; for in
scornfulness is destruction and much
trouble, and in waywardness is decay and
great lack; for waywardness is the mother
of famine. 14 Do not let the wages of any
man who works for you wait with you, but
give it to him out of your hand. If you serve
Elohim, you will be rewarded. Guard
yourself, my son, in all your works, and be
discreet in all your behavior. 15 And do not
do to man what you yourself hate. Do not
drink wine to drunkenness, and do not let
drunkenness go with you on your way.
16 Give of your bread to the hungry, and of
your garments to those who are naked.
Give tsedaqqah from all your abundance.
Do not let your eye be envious when you
give tsedaqqah. 17 Pour out your bread on
the burial of the just, and give nothing to
sinners.

18 "Ask counsel of every man who is wise,
and do not despise any counsel that is
profitable. 19 Bless יהוה your Elohim at all
times, and ask of Him that your ways may
be made straight, and that all your paths
and counsels may prosper; for every nation
has no counsel; but יהוה Himself gives all
good things, and He humbles whom He

will, as He will. And now, my son,
remember my commands, and do not let
them be blotted out of your mind.

20 "And now I will explain to you about the
ten talents of silver, which I left in trust
with Gava'el the son of Gaviyah at Ragesh
of Media. 21 And do not fear, my son,
because we are made poor. You have much
wealth, if you fear your Elohim, and depart
from all sin, and do that which is pleasing
in His eyes."

5 1 Then Toviyah answered and said to
him, "Father, I will do all things, whatever
you have commanded me. 2 But how will I
receive the money, since I do not know
him?"

3 He gave him the handwriting, and said to
him, "Seek a man who will go with you,
and I will give him wages, whiles I still
live; and go and receive the money."

4 He went to seek a man, and found
Rapha'el who was a messenger, and he did
not know it. 5 He said to him, "Can I go
with you to Ragesh of Media? Do you
know those places well?"

6 The messenger said to him, "I will go
with you. I know the way well. I have
lodged with our brother Gava'el."

7 Toviyah said to him, "Wait for me, and I
will tell my father."

8 He said to him, "Go, and do not wait."
And he went in and said to his father,
"Behold, I have found someone who will
go with me." But *his father* said, "Call him
to me, that I may know of what tribe he is,
and whether he be a trustworthy man to go
with you."

9 So he called him, and he came in, and
they saluted one another. 10 And Tovi said
to him, "Brother, of what tribe and of what
family are you? Tell me."

11 He said to him, "Do you seek a tribe and
a family, or a hired man which will go with
your son?" And Tovi said to him, "I want to
know, brother, your family and your
name."

12 And he said, "I am Azaryah, the son of
Ḥananyah the great, of your family."

13 And he said to him, "Welcome, brother.
Do not be angry with me, because I sought
to know your tribe and family. You are my
brother, of an honest and good lineage; for
I knew Ḥananyah and Yathan, the sons of
Shemayah the great, when we went
together to Yerushalayim to worship, and
offered the firstborn, and the tithes of our
increase; and they did not go astray in the
error of our brethren. My brother, you are
of a great stock. 14 But tell me, what wages
shall I give you? A drachma a day, and
those things that be necessary for you, as to
my son? 15 And moreover, if you both
return safe and sound, I will add something
to your wages."

16 And so they agreed. And he said to
Toviyah, "Prepare yourself for the journey.
May Elohim prosper you." So his son
prepared what was needed for the journey,
and his father said to him, "Go with this
man; but Elohim, who dwells in the
heavens, will prosper your journey. May
His messenger go with you." Then they
both departed, and the young man's dog
went with them. 17 But Ḥannah his mother
wept, and said to Tovi, "Why have you sent
away our child? Is he not the staff of our
hand, in going in and out before us? 18 Do
not be greedy to add money to money; but

let it be as refuse compared to our child.
19 For what יהוה has given us to live is
enough for us."

20 Tovi said to her, "Do not worry, my
sister. He [will leave in peace and he][a] will
return to us in peace, and your eyes will see
him. 21 For a good messenger will go with
him. His journey will be prospered, and he
will return to us in peace."

22 So she stopped weeping.

[So the young man left, along with the messenger, and the dog left with them, and the two walked together.][b]

6 1 Now as they went on their journey,
they came at evening to the river Ḥiddeqel[c],
and they lodged there. 2 But the young man
went down [to the River Ḥiddeqel][d] to
wash his feet, and a great fish leaped out of
the water, and tried to swallow the young
man's foot.[e] 3 The young man shouted, but
the messenger said to him, "Grab the fish!"
So the young man grabbed the fish, and
hauled it up onto the land.

4 And the messenger said to him, "Cut the
fish open, and take the heart, the liver, and
the gall, and keep them with you; [but
throw away the guts; for the gall, the heart
and the liver are a good remedy][f]." 5 And
the young man [split the fish and removed
the gall, the heart, and the liver; and they
roasted the fish, and ate it][g]. And they both
went on their way, until they drew near to
Aḥmetha.

6 The young man said to the messenger,
"Brother Azaryah, of what use is the heart,
the liver, and the gall of the fish?"

7 He said to him, "About the heart and the
liver: If a demon or an evil spirit troubles
anyone, we must burn those and make
smoke from them before the man or the
woman, and the attack will stop. 8 But as
for the gall, it is good to anoint a man that
has white films in his eyes, and he will be
healed."

9 But when they drew near to Ragesh,
10 Rapha'el said to the young man, "
Toviyah, my brother, today we will spend
the night in the house of Ragu'el. He is our
family. He has a beautiful daughter named
Sarah. 11 He has no son or daughter besides
her. And you are her closest relative to her
from all men to have her, and all that
belongs to her father. Take her for yourself
as a wife, for you have the right to inherit
all the possessions of her father. 12 The girl
is sensible and vibrant and very beautiful,
and her father loves her and all he has he
gives to her. And as for you, the lawful
right is yours to take her. Now listen to me,

---

[a] 5:20 Bracketed section indicates reading present in Aramaic fragment, but absent from Greek and Latin texts.
[b] 5 Bracketed section indicates reading present in Aramaic fragment but absent from Greek and Latin texts. The Latin does contain a similar statement regarding the dog following, however.
[c] 6:1 Ḥiddeqel – Hebrew name of the Tigris River.
[d] 6:2 Bracketed section indicates reading present in Aramaic fragment but absent from Greek and Latin texts.
[e] 6:2 Greek texts do not contain any references to his feet. Rather, they state that the fish wanted to swallow Toviyah.
[f] 6:4 Bracketed section indicates reading present in Aramaic fragment and (roughly) the Latin text, but absent from Greek texts.
[g] 6:5 Bracketed section indicates reading present in Aramaic fragment. Greek and Latin texts read, "did as he was commanded."

my brother. Speak to this young woman tonight, and betroth her and take her for a wife. For when we return from Ragesh we will celebrate the wedding feast; for I know that Ragu'el will in no way deny her to you, as he knows it is yours to take his daughter according to the Torah of Mosheh, or else he would be liable to death, because it belongs to you to take the inheritance, rather than any other. We will speak to her tonight, and betroth her to you."

13 Then Toyiyah said to Rapha'el, "Brother Azaryah, I have heard that she has already been given to seven men, and that they all died in the bride-chamber. They died when they went in to her. And I have heard that the people said it was a demon who killed them. And now, I fear the demon who loves her, for the demon kills those who approach her. **14** Now I am the only son of my father and my mother, and I am afraid of dying and the sorrow that would bring on my father and my mother on my account. They have no other son who could bury them."

15 But he said to him, "Do you not remember the words which your father commanded you, that you take a wife of your own family? Now hear me, my brother; do not fear this woman, but take her *as your wife*. For I know that in this night she will be given to you as a wife. **16** And when you come into the bride-chamber, you shall take some of the heart and liver of the fish, and lay them on the ashes of incense, and the aroma will rise. **17** Then the demon will smell it, and he will flee and not appear to her again. **18** And when you go near to her, both of you rise up, and cry to Elohim who is kind. He will save you, and be kind to you. Do not be afraid, for she was prepared for you from the beginning; and you will save her, and she will go with you. And I am sure that you will have children with her, and they will be like brothers for you."

19 When Toviyah heard the words of Rapha'el, that she was his sister and from the descendants of his father's house, he loved her exceedingly, and his heart grew greatly fond of her.[a]

7 **1** They came to Aḥmetha, [and Toviyah said to him, "Azaryah, take me straight to the house of Ragu'el, our brother." And he took him,][b] and arrived at the house of Ragu'el. [They found Ragu'el seated in front of the doo to the courtyard, and they spoke peace to him. He said to them, "In peace you come, and in peace you shall go, my brothers."][c] **2** Ragu'el said to Edna his wife, "This young man really resembles Tovi my cousin!" **3** And Edna[d] asked them, "Where are you two from, kindred?" They said to her, "We are of the sons of Naphtali, who are exiles in Nineveh."

---

[a] 6 Most of chapter 6 has been amended in light of the Aramaic fragments. Included in Appendix E is a list of textual variants including chapter 6 the way it is translated from Greek.
[b] 7:1 Bracketed section indicates reading present in Aramaic fragment but absent from Greek and Latin texts.
[c] 7:1 Bracketed section indicates reading present in Aramaic fragment. Greek text reads, "But Sarah met them; and she greeted them, and they her. Then she brought them into the house."
[d] 7:3 Greek and Latin texts read "Ragu'el" instead of "Edna" here. Likewise all personal pronouns in verses 3 and 4 are masculine in those texts. The Latin texts read, "Anna" instead of "Edna" most likely due to scribal error, transposing the name of Tovi's wife for the name of Ragu'el's.

4 She said to them, "Do you know Tovi our brother?" They said, "We know him." Then she said to them, "Is he in good health?"

5 They said, "He is both alive, and in good health." Toviyah said, "He is my father."

6 And Ragu'el sprang up, and kissed him, wept, 7 blessed him, and said to him, "You are the son of an honest and good man." When he had heard that Tovi had lost his sight, he was grieved, and [he fell on Toviyah's neck and][a] wept; 8 and Edna his wife and Sarah his daughter wept also. They received them gladly; and they killed a ram of the flock, and served them meat. But Toviyah said to Rapha'el, "Brother Azaryah, tell Ragu'el that he should give me Sarah, my sister."

9 So he spoke the word to Ragu'el. Ragu'el said to Toviyah, "Eat, drink, and be joyful: 10 for it belongs to you to take my daughter. However I will tell you the truth. 11 I have given my daughter to seven men, and whenever they came in to her, they died in the night. But for now, be joyful." And Toviyah said, "I will taste nothing here, until you all cut a covenant and enter into that covenant with me."

12 Ragu'el said, "Take her to yourself from now on, according to the custom. You are her relative, and she is yours. The kind Elohim will give all good success to you."

13 And he called his daughter Sarah, and took her by the hand, and gave her to be wife of Toviyah, and said, "Behold, take her to yourself after the Torah of Mosheh, and lead her away to your father." And he blessed them. 14 He called Edna his wife, then took a book, wrote a contract, and sealed it. 15 Then they began to eat.

16 And Ragu'el called his wife Edna, and said to her, "Sister, prepare the other chamber, and bring her in there." 17 She did as he asked, and brought her in there. She wept, and she received the tears of her daughter, and said to her, 18 "Be comforted, my child. May the Master of heaven and earth give you favor for this sorrow of yours. Be comforted, my daughter."

8 1 When they had finished their supper, they brought Toviyah in to her. 2 But as he went, he remembered the words of Rapha'el, and took the ashes of the incense, and put the heart and the liver of the fish on them, and made smoke with them. 3 When the demon smelled the aroma, it fled into the uppermost parts of Mitsrayim, and the messenger bound him. 4 But after they were both shut in together, Toviyah rose up from the bed, and said, "Sister, arise, and let us pray that יהוה may be kind to us."

5 And Toviyah began to say, "Blessed are You, O Elohim of our fathers, and blessed is Your set-apart and glorious Name forever. Let the heavens bless You, and all Your creatures *bless You.* 6 You made Adam, and gave him Ḥavvah his wife as a helper and support. From them came the seed of men. You said, 'It is not good that the man should be alone. Let us make him a helper like him.' 7 And now, O יהוה, I do not take this my sister for lust, but in truth.

---

[a] 7:7 Bracketed section indicates reading present in Aramaic fragment but absent from Greek texts.

Command that I may find kindness and
grow old with her."

8 She said with him, "Amein." And they
both slept that night.

9 Ragu'el arose, and went and dug a grave,
10 saying, "Lest he also should die." 11 And
Ragu'el came into his house, 12 and said to
Edna his wife, "Send one of the
maidservants, and let them see if he is
alive. If not, we will bury him, and no one
will know about it."

13 So the maidservant opened the door, and
went in, and found them both sleeping,
14 and came out, and told them that he was
alive.

15 Then Ragu'el blessed Elohim, saying,
"Blessed are You, O Elohim, with all pure
and set-apart blessing! Let Your set-apart
ones bless You, and all Your creatures! Let
all Your messengers and Your elect bless
You forever! 16 Blessed are You, because
You have made me glad; and it has not
happened to me as I suspected; but You
have dealt with us according to Your great
kindness. 17 Blessed are You, because You
have been kind to two that were the only
begotten children of their parents. Show
them mercy, O יהוה. Fulfill their life in
health with gladness and kindness."

18 He commanded his servants to fill the
grave. 19 He kept the wedding feast for
them fourteen days. 20 Before the days of
the wedding feast were finished, Ragu'el
swore to him that he should not depart until
the fourteen days of the wedding feast were
fulfilled; 21 and that then he should take
half of his goods, and go in peace to his
father; and the rest *he could have*, he said,
when my wife and I die.

9 1 And Toviyah called Rapha'el, and said
to him, 2 "Brother Azaryah, take with you
[four][a] servants and two camels, and go to
Ragesh of Media to Gava'el, and receive
the money for me, and bring it to the
wedding feast, 3 because Ragu'el has sworn
that I must not depart. 4 My father counts
the days; and if I wait long, he will be very
grieved."

5 So Rapha'el went on his way, and lodged
with Gava'el, and gave him the
handwriting; so he brought forth the bags
with their seals, and gave them to him.
6 Then they rose up early in the morning
together, and came to the wedding feast.
Toviyah blessed his wife.

10 1 Tovi his father counted every day.
When the days of the journey were expired,
and they did not return, 2 he said, "Perhaps
he is detained? Or perhaps Gava'el is dead,
and there is no one to give him the
money?" 3 He was very grieved.

4 But his wife said to him, "The child has
died, seeing he waits long." She began to
wail for him, and said, 5 "I do not care
about anything, my son, since I have let
you go, the light of my eyes." 6 Tovi said to
her, "Hold your peace. Do not worry. He is
in good health."

7 And she said to him, "Hold your peace.
Do not deceive me. My son has perished."
And she went out every day into the way

---

[a] 9:2 Aramaic fragment reads, "four" here, while the Greek texts do not specify. The Latin paraphrases this as, "…take with you servants and beasts."

by which they went, and ate no bread in the
day-time, and did not stop mourning her
son Toviyah for entire nights. When the
fourteen days of the wedding feast were
expired, which Ragu'el had sworn that he
should spend there, Toviyah said to
Ragu'el, "Send me away, for my father and
my mother no longer believe they will see
me again. [And now I beg you, my father,
allow me to leave so that I may go to my
father. I have already told you how I left
them.][a]" **8** But his father-in-law said to him,
"Stay with me, and I will send messengers
to your father, and they will declare to him
how things go with you." **9** Toviyah said,
"No. Send me away to my father."

10 Ragu'el arose, and gave him Sarah his
wife, and half his goods, servants, cattle,
and money; **11** and he blessed them, and
sent them away, saying, "The Elohim of
heaven will prosper you, my children,
before I die." **12** And he said to his
daughter, "Honor your father-in-law and
your mother-in-law. They are now your
parents. Let me hear a good report of you."
Then he kissed her. Edna said to Toviyah,
"May the Master of heaven restore you,
dear brother, and grant to me that I may see
your children of my daughter Sarah, that I
may rejoice before יהוה. Behold, I commit
my daughter to you in special trust. Do not
cause her grief."

11 **1** After these things Toviyah also went
his way, blessing Elohim because He had
prospered his journey; and he blessed
Ragu'el and Edna his wife. Then he went
on his way until they drew near to Nineveh.
2 Rapha'el said to Toviyah, "Do you not
know, brother, how you left your father?
3 Let us run forward before your wife, and
prepare the house. **4** But take in your hand
the gall of the fish." So they went their
way, and the dog went after them.

5 Ḥannah sat looking around toward the
path for her son. **6** She saw him coming,
and said to his father, "Behold, your son is
coming with the man that went with him!"

7 Rapha'el said, "I know, Toviyah, that your
father will open his eyes. **8** Therefore
anoint his eyes with the gall, and being
pricked because of it, he will rub *them*, and
will make the white films fall away. Then
he will see you."

9 Ḥannah ran to him, and fell upon the neck
of her son, and said to him, "I have seen
you, my son! I am ready to die." They both
wept.

10 Tovi went toward the door and stumbled;
but his son ran to him, **11** and took hold of
his father. He scattered the gall of the fish
in his father's eyes, saying, "Do not fear,
my father." **12** When his eyes began to
sting, he rubbed them. **13** Then the white
films scaled away from the corners of his
eyes; and he saw his son, and fell upon his
neck.

14 He wept, and said, "Blessed are You, O
Elohim, and blessed is Your Name forever!
Blessed are all Your set-apart messengers!
15 For You chastised, and were kind to me.
Behold, I see my son Toviyah." And his
son went in rejoicing, and told his father

---

[a] 10:7 Bracketed section indicates reading present in Aramaic fragment, but absent from Greek and Latin texts.

the great things that had happened to him in
Media.

16 Tovi went out to meet his daughter-in-
law at the gate of Nineveh, rejoicing, and
blessing Elohim. Those who saw him go
marveled, because he had received his
sight. 17 Tovi gave thanks before them,
because Elohim had shown kindness to
him. When Tovi came near to Sarah his
daughter-in-law, he blessed her, saying,
"Welcome, daughter! Blessed is Elohim
who has brought you to us, and blessed are
your father and your mother." And there
was joy among all his brethren who were at
Nineveh. 18 Aḥiqar and Nasbas his
nephews came. 19 Toviyah's wedding feast
was kept seven days with great gladness.

12 1 And Tovi called his son Toviyah, and
said to him, "See, my son, that the man
who went with you have his wages, and
you must give him more."

2 And he said to him, "Father, it is no harm
to me to give him the half of those things
which I have brought; 3 for he has led me
for you in peace, and he cured my wife, and
brought my money, and likewise cured
you."

4 The old man said, "It is due to him."

5 And he called the messenger, and said to
him, "Take half of all that you all have
brought."

6 Then he called them both privately, and
said to them, "Bless Elohim, and give Him
thanks, and magnify Him, and give Him
thanks in the sight of all that live, for the
things which He has done with you. It is
good to bless Elohim and exalt His Name,
showing forth with honor the works of
Elohim. Do not be slack to give Him
thanks. 7 It is good to keep close the secret
of a king, but to reveal gloriously the works
of Elohim. Do good, and evil will not find
you. 8 Prayer with fasting, tsedaqqah, and
righteousness is good. A little with
righteousness is better than much with
unrighteousness. It is better to give
tsedaqqah than to lay up gold. 9 Alms
delivers from death, and it purges away all
sin. Those who give tsedaqqah and do
righteousness will be filled with life; 10 but
those who sin are enemies to their own life.
11 Surely I will keep nothing closed from
you. I have said, 'It is good to keep close
the secret of a king, but to reveal gloriously
the works of Elohim.'

12 "And now, when you prayed, along with
Sarah your daughter-in-law, I brought the
memorial of your prayer before the Set-
Apart One. When you buried the dead, I
was with you likewise. 13 And when you
did not delay to rise up, and leave your
dinner, that you might go and cover the
dead, your good deed was not hidden from
me. I was with you. 14 And now Elohim
sent me to heal you and Sarah your
daughter-in-law. 15 I am Rapha'el, one of
the seven set-apart messengers, who
present the prayers of the set-apart ones,
and go in before the glory of the Set-Apart
One."[a]

16 And they were both troubled, and fell
upon their faces; for they were afraid.
17 And he said to them, "Do not be afraid.
You will all have peace; but bless Elohim
forever. 18 For I did not come of any favor
of my own, but by the will of your Elohim.

---

[a] 12:15 See Galah [Revelation] 1:4.

Therefore bless Him forever. 19 All these
days I appeared to you. I did not eat or
drink, but you all saw a vision. 20 Now give
thanks to Elohim, because I ascend to Him
that sent me. Write all the things which
have been done in a book."

21 Then they rose up, and saw him no more.
22 They confessed the great and wonderful
works of Elohim, and how the messenger
of the Lord had appeared to them.

13 1 And Tovi wrote a prayer for
rejoicing, and said,
"Blessed is Elohim who lives forever!
Blessed is His kingdom!
2 For He chastises, and shows kindness. He
leads down to Sheol, and brings up from
the abyss again. There is no one that will
escape His hand.
3 Give thanks to Him before the nations
among whom He has scattered you, all you
children of Yisra'el.
4 Declare His greatness there. Extol Him
before all the living; because He is our
Master, and Elohim is our Father forever.
5 He will chastise us for our iniquities, and
will again show kindness, and will gather
us out of all the nations among whom you
are all scattered.
6 If you turn to Him with your whole heart
and with your whole being, to do truth
before Him, then He will turn to you, and
will not hide His face from you. See what
He has done for you. Give Him thanks with
your whole mouth. Bless the Master of
righteousness. Exalt the everlasting King. I
give Him thanks in the land of my exile,
and show His strength and majesty to a
nation of sinners. Turn, you sinners, and do
righteousness before Him. Who can tell if
He will accept you and be kind to you?
7 I exalt my Elohim. My being exalts the
King of heaven, and rejoices in His
greatness all the days of my life.
8 Let all men speak, and chant psalms, and
let them give Him thanks in Yerushalayim.
9 O Yerushalayim, the set-apart city, He
will chastise you for the works of your
sons, and will again be kind to the sons of
the righteous.
10 Give thanks to יהוה with goodness, and
bless the everlasting King, that His
Tabernacle may be built in you again with
joy, and that He may make glad in you
those who are exiles, and forever love in
you those who are miserable.
11 Many nations will come from far off to
the Name of יהוה Elohim with gifts in their
hands, even gifts to the King of the
heavens. Generations of generations will
praise You, and sing songs of rejoicing.
12 [Cursed are all those who say harsh
things, and all those who are against You.]
Cursed are all those who hate You, [and all
those who speak against You][a]. All those
who love You forever will be blessed.
13 Rejoice and be exceedingly glad for the
sons of the righteous, for they will be
gathered together and will bless the Master
of the righteous.
14 Oh blessed are those who love You.
They will rejoice for Your peace. Blessed
are all those who sorrowed for all Your
chastisement, because they will rejoice for
You when they have seen all Your glory.
They will be made glad forever.

[a] 13:12 Bracketed sections indicate readings present in Aramaic fragment but absent from Greek texts. Latin texts paraphrase this to, "They shall be cursed that despise You, and condemned that blaspheme You."

15 Let my being bless [a]יהוה the great King.
16 For Yerushalayim will be built with
sapphires, emeralds, and precious stones;
your walls and towers and battlements with
pure gold.
17 The streets of Yerushalayim will be
paved with beryl, carbuncle, and stones of
Ophir.
18 All her streets will say, "Halleluyah!"
and give praise, saying, "Blessed be
Elohim, who has exalted you forever!"

14 1 Then Tovi finished giving thanks.
2 He was fifty-eight years old when he lost
his sight. After eight years, he received it
again. He gave tsedaqqah and he feared
יהוה Elohim more and more, and gave
thanks to Him.

3 Now he grew very old; and he called
Toviyah his son with the seven[b] sons of his
son, and said to him, "My child, take your
sons. Behold, I have grown old, and am
ready to depart out of this life. 4 Go into
Media, my son, for I surely believe all the
things which Yonah the prophet spoke of
Nineveh, that it will be overthrown, but in
Media there will rather be peace for a
season. Our brethren [who dwell in the land
of Yisra'el will be deserted, along with
Shomeron] will be scattered in the earth
from the good land. Yerushalayim will be
desolate, and the house of Elohim in it will
be burned up, and will be desolate for a
time. 5 Elohim will again be kind to them,
and bring them back into the land, and they
will build the house, but not like to the
former house, until the times of that age are
fulfilled. Afterward they will return from
the places of their exile, and build up
Yerushalayim with honor. The house of
Elohim will be built in it forever with a
glorious building, even as the prophets
spoke concerning it. 6 And all the nations
will turn to fear יהוה Elohim in truth, and
will bury their idols. 7 All the nations will
bless יהוה, and His people will give thanks
to Elohim, and יהוה will exalt His people;
and all those who love יהוה Elohim in
truth and righteousness will rejoice,
showing kindness to our brethren.

8 "And now, my son, depart from Nineveh,
because those things which the prophet
Yonah spoke will surely happen. 9 But you
must guard the Torah and the judgments,
and show yourself kind and righteous, that
it may be well with you. 10 Bury me
decently, and your mother with me. Do not
stay at Nineveh. See, my son, what Amon
did to Aḥiqar that nourished him, how out
of light he brought him into darkness, and
all the recompense that he made him.
Aḥiqar was saved, but the other had his
recompense, and he went down into
darkness. Menasheh gave tsedaqqah, and
escaped the snare of death which he set for
him; but Amon fell into the snare, and
perished. 11 And now, my children,
consider what tsedaqqah does, and how
righteousness delivers." While he was
saying these things, he gave up the spirit in
the bed; but he was one hundred fifty eight

---

[a] 13:15 In the Hebrew fragment, the Name of יהוה is not written, nor is מריא (*Mar-ya*) used as it is in some Aramaic texts. Instead, four dots **** are written in the text, indicating the placement of the Name. In this verse, the Hebrew fragment includes these dots, while the Greek texts read Θεος (*Theos*) or "Elohim" here.
[b] 14:3 Greek reads "six" here. Aramaic and Latin read "seven."

years old. Toviyah buried him
magnificently.

12 When Ḥannah died, he buried her with
his father. But Toviyah departed with his
wife and his sons to Aḥmetha to Ragu'el his
father-in-law, 13 and he grew old in honor,
and he buried his father-in-law and mother-
in-law magnificently, and he inherited their
possessions, and his father Tovi's. 14 He
died at Aḥmetha of Media, being one
hundred and twenty-seven years old.
15 Before he died, he heard of the
destruction of Nineveh, which
Nevuchadnetstsar and Aḥashverosh took
captive. Before his death, he rejoiced over
Nineveh.

יְהוּדִית

Yehudith [Judith]

1 1 In the twelfth year of the reign of
Nevukhadnetstsar, who reigned over the
Ashuwrites in Nineveh, the great city, in
the days of Arpakhshad, who reigned over
the Medes in Aḥmetha, 2 and built around
Aḥmetha walls of hewn stones three cubits
broad and six cubits long, and made the
height of the wall seventy cubits, and its
width fifty cubits; 3 and set its towers at its
gates, one hundred cubits high, and its
width in the foundation was sixty cubits;
4 and made its gates, even gates that were
raised to the height of seventy cubits, and
their width forty cubits, for his mighty
army to go out of, and the setting in array
of his footmen— 5 even in those days king
Nevukhadnetstsar made war with king
Arpakhshad in the great plain. This plain is
on the borders of Ragesh. 6 All that lived in
the hill country came out to meet him,
along with all that lived by *the rivers*
Perath, Ḥiddeqel, and Hydaspes[a], and in the
plain of Ariokh the king of the Elamites.
Many nations of the sons of Ḥeloud
assembled themselves to the battle.

7 And Nevukhadnetstsar king of the
Ashuwrites sent to all who lived in Paras,
and to all who lived westward, to those
who lived in Kilikia, Dammeseq, Levanon,
and Antilevanon, and to all who lived along
the sea coast, 8 and to those among the
nations that were of Karmel and Gilad, and
to the higher Galil and the great plain of
Yizreel, 9 and to all who were in Shom'ron
and its cities, and beyond Yarden to
Yerushalayim, Betane, Ḥalutsah, Qadesh,
the river of Mitsrayim, Taḥpanḥes,
Rameses, and all the land of Goshen,
10 until you come above Tsoan and Noph,
and to all that lived in Mitsrayim, until you
come to the borders of Kush.

11 All those who lived in all the land did
not regard the command of
Nevukhadnetstsar king of the Ashuwrites,
and did not go with him to the war; for they
did not fear him, but he was before them as
one man. They turned away his messengers
from their presence without effect, and with
disgrace. 12 And Nevukhadnetstsar was
exceedingly angry with all this land, and he
swore by his throne and kingdom, that he
would surely be avenged upon all the
coasts of Kilikia, Dammeseq, and Aram,
that he would kill with his sword all the
inhabitants of the land of Moav, and the
children of Ammon, all Yehudah, and all
that were in Mitsrayim, until you come to
the borders of the two seas.

13 And he set the battle in array with his
army against king Arpakhshad in the
seventeenth year; and he prevailed in his
battle, and turned to flight all the army of
Arpakhshad, with all his horses and all his
chariots. 14 He became master of his cities,
and he came even to Aḥmetha, and took the
towers, plundered its streets, and turned its
beauty into shame. 15 He took Arpakhshad
in the mountains of Ragesh, struck him
through with his javelins, and utterly
destroyed him, to this day. 16 He returned
with them to Nineveh, he and all his
company of sundry nations, an exceedingly
great multitude of men of war, and there he

[a] 1:6 Hydaspes – Unknown river.

took his ease and banqueted, he and his
army, for one hundred and twenty days.

2 1 In the eighteenth year, the twenty-
second day of the first month, there was
talk in the house of Nevukhadnetstsar king
of the Ashuwrites, that he should be
avenged on all the land, even as he spoke.
2 He called together all his servants and all
his great men, and communicated with
them his secret counsel, and concluded the
afflicting of all the land out of his own
mouth. 3 They decreed to destroy all flesh
which did not follow the word of his
mouth. 4 It happened, when he had ended
his counsel, Nevukhadnetstsar king of the
Ashuwrites called Olofernes the chief
captain of his army, which was next after
himself, and said to him, 5 "Thus says the
great king, the master of all the earth:
'Behold, you shall go out from my
presence, and take with you men who trust
in their strength, *even up* to one hundred
and twenty thousand footmen and twelve
thousand horsemen. 6 And you shall go out
against all the west country, because they
disobeyed the command of my mouth.
7 You shall declare to them that they should
prepare earth and water, because I will go
out in my wrath against them, and will
cover the whole face of the earth with the
feet of my army, and I will give them as
plunder to them. 8 Their slain will fill their
valleys and brooks, and the river will be
filled with their dead until it overflows. 9 I
will lead them captives to the utmost parts
of all the earth. 10 But you shall go forth,
and take all their coasts for me first. If they
will yield themselves to you, then you must
reserve them for me until the day of their
reproof. 11 As for those who are
disobedient, your eye shall not spare; but
you shall give them up to be slain and to be
plundered in all your land. 12 For as I live,
and by the power of my kingdom, I have
spoken, and I will do this with my hand.
13 Moreover, you shall not transgress
anything of the commands of your master,
but you shall surely accomplish them, as I
have commanded you. You shall not defer
to do them.'"

14 So Olofernes went out from the presence
of his master, and called all the governors,
the captains, and officers of the army of
Ashuwr. 15 He counted chosen men for the
battle, as his master had commanded him,
even one hundred and twenty thousand,
with twelve thousand archers on horseback.
16 He arranged them as a great multitude is
ordered for war. 17 He took camels and
donkeys and mules for their equipment, an
exceedingly great multitude, and sheep and
oxen and goats without number for their
provision, 18 and great stores of rations for
every man, and exceedingly much gold and
silver out of the king's house. 19 He went
out, he and all his army, on their journey, to
go before king Nevukhadnetstsar, and to
cover all the face of the earth westward
with their chariots, horsemen, and chosen
footmen. 20 A great company of various
nations went out with them like locusts,
and like the sand of the earth. For there
were so many that they could not be
counted.

21 And they departed out of Nineveh three
days' journey toward the plain of Beth-

Qetilath[a], and encamped from Beth-
Qetilath near the mountain which is at the
left hand of the upper Kilikia. 22 And he
took all his army, his footmen, horsemen,
and chariots, and went away from there into
the hill country, 23 and destroyed Put and
Lud, and plundered all the children of
Rhasseis and the children of Yishma'el,
which were along the wilderness to the
south of the land of the Ḥalutsites. 24 And
he went over *the River* Perath, and went
through Aram-Naharayim, and broke down
all the high cities that were upon the river
Arbonai, until you come to the sea.

25 And he took possession of the borders of
Kilikia, and killed all that resisted him, and
came to the borders of Yepheth, which
were toward the south, opposite Aravia.
26 He surrounded all the children of
Midian, and set their tents on fire, and
plundered their sheepfolds. 27 He went
down into the plain of Dammeseq in the
days of wheat harvest, and set all their
fields on fire, and utterly destroyed their
flocks and herds, and plundered their cities,
laid their plains waste, and struck all their
young men with the edge of the sword.
28 And the fear and the dread of him fell
upon those who lived on the sea coast,
upon those who were in Tsidon and Tsor,
those who lived in Sur and Okeina, and all
who lived in Yavni'el. Those who lived in
Ashdod and Ashqelon feared him
exceedingly.

3 1 And they sent messengers to him with
words of peace, saying, 2 "Behold, we the
servants of Nevukhadnetstsar the great king
lie before you. Use us as it is pleasing in
your eyes. 3 Behold, our dwellings, and all
our country, and all our fields of wheat, and
our flocks and herds, and all the sheepfolds
of our tents, lie before your face. Use them
as it may please you. 4 Behold, even our
cities and those who dwell in them are your
servants. Come and deal with them as it is
good in your eyes."

5 So the men came to Olofernes, and
declared to him according to these words.

6 He came down toward the sea coast, he
and his army, and set garrisons in the high
cities, and took out of them chosen men for
allies. 7 They received him, they and all the
country round about them, with wreaths
and dances and timbrels. 8 He cast down all
their borders, and cut down their sacred
groves. It had been given to him to destroy
all the elohim of the land, that all the
nations would worship Nevukhadnetstsar
only, and that all their languages and their
tribes would call upon him as el. 9 Then he
came towards Yizreel near to Dothan,
which is opposite the great ridge of
Yehudah. 10 He encamped between Geba
and Beth-Shean. He was there a whole
month, that he might gather together all the
equipment of his army.

4 1 The children of Yisra'el that lived in
Yehudah heard all that Olofernes the chief
captain of Nevukhadnetstsar king of the
Ashuwrites had done to the nations, and
how he had plundered all their temples and
destroyed them utterly. 2 They were
exceedingly afraid of him, and were

---

[a] 2:21 Beth-Qetilath – In Greek this is given as Βεκτιλὲθ (*Bektileth*). However, this is most likely a corruption of an Aramaic phrase, Beth (ܒܝܬ) meaning "house" and Qetilath (ܩܛܝܠܬ) meaning "slaughter."

troubled for Yerushalayim, and for the
Temple of יהוה their Elohim; 3 because
they had recently come up from the
captivity, and all the people of Yehudah
were recently gathered together; and the
vessels, the altar, and the house were set
apart after being profaned.

4 And they sent into every coast of
Shom'ron, to Yoqneam, to Beth-Ḥoron,
Yivleam, Yeriḥo, to Ḥoba, Aesora, and to
the valley of Salem; 5 and they occupied
beforehand all the tops of the high
mountains, fortified the villages that were
in them, stored supplies for the provision of
war; for their fields were newly reaped.

6 Yoyaqim the high priest, who was in
those days at Yerushalayim, wrote to those
who lived in Bethulyah, and Beth-
Omesthayim, which is opposite Yizreel
toward the plain that is near to Dothan,
7 charging them to seize upon the ascents
of the hill country; because the entrance
into Yehudah was by them, and it was easy
to stop them from approaching as the
approach was narrow, with space for not
more than two men. 8 And the children of
Yisra'el did as Yoyaqim the high priest had
commanded them, as did the council of all
the people of Yisra'el, which lived at
Yerushalayim.

9 And every man of Yisra'el cried to
Elohim with great sincerity, and with great
sincerity they humbled their beings.
10 They, their wives, their children, their
cattle, and every sojourner, hired worker,
and servant bought with their money put
sackcloth on their loins. 11 Every man and
woman of Yisra'el, and the little children,
and the inhabitants of Yerushalayim, fell
down before the Temple, and cast ashes
upon their heads, and spread out their
sackcloth before יהוה. They put sackcloth
around the altar. 12 They cried to the
Elohim of Yisra'el sincerely with one
accord, that He would not give their
children as plunder, their wives as spoil, the
cities of their inheritance to destruction,
and the set-apart place to being profaned
and being made a reproach, for the nations
to rejoice at. 13 יהוה heard their voice, and
looked at their affliction. The people
continued fasting many days in all
Yehudah and Yerushalayim before the set-
apart place of יהוה Almighty.

14 And Yoyaqim the high priest, and all the
priests that stood before יהוה, and those
who attended to יהוה, had their loins
dressed in sackcloth, and offered the
continual burnt offering, the vows, and the
free gifts of the people. 15 They had ashes
on their turbans. They cried to יהוה with
all their might, that He would look upon all
the house of Yisra'el for good.

5 1 Olofernes, the chief captain of the army
of Ashuwr, was told that the children of
Yisra'el had prepared for war, had shut up
the passages of the hill country, had
fortified all the tops of the high hills, and
had laid traps in the plains. 2 Then he was
exceedingly angry, and he called all the
princes of Moav, and the captains of
Ammon, and all the governors of the sea
coast, 3 and he said to them, "Tell me now,
you sons of Kana'an, who are these people
who dwell in the hill country? What are the
cities that they inhabit? How large is their
army? Where is their power and their
strength? What king is set over them, to be
the leader of their army? 4 Why have they
turned their backs, that they should not

come and meet me, more than all that dwell
in the west?"

5 Then Aḥihud, the leader of all the
children of Ammon, said to him, "Let my
master now hear a word from the mouth of
your servant, and I will tell you the truth
concerning these people who dwell in this
hill country, near to the place where you
dwell. No lie will come out of the mouth of
your servant. 6 These people are descended
from the Kaldeans. 7 They sojourned before
this in Aram-Naharayim, because they did
not want to follow the elohim of their
fathers, which were in the land of the
Kaldeans. 8 They departed from the way of
their parents, and worshiped the Elohim of
heaven, the Elohim whom they knew. Their
parents cast them out from the face of their
elohim, and they fled into Aram-
Naharayim, and sojourned there many
days. 9 Then their Elohim commanded
them to depart from the place where they
sojourned, and to go into the land of
Kana'an. They lived there, and prospered
with gold and silver, and with exceedingly
much cattle. 10 Then they went down into
Mitsrayim, for a famine covered all the
land of Kana'an. They sojourned there until
they had grown up. They became a great
multitude there, so that one could not count
the population of their nation.

11 "Then the king of Mitsrayim rose up
against them, and dealt subtly with them,
and brought them low, making them labor
in bricks, and made them slaves. 12 They
cried to their Elohim, and He struck all the
land of Mitsrayim with incurable plagues;
so the Mitsrites cast them out of their sight.
13 Elohim dried up the Sea of Reeds before
them, 14 and brought them into the way of
Sinai Qadesh-Barnea, and they cast out all
that lived in the wilderness. 15 They lived
in the land of the Amorites, and they
destroyed by their strength everyone in
Ḥeshbon. Passing over *the* Yarden, they
possessed all the hill country. 16 They cast
out the Kana'anite, the Perizzite, the
Yevusite, the Shekhemite, and all the
Girgashites before them, and they lived in
that country many days. 17 And when they
did not sin before their Elohim, they
prospered, because Elohim who hates
lawlessness was with them.

18 "But when they departed from the way
which He appointed for them, they were
destroyed in many severe battles, and were
led as captives into a land that was not
theirs. The Temple of their Elohim was cast
to the ground, and their cities were taken by
their adversaries. 19 And now they have
returned to their Elohim, and have come up
from the dispersion where they were
dispersed, and have possessed
Yerushalayim, where their set-apart place
is, and are seated in the hill country, for it
was desolate. 20 And now, my master and
ruler, if there is any error in this people,
and they sin against their Elohim, we will
consider this thing in which they stumble,
and we will go up and overcome them.
21 But if there is no lawlessness in their
nation, let my master now pass by, lest
their Master defend them, and their Elohim
be for them, and we will be a reproach
before all the earth."

22 It happened, when Aḥihud had finished
speaking these words, all the people
standing around the tent began to murmur.
The great men of Olofernes, and all that
lived by the seaside and in Moav, all saying
that he should kill him. 23 For, they said,
"We will not be afraid of the children of
Yisra'el; for behold, they are a people that
have no power nor might to make the battle

strong. 24 Therefore now we will go up,
and they will be plunder to be devoured by
all your army, Master Olofernes."

6 1 And when the disturbance of the men
that were around the council had ceased,
Olofernes the chief captain of the army of
Ashuwr said to Aḥihud and to all the
children of Moav before all the people of
the foreigners,

2 "And who are you, Aḥihud, and the hired
workers of Ephrayim, that you have
prophesied among us as today, and have
said that we should not make war with the
race of Yisra'el, because their Elohim will
defend them? And who is Elohim but
Nevukhadnetstsar? 3 He will send forth his
might, and will destroy them from the face
of the earth, and their Elohim will not
deliver them; but we his servants will strike
them as one man. They will not withstand
the might of our horses. 4 For with them we
will burn them up. Their mountains will be
drunken with their blood. Their plains will
be filled with their dead bodies. Their
footsteps will not stand before us, but they
will surely perish, says king
Nevukhadnetstsar, master of all the earth;
for he said, 'The words that I have spoken
will not be in vain.' 5 But you, Aḥihud,
hireling of Ammon, who have spoken these
words in the day of your iniquity, will see
my face no more from this day, until I am
avenged of the race of those that came out
of Mitsrayim. 6 And then the sword of my
army, and the multitude of those who serve
me, will pass through your sides, and you
will fall among their slain when I return.
7 Then my servants will bring you back
into the hill country, and will set you in one
of the cities of the ascents. 8 You will not
perish until you are destroyed with them.
9 And if you hope in your heart that they
will not be taken, do not let your
countenance fall. I have spoken it, and none
of my words will fall to the ground."

10 Then Olofernes commanded his servants
who waited in his tent to take Aḥihud, and
bring him back to Bethulyah, and deliver
him into the hands of the children of
Yisra'el. 11 So his servants took him, and
brought him out of the camp into the plain,
and they moved from the midst of the
plains into the hill country, and came to the
springs that were under Bethulyah.
12 When the men of the city saw them on
the top of the hill, they took up their
weapons, and went out of the city against
them to the top of the hill. Every man that
used a sling kept them from coming up, and
cast stones against them. 13 They took
cover under the hill, bound Aḥihud, cast
him down, left him at the foot of the hill,
and went away to their master.

14 But the children of Yisra'el descended
from their city, and came to him, untied
him, led him away into Bethulyah, and
presented him to the rulers of their city,
who 15 were in those days Uzziyah the son
of Mikhah, of the tribe of Shimon, and
Ḥabris the son of Othni'el, and Ḥarmis the
son of Melkhi'el. 16 Then they called
together all the elders of the city; and all
their young men ran together, with their
women, to the assembly. They set Aḥihud
in the midst of all their people. Then
Uzziyah asked him what had happened.
17 He answered and declared to them the
words of the council of Olofernes, and all
the words that he had spoken in the midst
of the princes of the children of Ashuwr,
and all the great words that Olofernes had
spoken against the house of Yisra'el.

18 Then the people fell down and
worshiped Elohim, and cried, saying, 19 "O
יהוה Elohim of heaven, behold their
arrogance, and pity the low estate of our
race. Look upon the face of those who are
set apart to You this day."

20 They comforted Aḥihud, and praised him
exceedingly. 21 Then Uzziyah took him out
of the assembly into his house, and made a
banquet for the elders. They called on the
Elohim of Yisra'el for help all that night.

7 1 The next day Olofernes commanded all
his army and all the people who had come
to be his allies, that they should move their
camp toward Bethulyah, take beforehand
the ascents of the hill country, and make
war against the children of Yisra'el. 2 Every
mighty man of them moved that day. The
army of their men of war was one hundred
and seventy thousand footmen, plus twelve
thousand horsemen, besides the equipment,
and the men that were on foot among them:
an exceedingly great multitude. 3 They
encamped in the valley near Bethulyah, by
the fountain. They spread themselves in
width over Dothan even to Yivleam, and in
length from Bethulyah to Cyamon, which is
near Yizreel.

4 But the children of Yisra'el, when they
saw the multitude of them, were troubled
exceedingly, and everyone said to his
neighbor, "Now these men will lick up the
face of all the earth. Neither the high
mountains, nor the valleys, nor the hills
will be able to bear their weight." 5 Every
man took up his weapons of war, and when
they had kindled fires upon their towers,
they remained and watched all that night.

6 But on the second day Olofernes led out
all his cavalry in the sight of the children of
Yisra'el which were in Bethulyah, 7 viewed
the ascents to their city, and searched out
the springs of the waters, seized them, and
set garrisons of men of war over them.
Then he departed back to his people.

8 All the rulers of the children of Esav, all
the leaders of the people of Moav, and the
captains of the sea coast came to him and
said, 9 "Let our master now hear a word, so
that there will not be any losses in your
army. 10 For this people, the children of
Yisra'el, do not trust in their spears, but in
the height of the mountains in which they
dwell, for it is not easy to come up to the
tops of their mountains. 11 And now, my
master, do not fight against them as men
fight who join battle, and there will not so
much as one man of your people perish.
12 Remain in your camp, and keep every
man of your army safe. Let your servants
take possession of the water spring, which
flows from the foot of the mountain,
13 because all the inhabitants of Bethulyah
get their water from there. Then thirst will
kill them, and they will give up their city.
Then we and our people will go up to the
tops of the mountains that are near, and will
encamp upon them, to watch that not one
man gets out of the city. 14 They will be
consumed with famine, they and their
wives and their children. Before the sword
comes against them they will be laid low in
the streets where they dwell. 15 And you
will pay them back with evil, because they
rebelled, and did not meet your face in
peace."

16 Their words were pleasing in the eyes of
Olofernes and in the sight of all his
servants; and he ordered them to do as they
had spoken. 17 And the army of the

children of Ammon moved, and with them
five thousand of the children of Ashuwr,
and they encamped in the valley. They
seized the waters and the springs of the
waters of the children of Yisra'el. 18 The
children of Esav went up with the children
of Ammon, and encamped in the hill
country near Dothan. They sent some of
them toward the south, and toward the east,
near Akrabeh, which is near Quzah, that is
upon the brook Makhphuryeh. The rest of
the army of the Ashuwrites encamped in
the plain, and covered all the face of the
land. Their tents were pitched upon it in a
great crowd, with their equipment. They
were an exceedingly great multitude.

19 The children of Yisra'el cried to יהוה
their Elohim, for their spirit fainted; for all
their enemies had surrounded them. There
was no way to escape out from among
them. 20 All the army of Ashuwr remained
around them, their footmen and their
chariots and their horsemen, thirty-four
days. All their vessels of water ran dry for
all the inhabitants of Bethulyah. 21 The
cisterns were emptied, and they had no
water to drink their fill for one day; for they
rationed drink by measure. 22 Their young
children were discouraged. The women and
the young men fainted for thirst. They fell
down in the streets of the city, and in the
passages of the gates. There was no longer
any strength in them.

23 All the people, including the young men,
the women, and the children, were gathered
together against Uzziyah, and against the
rulers of the city. They cried with a loud
voice, and said before all the elders,
24 "Elohim be judge between all of you and
us, because you have done us great wrong,
in that you have not spoken words of peace
with the children of Ashuwr. 25 Now we
have no helper; but Elohim has sold us into
their hands, that we should be laid low
before them with thirst and great
destruction. 26 And now summon them, and
deliver up the whole city as plunder to the
people of Olofernes, and to all his army.
27 For it is better for us to be made a spoil
to them. For we will be servants, and our
beings will live, and we will not see the
death of our infants before our eyes, and
our wives and our children fainting in
death. 28 We bring the heaven and the earth
to witness against you, and our Elohim and
the Master of our fathers, who punishes us
according to our sins and the sins of our
fathers. Do what we have said today!"

29 And there was great weeping of all with
one accord in the midst of the assembly;
and they cried to יהוה Elohim with a loud
voice. 30 And Uzziyah said to them,
"Brothers, take courage! Let us endure five
more days, during which *time* יהוה our
Elohim will turn His kindness toward us;
for He will not forsake us completely.
31 But if these days pass, and no help
comes to us, I will do what you say."

32 Then he dispersed the people, everyone
to his own camp; and they went away to the
walls and towers of their city. He sent the
women and children into their houses. They
were brought very low in the city.

8 1 In those days Yehudith heard about
this. She was the daughter of Merari, the
son of Aḥ, the son of Yoseph, the son of
Uzzi'el, the son of Elqiyah, the son of
Ḥananyah, the son of Gidon, the son of
Raphayim, the son of Aḥituv, the son of
Elihu, the son of Eliav, the son of
Nathana'el, the son of Shelumi'el, the son

of Tsurishaddai,[a] the son of Yisra'el. 2 Her
husband was Menasheh, *who was* of her
tribe and of her family. He died in the days
of barley harvest. 3 For he stood over those
who bound sheaves in the field, and the
heat came upon his head, and he fell on his
bed, and died in his city Bethulyah. So they
buried him with his fathers in the field
which is between Dothan and Ba'al-
Hamon.

4 Yehudith was a widow in her house three
years and four months. 5 She made herself
a tent upon the roof of her house, and put
on sackcloth upon her loins. The garments
of her widowhood were upon her. 6 And
she fasted all the days of her widowhood,
except the eves of the Sabbaths, the
Sabbaths, the eves of the new moons, the
new moons, and the Feasts and joyful days
of the house of Yisra'el. 7 She was of a fair
appearance and *was* exceedingly beautiful
to look upon. Her husband, Menasheh, had
left her gold, silver, manservants,
maidservants, cattle, and lands. She
remained on those lands. 8 No one said
anything evil about her; for she feared
Elohim greatly.

9 She heard the evil words of the people
against the governor, because they fainted
for lack of water; and Yehudith heard all
the words that Uzziyah spoke to them, how
he swore to them that he would deliver the
city to the Ashuwrites after five days. 10 So
she sent her maid, who was over all things
that she had, to summon Uzziyah, Ḥabris,
and Ḥarmis, the elders of her city.

11 They came to her, and she said to them,
"Hear me now, O you rulers of the
inhabitants of Bethulyah: for your word
that you have spoken before the people this
day is not right. You have set the oath
which you have pronounced between you
and Elohim, and have promised to deliver
the city to our enemies, unless within these
days יהוה turns to help you. 12 Now who
are you, that you have tried Elohim today,
and stand in the place of Elohim among the
children of men? 13 Now try יהוה
Almighty, and you will never know
anything. 14 For you will not find the depth
of the heart of man, and you do not
perceive the things that he thinks; how then
will you search out Elohim, who has made
all these things, and know His mind, and
understand His purpose? No, my brothers,
do not provoke יהוה our Elohim to anger!
15 For if He has not decided to help us
within these five days, He has power to
defend us in such time as He will, or to
destroy us before the face of our enemies.

16 "But do not pledge the counsels of יהוה
our Elohim! For Elohim is not like man,
that He can be threatened; nor *is He* like the
son of man, that He can be turned by
appeal. 17 Therefore let us wait for the
salvation that comes from Him, and call
upon Him to help us. He will hear our
voice, if it pleases Him. 18 For none in our
age have arisen, neither are there any of us
today, tribe, or brethren, or family, or city,
which bow down to elohim made with
hands, as it was in the former days; 19 for
which cause our fathers were given to the
sword, and for plunder, and fell with a
great fall before our enemies. 20 But we
know no other el beside Him. Therefore we
hope that He will not despise us, nor any of
our race. 21 For if we are taken thus, all

---

[a] 8:1 A few generations are omitted here, but this is the lineage of Shimon, one of the 12 tribes of Yisra'el. Compare Bemidbar [Numbers] 1:6; Yehudith 9:2.

Yehudah will sit upon the ground, and our
set-apart place will be plundered; and He
will require our blood for profaning it.
22 And the slaughter of our brothers, and
the captivity of the land, and the desolation
of our inheritance, He will turn upon our
heads among the nations, wherever we will
be in bondage. We will be an offense and a
reproach before those who take possession
of us. 23 For our bondage will not be
ordered to favor; but יהוה our Elohim will
turn it to dishonor.

24 "And now, brothers, let us show an
example to our brethren, because their
being hangs upon us, and the set-apart
place, the House, and the altar rest upon us.
25 Besides all this, let us give thanks to
יהוה our Elohim, who tries us, even as He
did our fathers also. 26 Remember all the
things which He did to Avraham, and all
the things in which He tried Yitschaq, and
all the things which happened to Ya'aqov in
Aram-Naharayim of Syria, when he kept
the sheep of Lavan his mother's brother.
27 For He has not tried us in the fire, as He
did them, to search out their hearts, neither
has He taken vengeance on us; but יהוה
does chastise them that come near to Him,
to admonish them."

28 And Uzziyah said to her, "All that you
have spoken, you have spoken with a good
heart. There is no one who will deny your
words. 29 For this is not the first day in
which your wisdom is manifested; but from
the beginning of your days all the people
have known your understanding, because
the disposition of your heart is good. 30 But
the people were exceedingly thirsty, and
compelled us to do as we spoke to them,
and to bring an oath upon ourselves, which
we will not break. 31 And now pray for us,
because you are a reverent woman, and
יהוה will send us rain to fill our cisterns,
and we will faint no more."

32 Then Yehudith said to them, "Hear me,
and I will do a thing, which will go down to
all generations among the children of our
race. 33 You shall all stand at the gate
tonight. I will go out with my maid. Within
the days after which you said that you
would deliver the city to our enemies; יהוה
will visit Yisra'el by my hand. 34 But you
shall not inquire of my act; for I will not
declare it to you, until the things are
finished that I will do."

35 Then Uzziyah and the rulers said to her,
"Go in peace. May יהוה Elohim be before
you, to take vengeance on our enemies."
36 So they returned from the tent, and went
to their stations.

9 1 But Yehudith fell upon her face, and
put ashes upon her head, and uncovered the
sackcloth with which she was clothed. The
incense of that evening was now being
offered at Yerushalayim in the House of
Elohim, and Yehudith cried to יהוה with a
loud voice, and said, 2 "O יהוה Elohim of
my father Shimon, into whose hand You
gave a sword to take vengeance on the
foreigners who loosened the belt of a virgin
to defile her, uncovered the thigh to her
shame, and profaned the womb to her
reproach; for You said, 'It shall not be so;'
and they did so.[a] 3 Therefore You gave

---

[a] 9:2 The story of the violation of the virgin is most likely a reference to Dinah, the daughter of Ya'aqov, sister of Shimon. According to B'reshiyt [Genesis] 34, Shimon and Levi

their rulers to be slain, and their bed, which
was ashamed for her who was deceived, to
be dyed in blood, and struck the servants
with their masters, and the masters upon
their thrones; **4** and gave their wives for
plunder, and their daughters to be captives,
and all their spoils to be divided among
Your dear children; which were moved
with zeal for You, and abhorred the
pollution of their blood, and called upon
You for aid. O Elohim, O my Elohim, hear
me also who is a widow.

5 "For You did that which was before those
things, and those things, and things that
come after; and You planned the things
which now occur, and the things which are
to come. The things which You planned
happened. **6** Yes, the things which You
determined stood before You, and said,
'Behold, we are here; for all Your ways are
prepared, and Your judgment is known
beforehand.'

7 "For, behold, the Ashuwrites are
multiplied in their power. They are exalted
with horse and rider. They were proud of
the strength of their footmen. They have
trusted in shield, spear, bow, and sling.
They do not know that You are יהוה, who
breaks the battles. יהוה is Your Name.
8 Break their strength in Your power, and
bring down their force in Your wrath; for
they intend to profane Your set-apart place,
and to defile the Tabernacle where Your
glorious Name rests, and to destroy the
horn of Your altar with the sword. **9** Look
at their pride, and send Your wrath upon
their heads. Give into my hand, who is a
widow, the might that I have conceived.
10 Strike the servant with the prince by the
deceit of my lips, and the prince with his
servant. Break down their arrogance by the
hand of a woman. **11** For Your power
stands not in multitude, nor Your might in
strong men. But You are the Elohim of the
afflicted. You are a helper of the minorities,
a helper of the weak, a protector of the
forsaken, a savior of those who are without
hope. **12** Yes, yes, Elohim of my father, and
Elohim of the inheritance of Yisra'el,
Master of the heavens and of the earth.
Creator of the waters, King of every
creature, hear my prayer. **13** Make my
speech and deceit to be their wound and
stripe, who intend hard things against Your
covenant, Your set-apart House, the top of
Tsion, and the house of the possession of
Your children. **14** Make every nation and
tribe of Yours to know that You are
Elohim, the Elohim of all power and might,
and that there is none other that protects the
race of Yisra'el but You."

10 **1** It happened, when she had ceased to
cry to the Elohim of Yisra'el, and had
finished saying all these words, **2** that she
rose up where she had fallen down, called
her maid, and went down into the house
that she used to live in on the Sabbath days
and on her Feast days. **3** She pulled off the
sackcloth which she had put on, took off
the garments of her widowhood, washed
her body all over with water, anointed
herself with precious ointment, braided the
hair of her head, and put a tiara[a] upon it.
She put on her garments of gladness, which

---

destroyed the entire city of Shekhem because the prince had violated their sister.

[a] 10:3 Tiara – Greek word μιτραν (*mitran*), meaning "miter." This is usually understood as a sort of headdress, or more commonly a turban. However women were not often seen with a turban, thus it most likely refers to some sort of jeweled headdress.

she used to wear in the days of the life of Menasheh her husband. 4 She took sandals for her feet, and put her necklace around her, and her bracelets, her rings, her earrings, and all her ornaments, and decked herself greatly, to deceive the eyes of all men who would see her. 5 She gave her maid a leather container of wine and a flask of oil, and filled a bag with parched corn, lumps of figs, and fine bread. She packed all her vessels together, and laid them upon her.

6 They went out to the gate of the city of Bethulyah, and found Uzziyah and the elders of the city, Ḥabris and Ḥarmis standing by it. 7 But when they saw her, that her countenance was altered and her apparel was changed, they wondered greatly at her beauty, and said to her, 8 "May the Elohim of our fathers give you favor, and accomplish your purposes to the glory of the children of Yisra'el, and to the exaltation of Yerushalayim." Then she bowed down to Elohim.

9 She said to them, "Command that they open the gate of the city for me, and I will go out to accomplish the things you spoke with me about." And they commanded the young men to open to her, as she had spoken; 10 and they did so. Then Yehudith went out, she, and her handmaid with her. The men of the city watched her until she had gone down the mountain, until she had passed the valley, and they could see her no more. 11 They went straight onward in the valley. The watch of the Ashuwrites met her; 12 and they took her, and asked her, "Of what people are you? Where are you coming from? Where are you going?" She said, "I am a daughter of the Hebrews. I am fleeing away from their presence, because they are about to be given you to be consumed. 13 I am coming into the presence of Olofernes the chief captain of your army, to declare words of truth. I will show him a way that he can go and win all the hill country, and not one of his men will be lacking, nor one life *lost*."

14 Now when the men heard her words, and considered her countenance, her beauty was exceedingly great in their eyes. They said to her, 15 "You have saved your life, in that you have hurried to come down to the presence of our master. Now come to his tent. Some of us will guide you until they deliver you into his hands. 16 But when you stand before him, do not be afraid in your heart, but declare to him according to your words; and he will treat you well." 17 They chose out of them a hundred men, and appointed them to accompany her and her maid; and they brought them to the tent of Olofernes.

18 And there was great excitement throughout all the camp, for her coming was reported among the tents. They came and surrounded her as she stood outside Olofernes' tent, until they told him about her. 19 They marveled at her beauty, and marveled at the children of Yisra'el because of her. Each one said to his neighbor, "Who would despise this people, that have among them such women? For it is not good that one man of them be left, seeing that, if they are let go, they will be able to deceive the whole earth."

20 Those who lay near Olofernes, and all his servants, went out and brought her into the tent. 21 And Olofernes was resting upon his bed under the canopy, which was woven with purple, gold, emeralds, and precious stones. 22 And they told him about her; and he came out into the space before

his tent, with silver lamps going before
him. 23 But when Yehudith had come
before him and his servants, they all
marveled at the beauty of her countenance.
She fell down upon her face, and bowed
down to him, but his servants raised her up.

11 1 Olofernes said to her, "Woman, take
courage. Do not be afraid in your heart; for
I never hurt anyone who has chosen to
serve Nevukhadnetstsar, the king of all the
earth. 2 And now, if your people who dwell
in the hill country had not insulted me, I
would not have lifted up my spear against
them; but they have done these things to
themselves. 3 And now tell me why you
fled from them and came to us; for you
have come to save yourself. Take courage!
You will live tonight, and hereafter; 4 for
there is no one that will wrong you, but all
will treat you well, as is done to the
servants of King Nevukhadnetstsar my
master."

5 And Yehudith said to him, "Receive the
words of your servant, and let your
handmaid speak in your presence, and I
will declare no lie to my master this night.
6 If you will follow the words of your
handmaid, Elohim will make this thing
happen perfectly with you; and my master
will not fail to accomplish his purposes.
7 As Nevukhadnetstsar king of all the earth
lives, and as his power lives, who has sent
you for the preservation of every living
thing, not only do men serve him by you,
but also the beasts of the field, the cattle,
and the birds of the heavens will live
through your strength, in the time of
Nevukhadnetstsar and of all his house.
8 For we have heard of your wisdom and
the subtle plans of your being. It has been
reported in all the earth that you alone are
brave in all the kingdom, mighty in
knowledge, and wonderful in feats of war.
9 And now as concerning the matter which
Aḥihud spoke in your council, we have
heard his words; for the men of Bethulyah
saved him, and he declared to them all that
he had spoken before you.

10 "Therefore, O master and ruler, do not
neglect his word; but lay it up in your heart,
for it is true; for our race will not be
punished, neither will the sword prevail
against them, unless they sin against their
Elohim. 11 And now, that my master be not
defeated and frustrate of his purpose, and
that death may fall upon them, their sin has
overtaken them, with which they will
provoke their Elohim to anger, whenever
they do wickedness. 12 Since their food
failed them, and all their water was scant,
they took counsel to lay hands upon their
cattle, and determined to consume all those
things which Elohim charged them by His
laws that they should not eat. 13 They are
resolved to spend the first fruits of the corn,
and the tenths of the wine and the oil,
which they had set apart and reserved for
the priests who stand before the face of our
Elohim in Yerushalayim; things which are
not fitting for any of the people so much as
to touch with their hands. 14 They have sent
some to Yerushalayim, because they also
that dwell there have done this thing, to
bring them permission from the council of
elders.

15 "It will be, when word comes to them
and they do it, they will be given to you to
be destroyed the same day. 16 Therefore I
your servant, knowing all this, fled away
from their presence. Elohim sent me to
work things with you, at which all the earth
will be astonished, even as many as hear it.

17 For your servant is reverent, and serves
the Elohim of heaven day and night. Now,
my master, I will stay with you, and your
servant will go out by night into the valley.
I will pray to Elohim, and He will tell me
when they have committed their sins.
18 Then I will come and show it also to
you. Then you shall go out with all your
army, and there will be none of them that
will resist you. 19 And I will lead you
through the midst of Yehudah, until you
come to Yerushalayim. I will set your seat
in the midst of it. You will drive them as
sheep that have no shepherd, and a dog will
not so much as open his mouth before you;
for these things were told to me according
to my foreknowledge, and were declared to
me, and I was sent to tell you."

20 Her words were pleasing in the eyes of
Olofernes and of all his servants. They
marveled at her wisdom, and said,
21 "There is not such a woman from one
end of the earth to the other, for beauty of
face and wisdom of words."

22 Olofernes said to her, "Elohim did well
to send you before the people, that might
would be in our hands, and destruction
among those who insulted my master.
23 And now you are beautiful in your
appearance, and wise in your words. If you
will do as you have spoken, your Elohim
will be my Elohim, and you will dwell in
the house of King Nevukhadnetstsar, and
will be renowned through the whole earth."

12 1 He commanded that she should be
brought in where his silver vessels were
set, and asked that his servants should
prepare some of his own meats for her, and
that she should drink from his own wine.

2 And Yehudith said, "I will not eat of it,
lest there be an occasion of stumbling; but
provision will be made for me of the things
that have come with me."

3 And Olofernes said to her, "But if the
things that are with you should fail, from
where will we be able to give you more like
it? For there is none of your race with us."

4 And Yehudith said to him, "As your
being lives, my master, your servant will
not spend those things that are with me,
until יהוה works by my hand the things
that He has determined."

5 Then Olofernes' servants brought her into
the tent, and she slept until midnight. Then
she rose up toward the morning watch,
6 and sent to Olofernes, saying, "Let my
master now command that they allow your
servant to go out to pray."

7 Olofernes commanded his guards that
they should not stop her. She stayed in the
camp three days, and went out every night
into the valley of Bethulyah, and washed
herself at the fountain of water in the camp.
8 And when she came up, she asked יהוה
Elohim of Yisra'el to direct her way to the
raising up of the children of His people.
9 She came in clean, and remained in the
tent, until she ate her food toward evening.
10 It happened on the fourth day, that
Olofernes made a banquet for his own
servants only, and called none of the
officers to the it.

11 And he said to Bagoas the eunuch, who
had charge over all that he had, "Go now,
and persuade this Hebrew woman who is
with you that she come to us, and eat and
drink with us. 12 For, behold, it is a shame
for us, if we shall let such a woman go, not

having had her company; for if we do not
draw her to ourselves, she will laugh us to
contempt."

13 Bagoas went from the presence of
Olofernes, and came in to her, and said,
"Let this fair lady not fear to come to my
master, and to be honored in his presence,
and to drink wine and be joyful with us,
and to be made this day as one of the
daughters of the children of Ashuwr, which
wait in the house of Nevukhadnetstsar."

14 Yehudith said to him, "Who am I, that I
should oppose my master? For whatever
would be pleasing in his eyes, I will do
quickly, and this will be my joy to the day
of my death." 15 She arose, and decked
herself with her apparel and all her
womanly attire; and her servant went and
laid fleeces on the ground for her next to
Olofernes, which she had received from
Bagoas for her daily use, that she might sit
and eat upon them.

16 Yehudith came in and sat down, and
Olofernes' heart was ravished with her. His
being was moved, and he exceedingly
desired her company. He was watching for
a time to deceive her, from the day that he
had seen her. 17 Olofernes said to her,
"Drink now, and be joyful with us."

18 Yehudith said, "I will drink now, my
master, because my life is magnified in me
this day more than all the days since I was
born." 19 Then she took and ate and drank
before him what her servant had prepared.
20 Olofernes took great delight in her, and
drank a vast amount of wine, more than he
had drunk at any time in one day since he
was born.

13 1 But when the evening had come, his
servants hurried to depart. Bagoas shut the
tent outside, and dismissed those who
waited from the presence of his master.
They went away to their beds; for they
were all weary, because the banquet had
been long. 2 But Yehudith was left alone in
the tent, with Olofernes lying along upon
his bed; for he was drunk with wine.
3 Yehudith had said to her servant that she
should stand outside her bedchamber, and
wait for her to come out, as she did daily;
for she said she would go out to her prayer.
She spoke to Bagoas according to the same
words. 4 All went away from her presence,
and none was left in the bedchamber, small
or great. Yehudith, standing by his bed,
said in her heart, "O יהוה Elohim of all
power, look in this hour upon the works of
my hands for the exaltation of
Yerushalayim. 5 For now is the time to help
Your inheritance, and to do the thing that I
have purposed to the destruction of the
enemies which have risen up against us."

6 She came to the rail of the bed, which was
at Olofernes' head, and took down his
akinakes[a] from there. 7 She drew near to the
bed, took hold of the hair of his head, and
said, "Strengthen me, O יהוה Elohim of
Yisra'el, this day."

8 She struck twice upon his neck with all
her might, and took away his head from
him, 9 tumbled his body down from the
bed, and took down the canopy from the

[a] 13:6 Akinakes – Greek word for a type of short sword used initially by Parasians, but subsequently adopted by Scythians and Greeks. It is often compared to a scimitar due to its curved blade, or to a katana due to its short length.

pillars. After a little while she went out,
and gave Olofernes' head to her maid;
10 and she put it in her bag of food. They
both went out together to prayer, according
to their custom. They passed through the
camp, circled around that valley, and went
up to the mountain of Bethulyah, and came
to its gates.

11 Yehudith said afar off to the watchmen
at the gates, "Open, open the gate now.
Elohim is with us, even our Elohim, to
show His power again in Yisra'el, and His
might against the enemy, as He has done
even today."

12 It happened, when the men of her city
heard her voice, they made haste to go
down to the gate of their city, and they
called together the elders of the city.
13 They all ran together, both small and
great, for it was strange to them that she
had come. They opened the gate and
received them, making a fire to give light,
and surrounded them.

14 She said to them with a loud voice,
"Praise Elohim! Praise Him! Praise Elohim,
who has not taken away His kindness from
the house of Yisra'el, but has destroyed our
enemies by my hand tonight!"

15 Then she took the head out of the bag
and showed it, and said to them, "Behold,
the head of Olofernes, the chief captain of
the army of Ashuwr, and behold, the
canopy, in which he laid in his
drunkenness. יהוה struck him by the hand
of a woman. 16 And as יהוה lives, who
preserved me in the way that I went, my
appearance deceived him to his destruction,
and he did not commit sin with me, to
defile and shame me."

17 All the people were exceedingly amazed,
and stooped low, and bowed before
Elohim, and said with one accord, "Blessed
are You, O our Elohim, who has brought
the enemies of Your people to nothing
today."

18 Uzziyah said to her, "Blessed are you,
daughter, in the sight of El Elyon, above all
the women upon the earth; and blessed is
יהוה Elohim, who created the heavens and
the earth, who directed you to cut off the
head of the prince of our enemies. 19 For
your hope will not depart from the heart of
men that remember the strength of Elohim
forever. 20 May Elohim turn these things to
you for a perpetual praise, to visit you with
good things, because you did not spare
your life by reason of the affliction of our
race, but avenged our fall, walking a
straight way before our Elohim." And all
the people said, "Amein! Amein!"

14 1 Yehudith said to them, "Hear me
now, my brethren, and take this head, and
hang it upon the battlement of your wall.
2 It will be, as soon as the morning appears
and the sun rises upon the earth, you shall
each take up his weapons of war, and every
valiant man of you go out of the city. You
shall set a captain over them, as though you
would go down to the plain toward the
watch of the children of Ashuwr; but you
men shall not go down. 3 These shall take
up their full armor, and shall go into their
camp and rouse up the captains of the army
of Ashuwr. They will run together to
Olofernes' tent, but they will not find him.
Fear will fall upon them, and they will flee
before your face. 4 You men, and all that
inhabit every coast of Yisra'el, shall pursue
them and overthrow them as they go. 5 But

before you do these things, summon
Aḥihud the Ammonite to me, that he may
see and know him that despised the house
of Yisra'el, and that sent him to us, as it
were to death."

6 And they called Aḥihud out of the house
of Uzziyah; but when he came, and saw the
head of Olofernes in a man's hand in the
assembly of the people, he fell upon his
face, and his spirit failed[a]. 7 But when they
had recovered him, he fell at Yehudith's
feet, and bowed down to her, and said,
"Blessed are you in every tent of Yehudah,
and in every nation, which will be troubled
upon hearing your name. 8 Now tell me all
the things that you have done in these
days." And Yehudith declared to him in the
midst of the people all the things that she
had done, from the day that she went out
until the time that she spoke to them.

9 But when she finished speaking, the
people shouted with a loud voice, and made
a joyful noise in their city. 10 But when
Aḥihud saw all the things that the Elohim
of Yisra'el had done, he believed in Elohim
exceedingly, and circumcised the flesh of
his foreskin, and was joined to the house of
Yisra'el, to this day.

11 And as soon as the morning arose, they
hanged the head of Olofernes upon the
wall, and every man took up his weapons,
and they went forth by bands to the ascents
of the mountain. 12 But when the children
of Ashuwr saw them, they sent word to
their leaders; but they went to their captains
and tribunes, and to every one of their
rulers. 13 They came to Olofernes' tent, and
said to him that was over all that he had,
"Wake our master up now; for the slaves
have been bold to come down against us to
battle, that they may be utterly destroyed."

14 Bagoas went in, and knocked at the outer
door of the tent; for he supposed that he
was sleeping with Yehudith. 15 But when
no one listened to him, he opened it, and
went into the bedchamber, and found him
cast upon the threshold dead, and his head
had been taken from him. 16 He cried with
a loud voice, with weeping and groaning
and a mighty cry, and tore his garments.
17 He entered into the tent where Yehudith
lodged, and he did not find her. He leaped
out to the people, and cried aloud, 18 "The
slaves have dealt treacherously! One
woman of the Hebrews has brought shame
upon the house of King Nevukhadnetstsar;
for, behold, Olofernes lies upon the ground,
and his head is not on him!"

19 But when the rulers of the army of
Ashuwr heard the words, they tore their
coats, and their being was troubled
exceedingly. There was a cry and an
exceedingly great noise in the midst of the
camp.

15 1 When those who were in the tents
heard, they were amazed at what happened.
2 Trembling and fear fell upon them, and
no man dared stay any more in the sight of
his neighbor, but rushing out with one
accord, they fled into every way of the
plain and of the hill country. 3 Those who
had encamped in the hill country around
Bethulyah fled away. And then the children
of Yisra'el, everyone who was a warrior,
rushed out upon them.

---

[a] 14:6 Spirit failed – That is, he fainted.

4 Uzziyah sent to Betomasthaim, Bebai,
Ḥoba, and Ḥola, and to every coast of
Yisra'el, to tell about the things that had
been accomplished, and that all should rush
upon their enemies to destroy them. 5 But
when the children of Yisra'el heard, they all
fell upon them with one accord, and struck
them to Ḥoba. Yes, and in the same way
those of Yerushalayim and of all the hill
country came – for men had told them
about what happened in their enemies'
camp – and those who were in Gilad and in
the Galil fell upon their flank with a great
slaughter, until they were past Dammeseq
and its borders. 6 The rest of the people
who lived at Bethulyah fell upon the camp
of Ashuwr, and plundered them, and were
enriched exceedingly. 7 The children of
Yisra'el returned from the slaughter, and
took possession of that which remained.
The villages and the cities that were in the
hill country and took many spoils in the
plain country; for there was an exceedingly
great supply.

8 Yoyaqim the high priest, and the elders of
the children of Yisra'el who lived in
Yerushalayim, came to see the good things
which יהוה had showed to Yisra'el, and to
see and salute Yehudith. 9 When they came
to her, they all blessed her with one accord,
and said to her, "You are the exaltation of
Yerushalayim! You are the great glory of
Yisra'el! You are the great rejoicing of our
race! 10 You have done all these things by
your hand. You have done with Yisra'el the
things that are good, and Elohim is pleased
with it. Blessed be you with יהוה Almighty
forever." And all the people said, "Amein!"

11 And the people plundered the camp for
the space of thirty days; and they gave
Olofernes' tent to Yehudith, along with all
his silver cups, his beds, his bowls, and all
his furniture. She took them, and placed
them on her mule, and prepared her
wagons, and heaped them on it. 12 And all
the women of Yisra'el ran together to see
her; and they blessed her, and made a dance
among them for her. She took branches in
her hand, and distributed them to the
women who were with her. 13 Then they
made themselves wreaths of olive
branches, she and those who were with her,
and she went before all the people in the
dance, leading all the women. All the men
of Yisra'el followed in their armor with
wreaths, and with songs in their mouths.

16 1 And Yehudith began to sing this song
of thanksgiving in all Yisra'el, and all the
people sang with loud voices this song of
praise.

2 Yehudith said, "Begin a song to my
Elohim with timbrels. Sing to my Master
with cymbals. Make music to Him with
psalm and praise. Exalt Him, and call upon
His Name.
3 For יהוה is the Elohim that crushes
battles. For in His armies in the midst of
the people, He delivered me out of the hand
of those who persecuted me.
4 Ashuwr came out of the mountains from
the north. He came with ten thousands of
his army. Its multitude stopped the torrents.
Their horsemen covered the hills.
5 He said that he would burn up my
borders, kill my young men with the sword,
throw my nursing children to the ground,
give my infants up as prey, and make my
virgins a plunder.
6 The יהוה Almighty brought them to
nothing by the hand of a woman.
7 For their mighty one didn't fall by young

men, neither did sons of the Titans[a] strike
him. Tall giants[b] did not attack him, but
Yehudith the daughter of Merari made him
weak with the beauty of her face.
8 For she put off her widow's garments, for
the exaltation of those who were distressed
in Yisra'el. She anointed her face with
ointment, bound her hair in a tiara, and
took a linen garment to deceive him.
9 Her sandal ravished his eye. Her beauty
took his soul prisoner. The akinakes passed
through his neck.
10 The Parasians quaked at her daring. The
Medes were daunted at her boldness.
11 Then my lowly ones shouted aloud. My
weak ones were terrified and trembled for
fear. They lifted up their voice, and they
fled.
12 The sons of young women pierced them
through, and wounded them as fugitives'
children. They perished by the battle of my
Master.

13 "I will sing to my Elohim a new song: O
יהוה, You are great and glorious,
marvelous in strength, invincible.
14 Let all Your creation serve You; for You
spoke, and they were made. You sent out
Your Ruaḥ, and it built them. There is no
one who can resist Your voice.
15 For the mountains will be moved from
their foundations with the waters, and the
rocks will melt as wax at Your presence;
But You are still kind to those who fear
You.
16 For all slaughtering is little for a sweet
savor, and all the fat is very little for a
whole burnt offering to You. But he who
fears יהוה is great continually.

17 "Woe to the nations who rise up against
my race! יהוה Almighty will take
vengeance on them in the day of judgment,
to put fire and worms in their flesh; and
they will weep and feel their pain forever."

18 Now when they came to Yerushalayim,
they bowed down to Elohim. When the
people were cleansed, they offered their
burnt offerings, their free will offerings,
and their gifts. 19 Yehudith dedicated all
Olofernes' things, which the people had
given to her, and gave the canopy, which
she had taken for herself out of his
bedchamber, as a gift to יהוה.

20 And the people continued feasting in
Yerushalayim before the set-apart place for
three months, and Yehudith remained with
them. 21 But after these days, everyone
departed to his own inheritance. Yehudith
went away to Bethulyah, and remained in
her own possession, and was honorable in
her time in all the land.

22 Many desired her, and no man knew her
all the days of her life, from the day that
Menasheh her husband died and was
gathered to his people. 23 She increased in
greatness exceedingly; and she grew old in
her husband's house, to one hundred and
five years, and let her maid go free. Then
she died in Bethulyah. They buried her in
the cave of her husband Menasheh. 24 The
house of Yisra'el mourned for her seven

---

[a] 16:7 sons of the Titans – Most likely a reference to the Rephaim, a group descended from the Nephilim. In the LXX in Shemu'el ב [2 Samuel] 5:18-20 the Hebrew phrase עמק רפאים (*emeq re'pha'im*) meaning "valley of Rephaim" is rendered as κοιλάδα τῶν Τιτάνων (*loi'lada ton Ti'tan'on*). This is rendered as "valley of the Titans."

[b] 16:7 Giants – Greek word γιγαντης (*gi'gan'tes*) meaning "giant" is the equivalent of the Hebrew נפלים (*Nephilim*).

days. She distributed her goods before she died to all those who were nearest of kin to Menasheh her husband, and to those who were nearest of her own family.
25 There
was no one that made the children of Yisra'el afraid any more in the days of Yehudith, nor a long time after her death.

תְּפִילַּת מְנַשֶּׁה

T'fillat Menasheh [Prayer of Manassas]

1 1 O יהוה Almighty, who is in heaven, Elohim of our fathers, of Avraham, and Yitschaq, and Ya'aqov, and of their righteous seed; 2 who made heaven and earth, with all their host; 3 who bound the sea by the word of Your command; who shut up the deep, and sealed it by Your terrible and glorious Name; 4 whom all things fear, yes, *they* tremble before Your power; 5 for the majesty of Your glory cannot be borne, and the anger of Your threatening toward sinners is importable. 6 Your kind promise is unmeasurable and unsearchable; 7 for You are יהוה Elyon, of great compassion, longsuffering and abundant in kindness, and relent from bringing evils upon men. 8 You, O יהוה, according to Your great goodness have promised repentance and forgiveness to those who have sinned against You: and of Your infinite kindnesses *You* have appointed repentance to sinners, that they may be saved. You therefore, O יהוה, Elohim of the just, have not appointed repentance to the just, to Avraham, and Yitschaq, and Ya'aqov, which have not sinned against You; but You have appointed repentance to me, for I am a sinner. 9 For I have sinned above the number of the sands of the sea. My transgressions are multiplied, O יהוה: my transgressions are multiplied, and I am not worthy to behold and see the height of heaven for the multitude of my iniquities. 10 I am bowed down with many iron bands, that I cannot lift up my head because of my sins, and I do not have any rest; for I have provoked Your wrath, and done that which is evil before You. I did not do Your will, neither did I guard Your commands. I set up abominations, and multiplied detestable things. 11 Now therefore I bow the knee of my heart, asking for Your kindness. 12 I have sinned, O יהוה, I have sinned, and I acknowledge my iniquities; 13 but, I humbly ask You: forgive me, O יהוה, forgive me, and do not destroy me with my iniquities. Do not be angry with me forever, by reserving evil for me; neither condemn me into the lower parts of the earth. For You, O יהוה, are the Elohim of those who repent; 14 and in me You will show all Your goodness; for You will save me, who is unworthy, according to Your great kindness. 15 And I will praise You forever all the days of my life, for all the army of heaven sings Your praise, and Yours is the glory forever and ever. Amein.

בֵּן סִירָא

Ben Sira [Sirach {Ecclesiasticus}]

The Prologue of the Wisdom of Yeshua, the Son of Sira.

While numerous and great things have been delivered to us by the Torah and the prophets, and by the others that have followed in their steps – for which things we must give Yisra'el the praise of instruction and wisdom – and since not only the readers need to become skillful themselves, but also those who love learning must be able to profit those who are outside, both by speaking and writing; my grandfather Yeshua, having much given himself to the reading of the Torah, and the prophets, and the other books of our fathers, and having gained great familiarity in them, was also drawn on himself to write something pertaining to instruction and wisdom, in order that those who love learning, and are dependent upon these things, might make progress much more by living according to the Torah.

You are asked, therefore, to read with favor and attention, and to pardon us, if in any parts of what we have labored to interpret, we may seem to fail in some of the phrases. For things originally spoken in Hebrew do not have the same force in them when they are translated into another tongue; and not only these, but the Torah itself, and the prophets, and the rest of the books, have no small difference, when they are spoken in their original language.

For having come into Mitsrayim in the thirty-eighth year of Energetes[a] the king, and having continued there some time, I found a copy affording no small instruction. I thought it therefore most necessary for me to apply some diligence and toil to translate this book, indeed being quite watchful and skillful in that space of time to bring the book to an end, and set it forth for them also, who in the land of their sojourning desire to learn, fashioning their manners beforehand, so as to live according to the Torah.[b]

1 1 All wisdom comes from יהוה, and is
with Him forever.
2 The sand of the seas, and the drops of
rain, and the days of eternity: who can
count *them*?
3 The height of the heavens, and the
breadth of the earth, [and the deep, and
wisdom]:[c] who can search them out?
4 Wisdom has been created before all
things, and the understanding of caution
from everlasting.
5 [The word of El Elyon is the fountain of
wisdom; and her ways are everlasting
commands.][d]

---

[a] There were two Ptolemaic rulers who bore the title Energetes: Ptolemy III and Ptolemy VIII. Given the supposed date of composition, it most likely refers to Ptolemy VIII.

[b] This Prologue is found in the Greek version only. The original Book of Yeshua ben Sira was written in Hebrew, as many fragments and Semitic idioms attest. The author of the Prologue claims to be the grandson of Yeshua ben Sira, and states that it was he who translated the Hebrew book into Greek.

[c] 1:3 Bracketed section indicates reading present in Greek text, but absent from Latin, Ethiopic, and Coptic.

[d] 1:5 Bracketed section indicates reading present in some Greek and Latin texts but absent from

6 To whom has the root of wisdom been
revealed? And who has known her private
counsels?
7 [To whom has the knowledge of wisdom
been made manifest? And who has
understood her great experience?][a]
8 There is one wise, *who is* greatly to be
feared: יהוה, sitting upon His throne.
9 He created her, and saw *her*, and counted
her, and poured her out upon all His works.
10 He has poured forth upon all His works,
upon every living thing, according to His
abundance; He has lavished her upon those
who fear Him. [The love of יהוה makes
noble wisdom, and He grants her to those
to whom He appears, that they may see
Him.][b]
11 The fear of יהוה is glory, and exultation,
and gladness, and a crown of rejoicing.
12 The fear of יהוה will delight the heart,
and will give gladness, and joy, and length
of days[c].
13 Whoever fears יהוה, it will go well with
him at the end, and in the day of his death
he will be blessed.
14 To fear יהוה is the beginning of
wisdom; and it was created together with
the faithful in the womb.
15 With men she laid an eternal foundation;
and with their seed she will be had in trust.
16 To fear יהוה is the fullness of wisdom;
and she satisfies men with her fruits.
17 She will fill all her house with desirable
things, and her garners with her produce.
18 The fear of יהוה is the crown of
wisdom, making peace and perfect health
to flourish. [Both are gifts from Elohim for
peace; glory opens out for those who love
Him.][d]
19 He both saw and counted her; He rained
down skill and knowledge of
understanding, and exalted the honor of
those who hold fast to her.
20 To fear יהוה is the root of wisdom,[e] and
her branches are length of days.
21 [The fear of יהוה drives away sins, and
where it is present, it turns away wrath.][f]
22 Unjust wrath can never be declared right;
for the sway of his wrath is his downfall.
23 A man that is forgiving will bear[g] for a
season, and afterward gladness will spring
up to him.
24 He will hide his words for a season, and
the lips of many will tell of his
understanding.
25 A parable of knowledge is in the
treasures of wisdom; but reverence is an
abomination to a sinner.
26 If you desire wisdom, keep the
commands, and יהוה will give her to you
freely.
27 For the fear of יהוה is wisdom and
instruction, and His good pleasure is in
faith and gentleness.

---

others. Also absent from Ethiopic, Coptic, and Syriac.

[a] 1:7 Bracketed section indicates reading present in some Greek and Latin texts but absent from others. Also absent from Ethiopic, Coptic, and Syriac.

[b] 1:10 Bracketed section indicates reading present in Greek and Latin texts, but absent from Ethiopic, Coptic, and Syriac.

[c] 1:12 Syriac reads, "eternal life" here.

[d] 1:18 Bracketed section indicates reading present in Greek, Latin, and Coptic texts, but absent from Ethiopic and Syriac.

[e] 1:20 Syriac reads, "Eternal life is the root of wisdom."

[f] 1:21 Bracketed section indicates reading present in some Greek and Latin texts but absent from others.

[g] 1:23 Some Greek texts read, "resist" here.

28 Do not disobey the fear of יהוה, and do not come to Him with a double heart.
29 Do not be a hypocrite in the mouths of men, and beware of your lips.
30 Do not exalt yourself, lest you fall, and bring dishonor upon your being, and so יהוה will reveal your secrets, and will cast you down in the midst of the assembly, because you did not come to the fear of יהוה, and your heart was full of deceit.

2 1 My son, if you come to serve יהוה, prepare your being for temptation.
2 Set your heart right, and constantly endure, and do not hurry in time of calamity.
3 Cling to Him, and do not depart, that you may be increased at your latter end.
4 Accept whatever is brought upon you, and be forgiving when you pass into humiliation.
5 For gold is tried in the fire, and acceptable men in the furnace of humiliation.
6 Put your trust in Him, and He will help you; order your ways correctly, and set your hope on Him.
7 You that fear יהוה, wait for His kindness, and do not turn aside, lest you fall.
8 You that fear יהוה, put your trust in Him, and your reward will not fail.
9 You that fear יהוה, hope for good things, and for eternal gladness and kindness[a].
10 Look at the generations of old, and see: did anyone put his trust in יהוה, and become ashamed? Or who abided in His fear, and was forsaken? Or who called upon Him, and was despised by Him?
11 For יהוה is full of compassion and kindness, and He forgives sins, and saves in time of affliction.
12 Woe to fearful hearts, and to weak hands, and to the sinner that goes two ways!
13 Woe to the faint heart! For it does not believes, therefore it will not be defended.
14 Woe to you that have lost your patience! And what will you do when יהוה visits you?
15 They that fear יהוה will not disobey His words; and those who love Him will guard His ways.
16 They that fear יהוה will seek His good pleasure, and those who love Him will be filled with the Torah.
17 They that fear יהוה will prepare their hearts, and will humble their beings in His eyes,
18 saying, "We will fall into the hands of יהוה, and not into the hands of men, for as His majesty is, so also is His kindness[b]."

3 1 Hear me your father, O my children, and do as I say, that you may be saved.
2 For יהוה has given the father glory concerning the children, and has confirmed the judgment of the mother concerning the sons.
3 He that honors his father will make atonement for sins;
4 and he that gives glory to his mother is as one that lays up treasure.
5 Whoever honors his father will have joy of his children, and in the day of his prayer

[a] 2:9 Syriac reads, "Salvation."

[b] 2:18 Syriac adds, "And His Name is equal to His works."

he will be heard.
6 He that gives honor to his father will have length of days; and he that honors his mother obeys יהוה,
7 and will do service under his parents, as to masters.
8 My son, honor your father in word and deed, that all blessings may come upon you.
9 For the blessing of a father establishes the root, but the curse of the mother uproots the plant.
10 Do not honor yourself in the shame of your father; for such is not your glory.
11 The glory of a man is from the glory of his father, but the one who curses his mother increases sin.
12 My son, strengthen the honor of your father in his old age, and do not forsake him all the days of your life.
13 And if he fails in understanding, have patience with him; and do not dishonor him while you are in your full strength.
14 For kindness to a father will not be blotted out, and instead of sins it will be planted.
15 In the day of your affliction it will remember you; as heat upon ice, so will your iniquities be melted away.
16 The presumptuous man hates his father, and he that curses his mother arouses the anger of his Creator[a].
17 My son, go on with your business in gentleness, and you will be loved more than one who gives *many* gifts.
18 The greater you are, humble your being the more, and you will find compassion before Elohim.
19 [Many are in high places and of renown, but mysteries are revealed to the humble.][b]
20 For great is the compassion of Elohim, and He reveals His counsel to those who are humble.
21 Do not seek things that are too difficult for you, and do not search out things that are concealed from you.
22 Dwell upon the things that you have been permitted, for you have no need of the things that are hidden.
23 Do not be bitter about that which is kept from you, for you have already been shown things that are greater than you.
24 For the conceit of many has led them astray, and evil presumption has caused their judgment to slip.
25 [When the eye has no pupil, there is a lack of light; when there is no knowledge, there is a lack of wisdom.][c]
26 A hard heart will grow ill in the end, and he that loves good *things* will be led by them.
27 A hard heart will be loaded with pains, and the one who heaps sin upon sin is a madman.
28 [Do not hurry to heal a scoffer's wound: there is no remedy for it. For he is a shoot from an evil plant.][d]
29 The heart of the wise will understand the

---

[a] 3:16 Hebrew text reads בוראו (*bo'ro*) meaning "his creator." Greek text reads Κυριου (*Kuriou*) meaning "of יהוה." Latin text reads Deo meaning "Elohim."

[b] 3:19 Bracketed section indicates reading present in some Greek and Latin texts but absent from others. Not present in Hebrew text.

[c] 3:25 Bracketed section indicates reading from Hebrew text, though it is placed after verse 27. Greek and Latin read, "Without eyes, you will lack light; therefore, do not profess knowledge which you do not have."

[d] 3:28 Bracketed section indicates reading from Hebrew text. Greek and Latin texts read, "In the punishment of the proud there is no remedy; for the plant of wickedness hath taken root in him."

proverbs of the wise, and the ear that hears
wisdom will rejoice.
30 Water will quench a blazing fire, and
tsedaqqah will atone for sins.[a]
31 The deeds of the good will meet him on
his way, and he will find support in time of
weakness.

4 1 My son, do not mock the life of the
poor, nor deprive the being of the poor or
the one who is bitter of being.
2 Do not make a hungry being sad, neither
turn away the one who is oppressed.
3 Do not add more trouble to a heart that is
oppressed, nor grieve the heart of the poor.
4 Do not withhold a gift from the
unfortunate, and do not turn away your
eyes from the needy,
5 [lest you give him cause to curse you.
6 For his Rock will hear the voice of his
cry, as he cries from the bitterness of his
spirit and the anguish of his being.][b]
7 Get the love of the assembly to yourself,
and bow your head before the city ruler.
8 Incline your ear to a poor man, and
answer him with peaceful words in
humility.
9 Deliver him that is oppressed from the
hand the oppressor, and do not be afraid in
giving judgment.
10 Be as a father to the fatherless, and
regarded as a husband to widows: so will
you be called a son; and show favor, and
defend the anointed.[c] [d]
11 Wisdom teaches her sons, and takes hold
of those who seek her.
12 Those that love her love life; and those
who seek her obtain favor from יהוה.
13 Those who support her will find honor
from יהוה and will encamp in the blessing
of יהוה.
14 The servants who attend to the Set-Apart
One, and His Tabernacle, and those who
love her, Elohim loves.
15 He that listens to her will judge the
nations in truth, and he that gives heed to
her will dwell in the chambers of the
Temple.
16 [If he trust her, he will inherit her, and
his generations will have her in
possession.][e]
17 For though treating him as a foreigner, I
will still walk with him, and he will first be
proven through trials.
18 I will continue returning to him, until his
heart is filled with me, so that I may reveal
my secret to him.
19 If he goes astray, [I will lead him back,
and teach him with bit and bridle.] If he
goes astray [again], I will cast him off, and
give him over to robbers.[f]

---

[a] 3:30 See Tovi 4:7-11.

[b] 4:5-6 Bracketed section indicates reading present in Hebrew text. Greek and Latin texts read, "5 Do not turn your eye away from the needy, and do not give him occasion to curse you; 6 For if he curses you in the bitterness of his being, his prayer shall be heard by Him that made him."

[c] 4:10 Verse above follows the reading of the Hebrew text. Greek text reads, "Be as a father unto the fatherless, and instead of a husband unto their mother: so you shall be as the son of Elyon, and He shall love you more than your own mother does."

[d] 4:10 Hebrew text contains a large blank space following verse 10 prior to the beginning of verse 11. This may be indication of a new topic or chapter.

[e] 4:16 Bracketed section indicates reading present in Greek, Latin, and Syriac texts, but absent from Hebrew text.

[f] 4:19 Bracketed sections indicate readings present in Hebrew text but absent from Greek, Latin, and Syriac texts. Both Hebrew and Syriac

20 [My son,][a] Guard the opportunity, and
beware of evil and fear, and do not be
ashamed concerning your being.
21 For there is a shame that brings iniquity,
and there is a shame that is glory and favor.
22 Do not accept the person of any against
your being, and reverence no man to your
falling.
23 Do not refrain from speaking when it
would do good, and do not hide your
wisdom [for the sake of fair appearance.][b]
24 For wisdom will be known by speech,
and instruction by the word of the tongue.
25 Do not rebel against Elohim, but be
humble towards Elohim.[c]
26 Do not be ashamed to repent of your
iniquity, and do not stand before a river.
27 Do not lay yourself down for a fool to
tread upon, and do not refuse judges to
their face.[d] [e]
28 Counsel on behalf of righteousness, and
יהוה will fight for you; do not be known as
double-tongued, and do not seek gossip.
29 Do not be hasty in your tongue, nor slack
and careless in your deeds.
30 Do not be as a lion[f] in your house, nor
look strange in your work, nor be in fear of
it.
31 Do not let your hand be stretched out to
receive, and closed when you should give.

5 1 Do not set your heart upon your
possessions, and then say, "Elohim
provides for my welfare." Do not rely on
strength to acquire what you desire.
2 Do not follow your own heart and your
own eyes, to walk in evil desires.
3 Do not say, "Who will have dominion
over me?" For יהוה will surely take
vengeance.
4 Do not say, "I sinned, and what will
happen to me?" For Elohim is slow to
anger. [Do not say, "יהוה is
compassionate, He will erase all my
iniquities."][g]
5 Concerning forgiveness, do not be
without fear, to add iniquity upon iniquity.
6 And so say, "His compassion is great, He
will forgive my many iniquities." For
compassion and wrath are with Him, and
His anger will rest upon the wicked.
7 Do not be late in returning to Him, and do
not put off from day to day. For suddenly
His wrath will come forth, and you will
perish in the day of vengeance.
8 Do not set your heart on unrighteous gain,
for you will profit nothing in the day of
wrath.
9 Do not inspect every wind, and do not

---

read in the first person, while Greek and Latin read third person.

[a] 4:20 Bracketed section indicates reading present in Hebrew and Latin texts, but absent from Greek and Syriac.

[b] 4:23 Bracketed section indicates reading present in Greek and Latin text, but absent from Hebrew text.

[c] 4:25 Greek and Latin texts read, "Do not speak against the truth; but be abashed of the error of your ignorance." Syriac text reads, "Do not speak against the truth; rather, keep yourself away from your own foolishness."

[d] 4:26-27 In the Hebrew text, a set of three dots (∴) appears at the beginning of verse 26 and again at the end of 27. The reason remains unknown, though it may have been a way to highlight a specific passage as either doubtful of authenticity, or of special importance.

[e] 4:27 Hebrew text adds the text of 8:14 here.

[f] 4:30 Greek, Latin, and some Hebrew texts read "lion" as it is here. Other Hebrew, with the Syriac, reads "dog."

[g] 5:4 Bracketed section indicates reading present in Hebrew text but absent from Greek, Latin, and Syriac texts.

[change the channel of a stream.][a]
10 Be steadfast in your understanding, and let your word come to pass.
11 Be swift to hear, but give answer with a slow spirit.
12 If you have understanding, answer your neighbor; and if not, let your hand be upon your mouth.
13 Glory and dishonor is in the [hand of the idle][b] speaker, and the tongue of a man is his fall.
14 Do not be called double-tongued, and do not speak evil; for shame is made for the thief, and condemnation is for the double-tongued.
15 Do not speak corruptly, either in small or great things.[c]
16 An evil name is a disgrace, and will get you condemnation. So the evil man will receive double.[d]

6 1 Do not become an enemy instead of a friend, for an evil name will inherit shame and reproach. Even so will the evil receive double.
2 Do not fall under the power of your own being, lest you besiege yourself.
3 You will eat up your leaves, and scatter your fruits, and leave yourself as a dry tree.
4 [The being of a strong owner was laid waste by a wicked being, and made into a joy of exaltation to those who overtook him.][e]
5 Sweet words will multiply a man's friends; favorable lips will increase peace.
6 Let those that are at peace with you be many, but your counselors one of a thousand.
7 If you gain a friend, gain him by proving, and do not be quick to trust him.
8 For there is a friend that is only *a friend* for his own sake, and he will not continue in the day of affliction.
9 And there is a friend that turns to enmity; and he will expose the strife of your reproach.
10 And there is a friend that is a companion at the table, and he will not continue in the day of your need.
11 And in your prosperity he will be as yourself, [but in harsh times he will look down upon you.][f]
12 If you are brought low, he will be against you, and will hide himself from before you.
13 Separate yourself from your enemies, and beware of your friends.
14 A faithful friend is a strong defense, and he that has found him has found a treasure.
15 There is nothing that can be paid in exchange for a faithful friend, and his goodness is priceless[g].

---

[a] 5:9 Bracketed section indicates reading present in Hebrew text. Greek text reads, "walk in every path, for the sinner that has a double tongue does such."
[b] 5:13 Bracketed section indicates reading present in Hebrew text, but absent from Greek and Latin.
[c] 5:15 So the Hebrew and Syriac texts. Greek text reads, "In a great matter and in a small, be not hate, but love."
[d] 5:16 Verse 16 is present in the Hebrew text but absent from Greek and Latin texts. It begins with a slight indentation in the manuscript.
[e] 6:4 Bracketed section indicates reading present in Hebrew text. Greek and Latin texts read, "A wicked being will destroy him that has gained it, and will make him a laughing stock to his enemies."
[f] 6:11 Bracketed section indicates reading present in Hebrew and Syriac texts, but absent from Greek texts. Latin adds, "and will act with confidence among those of your house."
[g] 6:15 Priceless – In Greek this is σταθμος (*stath'mos*) meaning "invaluable, priceless." In Hebrew this is a phrase, ואין משקל (*ve'ein me'sheqel*) meaning "without sheqel." This

16 A faithful friend is a medicine of life,
and those who fear El will find Him.
17 For as he is, so his neighbor is also in his
deeds.
18 [My son, gather instruction from your
youth up, so that even in old age you will
find wisdom.][a]
19 Come to her as one that reaps and sows,
and wait for her good fruits. For your work
will be little in her work, and tomorrow you
will eat of her fruits.
20 How exceedingly harsh she is to the
foolish! And he that is without
understanding will not take her to heart.
21 As a mighty stone of trial she will rest
upon him, and he will quickly cast her
away from him.
22 For correction is according to her name,
and she is not accepted by many as the
right way to life.[b]
23 [Give ear, my son, and accept my
judgment, and do not refuse my counsel.
24 Bring your feet into her fetters, and your
neck into her chain.][c]
25 Put your shoulder under her, and carry
her, and do not be grieved with her bonds.
26 [Come to her with all your being, and
guard her ways with your whole might.][d]
27 Search, and seek, and she will be made
known to you. And when you have found
her, do not let her go.
28 For in the end, you will find her rest, and
she will be turned into gladness for you.
29 And her fetters will be to you for a
covering of strength, and her chains for a
spotless garment.
30 For her yoke is a golden ornament upon
her, and her corrections are a cord of blue.[e]
31 You shall put her on as a garment of
glory, and shall crown yourself with her as
a crown of splendor.
32 My son, if you will, you shall be wise.
And if you will yield your being, you will
be practical.
33 If you love to hear, you will receive, and
if you incline your ear, you will be
disciplined.
34 [Stand in the multitude of the elders, and
whoever is wise, cling to him.][f]
35 Be willing to listen to every desirous
discourse, and do not let the proverbs of
understanding escape you.
36 If you see a son of understanding, go to
him often, and let your foot wear out the
steps of his doors.
37 Let your mind dwell in fear upon Elyon,
and meditate continually on His
commands. He will enlighten your heart,
and your desire of wisdom will be given to
you.

7 1 Do no evil, so that no evil will
overtake you.

---

idiom implies something that is "without a price."

[a] 6:18 Verse 18 is absent from the Hebrew text. However, given that verse 19 begins speaking of "her" (wisdom), it is reasonable to assume the passage is original.

[b] Hebrew text contains 27:5-6 here.

[c] 6:23-24 Bracketed section indicates reading present in Greek and Latin texts but absent from Hebrew text. However, given the context of the "bonds" of wisdom, it is reasonable to assume the passage is original.

[d] 6:26 Bracketed section indicates reading present in Greek and Latin, but absent from Hebrew text. Syriac reads, "heart" instead of "being."

[e] 6:30 Hebrew phrase "cord of blue" is פתיל תכלת (*pa'thil te'khelet*), which is the same as the cord of blue described in Bemidbar [Numbers] 15:37-41.

[f] 6:34 Bracketed section indicates reading present in Greek and Latin texts but absent from Hebrew text.

2 Depart from iniquity, and it will turn away from you.
3 My son, do not sow evil upon a brother, lest you reap sevenfold.
4 Do not seek preeminence from El, neither the seat of honor from the king.
5 Do not declare yourself right before the king, and do not display your wisdom before the king.
6 Do not seek to be a governor, unless you are valiant, unless you possess the strength to put down rebellion. Or else you will be afraid before a nobleman, and receive a spot on your integrity.
7 Do not sin not against the congregation of the gates of the Temple of Elohim, and do not cast yourself down in the assembly.
8 Do not plot to sin twice; for in one sin you will not go unpunished.
9 [Do not say, "He will look upon the multitude of my gifts, and when I offer to El Elyon, He will accept it."][a]
10 Do not be cut short in your prayer, and in your righteousness.
11 Do not laugh a man to scorn when he is in the bitterness of his being, for there is One who humbles and exalts.
12 Do not devise violence against a brother, neither do the like to a companion or a friend.
13 Do not love to make any manner of lie, for that habit is not for good.
14 Do not speak foolishly in the multitude of princes, and do not be repetitious in your prayer.[b]
15 Do not hate servile work, nor the raising of cattle, as El has ordained.
16 Do not be counted among the [chiefs of the people][c]. Remember that the time of trouble will not pass by.
17 Humble yourself greatly, for the only expectation of man is the worm [and fire; and do not make haste, saying "Rely on El, and be pleased with his way."][d]
18 Do not trade a friend for something indifferent, neither a true brother for the gold of Ophir.
19 Do not reject a wise and good wife, for her favor is above rubies[e].
20 Do not render evil to a servant that works in truth, nor a hireling that gives his being to work.
21 Let your being love a wise servant, and do not withhold his freedom from him.
22 Do you have sheep? Keep your eye on them; if you value them, let them stay near you.
23 Do you have sons? Correct them, and get wives for them in their youth.
24 Do you have daughters? Protect their body,[f] and do not make your face shine to them.[g]
25 Give your daughter in marriage, and you will have given over responsibility; but give her to a man of understanding, whom you know well.

---

[a] 7:9 Bracketed section indicates reading present in Greek, Latin and Syriac texts but absent from Hebrew text. Hebrew text places verse 15 here instead.

[b] 7:14 See Qoheleth [Ecclesiastes] 5:2; Mattithyahu [Matthew] 6:7.

[c] 7:16 Bracketed section indicates reading present in Hebrew text. Greek text reads, "multitude of sinners."

[d] 7:17 Bracketed section indicates reading present in Hebrew text, but absent from Greek and Latin texts.

[e] 7:19 Rubies – Hebrew word פנינים (*pe'ni'nim*) meaning "rubies" or "pearls." Same word used in Mishlei [Proverbs] 31:10. Greek and Latin both read "gold" here.

[f] 7:24 Protect their body – idiom meaning "their virginity."

[g] 7:24 Do not make your face shine to them – Idiom for "do not be indulgent with them."

26 Do you have a wife? Do not despise her;
and if you do not love her, do not entrust
yourself to her.
27 [Give glory to your father with your
whole heart, and do not forget the pangs of
your mother.
28 Remember that you were born from
them; and what will you repay them for the
things that they have done for you?][a]
29 Fear Elohim with all your heart, and set
apart His priests.
30 With all your strength, love Him that
made you, and do not forsake His
attendants.
31 Fear Elohim, and honor the priests; give
them their heave-offering, as it is
commanded of you. The first-fruits, and the
trespass offering, and the gift of the
shoulders, and the heave-offering of
righteousness, and the first-fruits of set-
apart *things* of the Temple.
32 Also stretch out your hand to the needy,
that your blessing may be perfected.
33 Give openly to every living creature, and
do not withhold kindness from a dead man.
34 Do not avoid visiting those who weep,
and mourn with those who mourn.
35 Do withdraw your heart from your
friend, for by such things you will gain
love.
36 In all your works remember your latter
end, and you will never see corruption.

8

1 Do not strive with a great man, lest
perhaps you fall into his hands.
2 Do not strive with a rich man, lest
perhaps he weigh out the price of your
demise. For gold has destroyed many, and
turned away the hearts of noblemen.
3 Do not strive with a man that is full of
tongue, and do not heap wood upon his
fire.
4 Do not jest with a fool, lest he dishonor
your fathers.
5 Do not reproach a man when he repents;
remember that we are all to receive
punishment.
6 Do not dishonor a man in his old age, for
we are all growing old.
7 Do not rejoice over one that is dead;
remember that we die all.
8 Do not neglect the discourse of the wise,
and analyze their proverbs; for you will
learn instruction from them, and how to
stand before princes.
9 Do not miss the discourse of elders, for
they also learned from their fathers. For
you will learn understanding from them, as
well as *how* to give answer in *the* time of
need.
10 Do not kindle the coals of a sinner, lest
you be burned with the flame of his fire.
11 Do not rise up from the presence of an
insolent man, lest he lie in wait as an
ambush before you.
12 Do not lend to a man that is mightier
than yourself. And if you lend, it will be as
though it is lost.
13 Do not be collateral above your might,
and if you are collateral, think as one that
will have to pay back.
14 Do not enter into judgment with a
[wicked][b] judge; for he will judge the
matter.
15 Do not go in the way with a rash man,
lest you be weighed with an evil burden.
For he will do according to his own desire,

---

[a] 7:27-28 Bracketed section indicates reading present in Greek, Latin, and Syriac texts, but absent from Hebrew text.

[b] 8:14 Bracketed section indicates reading present in Syriac text, but absent from Greek, Latin, and Hebrew texts.

and you will perish with his folly.
16 Do not defy a wrathful man, and do not
travel with him along the way. For blood is
as nothing in his sight, and he will
overthrow you where there is no help.
17 Do not take counsel with a fool, for he
will not be able to conceal the matter.
18 Do not reveal a secret thing before a
stranger, for you do not know what he will
bring forth later on.
19 Do not open your heart to everyone, lest
you drive good things away from you.

9 1 Do not be jealous over the wife of your
bosom, lest you teach an evil lesson against
yourself.
2 Do not be eager to give your being to a
woman, to bear her *burden* upon your
shoulders.
3 Do not be eager to give yourself to a
foreign woman, lest you fall into her
snares. Do not become intimate with a
whore, lest you become trapped in her
corruption.[a]
4 Do not lie with a woman that is a singer[b],
lest you be caught by her double-
mindedness.[c]
5 Do not stare at a virgin, lest you incur her
penalty.[d]
6 Do not give not yourself to a whore, lest
you lose your inheritance.
7 Your eyes will cause you to be a fool on
account of a beautiful woman, and your
house will be laid waste.[e]
8 Turn away your eye from a woman of
favor, and do not stare at her beauty [if she
is not your wife][f]. By the beauty of a
woman many have been led astray, and
with it her lovers are burned as in a fire.
9 Do not taste another man's wife. Do not
revel with her when you are drinking, lest
you hand your heart over to her, and your
blood over to the pit.
10 Do not forsake an old friend, for the new
is not comparable to him. As new wine, so
is a new friend. If it becomes old, you will
drink it.
11 Do not envy the glory of a sinner, for
you do not know what his day of judgment
will be like.
12 Do not delight in the delights of the
arrogant. Remember they will not go to
death unpunished.
13 Keep far from the man that has power to
kill, and do not fear death. And if you come
near to him, commit no fault, lest he take
away your life. Know surely that you go
about in the midst of snares, and walk upon
the fence of a city.
14 Answer your neighbor the best that you
can, and take counsel with the wise.
15 Let your conversation be with men of
understanding, and let all your secrets be

[a] 9:3 Reading present from Hebrew text. Greek text gives a condensed version: "Do not offer to meet a woman who is a whore, lest you fall into her snares."

[b] 9:4 Singer – Hebrew word מנגינה (*man'ginah*), which literally means "mocking, derisive song." It appears once in the Bible in Eikhah [Lamentations] 3:63; there it is usually translated as "song" or "mocking-song."

[c] 9:4 So the Hebrew, Greek, and Latin read. Syriac reads, "lest she destroy you by association with her."

[d] 9:5 Possible reference to Devarim [Deuteronomy] 22:28-29.

[e] 9:7 Reading present from Hebrew text. Greek text reads, "Do not look around in the streets of the city, and do not wander in its solitary places."

[f] 9:8 Bracketed section indicates reading present in Hebrew text, but absent in Greek and Latin texts.

shared with them alone.
16 Let righteous men be the companions of
your board, and glory in the fear of Elohim.
17 For the hand of the craftsman, a work
will be commended; he that rules the
people will be counted wise for his speech.
18 A man of idle tongue is feared in his
city, and he that takes matters upon his
mouth will be hated.

10 1 A wise judge will instruct his people,
and the government of a man of
understanding will be well ordered.
2 As the judge of his people, so are his
attendants; as the ruler of the city, so are all
those who dwell in it.
3 An uncovered king will destroy the city[a],
and a city will be established through the
understanding of the powerful.[b]
4 The kingdoms of the earth are in the hand
of Elohim, and in due time He will
establish over it one who is right for the
time.
5 The kingdoms of all men are in the hand
of Elohim, and He will lay His glory upon
the one whom He has decreed.[c]
6 Do not pay your neighbor back with evil
for every wrong, and do not walk in the
way of pride.
7 Pride is hateful before the Master and
before men, and in both oppression is even
more so.
8 Kingship is transferred from nation to
nation because of iniquity and pride.
9 Why are dust and ash proud, that it should
lift up its bowels[d] during its life?[e]
10 At the slightest illness he turns yellow,
and the physician mocks, "He is a king
today, but tomorrow he will die."
11 For when a man is dead, he will inherit
creeping things, and great beasts, and
worms.
12 It is the beginning of pride when a man
departs from Elohim, and in defiance he
turns away his heart.
13 For the cistern of presumption is sin, and
from that source will pour forth
abomination. For this cause Elohim
brought upon them strange calamities, and
utterly struck them, until they were no
more.
14 **Elohim has overthrown the thrones of
princes, and exalted the humble in their
place.**[f]
15 [יהוה plucked up the roots of nations,
and planted the lowly in their stead.][g]
16 יהוה overthrew the lands of nations;
Elohim dug[h] out their root to the ends of
the earth.
17 He has scraped them from the earth, and
uprooted them; He has made their memory

---

[a] 10:3 Greek, Latin, and Syriac texts read, "his people."
[b] 10:2-3 Hebrew text has verses 2 and 3 swapped.
[c] 10:4-5 Hebrew text has verses 4 and 5 swapped.
[d] 10:9 Bowels – that is, the innermost part of man.
[e] 10:9 In the Hebrew text there is a large blank space between the end of 9 and the beginning of 10. This may indicate a missing part of the verse.
[f] 10:14 This verse is quoted in Loukas [Luke] 1:52.
[g] 10:15 Bracketed section indicates reading present in Greek, Latin, and Syriac texts but absent from Hebrew text.
[h] 10:16 Hebrew word for "dug" here is קעקע (*qa'aqa*). This word appears only once in the Bible: in Vayyiqra [Leviticus] 19:28, where it is translated as "marks" or "tattoo." Given the cognates in other Semitic languages (Arabic, Nabataean, Syriac, Egyptian), it can be defined literally as "something that is dug out," ie. "a deep well."

to cease from *the* earth.
18 Pride has not been created for men, nor wrathful anger for those born of a woman.
19 What seed[a] is that which is a shame to people? The seed that is a shame is the transgressor of the commands.[b]
20 Among his brothers, the ruler has honor; and [with his eyes he will see Elohim][c].
21 [The fear of Elohim goes before the obtaining of authority, but roughness and pride will lose it.][d]
22 The sojourner, and the stranger, the foreigner and the poor *man*:[e] their honor is the fear of Elohim.
23 It is not right to despise a poor man that has understanding, and [not every man who is ruling deserves honor][f].
24 The great man, and the judge, and the honorable man will be glorified, *yet* none of them are greater than he that fears Elohim.
25 A practical servant should be exalted, and a servant that has knowledge will not complain.
26 Do not be overly wise[g] in doing your work, and do not glorify yourself in the time of your distress.
27 Better is he that labors and abounds in all things, than he that glorifies himself, and lacks bread.
28 My son, glorify your being in humility, and He will give you understanding when you go out, and when you come in.
29 Who will justify him that sins against his own being? And who will honor him that dishonors his own being?
30 A poor man is honored for his knowledge, and a rich man is honored for his riches.
31 Oh how much men are honored when they are rich, and how much they are dishonored when they are poor. If men honor themselves when they are poor, how much more will they honor themselves when they are rich! And if they are dishonored when they are rich, how much more will they be dishonored when they are poor![h]

11 1 The wisdom of the poor will lift up his head, and make him to sit among the great *men*.
2 Do not praise a man for his attractiveness, and do not despise an ugly a man for his appearance.
3 The bee is little among things that fly, and her fruit is the chief of produce.
4 Do not boast at the one who has but a

---

[a] 10:19 Given the context, the usage of "seed" here (Heb. זרע) implies race or people group.
[b] 10:19 So the Hebrew text reads. Greek, Latin, and Syriac texts read, "They that fear the Lord are a sure seed, and they that love him an honorable plant: they that regard not the law are a dishonorable seed; they that transgress the commands are a deceivable seed."
[c] 10:20 Bracketed section indicates reading present in Hebrew text. Greek text reads, "in the eyes of Elohim, those who fear Him."
[d] 10:21 Best Greek, Latin, Syriac, and Hebrew texts omit verse 21. Present in some Greek texts.
[e] 10:22 Greek texts read, "The rich man, and the poor, and the noble man."
[f] 10:23 So the Hebrew text reads. Greek text reads, "it is not fitting to glorify a man that is a sinner." Latin adds "rich" before "man."
[g] 10:26 Hebrew word translated here as "overly wise" is תתחכם (*tit'cha'kam*). This is a slang idiom, meaning something akin to the English phrase, "smart aleck."
[h] 10:31 So the Hebrew text reads. Greek and Latin texts read, "He that is honored in poverty, how much more in riches? And he that is dishonored in riches, how much more in poverty?" Latin reads, "let him fear poverty" in the last clause.

loincloth, and do not scoff at the day of his bitterness. For the works of יהוה are wonderful, and His works are hidden among men.
5 Many contrite ones[a] have sat down upon the ground, and one that was never thought of has worn a diadem.
6 Many great ones have been greatly disgraced and humiliated together, and men of renown have been delivered into other men's hands.
7 Do not *cast* blame before you have examined: understand first, and then rebuke.
8 My son, do not answer before you have heard, and do not interrupt *someone* in the middle of speech.
9 Do not strive in a matter that does not concern you, and do not judge with a band of sinners.
10 My son, should you increase your troubles? One who is eager to multiply wealth will not go unpunished. My son, if you do not run you will not reach the goal, and if you do not seek, you will not find.[b] [c]
11 There is one who toils, and labors, and runs, and is still behind for the same reason.
12 There is one that is sluggish, and perishing, lacking everything but life. But the eyes of יהוה looked upon him for good, and He will shake him from his filth.
13 He raises up his head and exalts him, and many have marveled at him greatly.
14 Good and evil, life and death, poverty and riches, are from יהוה.
15 [Wisdom and knowledge and the understanding of matters, each of these is from יהוה. Sin and the right ways, each are from יהוה.][d]
16 [Foolishness and darkness are formed for transgressors, and the evildoers are with them.][e]
17 The gift of Elohim remains with the righteous forever, and the one whom He has approved will prosper.
18 There is one who grows rich by his carefulness and pinching,[f] and this is the portion of his reward:
19 When he says, "I have found rest, and now I will eat of my goods;" yet he does not know what time will pass, and he will leave them to others, and die.

---

[a] 11:5 Contrite ones – Hebrew word נדכאים (*nid'kaim*), meaning literally "broken ones." Greek text reads τυραννος (*turannos*), meaning "tyrant, oppressor." This mistranslation most likely came about when the Greek translator mistook "broken [oppressed] ones" to mean "oppressors." Thus subsequent English translators have rendered it "kings." This word appears in this exact form in Yeshayahu [Isaiah] 57:15.

[b] 11:10 So the Hebrew text reads. Greek and Latin texts read, " My son, do not meddle with many matters: for if you meddle much, you shall not be innocent; and if you pursue, you shall not obtain, neither shall you escape by fleeing."

[c] 11:10 See also Korinthious A [1 Corinthians] 9:26; Philippesios [Philippians] 3:12-14; Mattithyahu [Matthew] 7:7; Loukas [Luke] 11:9; Devarim [Deuteronomy] 4:29; Yirmeyahu [Jeremiah] 29:13.

[d] 11:15 Verse not present in many Greek and Latin texts. It is partially damaged in the Hebrew text. Some Greek texts read as the Hebrew above, with a variation of the last sentence: "the way of good works, are from Him."

[e] 11:16 Verse not present in many Greek and Latin texts. It is partially damaged in the Hebrew text. Some Greek texts agree with the Hebrew above.

[f] 11:18 Carefulness and pinching – that is, he deprives himself for a time in order to store up goods.

20 My son, be steadfast in your occupation[a], and be conversant in it, and grow old in your work.
21 Do not marvel at the works of a sinner, but run to יהוה, and hope for His light. For it is right in the eyes of יהוה to suddenly to make a poor man rich.
22 The blessing of Elohim is in the reward of the righteous, and in the time of hope, it will come.
23 Do not say not, "What use is there for me? And what will be my belongings from now on?"
24 Do not say, "I have enough; from now on, what harm could happen to me?"
25 In the day of good things there is a forgetfulness of evil things; and in the day of evil things a man will not remember things that are good.
26 [For it is an easy thing in the eyes of Elohim to reward a man in the day of death according to his ways.][b]
27 The time of affliction causes pleasure to be forgotten, and in the end a man's deeds reveal the person he was.
28 Call no man blessed before he is examined, for the end of his life will declare him blessed. Do not call him blessed, for at the end of his life he will be known.
29 Do not bring every man into your house, for there are many plots of the deceitful man.
30 As a decoy bird in a cage, so is the heart of a proud man; [What rebellion will they multiply, like a wolf, lying in wait to tear into pieces? The transgressions of the one who seeks unjust gain are multiplied, as a dog entering every house *he finds*. So he comes with violence, and strives for all their possessions.][c] As one that spies, he looks upon your nakedness[d].
31 The slanderer will overthrow the good and make it evil, and will plot against your choice goods.
32 From a spark of fire a heap of many coals is kindled, and a worthless man lies in wait for blood.
33 Be on guard against the evildoer, for he brings forth wicked things; why should you bear blame forever?
34 Guard you way from the stranger, or he will separate you from your goods. Do not cling to a wicked man, for he will pervert your way, and make you strange to those whom are beloved by you.

12

1 If you do good, know to whom you do it, and your good will be hope for your sake.
2 Do good to *the* righteous, and you will find reward; if not from him, from יהוה.
3 No good will come to him that comforts the wicked, nor is doing so righteous.
4 Give to the good, and withhold from the evil.[e]

---

[a] 11:20 So the Hebrew text reads. Greek and Latin texts read, "covenant."

[b] 11:26 Bracketed section indicates reading present in Greek and Latin texts but absent from Hebrew text.

[c] 11:30 Bracketed section indicates reading present in Hebrew text, though absent from Greek and Latin texts. Latin fragment adds, "For as corrupted bowels send forth stinking breath;" to the beginning of the verse.

[d] 11:30 Nakedness – From the Hebrew word ערוה. Greek text uses πτωσιν (*p'tosin*), meaning "falling out." Latin text uses casum proximi sui, meaning "his neighbor's fall."

[e] 12:4 Hebrew texts place this verse after verse 6.

5 Withhold weapons of war from him,[a] and
do not give them to him, lest he overtake
you by them. For you will receive twice as
much evil in time of need, for all the good
you will have done to him.
6 For Elohim also hates evil men, and will
repay vengeance to the wicked.
7 Restore the poor, but do not give to the
proud.
8 A friend will not be known in prosperity,
and an enemy will not be hidden in
adversity.
9 In a man's prosperity even his enemies are
friends, and in his adversity even his friend
will be separated from him.
10 Never trust your enemy, for as copper
tarnishes, so does his wickedness.
11 Even if he humbles himself, and goes
with you peacefully, yet still take heed, and
beware of him. Treat him as one who will
betray you, and he will not discover a
means to destroy you. And know that in the
end, there will be jealousy.
12 Do not stand him beside you; why
should he overthrow you and stand in your
place? Do not let him sit on your right
hand; why should he take your seat? And in
the end you will acknowledge my words,
and lament at my lamentation.
13 Who will pity a charmer that is bitten by
a serpent, or any that come near wild
beasts?
14 So is he who joins himself to a proud
woman, and wallows in his iniquities.
15 When he travels with you, he will not
reveal his intentions to you. If you fall, he
will not bend down to save you. As long as
you stand he will control himself, but if you
stumble, he will prevail.
16 The enemy will speak sweetly with his
lips, and in his heart take counsel how to
overthrow you into a pit. The enemy will
weep with his eyes, and if he find
opportunity, he will not be satisfied with
blood.
17 If adversity meets you, you will find him
there before you, and as though he would
help you, he will supplant you.
18 He will shake his head, and clap his
hands, and change his form before you.

13 1 Pitch clings[b] to the one who touches
it, and he that has fellowship with a proud
man will become like him.
2 Why should you bear a burden too heavy
for you? And why should you fellowship
with a man who is richer than you? What
fellowship should the earthen pot have with
the iron kettle? Or why should the rich
fellowship with the poor?[c]
3 The rich man does wrong, and he boasts
about it; the poor is wronged, and he begs
for forgiveness.
4 If you seem profitable, he will make you
a slave, but if you are worn out, he will pity
you.
5 If you have possessions, he will speak

---

[a] 12:5 Weapons of war – Hebrew phrase כלי לחם (*k'li le'ḥem*), means literally "instruments of destruction." The Greek and Latin texts both read, "withhold bread" here instead. This arose from the Greek translator mistaking the Hebrew לחם (*laḥam*) meaning "devour, destroy" with the Hebrew *leḥem* (same consonants, different vowels), which means "bread."

[b] 13:1 So the Hebrew text reads. Greek and Latin texts read "defiles" here.

[c] 13:2 So the Hebrew and Syriac texts read. Greek and Latin texts read, "Do not burden yourself above your power while you live; and have no fellowship with one that is mightier and richer than yourself. For how shall agree the kettle and the earthen pot together? For if the one is struck against the other, it shall be broken."

kindly to you; but if you are poor, he will
not feel sorry.
6 When he has need, he will be with you,
and will be kind to you, and make promises
to you.
7 This he will do, for as long as he finds
you profitable. But then he will mock you,
and will harm you three times as much, and
will look at you in disarray, and will pass
you by, shaking his head.[a]
8 Beware: do not be arrogant, so as to die
from lack of knowledge.
9 If a mighty man invites you, act detached,
and he will invite you even more.
10 Do not press him on your own, or he
may refuse you; and do not stand far off,
lest you be forgotten.
11 Do not expect to speak freely with him
as an equal, and do not rely on his many
speeches. For from these many speeches he
will test you, all the while laughing with
you.
12 He will hand you over to a cruel ruler,
and he will not spare your being from being
bound with many bindings.
13 Guard yourself, and beware; do not
fellowship with men of violence.
14 [Love Elohim all your life, and call upon
Him for your salvation.][b]
15 Every living creature loves his kind, and
every man loves one who is like him.
16 All flesh keeps its own kind near, and
man will fellowship with his own kind.
17 What fellowship shall the wolf have with
the lamb? So is the wicked with the
righteous. [And so is the rich man keeping
close to the poor man.][c]
18 What peace is there between the hyena
and the dog? And what peace is there
between the rich man and the poor?
19 Wild donkeys are the prey of lions in the
wilderness, so poor men are pasture for the
rich.
20 Humility is an abomination to the proud,
and a poor man is an abomination to the
rich.[d]
21 A rich man, when he has fallen, is held
up by his friends; but a poor man is thrust
away from friend to friend.
22 A rich man speaks and he gains
attendants; though his words are deceitful,
they are perceived as beautiful. A poor man
is tripped and people mock, saying, "Fall
down, and lift yourself up, too." And
though his word is wise, the hearts of men
find no place for it.
23 A rich man speaks, and all keep silent;
and what he says they extol to the clouds.
A poor man speaks, and they say, "Who is
this?" And if he stumbles, they will help to
overthrow him.
24 Riches are good if there is no sin in
them; but poverty is evil in the mouth of
the proud.
25 The heart of a man changes his face,
whether it be for good or for evil.
26 A bright face is the mark of a heart that
is in prosperity; a distant look reveals
wearied thoughts.

---

[a] 13:7 So the Hebrew text reads. Greek and Latin texts read, "And he will shame you by his meats, until he makes you bare twice or thrice, and in the end he will laugh you to scorn, and afterward he will see you, and will forsake you, and shake his head at you."

[b] 13:14 Bracketed section indicates reading not present in many Greek texts, and also absent from the Hebrew text.

[c] 13:17 See Korinthious B [2 Corinthians] 6:14-16. Bracketed section indicates reading present in Hebrew text, but absent from Greek, Latin, and Syriac texts.

[d] 14:20 Verse not present in Syriac text.

14 1 Happy is the man whose mouth does not bring sorrow, and whose heart does not bring him judgment.
2 Happy is the man who does not condemn himself, and who has not fallen from his hope.
3 Riches are not beautiful for a stingy person, and gold is not beautiful to the envious one.
4 A stranger will revel in the goods of one who withholds from himself and gathers for another.
5 He that is evil to himself, whom will he please? He finds no pleasure in his possessions.
6 There is none more evil than he that envies himself, and this is a reward of his wickedness.
7 [Even if he does good, he does it in forgetfulness, and in the end, he shows forth his wickedness.
8 He that envies with his eye is evil; turning away the face, and despising the beings of men.][a]
9 The portion of the greedy is small in his eyes, but he who takes the portion of his neighbor shall lose his own.[b]
10 An evil eye keeps watch over his bread, and he is troubled at his table. [A good eye multiples bread, and even a dry well will flow upon his table.][c] [d]
11 My son, if you have possessions, let them be of use to your being. If you have possessions, let them be good to you, and let your hand be rich toward El.
12 Remember that death will not wait, and in Sheol there is no delight; and you have not been told when you will appointed to Sheol.
13 Do good to your friend before you die, and according to your ability stretch out your hand and give to him.
14 Do not defraud yourself of a good day, and do not desire any evil, to transgress.
15 Will you not leave your wealth to another, and your labor to those who cast lots for it?
16 Give to a brother, and you will receive. Deal with yourself well, for there is no seeking pleasure in Sheol, and everything is silent.
17 All flesh grows old like a garment, for the decree from the beginning is, "**They shall surely perish**."[e]
18 As of the leaves flourishing on a thick tree, one falls *off* while another springs up. So also are the generations of flesh and blood: one comes to an end, and another is born.
19 All of his work shall surely rot, and the work of his hands will be dragged to Sheol after him.
20 Happy is the man who meditates on wisdom, and fixes his eyes on

---

[a] 14:7-8 Bracketed section indicates reading present in Greek and Latin texts, but absent from Hebrew text.
[b] 14:9 So the Hebrew text reads. Greek and Latin texts read, "A covetous man's eye is not satisfied with his portion, and wicked injustice dries up his being."
[c] 14:10 Bracketed section indicates reading present in Hebrew text, but absent from Greek and Latin texts.
[d] 14:10 Compare Devarim [Deuteronomy] 15:9; Mattithyahu [Matthew] 6:23.
[e] 14:17 See Bereshiyt [Genesis] 2:17; 6:17. Note that Bereshiyt 2:17 contains the phrase מֹות תָּמוּת (*mowt ta'mut*), meaning "You shall surely die" (lit. "you will die death"). Here, however, we read גוע יגועו (*gawa yigwa'u*) meaning "you shall surely perish" (lit. "you will perish to perish"). While *mowt* means death in the most literal sense, *gawa* means perish, in the sense of expiration, or a "last breath."

understanding.
21 He that considers her ways in his heart shall also have knowledge of her secrets.
22 Go forth after her as one who tracks, and lie in wait in her ways.
23 He that watches at her windows shall also listen at her doors.
24 He that lodges close to her house shall also fasten a *tent* peg in her walls.
25 He shall pitch his tent near at hand to her, and will lodge as a good neighbor.
26 He will build his nest under the shadow of her wings, and spend the night in her branches.
27 He will take refuge from the heat in her shadow, and dwell in her habitations.

15 1 For he that fears יהוה will do this, and he who takes hold of the Torah will catch up to her.
2 She will go before him like a mother, and receive him like the wife of his youth.
3 She will feed him with bread of discernment, and give him water of understanding to drink.
4 He will lean on her, and will not be moved; he will rely on her, and will not be ashamed.
5 And she will exalt him above his neighbors, and she will open his mouth in the midst of the assembly.
6 He will find joy and gladness, and she will cause him to inherit an everlasting name.[a]
7 Vain men will not obtain her, and the prideful will not see her.
8 She is far from scoffers, and liars will not remember her.
9 She does not desire praise from the mouth of the wicked, for his lot is not from El.
10 Praise is spoken from the mouth of the wise, and she causes proverbs to be studied.
11 Do not say, "My transgression is from El." For He does not make that which He despises;
12 Lest you say, "He has made me accursed." For He does not need men of violence.
13 יהוה hates evil and abominations; He will not cause them to befall those who fear Him.
14 Elohim made man from the beginning, and placed him in the hand of his own inclination.
15 If you desire, you will guard the commands; doing His will is wisdom. If you are faithful in Him, you will [live][b].
16 He has poured out fire and water before you; you will stretch out your hand to whichever *one* you desire.
17 Life and death are before a man: whichever he desires, so it will be given to him.
18 The wisdom of יהוה is great; He is mighty in power, and sees all things.
19 The eyes of El see and behold; He knows every man's deeds.
20 He has not commanded any man to sin, [and He does not restore liars to strength. He does not show compassion to the one who works vanity, or to the one who reveals *secret* counsel.][c]

16 1 Do not desire the appearance of vain

[a] 15:6 Compare Yeshayahu [Isaiah] 56:5.
[b] 15:15 Bracketed section indicates reading present in Hebrew text. Greek, Latin, and Syriac texts read, "keep the commands."
[c] 15:20 So the Hebrew text reads. Greek and Latin texts read, "and he has not given any man license to sin" here.

youths, neither delight in children of
wickedness.
2 If they are fruitful, do not delight in them,
if there is no fear of יהוה in them.
3 Do not trust in their lives, neither rely on
their faithfulness; [for their end will not be
good.][a] For one who does his will shall be
better than a thousand, and to die childless
is better than having wicked children, and
better than the end of the proud.
4 For a city will be populated through a
single childless man who fears יהוה; but a
race of wicked men will be made desolate.
5 Many such things I have seen with my
eyes; and my ear has heard mightier things
than these.
6 A fire will be kindled in the congregation
of the wicked, and wrath is kindled in a
nation of profane ones.
7 He did not forgive the princes of old, who
trusted in their might.
8 He did not have pity on the place of Lot's
sojourning, those whom He abhorred for
their pride.
9 He did not pity the nations that were
under the ban, who were crushed because
of their iniquity.
10 And in like manner the six hundred
thousand footmen, who were gathered
together in their pride.
11 Even if there be one stiff-necked man, it
is a marvel if he will be unpunished: for
compassion and wrath are both with him.
He is mighty to forgive, and He pours out
wrath.
12 As great as His compassion is, so is His
punishment also. Each man will be judged
according to his works[b].
13 The unrighteous will not escape with his
plunder, and the perseverance of the
righteous will not be withheld forever.
14 Everyone who works righteousness will
have his wage, and every man stands before
Him according to his works.
15 [יהוה hardened the heart of Pharaoh,
who did not know Him whose works had
been made known under the heavens.][c]
16 [His compassion was seen by all His
creation, and His light and Glory He has
distributed to mankind.][d]
17 Do not say, "I shall be hidden from
יהוה. And who will remember me in the
heights? I will not be known among the
multitudes of people. And what is my being
compared to all the spirits of all mankind?
18 Behold the heavens, and the heavens of
heavens, and the deep, and the earth. When
He descended to the pillars to look, they
trembled.
19 The forms of the mountains and the
foundations of the earth will shake and
tremble under the gaze of Elohim.
20 "And who then can set his heart upon
Me? Who will consider My way?
21 If I sin, no eye will see Me; if I lie with
all sort of deception, who will know?
22 Who will declare the works of the
righteous? For I will pour out a decree."

---

[a] 16:3 Bracketed section indicates reading present in Hebrew text but absent from Greek and Latin texts.

[b] 16:12 Compare Mishlei [Proverbs] 24:12; Iyyov [Job 34:11]; Romaious 2:6; Galah [Revelation] 20:13; 22:12.

[c] 16:15 Bracketed section indicates reading present in Hebrew and some Greek texts, but absent from other Greek texts. Latin text reads, "Do not say, 'I shall be hidden from Elohim, and who shall remember me from on high?'"

[d] 16:16 Bracketed section indicates reading present in Hebrew and some Greek texts, but absent from other Greek texts. Latin text continues the previous reading with, "'In such a multitude I shall not be known: for what is my being in such an immense creation?'"

23 The ones who love their own hearts incline to such things, and a fool thinks this way.
24 My son, listen to me, and learn knowledge, and set your heart upon my words.
25 I will pour out my spirit in measure, and declare knowledge in humility.
26 As Elohim created His works from the beginning and assigned their tasks, from the time when He disposed of its parts.[a]
27 He adorned His works forever, and the beginnings of them to their generations; they neither hunger, nor are weary, and they do not cease from their works.
28 No one thrusts aside his neighbor, and they will never disobey His word.
29 After this also Elohim looked upon the earth, and filled it with His blessings.
30 All manner of living things covered the face *of the earth*, and they will return back into it.

17

1 Elohim created man from the earth, and turned him back to it again.
2 He gave them days by number, and a set time, and gave them authority over the things that are on *earth*.
3 He filled them with strength that suited them, and made them according to his own image.
4 He put the fear of him upon all flesh, and gave him to have dominion over beasts and fowls.
5 [They received the use of the five senses of Elohim, and in the sixth place He gave them understanding, and in the seventh *He gave them* speech, *and* an interpreter of the mind's considerations.][b]
6 He gave them counsel, and tongue, and eyes, ears, and heart, so that they may understand.
7 He filled them with the knowledge of wisdom, and showed them good and evil.
8 He set his eye upon their hearts, to show them the majesty of His works.
9 [He gave them to glory in His marvelous acts forever, that they might declare His works with understanding.][c]
10 And they will praise His Set-apart Name, that they may declare the greatness of His works.
11 He added knowledge to them, and gave them a law of life for a heritage.
12 He cut an everlasting covenant with them, and showed them His judgments.
13 Their eyes saw the majesty of His glory, and their ear heard the glory of His voice.
14 And He said to them, "Beware of all unrighteousness." And he gave them commands, each man, concerning his neighbor.
15 Their ways are always before Him, and they will not be hidden from His eyes.
16 [Every man from his youth is given to evil; and they could not exchange their hearts of stone for *hearts* of flesh.][d]
17 He appointed a ruler for every nation, and Yisra'el is the portion of Elohim.
18 [Who, being His firstborn, He nourished with discipline, and – giving him the light

---

[a] 16:26 Hebrew fragments end here for this section.
[b] 17:5 Bracketed section indicates reading not present in some Greek text. Latin text reads, "He created a helpmate like to himself from him;"
[c] 17:9 Bracketed section indicates reading absent from some Greek texts.
[d] 17:16 Bracketed section indicates reading absent from some Greek texts, as well as the Latin text.

of His love – does not forsake him.][a]
19 All their works are as the sun before Him, and His eyes are always watching their ways.
20 Their iniquities are not hidden from Him, and all their sins are before Elohim.
21 [But Elohim, being kind and knowing His creation, neither left nor forsook them, but spared them.][b]
22 With Him the righteousness of man is as a signet *ring*, and He will keep the good deeds of a man as the apple of His eye, [and give repentance to His sons and daughters.][c]
23 Afterwards He will rise up and reward them, and render their reward upon their head.[d]
24 But He grants a return to those that repent, and He comforts those who are losing patience.
25 Return to יהוה, and forsake your sins; make your prayer before His face, and lessen the offence.
26 Turn again to Elyon, and turn away from iniquity, and greatly hate the abominable thing.
27 Who will praise Elyon in Sheol, instead of those who live and give thanks?
28 [Thanksgiving perishes from the dead, as from one that is not;][e] he that is in life and health will praise Elohim.
29 How great is the kindness of יהוה, and His forgiveness to those who turn to Him!
30 For all things cannot be in men, because the son of man is not immortal.
31 What is brighter than the sun? Yet this fails; and flesh and blood will imagine evil.
32 He looks upon the power of the height of heaven, and all men are earth and ashes.

18 1 He that lives forever created all things in common.
2 Elohim alone will be declared right.
3 [He who governs the world with the palm of His hand, and all things obey His will: for he is the King of all, by His power: dividing set-apart things among them from profane.][f]
4 To whom has He given the power to declare His works? And who shall search out His noble acts?
5 Who shall number the strength of His majesty? And who shall tell of His kindness?
6 As for the wondrous works of Elohim, it is not possible to take from them nor add to them, nor is it possible to figure them out.
7 When a man has finished, then he is but at the beginning, and when he ceases, then he will be in doubt.
8 What is man, and what does he serve? What is his good, and what is his evil?
9 The number of man's days at the most are a hundred years.
10 As a drop of water from the sea, and a pebble from the sand, so are a few years in the day of eternity.
11 For this cause Elohim was patient with them, and poured out His kindness upon

---

[a] 17:18 Bracketed section indicates reading absent from some Greek texts.
[b] 17:21 Bracketed section indicates reading absent from some Greek texts, as well as the Latin text.
[c] 17:22 Bracketed section indicates reading absent from some Greek texts, as well as the Latin text.
[d] 17:23 Latin text adds, "and shall turn them down into the bowels of the earth."
[e] 17:28 Bracketed section indicates reading present in Greek and Latin texts, but absent from Syriac.
[f] 18:3 Bracketed section indicates reading absent absent from some Greek texts.

them.
12 He saw and perceived their end, that it is evil. Therefore He multiplied His forgiveness.
13 The kindness of a man is upon his neighbor, but the kindness of Elohim is upon all flesh. *It is* reproving, and disciplining, and teaching, and bringing *back* again, as a shepherd does his flock.
14 He is kind to those who accept discipline, and *to those* that diligently seek after His judgments.
15 My son, do not add blemish to your good deeds, and no words of grief in any of your giving.
16 Does the dew not soften the scorching heat? So is a word better than a gift.
17 Behold, is not a word better than a gift? And a kind man has both.
18 A fool will rebuke harshly, and the gift of an envious man consumes the eyes.
19 Learn before you speak, and take care of your health, or you will always be sick.
20 Examine yourself before judgment, and in the hour of visitation you will find forgiveness.
21 Humble yourself before you have fallen, and repent in the time of sin. [Do not delay in forsaking sins, and do not neglect it until you are in distress. Do not set a time for abandoning sin, and remember that death will not delay.][a]
22 Let nothing hinder you in paying your vows, and do not wait until death to be declared right.[b]
23 Before you make a vow, prepare yourself. Do not be as a man that tempts יהוה.
24 Consider the wrath that will be in the end of days, and the time of vengeance, when He turns away His face.
25 In the days of fullness, remember the time of hunger; in the days of wealth, *remember* poverty and lack.
26 From morning until evening the time changes; and all things are done quickly before יהוה.
27 A wise man will fear in everything, and in days of sinning he will beware of offence.
28 Every man of understanding knows wisdom, and will praise him that found her.
29 Those that understood sayings also became wise themselves, and poured forth appropriate proverbs.
30 Do not pursue your lusts, and refrain yourself from your cravings.
31 If you completely give your being the delight of her desire, she will make you the laughing-stock of your enemies.
32 Do not merry in excess luxury, nor be tied to its expense.
33 Do not be made into a beggar by feasting on borrowed *money*, when you have nothing in your purse.

19 1 A workman that is a drunkard will not become rich, and he that despises small things will fall little by little.
2 Wine and women will make men of understanding to fall away, [and he that clings to whores will be more reckless.][c]

[a] 18:21 Bracketed section indicates reading present in Syriac text, but absent from Greek and Latin texts.
[b] 18:22 Bracketed section indicates reading present in Greek and Latin texts, but absent from Syriac text.
[c] 19:2 Bracketed section indicates reading present in Greek, Latin, and Syriac texts, but absent from Hebrew fragment.

3 [Rottenness and worms will possess him,
and][a] a reckless being will be taken away.
4 He that trusts quickly is weak-minded,
and he that sins will offend against his own
being.
5 He that makes merry in his heart will be
condemned; [but he that resists pleasures
crowns his life. He that can rule his tongue
shall live without strife;][b]
6 And he that hates idle talk has less
wickedness.
7 Never repeat to others what is told to you,
and you will never fare worse.
8 Whether it pertains to friend or foe, do
not tell it; and unless it is a sin to you, do
not reveal it.
9 For he has heard you, and observed you,
and when the time comes he will hate you.
10 Have you heard a word? Let it die with
you. Be of good courage, for it will not
burst you.
11 A fool will cry out in pain with a word,
as a woman in labor with a child.
12 As an arrow that sticks in the flesh of the
thigh, so is a word in the belly of a fool.
13 Reprove a friend: he may not have done
it. But if he did something, *do so* that he
may do it no more.
14 Reprove your neighbor: he may not have
said it. But if he has said it, *do so* that he
may not say it again.
15 Reprove a friend: for many times there is
slander; and do not trust every word.
16 There is one that slips *in speech*, but not
from the heart. And who is he that has not
sinned with his tongue?
17 Reprove your neighbor before you
threaten him, and give place to the Torah of
Elyon.
18 [The fear of יהוה is the first step to be
accepted by Him, and wisdom obtains His
love.
19 The knowledge of the commands of
יהוה is the doctrine of life. Those that do
the things that please Him shall receive the
fruit of the tree of immortality.][c]
20 The fear of יהוה is all wisdom, and in all
wisdom is the doing of the Torah.
21 [If a servant says to his master, "I will
not do what pleases you;" though afterward
he does it, he angers him that nourishes
him.][d]
22 And the knowledge of wickedness is not
wisdom, and the discretion of sinners is not
counsel.
23 There is a wickedness, and it is
abomination. And the simple man may be
free from sin.
24 Better is one that has a little
understanding and fears, than one that has
much discretion, and transgresses the
Torah.
25 There is an exquisite subtlety, and it is
unjust. And there is one that perverts favor
to gain a judgment.
26 There is one that does wickedly, that
hangs down his head with mourning, but
inwardly he is full of deceit –
27 bowing down his face, and making as if
he were deaf of one ear; where he is not
known, he will be beforehand with you.
28 And even if he lacks power, which keeps
him from sinning, he will do mischief if he
finds the opportunity.
29 A man will be known by his look, and

---

[a] 19:3 Bracketed section indicates reading present in Greek and Latin texts, but absent from Syriac text and Hebrew fragment.
[b] 19:5 Bracketed section indicates reading absent from some Greek texts.
[c] 19:18-19 Bracketed section indicates reading absent from some Greek texts.
[d] 19:21 Bracketed section indicates reading absent from some Greek texts.

one that has understanding will be known by his face, when you meet him.
30 A man's garments, his hearty laughter, and the way he walks, will tell what sort *of man* he is.

20 1 There is a reproof that is not beautiful, and there is a man that keeps silence, and he is wise.
2 It is better to reprove, than to be angry. And he that makes confession will be kept back from hurt.
3 [How good is it, when you are reproved, to repent! For so you shall escape willful sin.][a]
4 As the eunuch lusts to deflower a virgin, so is he that executes judgments with violence.
5 There is one that keeps silence, and is found wise, and there is one that is hated for his excessive talk.
6 There is one that keeps silence, for he has no answer to make; and there is one that keeps silence, knowing his time.
7 A wise man will be silent until his time comes, but the babbler and fool will overpass his time.
8 He that uses many words will be abhorred, and he that takes authority into himself will be hated.
9 There is a prosperity that a man finds in misfortunes, and there is a gain that turns to loss.
10 There is a gift that will not profit you, and there is a gift whose reward is double.
11 There is an abasement because of glory, and there is an uplifting of the head from a low estate.
12 There is one that buys much for a little, and pays for it again sevenfold.
13 He that is wise in words will make himself beloved, but the pleasantries of fools will be wasted.
14 The gift of a fool will not profit you, for his eyes are many instead of one.
15 He will give little, and rebuke much. He will open his mouth like a crier; today he will lend, and tomorrow he will ask it again. One who does this is a hated man.
16 The fool will say, "I have no friend, and I have no thanks for my good deeds. They that eat my bread are of evil tongue."
17 How often, and how by many, he will be laughed to scorn! [For he does not clearly know what it is to have, and it is all to him as if he did not have it.][b]
18 A slip on the ground is better than a slip of the tongue. So the fall of the wicked will come speedily.
19 A man without favor is as a tale out of season: it will be continually in the mouth of the ignorant.
20 A wise sentence from a fool's mouth will be rejected, for he will not speak it in its season.
21 There is one who is hindered from sinning through lack, and when he takes rest he will not be troubled.
22 There is one that destroys his being through timidity, and by a foolish countenance he will destroy it.
23 There is one that is timid, and is such he promises to his friend, and he makes him his enemy for nothing.
24 A lie is a foul blot in a man: it will be continually in the mouth of the ignorant.
25 A thief is better than a man that is

[a] 20:3 Bracketed section indicates reading absent from some Greek texts, as well as the Latin text.

[b] 20:17 Bracketed section indicates reading absent from some Greek texts.

continually lying, but they both will inherit
destruction.[a]
26 The disposition of a liar is dishonor, and
his shame is with him continually.
27 He that is wise in words will advance
himself, and one that is prudent will please
great men.
28 He that tills his land will raise his storage
high, and he that pleases great men will get
pardon for iniquity.
29 Presents and gifts blind the eyes of the
wise, and as a muzzle on the mouth, turn
away reproofs.
30 Wisdom that is hidden, and treasure that
is out of sight, what profit is in them both?
31 Better is a man that hides his folly, than
a man that hides his wisdom.
32 [Necessary patience in seeking Elohim is
better than he that leads his life without a
guide.][b]

21

1 My son, have you sinned? Do not
add more to it; and make petition for your
former sins.
2 Flee from sin as from the face of a
serpent, for if you draw near it will bite
you. Its teeth are the teeth of a lion, slaying
the beings of men.
3 All iniquity is as a two-edged sword: its
stroke has no healing.
4 Terror and violence will lay waste to
riches; so the house of an arrogant man will
be laid waste.
5 Petitions from a poor man's mouth reach
to the ears of Elohim, and His judgment
comes quickly.
6 One that hates reproof is in the path of the
sinner, and he that fears יהוה will turn
again in his heart.
7 He that is mighty in tongue is known far
off, but the man of understanding knows
when he slips.
8 He that builds his house with other men's
money is like one that gathers himself
stones against winter.
9 The synagogue of wicked men is as a
cable bound together: the end of them is a
flame of fire.
10 The way of sinners is made smooth with
stones, and Sheol is at its end.
11 He that guards the Torah of יהוה gains
its knowledge, and the perfect fear of יהוה
is wisdom.
12 He that is not clever will not be
instructed, and there is a cleverness which
makes bitterness abound.
13 The knowledge of a wise man will be
made to abound as a flood, and his counsel
as a fountain of life.
14 The inward parts of a fool are like a
broken vessel: he will hold no knowledge.
15 If a man of knowledge hears a wise
word, he will commend it, and add to it.
When the immoral man hears it, and it
displeases him, he puts it away behind his
back.
16 The discourse of a fool is like a burden
in the way, but favor will be found on the
lips of the wise.
17 The mouth of the prudent man will be
sought for in the assembly, and they will
ponder his words in their heart.
18 As a house that is destroyed, so is
wisdom to a fool. And the knowledge of an
unwise man is as senseless talk.
19 Instruction is as fetters on the feet of an
unwise man, and as shackles on the right
hand.
20 A fool lifts up his voice with laughter,

---

[a] 20:25 Compare Korinthious A [1 Corinthians] 6:9-10.

[b] 20:32 Bracketed section indicates reading absent from most Greek and Latin texts.

but a clever man will scarcely smile
quietly.
21 Instruction is an ornament of gold to a
prudent man, and as a bracelet upon his
right arm.
22 The foot of a fool is quick to enter
another man's house, but a man of
experience will be ashamed of entering.
23 A foolish man spies into the door of
another man's house, but a man that is
instructed will stand outside.
24 It is a lack of instruction in a man to
listen at the door, but the prudent man will
be grieved with the disgrace.
25 The lips of strangers will be grieved at
these things, but the words of prudent men
will be weighed in the balance.
26 The heart of fools is in their mouth, but
the mouth of wise men is their heart.
27 When the wicked curses Satan, he curses
his own being.
28 A whisperer defiles his own being, and
will be hated wherever he sojourns.

22

1 A slothful man is compared to a
stone that is defiled, and everyone will hiss
him out in his disgrace.
2 A slothful man is compared to the filth of
a dunghill, and every man that takes it up
will shake out his hand.
3 A father has shame in having begotten an
undisciplined son, and a foolish daughter is
born to his loss.
4 A sensible daughter will inherit a husband
of her own, and she that brings shame is the
grief of her father.
5 She that is brash brings shame upon
father and husband, and she will be
despised by them both.
6 Unseasonable discourse is as music in
mourning, but stripes and correction are
wisdom at every season.
7 He that teaches a fool is as one that glues
a potsherd together, even as one that wakes
a sleeper out of a deep sleep.
8 He that converses with a fool is as one
speaking to a man that sleeps; by the end he
will say, "What is it?"
9 [If children live honestly, and have
ability, they shall cover the baseness of
their parents.
10 But children, being haughty, through
disdain and lack of nurturing stain the
nobility of their family.][a]
11 Weep for the dead, for light has failed
him. Weep for a fool, for understanding has
failed him. Weep more sweetly for the
dead, because he has found rest. But the life
of the fool is worse than death.
12 Seven days are the days of mourning for
the dead; but for a fool and a wicked man,
all the days of his life *are mourning*.
13 Do not talk much with a foolish man,
and do not go to one that has no
understanding. Beware of him, lest you
have trouble, and so you shall not be
defiled in his onslaught. Turn away from
him, and you will find rest. And so you
shall not be wearied in his madness.
14 What shall be heavier than lead? And
what is its name, but a fool?
15 Sand, and salt, and a mass of iron, is
easier to bear, than a man without
understanding.
16 Timber girded and bound into a building
will not be loosed with shaking. So a heart
established in due season on well-advised

---

[a] 22:9-10 Bracketed section indicates reading absent from most Greek texts, as well as the Latin text.

counsel will not be afraid.
17 A heart settled upon a thoughtful understanding is as an ornament of plaster on a polished wall.
18 Pales set on a high place will not stand against the wind, so a fearful heart in the imagination of a fool will not stand against any fear.
19 He that pricks the eye will make tears to fall, and he that pricks the heart causes it to show feeling.
20 Whoever casts a stone at birds scares them away, and he that rebukes a friend will dissolve friendship.
21 If you have drawn a sword against a friend, do not despair, for there may be a returning.
22 If you have opened your mouth against a friend, do not fear, for there may be reconciliation; except it be for rebuking, and arrogance, and disclosing of a secret, and a treacherous blow: for from these things every friend will flee.
23 Gain trust with your neighbor in his poverty, that in his prosperity you may have gladness. Remain steadfast to him in the time of his affliction, that you may be heir with him in his inheritance.
24 Before fire is the vapor and smoke of a furnace, so is reviling before bloodshed.
25 I will not be ashamed to shelter a friend, and I will not hide myself from his face.
26 If any evil happens to me because of him, every one that hears it will beware of him.
27 Who will set a watch over my mouth, and a seal of discernment upon my lips, that I will not fall from it, and that my tongue will not destroy me?

23 1 O יהוה, Father and Master of my life, do not abandon me not to their counsel, and do not allow me to fall by them.
2 *Those* who will set scourges over my thoughts, and a discipline of wisdom over my heart? They would not spare me because of my ignorance, and my heart will not pass by their sins;
3 that my ignorance will not be multiplied, and my sins not abound, and I will fall before my adversaries, and my enemy rejoice over me.
4 O יהוה, Father and El of my life, do not give me a proud look,
5 And turn away lust from me.
6 Do not let greed of stomach and lust of flesh overtake me, and do not give me over to a shameless mind.
7 Listen, my children, to the discipline of the mouth. He that keeps it will not be taken.
8 The sinner will be overtaken in his lips, and the reviler and the proud man will stumble.
9 Do not make a habit of taking an oath, nor make a habit of naming the Set-Apart One.
10 For as a servant that is continually scourged will not lack a bruise, so he also that swears and names Elohim continually will not be cleansed from sin.
11 A man of many oaths will be filled with iniquity, and the scourge will not depart from his house. If he offends, his sin will be upon him, and if he disregards it, he has sinned twice. If he has sworn in vain, he will not be declared right, for his house will be filled with calamities.
12 There is a manner of speech that is clothed about with death. Do not let it be found in the inheritance of Ya'aqov. For all these things will be far from the righteous, and they will not wallow in sins.
13 Do not make a habit of swearing excessively, for the word of sin is there.

14 Remember your father and your mother,
for you sit in the midst of great men, so that
you be not forgetful before them, and
become a fool by your custom. And so will
you desire that you had not been born, and
curse the day of your birth.
15 A man that is accustomed to words of
reproach will not be corrected all the days
of his life.
16 Two sorts of men multiply sins, and the
third will bring wrath. A hot mind, as a
burning fire, will not be quenched until it is
consumed. A fornicator in the body of his
flesh will never cease until he has burned
out the fire.
17 All bread is sweet to a fornicator, and he
will not quit until he is dead.
18 A man that goes astray from his own
bed, saying in his heart, "Who sees me?
Darkness surrounds me, and the walls hide
me, and no man sees me. Of whom should I
be afraid? Elyon will not remember my
sins."
19 And the eyes of men are his terror, and
he knows not that the eyes of יהוה are ten
thousand times brighter than the sun, seeing
all the ways of men, and looking into secret
places.
20 All things were known to Him before
they were even created, and in like manner
also after they were perfected.
21 This man will be punished in the streets
of the city, and he will be taken where he
did not suspect.
22 So also a wife that leaves her husband,
and brings in an heir by a stranger.
23 For first she was disobedient in the
Torah of the Elyon, and secondly she
trespassed against her own husband.
Thirdly she whored and brought forth a
child by a stranger.
24 She shall be brought out into the
assembly, and there will be visitation upon
her children.
25 Her children will not spread into roots,
and her branches will bear no fruit.
26 She will leave her memory for a curse,
and her reproach will not be blotted out.
27 And those who are left behind will know
that there is nothing better than the fear of
יהוה, and nothing sweeter than to guard the
commands of יהוה.
28 [It is great honor to follow יהוה, and to
be received by Him is long life.][a]

24 1 Wisdom will praise herself, and will
glory in the midst of her people.
2 She will open her mouth in the assembly
of Elyon, and glory in the presence of His
power.
3 "I came forth from the mouth of Elyon,
and covered the earth as a mist.
4 I lived in high places, and my throne is in
the pillar of the cloud.
5 I alone compassed the circuit of heaven,
and walked in the depth of the abyss.
6 In the waves of the sea, and in all the
earth, and in every people and nation, I
gained a possession.
7 With all these I sought rest; and in whose
inheritance shall I lodge?
8 Then the Creator of all things gave me a
command, and He that created me made my
tabernacle to rest, and said, 'Let your
tabernacle be in Ya'aqov, and your
inheritance in Yisra'el.'
9 He created me from the beginning before
the world, and to the end I will not fail.

---

[a] 23:28 Bracketed section indicates reading not present in most Greek texts.

10 I attended to Him in the set-apart
tabernacle, and so was I established in
Tsion.
11 Likewise in the beloved city He gave me
rest, and my authority was in
Yerushalayim.
12 And I took root in a people that was
glorified; even in the portion of the
inheritance of יהוה.
13 I was exalted like a cedar of Levanon,
and as a cypress tree on the mountains of
Ḥermon.
14 I was exalted like a palm tree on the sea
shore, and as rose plants in Yeriḥo, and as a
fair olive tree in the plain. I was exalted as
a plane tree.
15 As cinnamon and aspalathus, I have
given a scent of perfumes. And as choice
myrrh, I spread abroad a pleasant odor. As
galbanum, and onyx, and stacte, and as the
fume of frankincense in the Tabernacle.
16 As the terebinth I stretched out my
branches, and my branches are branches of
honor and favor.
17 I put forth favor as the vine, and my
flowers are the fruit of glory and riches.
18 [I am the mother of love, and fear, and
knowledge, and hope: I therefore, being
eternal, am given to all my children which
are named by Him.][a]
19 Come to me, you that desire me, and be
filled with my produce.
20 For my memorial is sweeter than honey,
and my inheritance *is sweeter* than the
honeycomb.
21 Those who eat me will hunger for more,
and those who drink me will thirst for
more.
22 He that obeys me will not be ashamed,
and those who work in me will not do
amiss."
23 All these things are the book of the
covenant of El Elyon, even the Torah
which Mosheh commanded us for an
inheritance to the synagogues of Ya'aqov.
24 [Do not lack strength in יהוה, that He
may confirm you; cling to Him, for יהוה
Almighty is Elohim alone, and besides Him
there is no other Savior.][b]
25 It is He that makes wisdom abundant, as
the river Pishon, and as Ḥiddeqel in the
days of new fruits,
26 that makes understanding full as Perath,
and as Yarden in the days of harvest;
27 that makes instruction to shine forth as
the light, as Giḥon in the days of vintage.
28 The first man did not know her perfectly.
In like manner the last has not figured her
out.
29 For her thoughts are filled from the sea,
and her counsels from the great deep.
30 "And I came out as a stream from a
river, and as a channel into a garden.
31 I said, 'I will water my garden, and will
water abundantly my garden bed, and,
behold, my stream became a river, and my
river became a sea.'
32 Yet I will bring instruction to light as the
morning, and will make these things to
shine forth afar off.
33 I will yet pour out doctrine as prophecy,
and leave it to generations of ages."
34 See that I have not labored for myself

---

[a] 24:18 Bracketed section indicates reading not present in some Greek texts.

[b] 24:24 Bracketed section indicates reading not present in some Greek texts. Latin text reads, "He appointed to David His servant to raise up of him a most mighty king, and set him on the throne of glory forever."

only, but for all those who diligently seek
her.

25 1 "In three things I was beautified, and
stood up beautiful before יהוה and men:
the harmony of brothers, friendship of
neighbors, and a woman and her husband
that walk together in agreement.
2 But three sorts of men my being hates,
and I am greatly offended by their life: a
poor man that is arrogant, a rich man that is
a liar, and an old man that is an adulterer
lacking understanding."
3 In your youth you have not gathered, and
how should you find in your old age?
4 How beautiful a thing is judgment for
gray hairs, and for elders to know counsel!
5 How beautiful is the wisdom of old men,
and thought and counsel to men that are in
honor!
6 Much experience is the crown of old men,
and their honor is the fear of יהוה.
7 There are nine things that I have thought
of, and in my heart counted happy, and the
tenth I will utter with my tongue: a man
that has joy in his children; a man that lives
and looks upon the fall of his enemies;
8 happy is he that dwells with a wife of
understanding; and he that has not slipped
with his tongue; and he that has not served
a man that is unworthy of him:
9 happy is he that has found discretion; and
he that discourses in the ears of those who
listen.
10 How great is he that has found wisdom!
Yet is there none above him that fears
יהוה.
11 The fear of יהוה surpasses all things. He
that holds it, to whom shall he be likened?
12 [The fear of יהוה is the beginning of His
love, and faith is the beginning of clinging
to Him.][a]
13 Give me any plague but the plague of the
heart, and any wickedness but the
wickedness of a woman.
14 Any calamity, but a calamity from those
who hate me, and any vengeance, but the
vengeance of enemies.
15 There is no head above the head of a
serpent, and there is no wrath above the
wrath of an enemy.
16 I would rather dwell with a lion and a
dragon, than keep house with a wicked
woman.
17 The wickedness of a woman changes her
look, and darkens her countenance as a bear
does.
18 Her husband will sit at meat among his
neighbors, and when he hears her, he sighs
bitterly.
19 All malice is small compared to the
malice of a *wicked* woman. Let the portion
of a sinner fall on her.
20 As going up a sandy way is *harsh* to the
feet of the aged, so is a wife full of words
to a quiet man.
21 Do not throw yourself upon the beauty
of a woman, and do not desire a woman for
her beauty.
22 There is anger, and rudeness, and great
reproach, if a woman has superiority over
her husband.
23 A wicked woman is an abasement of
heart, and sadness of face, and a wounded
heart. A woman that does not comfort her
husband is as hands that hang down, and
weak knees.
24 The beginning of sin came about from

---

[a] 25:12 Bracketed section indicates reading absent in some Greek texts.

woman, and because of her we all die.
25 Do not give water an outlet, nor freedom
of speech to a wicked woman.
26 If she does not go as you would have
her, cut her off from your flesh.

26 1 Happy is the husband of a good wife,
and the number of his days will be doubled.
2 A woman of valor rejoices in her
husband, and he will fulfil his years in
peace.
3 A good wife is a good portion, and she
will be given in the portion of those that
fear יהוה.
4 Whether a man be rich or poor, a good
heart makes at all times a cheerful
countenance.[a]
5 Of three things my heart was afraid, and
concerning the fourth kind I made petition:
the slander of a city, the assembly of a
multitude, and a false accusation. All these
are more grievous than death.
6 A grief of heart and sorrow is a woman
that is jealous of another woman, and the
scourge of a tongue communicating to all.
7 A wicked woman is as a yoke of oxen
shaken back and forth, and he that takes
hold of her is as one that grasps a scorpion.
8 A drunken woman causes great wrath,
and she will not cover her own shame.
9 The whoring of a woman is in the lifting
up of her eyes, and it will be known by her
eyelids.
10 Keep strict watch on a headstrong
daughter, lest she find liberty for herself,
and overuse it.
11 Look well after an evil eye, and do not
marvel if it trespasses against you.
12 She will open her mouth, as a thirsty
traveler, and drink of every water *source*
that is near. She will sit down at every post,
and open her quiver against any arrow.
13 The favor of a wife will delight her
husband, and her knowledge will fatten his
bones.
14 A silent woman is a gift from Elohim,
and there is nothing as valuable as a well-
instructed being.
15 A diligent woman is favor upon favor,
and a being of self-control is priceless.
16 As the sun when it arises in the highest
places of יהוה, so is the beauty of a good
wife in the ordering of a man's house.
17 As the lamp that shines upon the set-
apart menorah, so is the beauty of the face
in ripe age.
18 As the golden pillars are upon a base of
silver, so are beautiful feet with the chest of
one that is steadfast.
19 [My son, keep the flower of your age
sound; and do not give your strength to
strangers.
20 When you gain a fruitful possession
through all the field, sow it with your own
seed, trusting in the goodness of your stock.
21 So your race which you leave shall be
magnified, having the confidence of their
good descent.
22 A whore will be accounted as spit, but a
married woman is a tower against death to
her husband.
23 A wicked woman is given as a portion to
a wicked man, but a righteous woman is
given to him that fears יהוה.
24 A dishonest woman brings shame, but an
honest woman will honor her husband.
25 A shameless woman will be counted as a
dog, but she that is diligent will fear יהוה.
26 A woman that honors her husband will

[a] 26:4 Compare Mishlei [Proverbs] 15:13.

be considered wise by all, but she that
dishonors him in her pride will be
considered wicked by all.
27 A loud crying woman and a scold shall
be sought out to drive away the enemies.]
28 For two things my heart is grieved, and
for the third anger comes upon me: a man
of war that suffers for poverty, men of
understanding that are counted as refuse,
and one that turns back from righteousness
to sin; יהוה will prepare the sword for him.
29 A merchant shall hardly keep himself
from wrong doing, and a dealer will not be
acquitted of sin.

27 1 Many have sinned for profit, and he
that seeks to multiply gain will turn his eye
away.
2 A nail will stick fast between the joints of
stones, and sin will thrust itself in between
buying and selling.
3 Unless a man holds on diligently in the
fear of יהוה, his house will soon be
overthrown.
4 In the shaking of a sieve, the husk
remains; so do a man's sins when he
speaks.
5 The furnace will prove the potter's
vessels, and the trial of a man is in his
reasoning.
6 The fruit of a tree declares its maker; so is
the utterance of the thought of the heart of a
man.
7 Do not praise a man before you hear him
reason, for this is the trial of men.
8 If you follow righteousness, you will
obtain her, and put her on, as a long robe of
glory.
9 Birds will resort to their kind, and truth
will return to those who practice her.
10 As the lion lies in wait for prey, so does
sin *wait* for those who work iniquity.
11 The speech of a righteous man is always
wisdom, but the foolish man changes like
the moon *phases*.
12 Among men who lack understanding,
observe the opportunity, but stay
continually among the thoughtful.
13 The speech of fools is an offense, and
their laughter is in the depravity of sin.
14 The talk of a man of many oaths will
make the hair stand up, and their strife
makes one stop his ears.
15 The strife of the proud sheds blood, and
their reviling of each other is a grievous
thing to hear.
16 He that reveals secrets destroys
credibility, and will not find a friend to his
mind.
17 Love a friend, and keep faith with him;
but if you reveal his secrets, you shall not
pursue after him.
18 For as a man has destroyed his enemy,
so have you destroyed the friendship of
your neighbor.
19 And as a bird which you have released
from your hand, so have you let your
neighbor go, and you will not catch him
again.
20 Do not pursue him, for he is gone far
away, and has escaped as a gazelle out of
the snare.
21 For a wound may be bound up, and after
reviling there may be a reconciliation, but
he that reveals secrets has lost hope.
22 One that winks with the eye contrives
evil things, and no man will remove him
from it.
23 When you are present, he will speak
sweetly, and will admire your words. But
afterward he will twist his mouth, and set a
trap for you in your words.
24 I have hated many things, but nothing
like him: יהוה will hate him.

25 One that casts a stone on high casts it on his own head, and a deceitful stroke will open wounds.
26 He that digs a pit will fall into it, and he that sets a snare will be taken in it.
27 The evil things that he does will roll upon him, and he will not know why they have come.
28 Mockery and reproach are from the arrogant, and vengeance, as a lion, will lie in wait for him.
29 They that rejoice at the fall of the righteous will be taken in a snare, and anguish will consume them before they die.
30 Wrath and anger: these also are abominations, and a sinful man will possess them.

28 1 He that takes vengeance will find vengeance from יהוה, and He keeps account of his sins.
2 Forgive your neighbor the hurt that he has done you, and then your sins will be pardoned when you pray.[a]
3 Man cherishes anger against man, and does he seek healing from יהוה?
4 He has no compassion upon a man like himself; does he make petition for his own sins?
5 Being flesh, he nourishes himself with wrath. Who will atone for his sins?
6 Remember your latter end, and cease from enmity. Remember corruption and death, and [guard the commands][b].
7 Remember the commands, and do not be angry with your neighbor. Remember the covenant of Elyon, and overlook faults.
8 Avoid strife, and you your sins will diminish. For a passionate man will kindle
strife, 9 and a man that sins will trouble his
friends, and will sow discord among those who are at peace.
10 The greater the fuel, the greater the fire will burn. The greater the stoutness of the strife, the greater it will burn. The greater the strength of the man, the greater will be his wrath. And the greater his power, the greater will be his anger.
11 Pitch and tar kindle a fire, and a hasty fighting sheds blood.
12 If you blow a spark, it will burn. If you spit upon it, it will be quenched. And both of these shall come out of your mouth.
13 Curse the whisperer and double-tongued, for he has destroyed many that were at peace.
14 A meddlesome tongue has shaken many, and dispersed them from nation to nation. It has pulled down strong cities, and overthrown the houses of great men.
15 A meddlesome tongue has cast out brave women, and deprived them of their labors.
16 He that listens to it will not find rest, nor shall he dwell quietly.
17 The stroke of a whip makes a mark in the flesh, but the stroke of a tongue will break bones.
18 Many have fallen by the edge of the sword, yet not as many as have fallen because of the tongue.
19 Happy is he that is kept from it, that has not passed through its wrath, that has not drawn its yoke, and has not been bound with its bands.
20 For its yoke is a yoke of iron, and its bands are bands of copper.

---

[a] 28:2 See Mattithyahu [Matthew] 6:14-15.

[b] 28:6 Bracketed section indicates reading present in Greek and Latin texts. Syriac text reads, "cease from your sins."

21 Its death is an evil death, and Sheol is
greater than it.
22 It shall not have rule over righteous men,
and they shall not be burned in its flame.
23 They that forsake יהוה shall fall into it,
and it shall burn among them, and shall not
be quenched. It shall be sent forth upon
them as a lion, and as a leopard it shall
destroy them.
24 See to it that you hedge your possession
about with thorns, and bind up your silver
and your gold.
25 Make a balance and a weight for your
words, and make a door and a bar for your
mouth.
26 Take heed lest you slip in it, lest you fall
before one that lies in wait.

29 1 He that shows kindness will lend to
his neighbor, and he that strengthens him
with his hand keeps the commands.
2 Lend to your neighbor in time of his need,
and pay your neighbor back in due season.
3 Confirm your word, and keep faith with
him, and you will always find what you
need.
4 Many have asked for a loan, and have
given trouble to those that helped them.
5 When he borrows, he kisses the lender's
hand and speaks with respect of his
creditor's wealth; but when payment is due,
he will take too long, and return words of
heaviness, and complain of the times.
6 If he receives half *of what he loaned*, the
lender succeeds; if not, he is cheated of his
wealth and acquires an enemy at no greater
cost; the borrower will repay him with
curses and insults, and with contempt
instead of honor.
7 On account of this ill-dealing, many have
turned away: they have feared to be
defrauded for nothing.
8 However, be generous to a poor man, and
do not delay in acts of righteousness toward
him.
9 Help a poor man for the sake of the
command, and do not send him away
empty-handed because of his need.
10 Lose your money to a brother and a
friend, and do hide it under a stone to be
lost.
11 Let the commands of Elyon be your
treasure, and it will be better than gold.
12 Store up tsedaqqah in the hearts of the
poor, and it will gain you help against all
evil.
13 Better than a shield or lance of a
powerful man, it will fight for you against
your enemy.
14 A good man offers credit for his
neighbor, but he that has lost shame will
fail him.
15 Do not forget the good offices of your
patron, for he offers his life for you.
16 A sinner will overthrow the good estate
of his patron, 17 and he whose mind is not
thankful will fail the one that assisted him.
18 Patronage has ruined many that were
prospering, and shaken them as a wave of
the sea. It has driven mighty men from their
homes, and they wandered among strange
nations.
19 Through patronage, the wicked comes to
grief, and he who works too much comes to
lawsuits.
20 Help your neighbor as you are able, and
take heed to yourself that you fall not the
same way.
21 The chief *requirement* for life is water,
bread, and a garment, and a house to cover
shame.
22 Better is the life of a poor man under a
shelter of logs, than extravagant treatment
in another man's house.

23 Be content with what you have, be it
little or much; [and you will not hear
rebuke from your family][a].
24 It is a miserable life to go from house to
house. And where you are a sojourner, do
not dare to open your mouth.
25 You will entertain, and give to drink, and
have no thanks. And in addition to this, you
will hear bitter words *such as this*:
26 "Come here, sojourner; prepare a table,
and if you have anything in your hand, feed
me with it. 27 Go forth, sojourner, from the
face of honor, *for* my brother has come to
be my guest; I need my house."
28 These things are grievous to a man of
understanding: the rebuking of a
household, and the reproaching of the
money-lender.

30 1 He that loves his son will continue to
lay stripes upon him, that he may have joy
of him in the end.
2 He that disciplines his son will benefit
from him, and will boast about him among
his friends.
3 He that teaches his son shall provoke his
enemy to jealousy, and he will rejoice over
him among his friends.
4 His father dies, and is as though he had
not died, for he has one behind in his
likeness.
5 In his life, he saw and rejoiced in him.
And when he died, he did not sorrow.
6 He left behind him an avenger against his
enemies, and one to repay kindness to his
friends.
7 He that spoils his son will bind up his
wounds, and his heart will be troubled at
every cry.
8 An untamed horse becomes stubborn, and
a son left at large becomes headstrong.
9 Pamper your child, and he will be a terror
for you; indulge him, and he will grieve
you.
10 Do not share in his silliness, lest you
have sorrow because of him, and you will
gnash your teeth in the end.
11 Do not give him his own way in his
youth, and do not wink at his foolishness.
12 Bend him to the yoke in his youth, and
strike him on the sides while he is small,
lest he grow stubborn, and disobey you,
and leave you miserable.
13 Discipline your son, and [make his yoke
heavy][b], lest his foolishness humiliate you.
14 Better is a poor man, being strong and
robust, than a rich man that is plagued in
his body.
15 Health and well-being are better than all
gold, and a strong body than infinite
wealth.
16 There are no riches better than a healthy
body, and there is no gladness above the
joy of the heart.
17 Death is better than a bitter life, and
eternal sleep than a continual sickness.
18 Good things poured out upon a closed
mouth are like slabs of meat laid before an
idol[c].
19 What does an offering profit an idol? For
it does not eat it, nor smell it. So is he that
is punished by יהוה, 20 who groans at the
good things his eyes behold, like a eunuch

[a] 29:23 Bracketed section indicates reading present in some Greek and Latin texts, but absent from others.
[b] 30:13 So the Hebrew. Greek and Latin texts read, "take pains with him."
[c] 30:18 So the Hebrew text. Greek, Latin, and Syriac texts read, "grave."

embracing a virgin. So is he who does right
under compulsion, but יהוה will require it
at his hand.
21 Do not give your being over to sorrow,
and do not afflict yourself in your own
counsel.
22 A glad heart is the life of a man, and the
joy of a man is length of days.
23 Love your own being, comfort your
heart, and remove sorrow far from you: for
sorrow has destroyed many, and it is not
profitable.
24 Envy and wrath shorten a man's days,
and worry brings old age before its time.
25 A cheerful and good heart will benefit
from his meal.

31

1 Watching over riches wastes the
flesh, and the anxiety of it drives sleep
away.
2 Wakeful anxiety will crave slumber, and
sleep will be broken in a serious disease.
3 A rich man toils in gathering wealth
together, and his only rest is wanton
pleasure.
4 A poor man toils in lack of substance, and
if he rests he becomes needy.
5 He that loves gold shall not be freed from
sin, and he that pursues wealth will be led
astray by it.
6 Many have been ensnared by gold, and
their destruction meets them face to face.
[But their possessions were unable to save
them from disaster, or to save them on the
day of wrath.][a]
7 It is a stumbling block to those who
sacrifice to it, and every fool shall be taken
by it.
8 Blessed is the rich that is found
blameless, and that does not go after gold.
9 Who is he? We will call him blessed. For
he has done wonderful things among his
people.
10 Who has been tried by it, and found
perfect? Then let him glory. Who has had
the power to transgress, and has not
transgressed? And to do evil, and has not
done it?
11 His goods shall be secure, and the
congregation shall declare his
righteousness.
12 Do you sit at the table of the great? Do
not be greedy upon it, and do not say,
"There are many things upon it."
13 Elohim hates the evil eye; was any
created *thing* ever more wicked? And so it
shifts with everything it sees, and sends
tears streaming down the face.[b]
14 See that your neighbor feels as you do,
and remember your own dislikes.
15 Do not stretch your hand to what he
desires, and do not reach for what he does
in the same basket.
16 Eat that which is set before you like a
well-taught *man*, and do not be greedy, lest
you be hated.
17 Be the first to cease *eating* on account of
propriety, and do not be insatiable, lest you
offend.
18 And if you sit among many, do not reach
out your hand before them.
19 How sufficient to a well-mannered man
is a very little, and when he lies in his bed
his breathing is not labored.
20 Healthy sleep comes from moderate
eating: he rises early and his wits are with

[a] 31:6 Bracketed section indicates reading present in Syriac text, but absent from Hebrew, Greek, and Latin.

[b] 31:13 So the Hebrew and Syriac. Greek and Latin texts read, "Remember that an evil eye is a wicked thing. No created thing is more evil than the eye. Therefore it weeps for any cause."

him. *But* the pain of wakefulness, and
distress, and griping are with an insatiable
man.
21 And if you have been compelled to eat
too much, you shall have relief when your
stomach is empty.
22 Hear me, my son, and do not despise.
Later you shall find my words true: in all
your works be quick, and no disease shall
come to you.
23 Blessings are pronounced on a man
generous with food, and the witness of his
goodness lasts.
24 *But* he who is stingy with food is
rebuked in public, and the witness of his
stinginess lasts.
25 Do not show your strength in wine-
drinking, for wine has destroyed many.
26 As the furnace proves the temper of
steel, so does wine prove hearts in the
disputing of the proud.
27 Wine is as good as life to men, if you
drink it in its measure. What life is there to
a man that is without wine? And it has been
created to make men glad.
28 Wine drunk in season and to satisfy, is
joy of heart, and gladness of soul.
29 *But* drinking too much wine is bitterness
of soul, with provocation and conflict.
30 Drunkenness increases the rage of a fool
to his detriment; it diminishes strength, and
adds wounds.
31 Do not rebuke your neighbor at a
banquet of wine, nor shame him while he is
merry. Do not speak to him a word of
reproach, and do not press upon him by
asking back a debt.

32 1 Have they made you ruler of a feast?
Then do not be lifted up; act like one of
them. Remember them, and sit down.
2 And when you have fulfilled all your
duties, take your place, that you may be
made joyful on their account, and receive a
crown for your hospitality.
3 Speak, you that are the elder, for it suits
you, but do so with sound knowledge, and
do not hinder music.
4 Do not talk profusely [when wine is
present][a], and do not display your wisdom
out of season.
5 As a signet of carbuncle in a setting of
gold, so is a concert of music in a banquet
of wine.
6 As a signet of emerald in a work of gold,
so is a strain of music with pleasant wine.
7 Speak, young man, if you are needed, but
scarcely if you are asked twice.
8 Sum up your speech of many things in
few words, and be as one that knows, and
yet holds his tongue.
9 If you sit among great men, do not behave
as their equal. And when another is
speaking, refrain from whispering much.
10 Lightning speeds before thunder, and
favor shall go before a modest man.
11 When it is time to go home, go early,
and do not loiter.
12 There perform what is in your heart, and
enjoy your hobbies. And do not sin by
proud speech.
13 Bless Him that made you for these
things, He that gives you to drink freely of
His good things.
14 He that seeks Elohim will receive
correction from Him, and those who seek
Him early will find favor.
15 He that seeks the Torah will be filled
favor, but the hypocrite will stumble at it.

---

[a] 32:4 So the Hebrew text. Greek and Latin texts read, "where music is being performed."

16 They that fear יהוה will find judgment,
and will kindle righteous deeds as a light.
17 A sinful man shuns reproof, and will find
a judgment according to his own will.
18 A man of counsel will not neglect a
thought. A strange and proud man will not
crouch in fear, even after he has done a
thing by himself without counsel.
19 Do nothing without counsel, and when
you have done it, do not regret.
20 Do not go in a way of conflict, and do
not stumble in the same place twice.
21 Do not be over-confident in a smooth
road, 22 and beware in all your paths.
23 In every work trust your own being, for
this is the guarding of the commands.
24 He that [guards the Torah preserves
himself][a], and he that trusts in יהוה will not
be put to shame.

33

1 No evil happen to him that fears
יהוה; but He will deliver him from
temptation again and again.
2 He who hates the Torah is without
wisdom, but the hypocrite in it is as a ship
in a storm.
3 A man of understanding will put his trust
in the word of יהוה, and the Torah is
faithful to him, as a divine oracle.
4 Prepare your speech, and so shall you be
heard. Bind up instruction, and make your
answer.
5 The heart of a fool is as a cart wheel, and
his thoughts revolve in circles.
6 A stallion horse is as a mocking friend: he
neighs under every one that sits upon him.
7 Why is one day better than another, when
all the light of every day in the year is from
the sun?
8 By the knowledge of יהוה they were
distinguished, and He varied times and
feasts.
9 Some of them He exalted and set apart,
and some of them He made ordinary days.
10 All men are from the ground, and Adam
was created of earth.
11 In the abundance of His knowledge,
יהוה distinguished them, and made their
ways various.
12 Some of them He blessed and exalted,
and some of them He set apart and brought
near to Himself. Some of them He cursed
and brought low, and overthrew them from
their place.
13 As the clay of the potter is in his hand,
and he does all that he desires, so men are
in the hand of Him that made them, [to
render to them according to His
judgment.][b]
14 Good is the opposite of evil, and life is
the opposite of death. So the sinner is the
opposite of the righteous. [And darkness
with the light].[c]
15 And now look upon all the works of
Elyon: the two and two, one against
another.
16 I was the last to awake, as one that
gleans after the grape gatherers.
17 By the blessing of יהוה I got before
them, and filled my winepress as one that

---

[a] 32:24 So the Hebrew text. Greek and Latin texts read, "He that believes the Law, heeds the commandments."

[b] 33:13 So the Greek and Latin texts. Hebrew reads, "to assign their function to them;" Syriac reads, "to raise them up among all His works."

[c] 33:14 So the Hebrew and Syriac texts. Greek and Latin texts omit.

gathers grapes.
18 Consider that I labored not for myself
alone, but for all those who seek
instruction.
19 Hear me, O great men of the people, and
listen with your ears, O rulers of the
congregation.
20 Do not give power over you while you
live to son and wife, or to friend and
brother. And do not give your goods to
another, lest you repent and plead for them.
21 While you are living, and breath is in
you, do not give yourself over to anyone.
22 For it is better that your children should
plead with you, than that you should look
to the hand of your sons.
23 In all your works keep the upper hand,
and do not defile your honor.
24 In the end of the days of your life, and in
the time of death, distribute your
inheritance.
25 Fodder and whip and loads for a donkey;
the yoke and harness and the rod of his
master.
26 Bread, discipline, and work for a servant,
and punishment for a wicked servant.
27 Set your servant to work, and you shall
find rest. Leave his hands idle, and he will
seek to be freed.
28 Send him to labor, so that he is not idle,
29 for idleness teaches much mischief.
30 Set him to work, as is fit for him, and if
he does not obey, make his chains heavy.
Do nothing unjust.
31 If you have one servant, treat him as
yourself, for you have acquired him with
your lifeblood.
32 If you have one servant, deal with him as
a brother, for you need him as you need
your own life.
33 If you mistreat him and he runs away,
where will you look for him?

34 1 The hopes of a man who lacks
understanding are empty and vain, and
dreams give wings to fools.
2 As one that grasps at a shadow, and
follows after the wind, so is he who puts
his trust in dreams.
3 The vision of dreams is to this *reality*
what the reflection of a face is to the face
itself.
4 Can an unclean thing produce that which
is clean? Can the false one speak truth?
5 Divinations, and omens, and dreams are
meaningless, and the heart depicts what is
expected.
6 If visions are not sent from Elyon, do not
pay attention to them.
7 For dreams have led many astray, and
those that have put their hope in them have
perished.
8 The Torah is fulfilled without fail, and
perfect wisdom is found in the mouth of the
faithful man.
9 An educated man knows many things,
and he that has much experience will
declare understanding.
10 He that has no experience knows very
little,
11 but he that has wandered shall increase
his skill.
12 In my wandering I have seen many
things, and my understanding is more than
my words.
13 Many times I was in danger – even *close*
to death – and I was preserved because of
these things.
14 The spirit of those that fear יהוה shall
live,
15 for their hope is on Him who saves them.
16 Whoever fears יהוה shall not be afraid,
and shall not play the coward: for He is his
hope.

17 Happy is the one who fears יהוה.
18 In whom does he trust, and who is his support?
19 The eyes of יהוה are on those who love Him. A mighty shield and strong support. A shelter from the heat, and a shade from the noonday. A guard from stumbling, and a help against falling.
20 He raises up the being, and enlightens the eyes: He gives healing, life, and blessing.
21 He that sacrifices a thing wrongfully acquired, his offering is made in mockery.
22 The gifts[a] of wicked men are not well-pleasing.
23 Elyon has no pleasure in the offerings of the wicked, neither does He forgive their sins by the multitude of sacrifices.
24 As one that kills the son before his father's eyes, so is he that brings a sacrifice from the goods of the poor.
25 The bread of the needy is the life of the poor, *and* he that deprives him of it is a man of blood.
26 As one that slays his neighbor, so is he that takes away his living.
27 One that deprives a worker of his wage is a shedder of blood.
28 *If* one builds up and another pulls down, what profit have they had but toil?
29 *If* one is praying and another cursing, whose voice will יהוה hear?
30 He that washes himself after touching a dead body, and then touches it again, what profit has he in his washing?
31 Even so a man fasting for his sins, and going again to do the same, who will hear his prayer? And what does he gain in his humiliation?

35 1 He that guards the Torah multiplies offerings; he that takes heed to the commands sacrifices a peace offering.
2 He that repays a good turn offers *a* fine flour *offering*, and he that gives tsedaqqah sacrifices a thanksgiving offering.
3 To depart from wickedness is pleasing יהוה, and to depart from unrighteousness is an atoning sacrifice.
4 See that you not appear in the presence of יהוה empty-handed; for all these things are to be done because of the command.
5 The offering of the righteous makes the altar fat, and the soothing aroma if it is before Elyon.
6 The sacrifice of a righteous man is acceptable, and the memory of it shall not be forgotten.
7 Glorify יהוה with a good eye, and do not withhold the firstfruits of your hands.
8 In every gift display a cheerful face, and dedicate your tithe with gladness.
9 Give to Elyon as He has given to you, and as your hand has found, give with a good eye. [He who gives to the poor makes יהוה his debtor, and who else is the source of repayment?][b]
11 For יהוה repays, and He will repay you sevenfold.
12 Do not think that you can bribe Him with gifts, for He will not receive them. And do not set your mind on an unrighteous sacrifice. For יהוה is Judge, and He shows

[a] 34:22 So the Syriac, Latin, and some Greek. Other Greek read, "mockeries."

[b] 35:9 Bracketed section indicates reading present in Hebrew and Syriac texts, but absent from Greek text. Latin reads, "do according to the ability of your hands" instead.

no partiality for men.
13 He will not accept any man against a
poor man, and He will listen to the prayer
of him that is wronged.
14 He will in no way despise the petition of
the orphan, or the widow, when she pours
out her tale.
15 Do the tears of the widow not run down
her cheek? And is her cry not against him
that has caused them to fall?
16 He that serves Elohim according to His
good pleasure shall be accepted, and his
petition shall reach to the clouds.
17 The prayer of the humble pierces the
clouds, and he will not be comforted until it
comes near; and he will not depart until
Elyon visits. And He shall judge
righteously, and execute judgment.
18 And יהוה will not be slack, neither will
He be longsuffering toward them, until He
has crushed the loins of the unkind. And He
will repay vengeance to the heathen, until
He has taken away the multitude of the
arrogant, and broken in pieces the scepters
of the unrighteous.
19 Until **He has rendered to every man
according to his works**[a], and to the works
of men according to their plans. Until He
has judged the cause of His people. And He
shall make them to rejoice in His loving-
kindness.
20 Loving-kindness is seasonable in the
time of His afflicting them, as clouds of
rain in the time of drought.

36 1 Have compassion on us, O יהוה,
Elohim of all, and behold.
2 And send Your fear upon all the nations.
3 Lift up Your hand against the strange
nations, and let them see Your mighty
power.
4 As You were set apart in us before them,
so shall You be magnified in them before
us.
5 And let them know You, as we also have
known You, that there is no Elohim but
only You, O Elohim.
6 Show new signs, and work various
wonders. Glorify Your hand and Your right
arm.
7 Raise up indignation, and pour out wrath.
Take away the adversary, and destroy the
enemy.
8 Quicken the time, and remember the oath,
and let them declare Your mighty works.
9 Let him that escapes be devoured by the
rage of fire, and may those who harm Your
people find destruction.
10 Crush the heads of the rulers of the
enemies, those that say, "There is none but
us."
11 Gather all the tribes of Ya'aqov together,
and take them for Your inheritance as from
the beginning.
12 O יהוה, have compassion on the people
that is called by Your Name, and upon
Yisra'el, whom You made like a firstborn.
13 Have compassion on the city of Your
dwelling place, Yerushalayim, the place of
Your rest.
14 Fill Tsion; exalt Your prophecies, and
fill Your Temple[b] with Your glory.
15 Give testimony to those that were Your
creatures in the beginning, and raise up the
prophecies that have been in Your Name.
16 Give reward to those who wait for You,
and men shall put their trust in Your
prophets.
17 Listen to the prayer of Your servants,

[a] 35:19 See Romaious [Romans] 2:6; Mishlei [Proverbs] 24:12.

[b] 36:14 So the Hebrew and Syriac texts. Greek and Latin read, "people."

according to the blessing of Aharon
concerning Your people. And all those who
are on the earth shall know that You are the
eternal Elohim.
18 The throat[a] can consume any meat, yet
one meat is still better than another.
19 *As* the palate tastes meats taken in
hunting, so an understanding heart
perceives false speeches.
20 A perverse heart will cause grief, and a
man of experience will resist him.
21 A woman may receive any man, yet one
girl is better than another.
22 The beauty of a woman lights the face,
and a man desires nothing more.
23 If there is loving-kindness and humility
[and healing][b] on her tongue, her husband
is not like the sons of men.
24 He that acquires a wife gains his best
possession: a helper suitable for him, and a
pillar of rest.
25 Where there is no hedge, the possession
will be laid waste, and he that has no wife
will mourn as he wanders to and fro.
26 For who will trust a nimble robber, that
skips from city to city? Even so who shall
trust a man that has no nest, and lodges
wherever he finds himself at nightfall?

37 1 Every friend will say, "I also am his
friend;" but there is a friend who is only a
friend in name.
2 Is there not a grief in it even to death,
when a companion and friend is turned into
an enemy?
3 O wicked imagination, why did you come
rolling in? To cover the dry land with
deceitfulness?
4 There is a companion who rejoices in the
gladness of a friend, but in time of
affliction will be against him.
5 And there is a companion who, for the
sake of his belly, labors with his friend.
And in the face of battle will take up the
shield.
6 Do not forget a friend in your being, and
do not neglect him in your riches.
7 Every counsellor extols counsel, but there
is one that counsels for himself.
8 Let your being beware of *such* a
counsellor, and know beforehand what his
interest is – for he will take counsel for
himself – else he will cast the lot upon you,
9 and say to you, "Your way is good;" and
he will stand near you, to see what will
happen to you.
10 Do not take counsel with one that looks
suspiciously at you, and hide your counsel
from those that are jealous of you.
11 Do not take counsel with a woman about
her rival, nor with a coward about war; nor
with a merchant about exchange; nor with a
buyer about selling; nor with an envious
man about thankfulness; nor with an
unkind man about loving-kindness; nor
with a lazy man about any kind of work;
nor with a hireling in your house about
finishing his work; nor with an idle servant
about much business. Do not give heed to
these in any matter of counsel.
12 But rather, consult continually with a
righteous man, one whom you know guards
the commands, who in his being is as your
own being, and who will grieve with you if
you shall miscarry.
13 And make the counsel of your heart to
stand, for there is none more faithful to you
than it.
14 For a man's being sometimes desires to

[a] 36:18 So the Hebrew text. Greek and Latin texts read, "belly."

[b] 36:23 Some Hebrew and Greek texts add this section.

bring him news, more than seven
watchmen that sit on high on a watch-
tower.
15 And above all this, entreat Elyon, that
He may direct your way in truth.
16 Let reason be the beginning of every
work, and let counsel go before every
action.
17 As a token of the changing of the heart,
18 four kinds of things rise up: good and
evil, life and death. And that which rules
over them continually is the tongue.
19 There is one that is discerning and the
instructor of many, and yet is unprofitable
to his own being.
20 There is one that is subtle in words, and
is hated: he shall be destitute of all food.
21 For favor was not given to him from
יהוה, because he is deprived of all wisdom.
22 There is one that is wise to his own
being, and the fruits of his understanding
are trustworthy in the mouth.
23 A wise man will instruct his own people,
and the fruits of his understanding are
trustworthy.
24 A wise man will be filled with blessing,
and all those who see him will call him
happy.
25 The life of man is counted by days, and
the days of Yisra'el are innumerable.
26 The wise man shall inherit confidence
among his people, and his name shall live
forever.
27 My son, prove your being in your life,
and see what is evil for it, and do not give
that to it.
28 For all things are not profitable for all
men, nor does every being pleasure in
every thing.
29 Do not be insatiable in any luxury, and
do not be greedy on the things that you eat.
30 For in multitude of meats there shall be
disease, and gluttony leads to colic.
31 Many have perished because of gluttony,
but he that takes heed shall prolong his life.

38 1 Honor a physician according to your
need of him with the honors due to him.
For truly יהוה has created him.
2 For healing comes from Elyon, and he
shall receive a gift from the king.
3 The skill of the physician shall lift up his
head, and in the sight of great men he shall
be admired.
4 יהוה created medicines out of the earth,
and a sensible man will have no disgust at
them.
5 Was not water made sweet with wood,
that the virtue of it might be known?[a]
6 And he gave men skill, that they might be
glorified in His marvelous works.
7 He heals men with them, and takes away
his pain.
8 The pharmacist will make a medicine
with them, and His works shall not be
brought to an end. And from Him is peace
upon the face of the earth.
9 My son, do not be negligent in your
sickness, but pray to יהוה, and He shall
heal you.
10 Put away wrong doing, order your hands
correctly, and cleanse your heart from all
manner of sin.
11 Give *an offering for* a soothing aroma,
and a memorial *offering* of fine flour. Make
your offering fat, as one that is not.
12 Then give place to the physician, for
truly יהוה has created him, and do not let
him go from you, for you have need of him.

---

[a] 5 See Shemoth [Exodus] 15:22-27.

13 There is a time when the issue for good is in their hands.
14 For they also seek יהוה, that He may prosper them in giving relief and in healing for the maintenance of life.
15 He that sins before his Maker, let him fall into the hands of the physician.
16 My son, let your tears fall over the dead, and as one that suffers grievously, lament. Wrap up his body according to his due, and do not neglect his burial.
17 Make bitter weeping, and make passionate wailing, and let your mourning be according to his desert, for one day or two, lest you be evil spoken of, and so be comforted for your sorrow.[a]
18 For death comes from sorrow, and sorrow of heart will weaken strength.
19 Sorrow remains in calamity, and the poor man's life is grievous to the heart.[b]
20 Do not give your heart to sorrow: put it away, remembering the latter end.
21 Do not forget it, for there is no returning again. You will not profit him, and you will hurt yourself.
22 Remember the sentence upon him, for so also shall yours be. Yesterday for him, and today for you.
23 When the dead is at rest, let his memory rest, and be comforted for him, when his spirit departs from him.
24 [The profession of the scribe increases his wisdom][c], and he that has little business shall become wise.
25 How shall he become wise that holds the plow, that glories in the shaft of the goad, that drives oxen, and is occupied in their labors, and whose conversation is of the stock of bulls?
26 He will set his heart upon turning his furrows, and his wakefulness is to give his heifers their food.
27 So is every craftsman and taskmaster that passes his time by night as by day. They that cut engravings of signets, and his diligence is to make great variety. He will set his heart to preserve likeness in his portraiture, and will be wakeful to finish his work.
28 So is the smith sitting by the anvil, and considering the unformed iron. The flame[d] of the fire will waste his flesh, and in the heat of the furnace he will wrestle with his work. The noise of the hammer will always be in his ear, and his eyes are upon the pattern of the vessel. He will set his heart upon perfecting his works, and he will be careful to decorate them perfectly.
29 So is the potter sitting at his work, and turning the wheel about with his feet, who is always anxiously set at his work, and all his handiwork is by number.
30 He will fashion the clay with his arm, and will bend its strength in front of his feet. He will apply his heart to finish the glazing, and he will be careful to clean the furnace.
31 All these put their trust in their hands, and each becomes wise in his own work.
32 Without these *workers*, a city could not be inhabited, [and wherever they dwell,

---

[a] 38:17 Latin text omits this verse.
[b] 38:19 So the Greek text. Hebrew omits this verse. Syriac reads, "For thus the sad heart, rather than death, breaks the poor with cares and brings grief; because the life of the poor is the curse of the heart."
[c] 38:24 So the Hebrew text. Greek and Latin texts read, "The wisdom of the scribe comes by opportunity of leisure."
[d] 38:28 So the Syriac text. Greek and Latin texts read, "vapor."

they need not hunger][a].
33 They shall not be sought for in the council of the people, and in the assembly they shall not mount on high. They shall not sit on the seat of the judge, and they shall not understand the covenant of judgment. Nor shall they declare instruction and judgment, and they shall not be found where the parables are.
34 But they will maintain the fabric of the world, and their concern[b] is for the exercise of their craft.

39 1 Not so he that applies himself to the fear of Elohim, and meditates on the Torah of Elyon. He will seek out the wisdom of all the ancients, and will be occupied with the prophets of old.
2 He will keep the discourse of the men of renown, and will enter in amidst the deep things of parables.
3 He will seek out the hidden meaning of proverbs, and be conversant in the dark sayings of parables.
4 He will serve among great men, and appear before him that rules. He will travel through the land of strange nations, for he has tried good things and evil among men.
5 He is careful to seek his Maker, and will make petition before Elyon; and will open his mouth in prayer, and will make petition for his sins.
6 If it seems good to El Eyon, *then* he shall be filled with the spirit of understanding. He shall pour forth the words of his wisdom, and in prayer give thanks to יהוה.
7 He shall direct his counsel and knowledge, and in his secrets shall he meditate.
8 He shall show forth the instruction which he has been taught, and shall glory in the Torah of the covenant of יהוה.
9 Many shall commend his understanding, and so long as the world endures, it shall not be blotted out. His memory shall not depart, and his name shall live from generation to generation.
10 Nations shall declare his wisdom, and the congregation shall tell of his praise.
11 If he continue, he shall leave a greater name than a thousand, and if he die, he adds to it.
12 Yet more I will utter, which I have thought about. And I am filled as the moon at the full.
13 Listen to me, you set-apartchildren, and bud forth as a rose growing by a brook of
water; 14 and give a soothing aroma as frankincense, and put forth flowers as a lily. Spread abroad a soothing aroma, and sing a song of praise. Bless יהוה for all His works.
15 Magnify His Name, and give utterance to His praise with the songs of your lips, and with harps. And thus shall you say
when you utter His praise: 16 all the works
of יהוה are exceedingly good, and every command shall be accomplished in His timing.
17 None can say, "What is this? Why is that?" For in His timing they shall all be sought out. At His word the waters stood as a heap, and the receptacles of waters at the word of His mouth.
18 At His command is all His good pleasure done, and there is none that shall hinder His salvation.

---

[a] 38:32 So the Syriac text. Greek and Latin read, "and men would not sojourn, nor would they walk to and fro in it."

[b] 38:34 So the Hebrew text. Greek and Latin texts read, "prayer."

19 The works of all flesh are before Him, and it is not possible to be hidden from His eyes.
20 He sees from everlasting to everlasting, and there is nothing wonderful before Him.
21 None can say, "What is this? Why is that?" For all things are created for their uses.
22 His blessing covered the dry land as a river, and saturated it as a flood.
23 As He has turned the waters into saltiness; so shall the heathen inherit His wrath.
24 His ways are clear to the set-apart, and they are stumbling blocks to the wicked.
25 As good things are created from the beginning for the good, so are evil things for sinners.
26 The chief of all things necessary for the life of man are water, and fire, and iron, and salt, and wheat flour, and honey, and milk; the blood of the grape, and oil, and clothing.
27 All these things are for good to the righteous. So to the sinners they shall be turned into evil.
28 There are winds that are created for vengeance, and in their fury lay on their scourges heavily; in the time of consummation they pour out their strength, and shall appease the wrath of Him that made them.
29 Fire, and hail, and famine, and death: all these are created for vengeance.
30 Teeth of wild beasts, and scorpions and adders, and a sword punishing the wicked to destruction.
31 They shall rejoice in His command, and shall be made ready upon earth, when need be; and in their seasons they shall not transgress His word.
32 Therefore from the beginning I decided, and I thought this, and left it in writing:
33 all the works of יהוה are good, and He will supply every need in its time.
34 And none can say, "This is worse than that." For they shall all be well-approved in their time.
35 And now with all your heart and mouth sing praises, and bless the Name of יהוה.

40 1 Great travail is created for every man, and a heavy yoke is upon the sons of Adam[a], from the day of their coming forth from their mother's womb, until the day for their burial in the mother of all things.
2 The expectation of things to come, and the day of death, trouble their thoughts, and cause fear of heart.
3 From him that sits on a throne of glory, even to him that is humbled in earth and ashes.
4 From him that wears purple and a crown, even to him that is clothed with a hemp frock.
5 There is wrath, and jealousy, and trouble, and disquiet, and fear of death, and anger, and strife; and in the time of rest upon his bed his night-sleep does change his knowledge.
6 His rest is little to nothing, and afterward in his sleep, as in a day of keeping watch, he is troubled in the vision of his heart, as one that has escaped from the front of battle.
7 In the very time of his deliverance he awakens, and marvels that the fear is vain.
8 So it is with all flesh, from man to beast, and upon sinners sevenfold more.
9 Death, and bloodshed, and strife, and

[a] 40:1 Or "mankind."

sword; calamities, famine, tribulation, and
the scourge: 10 all these things were created
for the wicked, and because of them the
flood was brought.
11 All things that are of the earth return to
the earth again, and all things that are of the
waters return into the sea.
12 All bribery and injustice shall be blotted
out, and good faith shall stand forever.
13 The goods of the unjust shall be dried up
like a river, and like a great thunder in rain
shall go off in noise.
14 In opening his hands, a man shall be
made glad: so shall transgressors utterly
fail.
15 The children of the wicked shall not put
forth many branches, and are as unclean
roots upon a sheer rock.
16 The reed-stalks that grows upon every
water and bank of a river shall be plucked
up before all grass.
17 Bounty is as a garden of blessings, and
righteousness endures forever.
18 The life of one that labors and is
contented, shall be made sweet, and he that
finds a treasure is above both.
19 Children and the building of a city
establish a man's name, and a blameless
wife is counted above both.
20 Wine and music rejoice the heart, and
the love of wisdom is above both.
21 The flute and the lyre make pleasant
melody, and a pleasant tongue is above
both.
22 Your eye shall desire favor and beauty,
and above both *is* the green blade of corn.
23 A friend and a companion will each
conduct himself opportunely, and a discreet
wife is above both.
24 A brother and helper are for a time of
affliction, and righteousness is a deliverer
above both.
25 Gold and silver will make the foot stand
sure, and counsel is esteemed above them
both.
26 Riches and strength will lift up the heart,
and the fear of יהוה is above both. There is
nothing lacking in the fear of יהוה, and
there is no need to seek help in it.
27 The fear of יהוה is a very Eden of
blessing, and its canopy *stretches* above all
that is glorious.
28 My son, do not live as a beggar, for it is
better to die than to beg.
29 A man that looks to the table of another,
his life is not counted as a *real* life. He will
pollute his soul with another man's meats.
But to a wise man it is inward torture.
30 In the mouth of the shameless, begging
will be sweet, and in his belly a fire shall be
kindled.

41

1 O death, how bitter is your memory
to a man that is at peace in his possessions;
to the man that has nothing to distract him,
and has prosperity in all things, and that
still has strength to receive meat!
2 O death, acceptable is your sentence to a
man that is needy, and that fails in strength;
that is very old, and is distracted about all
things, and is perverse, and has lost
patience!
3 Do not be afraid of the sentence of death.
Remember those who have been before
you, and that come after, *for* this is the
sentence from יהוה over all flesh.
4 And why do you refuse, when it is the
good pleasure of Elyon? Whether it be ten,
or a hundred, or a thousand years, there is
no reproach concerning life in Sheol.
5 The children of sinners are abominable
children, and they frequent the dwellings of
the wicked.
6 The inheritance of sinners' children shall

perish, and with their posterity shall be a
perpetual reproach.
7 Children will complain about a wicked
father, because they shall be reproached for
his sake.
8 Woe to you, wicked men, which have
forsaken the Torah of El Elyon!
9 [If you increase, it shall be for mischief,
and if you bring forth children, it shall be
for sighing; if you stumble, it shall be for
everlasting joy, and if you die, it shall be
for a curse.][a]
10 All things that are of the earth shall go
back to the earth, and the profane *man* shall
go from nothingness to nothingness.
11 The vanity of men is concerning their
bodies, but the names of the devoted ones
shall not be cut off.
12 Have regard to your name, for it
continues with you longer than a thousand
great treasures of gold.
13 A good life has its number of days, and a
good name continues forever.
14 Hidden wisdom and a concealed
treasure: what is the use of either?
15 Better is a man that hides his foolishness
than a man that hides his wisdom.
16 Hear, O children, instruction concerning
shame[b],[c] and be abashed according to my
judgment. For not every kind of shame is
proper to keep, and not every kind of
abashment is to be approved.
17 Be ashamed of a father and mother of
whoredom, and of a prince and a ruler of
lies.
18 *Be ashamed* of master and a mistress of
deceit, *and* of iniquity before the
congregation and the people, *and of* unjust
dealing before a partner and friend, 19 and
of theft in regard of the place where you
sojourn, and in regard of the truth of
Elohim and His covenant, and of leaning
with your elbow at the table, and of
withholding in the matter of giving and
taking; 20 and of silence before those who
salute you, and of looking upon a woman
that is a whore, 21 and of turning away your
face from a kinsman, *and* of taking away a
portion or a gift, and of gazing upon a
woman that has a husband, *and* 22 of being
overly busy with his maid – and do not
come near her bed – of reproving speeches
before friends, and after you have given, do
not reprove *again*; 23 *and* of repeating and
speaking what you have heard, and of
revealing secrets.
24 So shall you be truly ashamed, and find
favor in the eyes of every man.

42 1 Do not be ashamed of these things,
and do not accept persons unto sin:
2 *Do not be ashamed* of the Torah of Elyon,
and His covenant; and of judgment to do
justice to the wicked; 3 of reckoning with a
partner and with a traveler, and of a gift
from the heritage of friends; 4 of the small
dust of balance and weights; and of testing
measure and weight; 5 of indifferent selling
of merchants; and of much correction of
children; and of striking the side of an evil
servant.
6 *Make* a seal for an evil wife, and shut up
closed where there are many hands.

---

[a] 41:9 So the Greek text. Latin text omits, "*and* if you bring forth…everlasting joy." Syriac contains an entirely different verse, reading, "A fruitful woman is the joy of her people, and if there die an unrighteous father, his sons will not grieve over him."

[b] 41:16 Some Greek texts read "peace."

[c] 41:16 In some Greek texts, this sentence is included at the beginning of verse 14.

7 Whatever you hand over, let it be by
number and weight, and in giving and
receiving let all be in writing.
8 *Do not be ashamed* to instruct the unwise
and foolish, and one of extreme old age that
contends with those that are young; so you
shall be well-instructed indeed, and
approved in the sight of every man living.
9 A daughter is a secret cause of worry to a
father, and caring for her puts away sleep.
In her youth, lest she pass the flower of her
age, and when she is married, lest she
should be hated.
10 In her virginity, lest she should be
defiled, and be with child in her father's
house;[a] and when she has a husband, lest
she should transgress; and when she is
married, lest she should be barren.
11 Keep a strict watch over a headstrong
daughter, lest she make you a laughing-
stock to your enemies, a byword in the city
and notorious among the people, and shame
you before the multitude.
12 Do not look upon every body in regard
to beauty, and do not sit in the midst of
women.
13 For from garments comes a moth, and
from a woman a woman's wickedness.[b] [c]
14 Better is the wickedness of a man than
the goodness of a woman, and a woman
who puts you to shameful reproach.
15 I will make mention now of the works of
יהוה, and will declare the things that I have
seen. The works of יהוה are in His words.
16 The sun that gives light looks upon all
things, and the work of יהוה is full of His
glory.
17 יהוה has not given power to the set-apart
ones to declare all His marvelous works;
which יהוה Almighty firmly settled; that
whatever is, might be established in His
glory.
18 He searches out the deep, and the heart,
and He has understanding of their cunning
plans. For Elyon knows all knowledge, and
He looks into the signs of the world,
19 declaring the things that are past, and the
things that shall be, and revealing the traces
of hidden things.
20 No thought escapes Him, and there is not
a word hidden from Him.
21 He has ordered the mighty works of His
wisdom, *He* who is from everlasting to
everlasting: nothing has been added to
them, nor diminished from them. He had no
need of any counsellor.
22 How desirable are all His works! One
may see this even to a spark.
23 All these things live and remain forever
in all manner of uses, and they are all
obedient.
24 All things are double one against
another, and He has made nothing
imperfect.
25 One thing establishes the good things of
another; and who can be satisfied with
beholding His glory?

43 1 The beauty of the *heavenly* height is

---

[a] 42:10 "in her father's house" that is, unmarried.
[b] 42:13 R. H. Charles notes: "The reference is to daughters. If such mix with married women on familiar terms, and listen to the conversation of the latter, sexual impulses and desires will be stirred which will lead to sin. The sentence is couched in proverbial form. The moth issuing from the garment is a figure of something emanating spontaneously from within."
[c] 42:13 Syriac reads, "For as a moth falls upon a garment, so does jealousy fall upon a woman from the wickedness of her companion."

the pure expanse[a], and the firm heavens
pour forth light.
2 The sun – when he appears, shining as he
goes forth – is a marvelous instrument, the
work of Elyon.
3 At his noon he dries up the land, and who
shall stand against his burning heat?
4 A man blowing a furnace is in works of
heat, but the sun three times more, burning
up the mountains, breathing out fiery
vapors; and sending forth bright beams, he
dims the eyes.
5 Great is יהוה who made him; and at His
word he quickens makes bright His mighty
one.
6 The moon also is in all things for her
season; to rule over periods[b] *of time*, and a
sign of the world.
7 From the moon is the sign of the Feast
day; a light that dims with her course.
8 The new moon, like her name, renews
herself.[c] An instrument of the host on high,
shining forth in the firmament of the
heavens.
9 The beauty of the heavens, the glory of
the stars, an ornament giving light in the
highest places of יהוה.
10 At the word of the Set-Apart One they
will stand in due order, and they will not
faint in their watches.
11 Look upon the rainbow, and praise Him
that made it; its brightness is exceedingly
beautiful.
12 It encircles the heavens round about with
a circle of glory; the hands of Elyon have
stretched it.
13 By His command He makes the snow to
fall, and sends the lightnings of His
judgment swiftly.
14 For this reason the treasure-houses are
opened, and clouds fly forth as birds.
15 By His mighty power He strengthens the
clouds, and the hailstones are broken small.
16 At His appearing, the mountains will be
shaken, and at His will the south wind will
blow.
17 The voice of His thunder makes the earth
travail;

so does the northern storm and the
whirlwind. As birds flying down He
sprinkles the snow, and as the lighting of
the locust is the falling down.
18 The eye will marvel at the beauty of its
whiteness, and the heart will be astonished
at its raining.
19 He also pours the hoar-frost on the earth
as salt, and when it is hardened it is as
points of thorns.
20 The cold north wind shall blow, and the
ice shall be hardened on the water. It shall
sit upon every gathering of water, and the
water shall put it on as if it were a
breastplate.
21 It shall devour the mountains, and burn
up the wilderness, and consume the green
herb as fire.
22 A mist coming speedily is the healing of
all things; a dew coming after heat shall
bring cheerfulness.
23 By His counsel He has stilled the deep,
and planted islands in it.
24 They that sail on the sea tell of its

---

[a] 43:1 That is, the firmament described in Bereshiyt 1.

[b] 43:6 Hebrew text here reads קץ (*qets*), meaning "end;" this could literally be read as, ends *of time*."

[c] 43:8 In Hebrew, the word for "new moon" (also commonly "month") is חודש (*hodesh*), which literally means "renewal." It is derived from the verb חדש (*hadash*) which means "to renew." This is a reference to the natural cycle of the moon to grow bright and then dim, to wax and wane.

danger, and when we hear it with our ears, we marvel.
25 There also are those strange and wondrous works, variety of all that has life, the race of sea-monsters.
26 Because of Him, His end has success, and by His word all things consist.
27 We may say many things, yet we shall not attain, and the sum of our words is this: He is all.
28 How shall we have strength to glorify Him? For He is Himself the great one above all His works.
29 יהוה is terrible and exceedingly great, and marvelous is His power.
30 When you glorify יהוה, exalt Him as much as you can; for even yet He will exceed. And when you exalt Him, put forth your full strength. Do not be weary; for you will never attain.
31 Who has seen Him, that he may declare Him?[a] And who shall magnify Him as He is?
32 Many things are hidden greater than these, for we have seen but a few of His works.
33 For יהוה made all things, and He gave wisdom to the righteous.[b]

44

1 Let us now sing praises for men of renown, and our fathers that brought us forth.
2 יהוה apportioned great glory to them, even His mighty power from the beginning.
3 These ruled in their kingdoms; men that were known for their power, giving counsel by their understanding; such as have brought news in prophecies.
4 Leaders of the people by their counsels, and by their understanding, *they are* men of learning for the people. Their words of instruction were wise.
5 These sought out musical tunes, and set forth verses in writing.
6 Rich men furnished with ability, living peaceably in their habitations.
7 All these were honored in their generations, and were a glory in their days.
8 Those *born* of them have left a name behind them, to declare their praises.
9 And there are some which have no memorial, who perished as though they had not been, and have become as though they had not been born, and their children after them.
10 But these were men of kindness, whose righteous deeds have not been forgotten.
11 A good inheritance shall remain with their seed continually. Their children are in the covenants.
12 Their seed stands fast, and their children for their sakes.
13 Their seed shall remain forever, and their glory[c] shall not be erased.
14 Their bodies were buried in peace, and their name lives to all generations.
15 Nations will declare their wisdom, and the assembly tells out their praise.
16 Ḥanokh walked with יהוה, and was taken, being an example of repentance to all generations.
17 Noaḥ was found perfect and righteous, and in the season of wrath he was taken in exchange for the world. Therefore a remnant was left to the earth when the flood came.

---

[a] 43:31 See Yoḥanan [John] 1:18.
[b] 43:11-33 Syriac text omits these verses.
[c] 44:13 So the Greek, Dead Sea Scrolls, Latin, and Syriac. Hebrew fragment reads "righteousness."

18 Everlasting covenants were made with
him, that all flesh would never again be
erased by a flood.
19 Avraham was a great father of a
multitude of nations, and there was none
found like him in glory,
20 who kept the Torah of Elyon, and was
taken into covenant with Him. In his flesh
he established the covenant, and when he
was proved, he was found faithful.
21 Therefore He assured him by an oath
that the nations should be blessed in his
seed, that He would multiply him as the
[dust of the earth][a], and exalt his seed as the
stars, and cause them to inherit from sea to
sea, and from the river to the utmost part of
the earth.
22 In Yitsḥaq also He [established the
same][b] – for Avraham his father's sake –
the blessing of all men, and the covenant.
23 And He made it rest upon the head of
Ya'aqov. He acknowledged him in His
blessings, and gave to him by inheritance,
and divided his portions, parting them
among twelve tribes.

45 1 And he brought out of him a man[c] of
kindness, who found favor in the sight of
all flesh; a man loved by Elohim and men:
Mosheh, whose memory is blessed.
2 He made his *glory* like the glory of the
set-apart ones, and magnified him in the
fears of his enemies.
3 By his words he [worked swift miracles][d].
He glorified him in the sight of kings; He
gave him commands for His people, and
showed him part of His glory.
4 He set him apart in his faithfulness and
humility. He chose him out of all flesh.
5 He caused him to hear His voice, and led
him into the thick darkness, and gave him
commands face to face – even the Torah of
life and knowledge – that he might teach
Ya'aqov the covenant, and Yisra'el His
judgments.
6 He exalted Aharon, a set-apart man
likened to him, even his brother, of the
tribe of Levi.
7 He established for him an everlasting
covenant, and gave him the priesthood of
the people. He outfitted him with beautiful
ornaments, and dressed him about with a
robe of glory.
8 He clothed him with the perfection of
exultation, and strengthened him with
garments of glory: the linen pants, the long
robe, and the ephod.
9 And He surrounded him with gold
pomegranates, and with many bells round
about, to send forth a sound as he went, to
make a sound that might be heard in the
Temple, for a memorial to the children of
his people.
10 With a set-apart garment, with gold and
blue and purple, the work of the
embroiderer, with an oracle of judgment,
even with the Urim and Thummim.
11 With twisted scarlet, the work of the
weaver; with precious stones engraved like
a signet, in a setting of gold, the work of
the jeweler, for a memorial engraved in
writing, after the number of the tribes of
Yisra'el.

---

[a] 44:21 So the Greek and Latin texts. Hebrew reads, "grains of dust"; Syriac reads, "sand of the seashore."
[b] 44:22 So the Greek, Latin, and Hebrew marginal note read. Hebrew primary text reads, "raised up a son."
[c] 45:1 So the Hebrew and Greek texts. Latin, Syriac, and Ethiopic read, "men."
[d] 45:3 So the Hebrew text. Greek and Latin texts read, " caused the wonders to cease."

12 With a crown of gold upon the turban,
having engraved on it, as on a signet, "Set-
Apart," an ornament of glory, a work of
might, the desires of the eyes, goodly and
beautiful.
13 There have never been any like him
before; no stranger put them on, but only
his sons, and his offspring, continually.
14 His sacrifices shall be entirely
consumed, twice daily, continually.[a]
15 Mosheh set him apart and anointed him
with set-apart oil. It was to him for an
everlasting covenant, and to his seed, all
the days of the heavens, to attend to Him,
and to execute the office of priest, and bless
His people in His Name.
16 He chose him out of all living *people t*o
offer ascension offerings, incense, and a
pleasing aroma, for a memorial, to make
reconciliation for your people.
17 He gave to him in His commands, yes,
authority in the covenants of judgments, to
teach Ya'aqov the testimonies, and to
enlighten Yisra'el in His Torah.
18 Strangers gathered themselves together
against him, and envied him in the
wilderness. Dathan and Aviram with their
company, and the congregation of Qoraḥ,
with wrath and anger.
19 יהוה saw it and it displeased Him. And
in the wrath of His anger they were
destroyed. He did a wondrous thing to
them, consuming them with flaming fire.
20 And He added glory to Aharon, and gave
him a heritage. He divided to him the first
fruits of the increase, and bread of the
presence is his portion.
21 For they shall eat the sacrifices of יהוה,
which He gave to him and to his seed.
22 Only in the land of the people he shall
have no inheritance, and he has no portion
among the people, for He Himself is his
portion and inheritance.
23 And Pineḥas the son of Elazar is the
third in glory, in that he was zealous in the
fear of יהוה, and stood and stood in the
breach for his people, while his heart
prompted him, and he made reconciliation
for Yisra'el.
24 Therefore was there a covenant of peace
established for him that he should be leader
of the set-apart ones and of His people.
That he and his seed should retain the
High-Priesthood forever.
25 Also he made a covenant with David the
son of Yishai, of the tribe of Yehudah, *and*
the inheritance of the king is his alone,
from son to son, just as the inheritance of
Aharon is to his seed.
26 And now, bless יהוה, [who has crowned
you with glory][b]; may He grant you
wisdom of heart to judge His people in
righteousness, that your prosperity may
never cease, nor your power for continual
generations.

46 1 Yehoshua the son of Nun was valiant
in war, and was the successor of Mosheh in
prophecies. He was formed according to his
name, a great salvation for His chosen,[c] to
take vengeance of the enemies that rose up
against them, that he might give Yisra'el
their inheritance.
2 How he was glorified in the lifting up his
hands, and in stretching out his sword
against the cities!

---

[a] 45:9-14 Syriac omits these verses.
[b] 45:26 So the Hebrew text. Greek and Latin texts omit.
[c] 46:1 The name Yehoshua means 'יהוה is salvation.'

3 Who before him stood fast thus? For יהוה Himself brought his enemies to him.
4 Did the sun not go back by his hand? And did not one day become as two?
5 For he called upon El Elyon, when he was oppressed by his enemies around him. And El Elyon answered him with hailstones and bolts *of lightning*.
6 He cast them down upon the hostile people, and in the going down *of the sun* he destroyed those that rose up, so that all those devoted to destruction might know that יהוה saw their fighting; and because he completely followed Elohim.
7 Also in the time of Mosheh he did a work of kindness: he and Kalev the son of Yephunneh, in that they stood firm when the congregation broke loose, to turn away wrath from the assembly and to cause the evil report to cease.
8 And of six-hundred thousand men on foot, they two alone were preserved to bring them into the inheritance, even into a land flowing with milk and honey.
9 And יהוה gave Kalev strength, and it remained with him into his old age, so that he entered upon the height of the land, and his seed obtained it for an inheritance.
10 That all the children of Yisra'el might see that it is good to walk after יהוה.
11 Also the judges, every one by his name, all whose hearts did not go whoring, and who did not turn away from יהוה: may their memory be blessed.
12 May their bones flourish again out of their place, and may the name of those who have been honored be renewed upon their children.
13 Shemu'el, the prophet of יהוה, beloved of his Maker, established a kingdom, and anointed rulers over His people.
14 By the Torah of יהוה he judged the congregation, and יהוה visited Ya'aqov.
15 By his faithfulness he was proved to be a prophet, and by his words he was known to be faithful in vision.
16 Also when his enemies pressed him round about he called upon Elohim, with the offering of the suckling lamb.
17 And יהוה thundered from the heavens, and with a mighty sound made His voice to be heard.
18 And he utterly destroyed the rulers of Tsor, and all the princes of the Philistines.
19 Also before the time of his long sleep he protested in the sight of יהוה and His anointed, *saying*, "I have not taken any man's goods, so much as a shoe;" and no man could accuse him.
20 And after he fell asleep he prophesied, and showed the king his way[a], and lifted up his voice from the earth in prophecy, to erase [iniquity by prophecy][b].

47

1 And after him Nathan rose up to prophesy in the days of David.
2 As is the fat when it is separated from the peace offering, so was David separated from the children of Yisra'el.
3 He played with lions as with *goat* kids, and with bears as with lambs of the flock.
4 In his youth did he not kill the giant, and take away reproach from the people, when he lifted up his hand with a sling stone, and beat down the boasting of Goliath?

---

[a] 46:20 "his way" ie. his destiny, a reference to Sha'ul's death.

[b] 46:20 So the Hebrew and Syriac. Greek and Latin texts read, "erase the wickedness of the people."

5 For he called upon El Elyon, and He gave him strength in his right hand, to kill a man mighty in war, *and* to exalt the horn of His people.
6 So the daughters sang of him, and glorified him with: "*Slayer* of ten thousand!"[a] When he put on the diadem he fought.
7 For he destroyed the enemies on every side, and brought to nothing the Philistines his adversaries, breaking their horn in pieces to this day.
8 In every work of his he gave thanks to El Elyon with words of glory. With his whole heart he sang praise, and loved Him who made him.
9 Also he set singers before the altar, and to make sweet melody by their music.
10 He gave beauty to the feasts, and set in order the appointed times to perfection, for he praised His Set-Apart Name, and the sanctuary sounded from early morning.
11 יהוה took away his sins, and exalted his horn forever, and gave him a covenant of kings, and a throne of glory in Yisra'el[b].
12 After him rose up a son, a man of understanding. And for his sake dwelled in safety.
13 Shelomoh reigned in days of peace, and Elohim gave him rest all around, so he might build a House for His Name, and prepare a dwelling-place forever.
14 How wise you were in your youth, [Shelomoh][c], and filled as a river with understanding!
15 Your being covered the earth, and you filled it with dark parables.
16 Your name reached to the aisles afar off, and for your peace you were beloved.[d]
17 For your songs and proverbs and parables, and for your interpretations, the countries marveled at you.
18 By the Name of יהוה Elohim, He who is called the Elohim of Yisra'el, you gathered in gold as *if it were* tin, and multiplied silver as *if it were* lead.
19 You bowed your loins to women, and by your body you were brought into subjection.
20 You stained your glory, and profaned your seed, to bring wrath upon your children, and I was grieved for your foolishness.
21 So that the kingdom was divided, and out of Ephrayim arose a rebellious kingdom.
22 But יהוה will never forsake His kindness, and He will not destroy any of His works, nor erase the legacy of His chosen. And He will not remove the seed of them that love Him. And He gave a remnant to Ya'aqov, and to David a root out of him.
23 And so Shelomoh rested with his fathers, and of his seed he left behind him Reḥavam, even the foolishness of the people, and one that lacked understanding, who made the people to revolt by his counsel. Also [Yarovam the son of Nevat][e],

---

[a] 47:6 So the Hebrew text. Syriac reads, "Therefore the women praised him in myriads." See also Shemu'el א [1 Samuel] 18:7.
[b] 47:11 So the Greek, Latin, and Syriac texts. Hebrew text reads, "Yerushalayim."
[c] 47:14 So the Syriac text. Greek, Latin, and Hebrew omit.
[d] 47:16 So the Greek and Latin texts. Hebrew omits this verse; Syriac reads, "...and you were loved for your happy estate." in place of the second sentence.
[e] 47:23 So the Greek and Latin texts. Hebrew and Syriac read, "the sinner." The variation is difficult; either it was added into Greek and Latin for clarification, or it was omitted from the

who made Yisra'el sin, and gave Ephraim a way of sin.
24 And their sins multiplied exceedingly, *enough* to remove them from their land.
25 For they sought out all manner of wickedness, until vengeance should come upon them.

48 1 Also Eliyahu the prophet arose as a fire, and his word burned like a torch.
2 He brought a famine upon them, and his zeal reduced their number.
3 By the word of יהוה he shut up the heavens, and three times he called down fire.
4 How you were glorified, O Eliyahu, in your wondrous deeds! And who shall glory like to you?
5 Who raised a dead man up from death, and from Sheol according to the good pleasure of יהוה.
6 Who brought down kings to destruction, and honorable men from their beds.
7 Who heard rebuke in Sinai, and judgments of vengeance in Ḥorev.
8 Who anointed kings for retribution, and prophets to succeed after him.
9 Who was taken up in a tempest of fire, in a chariot of fiery horses.
10 Who was recorded for reproofs at their appointed times, to quell anger before it breaks forth into wrath. **To turn the heart of the father to the son**, and to restore the tribes of Ya'aqov.
11 Blessed are those who saw you, for we also shall live again.[a]
12 Eliyahu is he who was wrapped in a tempest, and Elisha was filled with his spirit. And in all his days he was not moved by the fear of any ruler, and no one brought him into subjection.
13 Nothing was too high for him, and when he was laid on sleep his body prophesied.
14 As in life he did wonders, so in death were his works marvelous.
15 For all this the people did not repent, and they did not depart from their sins until they were carried away as a plunder from their land. And were scattered through all the earth, and the people were left very few in number, and a ruler was left in the house of David.
16 Some of them did that which pleased Elohim, and some multiplied sins.
17 Ḥizqiyahu fortified his city, and brought in water into the midst of them. He dug the sheer rock with iron, and built up wells for waters.
18 In his days Sanḥeriv came up, and sent Ravshaqeh, and departed. And he lifted up his hand against Tsion, and boasted great things in his arrogance.
19 Then their hearts and their hands were shaken, and they were in pain, as women in travail.
20 And they called upon יהוה who is kind, spreading forth their hands to Him; and the Set-apart One quickly heard them from the heavens, and delivered them by the hand of Yeshayahu.
21 He struck the camp of the Ashuwrites, and [His messenger utterly][b] destroyed them.
22 For Ḥizqiyahu did that which was pleasing to יהוה, and was strong in the

Semitic versions for fear of mentioning the name of Yarovam.

[a] 48:11 Syriac adds, "But he shall not die, but shall certainly live!"

[b] 48:21 So the Greek and Latin texts. Hebrew text reads, "with a plague."

ways of David his father, which Yeshayahu
the prophet commanded, who was great
and faithful in his vision.
23 In his days the sun went backward, and
he added life to the king.
24 He saw by an excellent spirit what
should come to pass at the last, and he
comforted those who mourned in Tsion.
25 He showed the things that should be to
the end of time, and the hidden things
before they came *to be*.

49 1 The memorial of Yoshiyahu is like
the composition of incense, prepared by the
work of the perfumer. It shall be sweet as
honey in every mouth, and as music at a
banquet of wine.
2 He behaved himself uprightly in the
conversion of the people, and took away
the abominations of iniquity.
3 He set his heart right toward יהוה. In the
days of wicked men he made righteousness
prevail.
4 Except David and Ḥizqiyahu and
Yoshiyahu, all committed trespass. For
they abandoned the Torah of Elyon, and the
kings of Yehudah failed.
5 For they gave their power to others, and
their glory to a strange nation.
6 They set the chosen city of the dwelling-
place on fire, and made her streets desolate,
as it was written by the hand of Yirmeyahu.
7 For they treated him evilly, and yet he
was set apart in the womb to be a prophet,
to root out, and to afflict, and to destroy,
and in like manner to build and to plant.
8 It was Yeḥezqel who saw the vision of
glory, which Elohim showed him upon the
chariot of the kerubim.
9 He also made mention of Iyyov, who
maintained all the ways of righteousness.[a]
10 Also of the twelve prophets: may their
bones flourish again out of their place. And
He comforted Ya'aqov, and delivered them
by confidence of hope.
11 How shall we magnify Zerubbavel? He
was as a signet on the right hand;
12 So was Yeshua the son of Yehotsadoq,
who in their days built the House, and
exalted a people *as* set-apart to יהוה,
prepared for everlasting glory.
13 Also the memory of Neḥemyah is great;
he who raised up for us the walls that were
fallen, and set up the gates and bars, and
raised up our homes again.
14 Few[b] have ever been created upon the
earth like Ḥanokh, *though*, for he was taken
up from the earth.
15 Neither was there a man born like
Yoseph, a governor of his brethren, a
stronghold of the people. Yes, his bones
were visited.
16 Shem and Sheth were glorified among
men, and above every living thing in
creation is Adam.

50 1 It was Shimon, the son of Ḥoniyo,
the High Priest, who in his life repaired the
House, and in his days strengthened the
Temple.
2 The double wall was built from the
foundation up by him; the lofty underworks
of the enclosure of the Temple.
3 In his days the cistern of waters

[a] 49:9 So the Hebrew text. Greek and Latin texts read, "For he made mention of the enemies under the figure of a storm, and of doing good to them that showed right ways."

[b] 49:14 So the Hebrew and Syriac. Greek and Latin read, "none."

diminished, the copper vessel as abundant
as the sea.
4 It was he that cared for his people that
they should not fall, and fortified the city
against siege.
5 How glorious was he when the people
gathered around him, at his coming forth
out of the dwelling-place!
6 As a star shining in the midst of a cloud,
as the moon at the full; 7 as the sun shining
forth upon the Temple of El Elyon, and as
the rainbow giving light in clouds of glory;
8 as the flower of roses in the days of new
fruits, as lilies of the brook, as the shoot of
the frankincense tree in the time of
summer; 9 as fire and incense in the censer,
as a vessel all of beaten gold adorned with
all manner of precious stones; 10 as an olive
tree budding forth fruits, and as a cypress
growing high among the clouds.
11 When he took up the robe of glory, and
put on the perfection of exultation, in the
ascent of the set-apart altar, he made the
complex of the dwelling-place glorious.
12 And when he received the portions out
of the priests' hands, himself also standing
by the hearth of the altar – his brethren as a
garland around him – he was as a young
cedar in Lavanon; and as stems of palm
trees they surrounded him, 13 and all the
sons of Aharon in their glory, and the
offering of יהוה in their hands, before all
the assembly of Yisra'el.
14 And finishing the service at the altars,
that he might adorn the offering of El
Elyon, 15 he stretched out his hand to the
cup, and poured out the cup of the grape.
He poured out at the foot of the altar a
soothing aroma to El Elyon, the King of all.
16 Then the sons of Aharon shouted, they
sounded the trumpets of beaten work, they
made a great noise to be heard, for a
remembrance before Elyon.
17 Then all the people together hurried, and
fell down upon the earth on their faces to
bow down to יהוה, El Shaddai.
18 The singers also praised Him with their
voices. In the whole house there was a
sweet melody.
19 And the people petitioned יהוה Elohim
in prayer before Him that is kind. Until the
worship of יהוה shall end, and so they
accomplished his service.
20 Then he went down, and lifted up his
hands over the whole congregation of the
children of Yisra'el, to bless יהוה with his
lips, and to glorify His Name.
21 And he lowered himself and bowed the
second time, to declare the blessing from El
Elyon.
22 Blessed is יהוה, the Elohim of Yisra'el,
who does great things everywhere, who
exalts our days from the womb, and deals
with us according to His kindness.
23 May He grant us joyfulness of heart, and
may peace be in our days, and in Yisra'el
for the days of eternity, 24 to entrust us with
His kindness: let Him deliver us in His
time!
25 My being is vexed by two nations, and
the third is not even a nation.
26 They that sit upon the mountain of
Shomeron, and the Philistines, and that
foolish people that dwells in Shekhem.
27 I have written in this book the instruction
of understanding and knowledge, I,
Yeshua, the son of Sira Elazar, of
Yerushalayim, who poured forth wisdom
out of his heart.
28 Blessed is he that does these things, and
he that takes them to heart shall become
wise.
29 For if he does them, he shall be strong in
all things, for the light of יהוה is his guide.

51 A Prayer of Yeshua the son of Sira.
1 I will give thanks to You, O Elohim of
my father, and will praise You, O Elohim
my Savior. I give thanks to Your Name.
2 For You were my protector and helper,
and delivered my body from destruction,
and out of the snare of a slanderous tongue:
from lips that forge lies, and *You* were my
helper before those who stood by.
3 You delivered me according to the
abundance of Your kindness and the
greatness of Your Name, from the gnashing
of teeth ready to devour; out of the hand of
those who sought my life; out of the many
afflictions which I had; 4 from the choking
of a fire on every side, and out of the midst
of fire which I did not kindle; 5 out of the
depth of the belly of Sheol, and from an
unclean tongue, and from lying words,
6 *even* the slander of an unrighteous tongue
to the king. My soul drew near even to
death, and my life was near to Sheol
beneath.
7 They surrounded me on every side, and
there was none to help me. I was looking
for the help of men, and it was not *there*.
8 And I remembered Your kindness, O
יהוה, and Your working which has been
from everlasting: how You deliver those
who wait for You, and save them out of the
hand of the enemies.
9 And I lifted up my petition from the earth,
and prayed for deliverance from death.
10 I called upon יהוה, the Father of my
Master, that He would not forsake me in
the days of affliction, in the time when
there was no help against the proud.
11 I will praise Your Name continually, and
will sing praise with thanksgiving. Then
my petition was heard.
12 For You saved me from destruction, and
delivered me from the evil time. Therefore
I will give thanks and praise to You, and
bless the Name of יהוה.

[Give thanks to יהוה, for He is good, and
His kindness endures forever.
Give thanks to the Elohim of glory, for His
kindness endures forever.
Give thanks to the guardian of Yisra'el, for
His kindness endures forever.
Give thanks to the creator of the universe,
for His kindness endures forever.
Give thanks to the redeemer of Yisra'el, for
His kindness endures forever.
Give thanks to Him who gathers the
dispersed of Yisra'el, for His kindness
endures forever.
Give thanks to Him who builds His city
and His dwelling-place, for His kindness
endures forever.
Give thanks to Him who makes a horn to
sprout forth for the house of David, for His
kindness endures forever.
Give thanks to Him who has chosen for His
priests the sons of Tsadoq, for His kindness
endures forever.
Give thanks to the shield of Avraham, for
His kindness endures forever.
Give thanks to the rock of Yitsḥaq, for His
kindness endures forever.
Give thanks to the mighty one of Ya'aqov,
for His kindness endures forever.
Give thanks to Him who has chosen Tsion,
for His kindness endures forever.
Give thanks to the kings of kings, for His
kindness endures forever.
He has lifted up the horn of His people;
praise Him, all you His faithful ones, from
the children of Yisra'el, the people close to

Him. Praise יהוה!][a]
13 When I was young, or whenever I traveled abroad, I sought wisdom openly in my prayer.
14 Before the Temple I asked for her, and I will seek her out even to the end.
15 From her flower as from the ripening grape my heart delighted in her; my foot walked in uprightness; from my youth I tracked her.
16 I bowed down my ear a little, and received her, and found for myself much instruction.
17 I profited in her. *She said,* "To him that gives me wisdom I will give glory."
18 For I decided to practice her, and I was zealous for that which is good, and I shall never be put to shame.
19 My being has wrestled in her, and I was precise in my works. I spread forth my hands to the heavens above, and lamented my ignorance of her.
20 I set my soul towards her, and I found her in purity. I gained a heart joined with her from the beginning, therefore I shall not be forsaken.
21 My inward part also was troubled to seek her: therefore I have gotten a good possession.
22 יהוה gave me a tongue for my reward, and I will praise Him with it.
23 Draw near to me, all you unlearned, and dwell in the house of instruction.
24 Say, "Why are you lacking in these things, and *why are* your beings so thirsty?"
25 I opened my mouth and spoke, "Get her
for yourselves without money. 26 Put your
neck under the yoke, and let your being receive instruction: she is difficult to find."
27 Behold with your eyes, how I labored a little, and found for myself much rest.
28 Get instruction with a great sum of silver, and gain much gold by her.
29 May your being rejoice in His kindness, and may you all not be put to shame in praising Him.
30 Work your work before the time comes, and in His time He will give you your reward.

Thus the words of Yeshua the son of Shimon who is called Sira. The Wisdom of Shimon, the son of Yeshua, the son of Elazar, the son of Sira. May the Name of יהוה be blessed from now on and forever.[b] [c]

---

[a] 51:12 Bracketed section is found only in the Hebrew text. It is doubtful that it is original to Ben Sira; it is most likely a hymn or traditional prayer (similar to Tehillim 136) that was added as a liturgical piece to the book, here being nearly at its close.

[b] So the Hebrew text. Some Greek and Syriac omit, while most Greek read, "*This is the* Wisdom of Yeshua, son of Sira." Most Syriac read, "The writing of the son of Sira is finished" with one text adding, "in the time of the Maqabiym."

[c] Two early Armenian, and Old Latin texts omit chapters 44 – 51.

חָכְמַת שְׁלֹמֹה

Ḥokhmat Shelomoh [Wisdom of Solomon]

1 1 Love righteousness, all you who are judges of the earth. Set your heart on יהוה in goodness, and seek Him in sincerity of heart.
2 For He is found by those who do not test Him, and is manifested to those who trust Him.
3 For crooked thoughts separate *a man* from Elohim. His Power convicts when it is tested, and exposes the foolish.
4 Because wisdom will not enter into a being that devises evil, nor dwell in a body that is enslaved by sin.
5 For a set-apart spirit of discipline will flee from deceit, and will depart from thoughts that are without understanding, and will be rebuked when unrighteousness comes in.
6 For wisdom is a spirit who loves man, and she will not hold a blasphemer guiltless for his lips; for Elohim is a witness of his kidneys, and is a true overseer of his heart, and a hearer of his tongue.
7 For the Ruaḥ of יהוה has filled the world, and the one who possesses all knows what is said.
8 Therefore no one who utters unrighteous things will go unnoticed, and neither will justice pass him by when it convicts.
9 For in his counsels the wicked will be searched out, and the sound of his words will come to יהוה to bring his lawless deeds to conviction.
10 For a jealous ear listens to all things, and the noise of complaints is not hidden.
11 Beware then of unprofitable complaining, and keep your tongue from slander; for no secret utterance will go on its way void, and a lying mouth destroys a being.
12 Do not court death in the error of your life, and do not draw destruction upon yourselves by the works of your hands.
13 For Elohim did not make death, nor does He delight when the living perish.[a]
14 For He created all things that they might have being. All creations of the world are wholesome, and there is no poison of destruction in them, nor does Sheol possess sovereignty upon earth.
15 For righteousness is immortal,
16 but wicked men summon death by their hands and their words; and considering it a friend, they were consumed by it. They made a covenant with him[b], because they are worthy to belong with him.

2 1 For they said within themselves, with unsound reasoning, "Our life is short and sorrowful. There is no healing when a man comes to his end, and no one was ever known that was released from Sheol.
2 "Because we were born simply by chance, and after this we will be as though we had never been. For the breath in our nostrils is smoke, and reason is a spark kindled by the beating of our heart;
3 "which when extinguished, turns the body into ashes, and the spirit will be dispersed as thin air.
4 "Our name will be forgotten in time. No one will remember our works. Our life will

[a] 1:13 Compare Yeḥezqel [Ezekiel] 18:23.

[b] 1:16 him – that is, death.

pass away as the traces of a cloud, and will
be scattered as is a mist, when it is chased
by the rays of the sun, and overcome by its
heat.
5 "For our allotted time is the passing of a
shadow, and our end does not wait; for it is
securely sealed, and no one turns it back.
6 "Come therefore and let us enjoy the good
things that now exist. Let us use the
creation earnestly as in our youth.
7 "Let us fill ourselves with costly wine and
cover ourselves with perfumes, and let no
Spring flower pass us by.
8 "Let us crown ourselves with rosebuds
before they wither.
9 "Let none of us go without his share in
our proud revelry. Let us leave tokens of
mirth everywhere, for this is our portion,
and this is our lot.
10 "Let us oppress the righteous poor. Let
us not spare the widow, nor honor the gray
hair of the old man.
11 "But let our strength be a law of
righteousness, for that which is weak is
proven useless.
12 "But let us lie in wait for the righteous
man, because he aggravates us, he is
contrary to our works, he rebukes us with
sins against the Torah, and charges us with
sins against our training.
13 "He claims to know Elohim, and calls
himself a child of יהוה.
14 "He became to us a reproof of our
thoughts.
15 "He is grievous to us even to look at,
because his life is unlike other men's, and
his paths are strange.
16 "We were regarded by him as worthless
metal, and he abstains from our ways as
from uncleanness. He calls the latter end of
the righteous happy. He boasts that Elohim
is his father.
17 "Let us see if his words are true. Let us
test what will happen at the end of his life.
18 **"For if the righteous man is the Son of
Elohim, He will uphold him, and He will
deliver him out of the hand of his
adversaries.**[a]
19 "Let us test him with outrage and torture,
that we may find out how gentle he is, and
test his patience.
20 "Let us condemn him to a shameful
death, for he will be overseen according to
his words."
21 Thus they reasoned, and they were led
astray; for their wickedness blinded them,
22 and they did not know the mysteries of
Elohim, neither did they hope for wages of
set-apartness, nor did they discern that
there is a reward for blameless beings.
23 Because Elohim created man for
incorruption, and made him an image of
His own nature;
24 but death entered into the world by the
envy of a slanderer, and those who belong
to him experience it.

3 1 But the beings of the righteous are in
the hand of Elohim, and no torment will
touch them.
2 In the eyes of the foolish they seemed to
have died. Their departure was considered
affliction,
3 and their travel away from us ruin; but
they are in peace.
4 For even if in the sight of men they are
punished, their hope is full of immortality.
5 Having borne a little discipline, they will
receive great good; because Elohim tested

---

[a] 2:18 See Mattithyahu [Matthew] 27:43;
Tehillim [Psalm] 22:8.

them, and found them worthy of Himself.
6 He tested them like gold in the furnace,
and He accepted them as an ascension
offering.
7 In the time of their visitation they will
shine. They will run back and forth like
sparks among stubble.
8 They will judge nations and have
dominion over peoples. יהוה will reign
over them forever.
9 Those who trust Him will understand
truth. The faithful will live with Him in
love, for favor and kindness are with His
chosen ones.
10 But the wicked – those who neglected
righteousness and rebelled against יהוה –
they will be punished even as they
reasoned.
11 For he who despises wisdom and
discipline is miserable. Their hope is void
and their toils unprofitable. Their works are
useless.
12 Their wives are foolish and their children
are wicked.
13 Their descendants are cursed, because
the barren woman who is undefiled is
happy, she who has not conceived in
transgression. She will have fruit in the
visitation of beings.
14 So is the eunuch who has done no
lawless deed with his hands, nor imagined
wicked things against יהוה; for a precious
gift will be given to him for his
faithfulness, a special favor, and a
delightful inheritance in the set-apart place
of יהוה.
15 For good labors have fruit of great
renown. The root of understanding cannot
fail.
16 But children of adulterers will not come
to maturity. The seed of a lawless bed will
vanish away.
17 For if they live long, they will not be
esteemed, and in the end, their old age will
be without honor.
18 If they die quickly, they will have no
hope, nor consolation in the day of
decision.
19 For the end of an unrighteous generation
is always grievous.

4 1 It is better to be childless with virtue,
for immortality is in the memory of virtue,
because it is recognized both before Elohim
and before men.
2 When it is present, people imitate it. They
long after it when it has departed.
Throughout all time it marches crowned in
triumph, victorious in the competition for
the prizes that are undefiled.
3 But the multiplying brood of the wicked
will be of no profit, and their illegitimate
offshoots will not take deep root, nor will
they establish a sure hold.
4 For even if they grow branches and
flourish for a season, standing unsure, they
will be shaken by the wind. They will be
uprooted by the violence of winds.
5 Their branches will be broken off before
they come to maturity. Their fruit will be
useless, never ripe to eat, and fit for
nothing.
6 For children conceived lawlessly are
witnesses of wickedness against parents
when they are investigated.
7 But a righteous man, even if he dies
before his time, will be at rest.
8 For honorable old age is not that which
stands in length of time, nor is its measure
given by number of years:
9 but understanding is gray hair to men, and
an unspotted life is ripe old age.
10 Being found well-pleasing to Elohim, he
was loved. While living among sinners he

was transported.
11 He was caught away, lest evil should change his understanding, or craftiness deceive his being.
12 For the sorcery of worthlessness obscures the things which are good, and the whirl of desire perverts an innocent mind.
13 Being made perfect quickly, he filled a long time.
14 For his being was pleasing to יהוה. Therefore he hurried out of the midst of wickedness.
15 But as for the peoples seeing and not understanding, not considering this, that favor and kindness are with His chosen ones, and that He visits His set-apart ones;
16 but a righteous man who is dead will condemn the wicked who are living, and a youth that is quickly perfected will condemn the many years of an unrighteous man's old age.
17 For the wicked will see a wise man's end, and will not understand what יהוה planned for him, and why He safely kept him.
18 They will see, and they will despise; but יהוה will laugh them to scorn. After this, they will become a dishonored carcass and a reproach among the dead forever;
19 for He will dash them speechless to the ground, and will shake them from the foundations. They will lie utterly waste. They will be in anguish and their memory will perish.
20 They will come with cowardly fear when their sins are counted. Their lawlessness will convict them to their face.

5 1 Then the righteous man will stand in great boldness before the face of those who afflicted him, and those who make his labors of no account.
2 When they see him they will be troubled with terrible fear, and will be amazed at the marvel of salvation.
3 They will speak among themselves repenting, and for distress of spirit they will groan, "This was he whom we used to revile, as a parable of reproach.
4 "We fools considered his life madness, and his end without honor.
5 "How was he counted among sons of Elohim? How is his lot among set-apart ones?
6 "Truly we went astray from the way of truth. The light of righteousness did not shine for us. The sun did not rise for us.[a]
7 "We took our fill of the paths of lawlessness and destruction. We traveled through trackless deserts, but we did not know the way of יהוה.
8 "What did our arrogance profit us? What good have riches and boasting brought us?
9 "Those things all passed away as a shadow, like a message that runs by,
10 "like a ship passing through the billowy water, which, when it has gone by, there is no trace to be found, no pathway of its keel in the billows.
11 "Or it is like when a bird flies through the air, no evidence of its passage is found, but the light wind, lashed with the stroke of its pinions, and torn apart with the violent rush of the moving wings, is passed through. Afterwards no sign of its coming remains.
12 "Or it is like when an arrow is shot at a mark, the air that was disturbed closes up

[a] 5:6 Compare Malakhi 4:2.

again immediately, so that men do not
know where it passed through.
13 "So we also, as soon as we were born,
ceased to be; and we had no sign of virtue
to show, but we were utterly consumed in
our wickedness."
14 Because the hope of the wicked man is
like chaff carried by the wind, and as foam
vanishing before a tempest; and is scattered
like smoke by the wind, and passes by as
the remembrance of a guest that waits but a
day.
15 But the righteous live forever. Their
reward is in יהוה, and Elyon will care for
them.
16 Therefore they will receive the crown of
royal dignity and the diadem of beauty
from the hand of יהוה; because He will
cover them with His right-hand, and He
will shield them with His arm.
17 He will take His jealousy as complete
armor, and will make the whole creation
His weapons to punish His enemies:
18 He will put on righteousness as a
breastplate, and will wear just judgment as
a helmet.[a]
19 He will take set-apartness as an
indestructible shield.
20 He will sharpen stern wrath for a sword.
The world will go with Him to fight against
His frenzied foes.
21 Shafts of lightning will fly with true aim.
They will leap to the mark from the clouds,
as from a well-drawn bow.
22 Hailstones full of wrath will be hurled
from an engine of war. The water of the sea
will be angered against them. Rivers will
sternly overwhelm them.
23 A mighty blast will encounter them. It
will winnow them away like a tempest. So
lawlessness will make all the land desolate.
Their evil-doing will overturn the thrones
of princes.

6 1 Hear therefore, you kings, and
understand. Learn, you judges of the ends
of the earth.
2 Give ear, you rulers who have dominion
over many people, and make your boast in
multitudes of nations,
3 for your dominion was given to you by
יהוה, and your sovereignty from Elyon. He
will search out your works, and will inquire
about your plans.
4 Being officers of his kingdom, you did
not judge rightly, nor did you guard the
Torah, nor did you walk according to the
counsel of Elohim.
5 He will come upon you awfully and
swiftly, because a stern judgment comes on
those who are in high place.
6 For the man of low estate may be
pardoned in kindness, but mighty men will
be mightily tested.
7 For Adonai יהוה Tsevaot will not be
impressed with anyone, neither will He
show partiality to the mighty; for it is He
who made both small and great, and cares
about them all;
8 but the scrutiny that comes upon the
powerful is strict.
9 Therefore, my words are to you, O
princes, that you may learn wisdom and not
fall away.
10 For those who have set apart the things
that are set-apart will be made set-apart.
Those who have been taught them will find
what to say in defense.

---

[a] 5:18 Compare Yeshayahu [Isaiah] 59:17;
Ephesious 6:14-17.

11 Therefore set your desire on my words.
Long for them, and you princes will be
instructed.
12 Wisdom is radiant and does not fade
away; she is easily seen by those who love
her, and found by those who seek her.
13 She anticipates those who desire her,
making herself known.
14 He who rises up early to seek her will
not have difficulty *finding her*, for he will
find her sitting at his gates.
15 For to think upon her is perfection of
understanding, and he who watches for her
will quickly be free from care;
16 for she herself goes around, seeking
those who are worthy of her, and in their
paths she appears to them kindly, and she
meets them in every purpose.
17 For her true beginning is desire for
instruction, and desire for instruction is
love.
18 And love is observance of her laws: to
guard her laws confirms immortality.
19 Immortality brings closeness to Elohim.
20 So then desire for wisdom promotes to a
kingdom.
21 If therefore you delight in thrones and
scepters, you princes of peoples, honor
wisdom, that you may reign forever.
22 But what wisdom is, and how she came
into being, I will declare. I will not hide
mysteries from you, but I will explore from
her first beginning, bring the knowledge of
her into clear light, and I will not pass by
the truth.
23 Indeed, I will not go with consuming
envy, for envy will have no fellowship with
wisdom.
24 But a multitude of wise men is salvation
to the world, and an understanding king is
stability for his people.
25 Therefore be instructed by my words,
and you will profit.

7 1 I myself am also mortal, like everyone
else, and am a descendant of one formed
first and born of the earth.
2 I molded into flesh in the time of ten
months in my mother's womb, being
compacted in blood from the seed of man
and pleasure that came with sleep.
3 I also, when I was born, drew in the same
air *as everyone else*, and fell upon the same
earth, uttering the same cry like everyone
else, for my first voice.
4 I was nursed with care in swaddling
clothes.
5 For no king had any other first beginning;
6 but all men have one entrance into life,
and a common departure.
7 For this cause I prayed, and
understanding was given to me. I asked that
spirit of wisdom would come to me.
8 I preferred her before scepters and
thrones. I considered riches nothing in
comparison to her.
9 Neither did I compare her to any priceless
gem, because all gold in her presence is as
a little sand, and silver is considered as clay
before her.
10 I loved her more than health and beauty,
and I chose to have her rather than light,
because her bright shining is never laid to
sleep.
11 All good things came to me with her,
and innumerable riches are in her hands.
12 And I rejoiced over them all because
wisdom leads them; although I did not
know that she was their mother.
13 As I learned without deceit, I impart
without grudging. I do not hide her riches.
14 For she is a treasure for men that does
not fail, and those who use it obtain
friendship with Elohim, commended by the
gifts which they present through discipline.

15 But may Elohim grant that I may speak
His judgment, and to conceive thoughts
worthy of what has been given me; for He
is one who even guides wisdom, and who
corrects the wise.
16 For both we and our words are in His
hand, with all understanding and skill in
various crafts.
17 For He Himself gave me an unerring
knowledge of the things that are, to know
the structure of the universe and the
operation of the elements;
18 the beginning, end, and middle of times;
the alternations of the courses and the
changes of seasons;
19 the circuits of years and the positions of
stars;
20 the natures of living creatures and the
raging of wild beasts. The violence of
winds and the thoughts of men; the
diversities of plants and the virtues of roots.
21 All things that are either secret or
manifest I learned,
22 for wisdom, which is the architect of all
things, taught me. For there is in her a spirit
that is: quick to understand, set-apart,
unique, diverse, subtle, freely moving, clear
in utterance, pure, distinct, unharmed,
loving what is good, acute, unhindered,
23 beneficent, loving toward man, steadfast,
sure, free from care, all-powerful, all-
surveying, and penetrating through all
spirits that are quick to understand, pure,
most subtle:
24 For wisdom is more mobile than any
motion. Yes, she pervades and penetrates
all things by reason of her purity.
25 For she is a breath of the power of
Elohim, and a clear essence of the glory of
the Almighty. Therefore nothing defiled
can find entrance into her.
26 For she is a reflection of everlasting
light, an unblemished mirror of the working
of Elohim, and an image of His goodness.
27 She, being one, has power to do all
things. Remaining in herself, she renews all
things. From generation to generation
passing into set-apart people, she makes
friends of Elohim and prophets.
28 For Elohim loves nothing as much as
one who dwells with wisdom.
29 For she is fairer than the sun, and above
all the constellations of the stars. She is
better than light.
30 For *though* daylight succeeds night, but
evil does not prevail against wisdom.

8 1 But she reaches from one end to the
other with full strength, and orders all
things well.
2 I loved her and sought her from my
youth. I sought to take her for my bride. I
became enamored by her beauty.
3 She glorifies her noble birth by living
with Elohim. Adonai יהוה Tsevaot loves
her.
4 For she is initiated into the knowledge of
Elohim, and she chooses His works.
5 But if riches are a desired possession in
life, what is richer than wisdom, which
makes all things?
6 And if understanding works, who more
than she is an architect of the things that
exist?
7 If a man loves righteousness, the fruits of
wisdom's labor are virtues, for she teaches
sobriety, understanding, righteousness, and
courage. There is nothing in life more
profitable for men than these.
8 And if anyone longs for wide experience,
she knows the things of old, and infers the
things to come. She understands subtleties
of speeches and interpretations of dark
sayings. She foresees signs and wonders,

and the issues of seasons and times.
9 Therefore I determined to take her to live with me, knowing that she is one who would give me good counsel, and encourage me in cares and grief.
10 Because of her, I will have glory among multitudes, and honor in the eyes of elders, even though I am young.
11 I will be found keen when I give judgment. I will be admired in the presence of rulers.
12 When I am silent, they will wait for me. When I open my lips, they will heed what I say. If I continue speaking, they will put their hands on their mouths.
13 Because of her, I will have immortality, and leave behind an eternal memory to those who come after me.
14 I will govern peoples. Nations will be subjected to me.
15 Dreaded kings will fear me when they hear of me. Among the people, I will show myself to be good, and courageous in war.
16 When I come into my house, I will find rest with her.
For conversation with her has no bitterness, and living with her has no pain, but gladness and joy.
17 When I considered these things in myself, and thought in my heart how immortality is in kinship to wisdom,
18 and in her friendship is good delight, and in the labors of her hands is wealth that does not fail, and understanding is in her companionship, and great renown in having fellowship with her words, I went about seeking how to take her to myself.
19 Now I was a clever child, and was allotted a good being.
20 Or rather, being good, I came into an undefiled body.
21 But perceiving that I could not otherwise possess wisdom unless Elohim gave her to me – yes, and to know and understand by whom favor is given – I pleaded with יהוה and asked Him, and with my whole heart I said,

9 1 "O Elohim of my fathers; Master of kindness, who made all things by Your word;
2 and by your wisdom you formed man, that he should have dominion over the creatures that were made by You,
3 and rule the world in set-apartness and righteousness, and execute judgment in uprightness of being:
4 give me wisdom, her who sits by You on Your thrones. Do not reject me from among Your servants,
5 because I am Your servant and the son of Your handmaid, a weak and short-lived man, with little power to understand judgments and statutes.
6 For even if a man is perfect among the sons of men, if the wisdom that comes from You is not with him, he will count for nothing.
7 You chose me to be king of Your people, and a judge for Your sons and daughters.
8 You gave a command to build a set-apart place on Your set-apart mountain, and an altar in the city where You pitch Your tent, a copy of the set-apart tent which You prepared from the beginning.
9 Wisdom is with You and knows Your works, and was present when You made the world, and understands what is pleasing in Your eyes, and what is right according to Your commands.
10 Send her from the set-apart heavens, and ask her to come from the throne of Your glory, that being present with me she may work, and I may learn what is pleases You

well.
11 For she knows all things and understands, and she will guide me soberly in my actions. She will guard me in her glory.
12 So my works will be acceptable. I will judge Your people righteously, and I will be worthy of my father's throne.
13 For what man will know the counsel of Elohim? Or who will conceive what יהוה decides?
14 For the thoughts of mortals are unstable, and our plans are prone to fail.
15 For a corruptible body weighs down the being. The earthy frame lies heavy on a mind that is full of cares.
16 We can hardly guess the things that are on earth, and we find the things that are close at hand with labor; but who has searched out the things that are in the heavens?
17 Who gained knowledge of Your counsel, unless You gave wisdom, and sent Your Set-Apart Ruaḥ from the highest?
18 It was thus that the ways of those who are on earth were corrected, and men were taught the things that are pleasing to You, and they were saved through wisdom."

10 1 Wisdom guarded (to the end) the first-formed father[a] of the world, that was created alone, and *she* delivered him out of his own transgression,
2 and gave him strength to get dominion over all things.
3 But when an unrighteous man[b] fell away from her in his anger, he caused himself to perish in the rage with which he killed his brother[c].
4 And when, for his cause, the earth was drowning with a flood, Wisdom saved it again, guiding the righteous man's[d] course by a poor piece of wood.
5 Moreover, when nations that consented together in wickedness had been confounded, Wisdom knew the righteous man[e], and preserved him blameless to Elohim, and kept him strong when his heart yearned toward his child[f].
6 While the wicked were perishing, Wisdom delivered a righteous man[g], when he fled from the fire that descended out of heaven on Pentapolis[h].
7 To whose wickedness a smoking waste still witnesses, and plants bearing fair fruit that will not ripen; yes and a disbelieving being has a memorial there, a pillar of salt still standing.[i]
8 For having passed Wisdom by, not only were they unable to recognize the things which are good, but they also left behind them for human life a monument of their foolishness, to the end that where they went astray they might fail even to be hidden.
9 But Wisdom delivered out of troubles those that waited on her.
10 When a righteous man[j] was a fugitive from a brother's wrath, Wisdom guided him

---

[a] 10:1 Adam.
[b] 10:3 Qayin.
[c] 10:3 Havel.
[d] 10:4 Noaḥ.
[e] 10:5 Avraham.
[f] 10:5 Yitsḥaq.
[g] 10:6 Lot. See Kepha ב [2 Peter] 2:7; both are references to Lot being called "righteous."
[h] 10:6 Pentapolis – Greek word meaning "five cities." This refers to Sedom and Gomorrah, as well as Segor, Admah, and Tsevoyim.
[i] 10:7 Historian Flavius Josephus claimed in his work *Antiquities of the Jews*, Book 1, Chapter 11, verse 4, that he saw the pillar of salt that was Lot's wife. Similar testimony is also cited by Clement of Rome and Irenaeus.
[j] 10:10 Ya'aqov.

in straight paths; she showed him the kingdom of Elohim, and gave him knowledge of set-apart things; she prospered him in his toils, and multiplied the fruits of his labor.
11 When, in their covetousness, men dealt harshly with him, she stood by him and made him rich.
12 She guarded him from enemies, and she kept him safe from those that lay in wait, and over his sore conflict she watched as judge, that he might know that righteousness is more powerful than all.
13 When a righteous man[a] was sold, Wisdom did not forsake him, but she delivered him from sin. She went down with him into a dungeon,
14 and even in bonds she would not leave him, until she brought him the scepter of a kingdom, and authority over those that dealt tyrannously with him. She showed them also to be false that had mockingly accused him, and gave him eternal glory.
15 Wisdom delivered a set-apart people[b] and a blameless seed from a nation of oppressors.
16 She entered into the being of a servant[c] of יהוה, and withstood terrible kings in wonders and signs.
17 She rendered a reward of toils to set-apart men. She guided them along a marvelous way, and became to them a covering in the day-time, and a flame of stars through the night.
18 She brought them over the Sea of Reeds, and led them through much water.
19 But she drowned their enemies, and out of the bottom of the deep she cast them up.
20 Therefore the righteous plundered the wicked. And they sang praise to Your Set-Apart Name, O יהוה, and extolled with one accord Your hand that fought for them.[d]
21 Because wisdom opened the mouth of the dumb, and made the tongues of babes to speak clearly.

11 1 She prospered their works in the hand of a set-apart prophet.
2 They traveled through a desert without inhabitant, and in trackless regions they pitched their tents.
3 They withstood enemies, and repelled foes.
4 They thirsted, and they called upon You, and there was given them water out of the flinty rock, and healing of their thirst out of the hard stone.
5 For by what things their foes were punished, by these they in their need were benefited.
6 When enemies were troubled with clotted blood instead of a river's ever-flowing fountain,
7 to rebuke the decree for the slaying of babies, You gave them abundant water beyond all hope,
8 having shown by the thirst which they had suffered how You punished the adversaries.
9 For when they were tried, although disciplined in kindness, they learned how the wicked were tormented, being judged with wrath.
10 For You tested these as a father admonishing them, but You searched out those as a stern king condemning them.
11 Yes and whether they were far off or near, they were equally distressed;

---

[a] 10:13 Yoseph.
[b] 10:15 Children of Yisra'el.
[c] 10:16 Mosheh.
[d] 10:20 See Shemoth [Exodus] 15.

12 for a double grief seized them, and a groaning at the memory of things past.
13 For when they heard that through their own punishments the others benefited, they recognized יהוה.
14 For him who long before was thrown out and exposed they stopped mocking. In the end of what happened, they marveled, having thirsted in another manner than the righteous.
15 But in return for the senseless inclinations of their unrighteousness, in which they were led astray to worship absurd reptiles and wretched vermin, You sent upon them a multitude of absurd creatures for vengeance,
16 that they might learn that by what things a man sins, by these he is punished.
17 For Your all-powerful hand, which created the world out of formless matter, did not lack means to send upon them a multitude of bears, fierce lions,
18 or newly-created and unknown wild beasts, full of rage, either breathing out a blast of fiery breath, or coughing out smoke, or flashing dreadful sparks from their eyes;
19 which had power not only to consume them by their violence, but to destroy them even by the terror of their sight.
20 Yes and without these they might have fallen by a single breath, being pursued by judgment, and scattered abroad by the breath of Your power. But You arranged all things by measure, number, and weight.
21 For to be greatly strong is Yours at all times. Who could withstand the might of Your arm?
22 Because the whole world before You is as a grain in a balance, and as a drop of dew that comes down upon the earth in the morning.
23 But You have mercy on all men, because You have power to do all things, and You overlook the sins of men to the end that they may repent.
24 For You love all things that are, and abhor none of the things which You made. For You never would have formed anything if You hated it *then.*
25 How would anything have endured, unless You had willed it? Or that which was not called by You, how would it have been preserved?
26 But you spare all things, because they are Yours, O Adonai יהוה, You who love lives.

12 1 For Your incorruptible Ruaḥ is in all things.
2 By which You convict – little by little – those who fall from the right way, and, putting them in remembrance by the things in which they sin, You admonish them, that escaping from their wickedness they may believe in You, O יהוה.
3 For truly the old inhabitants of Your set-apart land,
4 hating them because they practiced detestable works of sorcery and wicked
rituals, 5 evil slaughters of children and sacrificial banquets of men's flesh and blood;
6 confederates in a wicked fellowship, and murderers of their own helpless infants, it was Your counsel to destroy by the hands of our fathers;
7 that the land which in Your eyes is most precious of all might receive a worthy colony of the servants of Elohim.
8 Nevertheless You even spared these as men, and You sent hornets as forerunners of Your army, to cause them to perish little by little.

9 Not that You were unable to subdue the
wicked under the hand of the righteous in
battle, or by terrible beasts or by a stern
word to make away with them at once;
10 but judging them little by little You gave
them a chance to repent, not being ignorant
that their inclination by birth was evil, their
wickedness inborn, and that their manner of
thought would never be changed.
11 For they were a cursed seed from the
beginning. It was not through fear of any
that You left them unpunished for their
sins.
12 For who will say, "What have You
done?" Or "Who will withstand Your
judgment?" Who will accuse You for the
perishing of nations which You caused? Or
who will come and stand before You as an
avenger for unrighteous men?
13 For there is no Elohim besides You that
cares for all, that You might show that You
did not judge unrighteously.
14 No king or prince will be able to look
You in the face for those whom You have
punished.
15 But being righteous, You rule all things
righteously, deeming it far from Your
desire to condemn one that does not
deserve to be punished.
16 For Your strength is the beginning of
righteousness, and Your reign over all
makes You to forbear all.
17 For when men do not believe that You
are perfect in power, You show Your
strength, and in dealing with those who
think this, You confuse their boldness.
18 But You, being sovereign over strength,
judge in gentleness, and with great
forbearance do You govern us. For the
power is Yours whenever You desire it.
19 But You taught Your people by such
works as these, how the righteous must be a
lover of men. You made Your sons to have
good hope, because You give repentance
when men have sinned.
20 For if you took vengeance on those who
were enemies of Your servants, and due to
death, with so great deliberation and
indulgence, giving them times and
opportunities when they might escape from
their wickedness,
21 with how great carefulness You judged
Your sons, to whose fathers You gave
oaths and covenants of good promises!
22 Therefore while You discipline us, You
scourge our enemies ten thousand times
more, to the intent that we may ponder your
goodness when we judge. And when we are
judged, we may look for kindness.
23 Wherefore also the unrighteous that
lived in folly of life, You tormented
through their own abominations.
24 For truly they went astray very far in the
ways of error, taking as elohim those
animals which even among their enemies
were held in dishonor, deceived like foolish
children.
25 Therefore, as to unreasoning children,
You sent Your judgment to mock them.
26 But those who would not be admonished
by a mocking correction as of children will
experience a judgment worthy of Elohim.
27 For through the sufferings they were
indignant of, being punished in these
creatures which they supposed to be
elohim, they saw and recognized as the true
El Him whom they refused to know.
Therefore also the result of condemnation
came upon them.

13

1 For truly all men who had no
perception of Elohim were vain by nature,
and did not gain power to know Him who
exists from the good things that are seen.
They did not recognize the architect from

His works.[a]

2 But they thought that either fire, or wind, or swift air, or circling stars, or raging water, or lights of heaven were elohim that rule the world.[b]

3 If it was through delight in their beauty that they believed them to be elohim; let them know how much better Adonai יהוה is than these, for the first author of beauty created them.

4 But if it was through astonishment at their power and influence, then let them understand from them how much more powerful is He who formed them.

5 For from the greatness of the beauty of created things, mankind forms the corresponding image of their Maker.

6 But yet for these men there is but small blame, for they too perhaps go astray while they are seeking Elohim, and desiring to find Him.

7 For they diligently search while living among His works, and they trust their sight that the things that they look at are beautiful.

8 But again, even they are not to be excused.

9 For if they had power to know so much, that they should be able to explore the world, how is it that they did not find Adonai יהוה sooner?

10 But miserable were they, and in dead things were their hopes, who called them elohim which are works of men's hands; gold and silver, skillfully made, and likenesses of animals, or a useless stone, the work of an ancient hand.

11 Yes and if some woodcutter, having sawn down a tree that is easily moved, skillfully strips away all its bark, and fashioning it in attractive form, makes a useful vessel to serve his life's needs.

12 Burning the scraps from his handiwork to cook his food, he eats his fill.

13 Taking a discarded scrap which served no purpose, a crooked piece of wood and full of knots, carves it with the diligence of his zeal, and shapes it by the skill of his zeal. He shapes it in the image of a man,

14 or makes it like some paltry[c] animal, smearing it with red, painting it crimson, and smearing over every stain in it.

15 Having made a worthy chamber for it, he sets it in a wall, securing it with iron.

16 He plans for it that it may not fall down, knowing that it is unable to help itself (for truly it is an image, and needs help).

17 When he makes his prayer concerning goods and his marriage and children, he is not ashamed to speak to that which has no life.

18 Yes, for health, he calls upon that which is weak. For life, he implores that which is dead. For aid, he petitions that which has no experience. For a good journey, he asks that which cannot so much as move a step.

19 And for profit in business and good success of his hands, he asks ability from that which has hands with no ability.

14 1 Again, one preparing to sail, and about to journey over raging waves, calls upon a piece of wood more rotten than the vessel that carries him.

2 For the hunger for profit planned it, and wisdom was the craftsman who built it.

3 Your providence, O Father, guides it

---

[a] 13:1 See Romaious 1:20.

[b] 13:2 See Romaious 1:21-27.

[c] 13:14 Greek reads ευτελει (*eutelei*) meaning "mere, measly, paltry." Syriac text reads ܫܦܝܪܬܐ (*sapir'ata*) meaning "beautiful."

along, because even in the sea You gave a way, and in the waves a sure path,
4 showing that You can save out of every danger, that even a man without skill may put to sea.
5 It is Your will that the works of Your wisdom should not be idle. Therefore men also entrust their lives to a little piece of wood, and passing through the surge on a raft come safely to land.
6 For even in the beginning, when arrogant giants[a] were perishing, the hope of the world took refuge on a raft, and guided by Your hand left to the world the seed of a new generation.
7 For blessed is the wood through which comes righteousness;
8 but the idol made with hands is accursed, itself and he that made it; because his was the working, and the corruptible thing was called an el.
9 For both the wicked and his wickedness are alike hateful to Elohim;
10 for truly the deed will be punished together with him who committed it.
11 Therefore also there will be a visitation among the idols of the nation, because, though formed of things which Elohim created, they were made an abomination, stumbling blocks to the beings of men, and a snare to the feet of the foolish.
12 For the devising of idols was the beginning of whoring, and their invention was the corruption of life.
13 For they did not exist from the beginning, and they will not exist forever.
14 For by the vanity of men they entered into the world, and therefore a speedy end is planned for them.
15 For a father worn with untimely grief, making an image of the child quickly taken away, now honored him as an el which was then dead, and delivered to those that were under him mysteries and solemn rites.
16 Afterward the wicked custom, having been strengthened over time, was kept as a law, and the engraved images received worship by the commands of princes.
17 And when men could not honor them in presence because they lived far off, imagining the likeness from afar, they made a visible image of the king whom they honored, that by their zeal they might flatter the absent as if present.
18 But worship was raised to a yet higher pitch, even by those who did not know him, urged forward by the ambition of the architect;
19 for he, desiring to please one in authority, used his art to force the likeness toward a greater beauty.
20 So the multitude, allured by reason of the form of his handiwork, now consider him as an object of devotion – the same who, a little before, was honored as a man.
21 And this became an ambush, because men – in bondage either to calamity or to tyranny – called stones and wood an unspeakable name.
22 Afterward it was not enough for them to go astray concerning the knowledge of Elohim, but also while they live in sore conflict through ignorance of Him. That multitude of evils they call peace.
23 For either slaughtering children in solemn rites, or celebrating secret mysteries, or holding frantic revels of strange ordinances;

---

[a] 14:6 Syriac text reads ܓܢܒܪܐ (*g'nbara*), meaning "mighty men." Compare B'reshiyt [Genesis] 6:4.

24 No longer do they guard either life or purity of marriage, but one brings upon another either death by treachery, or grief by adultery.

25 And all things are filled with blood and murder, theft and deceit, corruption, faithlessness, tumult, perjury,

26 turmoil, ingratitude for benefits received, defiling of selves, alteration of nature, disorder in marriage, adultery, and debauchery.

27 For the worship of those nameless idols is a beginning and cause and end of every evil.

28 For their worshippers either make merry to madness, or prophesy lies, or live unrighteously, or take oaths lightly.

29 For putting their trust in lifeless idols, when they have sworn a wicked oath, they expect not to suffer harm.

30 But for both sins will the just end pursue them, for they had evil thoughts of Elohim by giving heed to idols, and swore unrighteously in deceit through contempt for set-apartness.

31 For it is not the power of them by whom men swear, but it is that justice, which has regard to those who sin, that always visits the transgression of the unrighteous.

15 1 But You, our Elohim, are kind and true, patient, and in kindness ordering all things.

2 For even if we sin, we are Yours, knowing Your dominion. But we will not sin, knowing that we have been accounted as Yours.

3 For to be acquainted with You is perfect righteousness, and to know Your dominion is the root of immortality.

4 For we were not led astray by any evil plan of men, nor yet by painters' fruitless labor, a form stained with varied colors,

5 the sight of which leads fools into lust. Their desire is for the breathless form of a dead image.

6 Lovers of evil things, and worthy of such hopes as these, are both those who do, and those who desire, and those who worship.

7 For a potter, kneading soft clay, laboriously molds each vessel for our service. See, he fashions out of the same clay both the vessels that minister to clean uses, and those of a contrary sort, all in like manner; but the use of each vessel of either sort is judged by the craftsman himself.

8 And also, laboring to an evil end, he molds a worthless el out of the same clay, he who, having but a little before been made of earth, after a short space goes his way to the earth out of which he was taken, when he is required to render back the being which was lent him.

9 Therefore he has anxious care; not because his powers will fail, nor because his span of life is short; but he matches himself against goldsmiths and silversmiths, and he imitates the formers of copper, and esteems it glory that he molds counterfeits.

10 His heart is ashes, and his hope of less value than earth, and his life of less honor than clay.

11 For he was ignorant of Him that molded him, and of Him that inspired the being into him, and breathed into him a living spirit.

12 But he accounted our very life to be a plaything, and our lifetime a gainful fair. "For," he says, "one must get gain where one can, even if by evil."

13 For this man beyond all others knows that he sins, out of earthy matter making brittle vessels and graven images.

14 But most foolish were they all, and of feebler being than an infant, the enemies of

Your people, who oppressed them.
15 For they even accounted all the idols of
the nations to be elohim, which have
neither the use of eyes for seeing, nor
nostrils for drawing breath, nor ears to hear,
nor fingers for handling, and their feet are
helpless for walking.
16 For a man made them, and one whose
own spirit is borrowed molded them. For
no one has power, being a man, to mold an
el like himself.
17 But, being mortal, he makes a dead thing
by the work of lawless hands. For he is
better than the objects of his worship, for as
he indeed had life, they never did.
18 Yes, and they worship the creatures that
are most hateful, for, being likened to lack
of sense, these are worse than all others.
19 Neither, as seen beside other creatures,
are they beautiful, so that one should desire
them. But they have escaped both the
praise of Elohim and His blessing.

16

1 Because of this these men were
worthily punished through creatures like
those which they worship, and tormented
through a multitude of vermin.
2 Instead of that punishment You,
bestowing benefits on Your people,
prepared quails for food, food of rare taste,
to satisfy the desire of their appetite.
3 To the end that Your enemies, desiring
food, might for the hideousness of the
creatures sent among them loathe even the
necessary appetite. But these, Your people,
having for a short space suffered lack,
might even partake of food of rare taste.
4 For it was necessary that upon those
should come unescapable lack in their
oppressive dealing, but that to these it
should only be showed how their enemies
were tormented.
5 For even when terrible raging of wild
beasts came upon Your people, and they
were perishing by the bites of fiery
serpents, Your wrath did not continue to
the end of them.
6 But they troubled as punishment *only* for
a short time, having a sign of salvation, to
put them in remembrance of the command
of Your Torah.
7 For he that turned toward it was not saved
because of that which was seen, but
because of You, the Savior of all.[a]
8 Yes, and in this You persuaded our
enemies, that You are He that delivers out
of every evil.
9 For them truly the bites of locusts and
flies did kill, and there was not found a
healing for their life, because they were
worthy to be punished by such as these.
10 But not even the very teeth of adders
overcame Your children, for Your mercy
passed by where they were, and healed
them.
11 For they were bitten, to put them in
remembrance of Your prophecies, and were
quickly saved, lest, falling into deep
forgetfulness, they should become unable
to be roused by Your generosity.
12 For truly it was neither root nor poultice
that cured them, but Your word, O יהוה,
which heals all things.
13 For You have authority over life and
death, and You lead down to the gates of
Sheol, and lead up again.
14 But if a man kills by his wickedness, and
when the spirit is gone it shall not return;
neither can he take back the being from

---

[a] 16:7 See Bemidbar [Numbers] 21:4-9; Yoḥanan [John] 3:14-15.

Sheol.
15 But a man cannot be removed from Your hand.
16 For wicked men, refusing to know You, were scourged in the strength of Your arm, pursued with strange rains and hails and unstoppable showers, and utterly consumed with fire.
17 For what was most marvelous of all, in the water which quenches all things, the fire worked yet more mightily. For the world fights for the righteous.
18 For at one time the flame lost its fury that it might not burn up the creatures sent against the wicked. But that these themselves, as they looked, might see that they were persecuted by the judgment of Elohim.
19 And at another time, even in the midst of water, it burns above the power of fire, that it may destroy the fruits of an unrighteous land.
20 Instead these, You gave Your people food of messengers[a] to eat, and You provided bread for their use from heaven without their toil; bread having the virtue of every pleasant savor, and agreeing to every palate.
21 For Your nature manifested Your sweetness toward Your children while that bread, ministering to the desire of the one eating, altered itself according to every man's choice.
22 But snow and ice endured fire, and did not melt, that men might know that fire was destroying the fruits of the enemies, burning in the hail and flashing in the rains.
23 And that this element again, in order that righteous men may be nourished, has even forgotten its own power.
24 For the creation, ministering to You its maker, strains its force against the unrighteous, for punishment, and slackens it on behalf of those who trust in You, for generosity.
25 Therefore at that time also, converting itself into all forms, it ministered to Your all-nourishing bounty, according to the desire of those who petitioned,
26 that Your sons, whom You loved, O יהוה, might learn that it is not the growth of the earth's fruits that nourishes a man, but that Your word preserves those who trust You.
27 For that which was not marred by fire, when it was simply warmed by a faint sunbeam melted away,
28 that it might be known that we must rise before the sun to give thanks to You, and must plead with You at the dawning of the light.
29 For the hope of the unthankful will melt as the winter's hoar frost, and will flow away as water that has no use.

17

1 For Your judgments are great, and hard to interpret. Therefore undisciplined beings went astray.
2 For when lawless men had supposed that they held a set-apart nation in their power, they, themselves, prisoners of darkness, and bound in the fetters of a long night, shut up beneath their roofs, lay exiled from the eternal providence.
3 For while they thought that they were unseen in their secret sins, they were divided one from another by a dark curtain of forgetfulness, stricken with terrible awe, and badly troubled by shadowy forms.
4 For neither did the dark recesses that held them guard them from fears, but sounds rushing down rang around them, and

[a] 16:20 Or, more commonly, "angels."

apparitions appeared, cheerless with
unsmiling faces.
5 And no force of fire prevailed to give
them light, neither were the brightest
flames of the stars strong enough to
illuminate that gloomy night.
6 But only there appeared to them the
glimmering of a self-kindled fire, full of
fear. And in terror they deemed the things
which they saw to be worse than that sight,
on which they could not gaze.
7 And they lay helpless, those who make
sport of sorcery, and a shameful rebuke of
their boast of understanding.
8 For those who promised to drive away
terrors and troubles from a sick being, these
were themselves sick with a ludicrous
fearfulness.
9 For even if no troublous thing frightened
them, yet still, scared with the creeping of
vermin and hissing of serpents, 10 they
perished for very trembling, refusing even
to look on the air which could not be
escaped on any side.
11 For wickedness, condemned by a witness
within, is a cowardly thing, and, being
pressed hard by conscience, always
forecasts the worst lot.
12 For fear is nothing else but a surrender of
the help which reason offers, 13 and from
within the heart the expectation of them
being less makes of greater account the
ignorance of the cause that brings the
torment.
14 But they, all through the night which was
powerless indeed, and which came upon
them out of the recesses of powerless
Sheol, all sleeping the same sleep, 15 now
were haunted by monstrous apparitions,
and now were paralyzed by the
surrendering of their being. For fear,
suddenly came upon them, without being
sought.
16 So then every man, whoever it might be,
sinking down in his place, was kept in ward
shut up in that prison which was barred
without iron.
17 For whether he were a husbandman, or a
shepherd, or a laborer whose toils were in
the wilderness, he was overtaken, and
endured that inevitable necessity, for with
one chain of darkness were they all bound.
18 Whether there were a whistling wind, or
a melodious noise of birds among the
spreading branches, or a measured fall of
water running violently, 19 or a harsh
crashing of rocks hurled down, or the swift
course of animals bounding along unseen,
or the voice of wild beasts harshly roaring,
or an echo rebounding from the hollows of
the mountains: all these things paralyzed
them with terror.
20 For the whole world beside was
enlightened with clear light, and was
occupied with unhindered works.
21 While over them alone was spread a
heavy night, an image of the darkness that
should afterward receive them. But they
were yet still heavier to themselves, than
was the darkness.

18 1 But for Your set-apart ones there was
great light; and the Mitsrites, hearing their
voice but not seeing their form, counted it a
happy thing that they too had suffered.
2 And they do not hurt them now for that,
though wronged by them before, they are
thankful. And because they had been at
odds with them *before*, they made petition
to them.
3 Whereas You provided for Your people a
burning pillar of fire, to be a guide for their
unknown journey, and a kindly sun for
their proud exile.
4 For the Mitsrites did well deserve to be

deprived of light and imprisoned by darkness, those who had kept in close ward Your sons, through whom the incorruptible light of the Torah was to be given to the race of men.
5 After they had taken counsel to kill the infants of the set-apart ones, and when a single child had been cast forth and saved to convict them of their sin, You took away from them their multitude of children, and destroyed all their army together in a mighty flood.
6 Our fathers were made aware of that night beforehand, that, having sure knowledge, they might be cheered by the oaths which they had trusted.
7 So Your people expected salvation of the righteous and destruction of the enemies.
8 For as You took vengeance on the adversaries, by the same means, calling us to Yourself, You glorified us.
9 For set-apart children of good men offered sacrifice in secret, and in one accord they took upon themselves the covenant of the Just Torah, that they would partake alike in the same good things and the same perils; the fathers already leading the songs of praise.
10 But there came back a sound of discord: the cry of the enemies. And a mourning voice of lamentation for children was lifted.
11 And servant along with master punished with a like just doom, and commoner suffering the same as king.
12 Yes, all the people together, under one form of death, had innumerable corpses with them. For there were not enough of the living *left* to bury them, since with a single stroke their nobler seed were consumed.
13 For while they were disbelieving all things by reason of the enchantments, upon the destruction of the firstborn they confessed the people to be children of Elohim.
14 For while peaceful silence enwrapped all things, and night, in her own swiftness, was
in mid-course, 15 Your all-powerful word leaped from heaven out of the royal throne, a stern warrior, into the midst of the
doomed land, 16 bearing Your sincere command as a sharp sword, and standing, it filled all things with death. And while it touched the heavens it trod upon the earth.
17 Then immediately apparitions in dreams terribly troubled them, and fears came upon them that they did not seek.
18 And one thrown here half dead, another there, and so each made manifest why he was dying.
19 For the dreams, disturbing them, did foreshow this, that they might not perish without knowing why they were afflicted.
20 But it happened to the righteous also to make trial of death, and a multitude were stricken in the wilderness. However, the wrath did not endure for long.
21 For a blameless man hurried to be their champion, [bringing the instrument of his own ministry][a], even prayer and petition and incense, he withstood the indignation, and set an end to the calamity, showing that he was Your servant.
22 And he overcame the anger, not by strength of body, nor by strength of weapons. But by word he subdued the minister of punishment, by bringing to remembrance oaths and covenants made with the fathers.
23 For when the dead were already fallen in

---

[a] 18:21 So the Greek text. Latin text reads, "bringing the shield of his ministry." The Syriac text reads, "clothed with the garments of the priesthood."

heaps one upon another, he stood between
the advancing wrath and stopped, and cut
off the way to the living.
24 For upon his long high-priestly robe was
the whole world, and the glories of the
fathers were upon the graving of the four
rows of precious stones, and Your majesty
was upon the diadem of his head.
25 To these the destroyer gave place, and
these the people feared: for it was enough
only to make trial of the wrath.

19
1 But upon the wicked there came to
the end indignation without compassion:
for Elohim foreknew their future also.
2 How that, having changed their minds to
let Your people go, and having speeded
them eagerly on their way, they would turn
themselves and pursue them.
3 For while they were still in the midst of
their mourning, and making lamentation at
the graves of the dead, they drew upon
themselves another counsel of foolishness,
and pursued as fugitives those whom with
entreaties they had cast out.
4 For the doom which they deserved was
drawing them to this end, and it made them
forget the things that happened to them,
that they might fill up the punishment
which was still lacking to their torments.
5 And that Your people might journey on
by a marvelous road, but they themselves
might find a strange death.
6 For all of creation, each part in its several
kinds, was fashioned again anew, attending
to Your several commands, that Your
servants might be guarded free from hurt.
7 Then the cloud that shadowed the camp
was seen, and dry land rising up out of
what before was water, out of the Sea of
Reeds, an unhindered highway, and a
grassy plain out of the violent surge.
8 They passed over with all their host by
this, these that were covered with Your
hand, having seen strange marvels.
9 For like horses they roamed at large, and
they skipped about like lambs, praising
You, O יהוה, who was their deliverer.
10 For they still remembered the things that
came to pass in the time of their
sojourning; how instead of bearing cattle
the land brought forth lice, and instead of
fish the river cast up a multitude of frogs.
11 But afterwards they saw also a new race
of birds, when, led on by desire, they asked
for luxurious dainties.
12 For, to appease them, quails came up for
them from the sea.
13 And upon the sinners came the
punishment; not without the tokens that
were given beforehand by the force of the
thunders. For they suffered justly through
their own wickednesses, for grievous
indeed was the hatred which they practiced
toward guests.
14 For whereas the men of Sedom did not
receive the strangers when they came
among them, the Mitsrites made slaves of
guests who were their benefactors.
15 And not only this, but Elohim will visit
the men of Sedom after another sort, since
they received as enemies those who were
foreigners.
16 Whereas these first welcomed with
feastings, and then afflicted with dreadful
toils, them that had already shared with
them in the same rights.
17 And moreover they were stricken with
blindness (even as were those others at the
righteous man's doors), when, being
surrounded with yawning darkness, each
one sought passage through his own door.
18 For as the notes of a lyre vary the
character of the rhythm, even so did the
elements, changing their order one with

another, continue always the same, each in
its several sounds. As may clearly be
determined from the sight of the things that
are come to pass.
19 For creatures of the dry land were turned
into creatures of the waters, and creatures
that swim trod now upon the earth.
20 Fire kept the mastery of its own power in
the midst of water, and water forgot its
quenching nature.
21 Conversely, flames did not waste the
flesh of perishable creatures that walked
among them; neither did they melt the good
food, which was prone to melt.
22 For in all things, O יהוה, You magnified
Your people, and You glorified them, and
regard them highly, standing by their side
in every time and place.

ⲈⲤⲆⲢⲀⲤ Ⲃ
Esdras B
[2 Esdras {4 Ezra}]

1 [a][1 The second book of the prophet Ezra,
Serayah, the son of Azaryah, the son of
Ḥilqiyahu, the son of Shallum, the son of
Tsadoq, the son of Aḥitov, 2 the son of
Aḥiyah, the son of Pineḥas, the son of Eli,
the son of Amaryah, the son of Oziyah, the
son of Meraioth, the son of Zerayah, the
son of Uzziyah, the son of Buqqi, the son
of Avishua, the son of Pineḥas, the son of
Elazar, 3 the son of Aharon, of the tribe of
Levi; which was captive in the land of the
Medes, in the reign of Artaḥshasta king of
the Parasians.

4 And the word of the Master came to me,
saying, 5 "Go your way, and show My
people their sinful deeds, and their children
their wickedness which they have done
against Me, *so* that they may tell their
children's children: 6 because the sins of
their fathers are increased in them; for they
have forgotten Me, and have sacrificed to
strange elohim.

7 "Did I not bring them out of the land of
Mitsrayim, out of the house of bondage?
Yet they have provoked Me to wrath, and
have despised My counsels. 8 Therefore,
shake the hair of your head, and cast all
evils upon them, for they have not obeyed
My Torah; rather, they are a rebellious
people. 9 How long shall I withhold
judgment from them, to whom I have done
so much good? 10 I have overthrown many
kings for their sakes; I have struck down
Pharaoh with his servants and all his army.
11 I have destroyed all nations *that were*
before them, and in the east I have scattered
the people of two provinces, even of Tsor
and Tsidon, and have slain all their
adversaries.

12 Therefore, speak to them, saying,
13 'Thus says the Master: truly, I brought
you through the sea, and I made for you
where there were no highways. I gave you
Mosheh for a leader, and Aharon for a
priest. 14 I gave you light in a pillar of fire,
and have done great wonders among you.
Still, you have forgotten Me,' says the
Master.

15 "Thus says El Shaddai: 'The quails were
for a token to you. I gave you a camp to
guard you, yet you still grumbled there;
16 and you did not triumph in My Name for
the destruction of your enemies, but even to
this day you still grumble. 17 Where are the
benefits that I have done for you? When
you were hungry and thirsty in the
wilderness, did you not cry to Me,
18 saying, "Why have You brought us into
this wilderness to kill us? It would have
been better for us to have served the
Mitsrites, than to die in this wilderness."
19 I had pity upon your mourning, and gave

---

[a] 1-2 Given the content of the first two chapters, along with the lack of support among the Eastern versions of 2 Esdras, it is believed by most scholars that these two chapters were penned by a second author that came much later. Though prevalent among the Latin copies, these two chapters are lacking among the other versions. They also present a somewhat biased view against Jews, which does not suit chapters 3-14, which are clearly Jewish in origin. Likewise although the author shows a knowledge of Hebrew (see footnote at 1:40), the Latin of this text is more refined than it should be if it were merely a translation of a Greek or Semitic original. For this reason these first two chapters are generally referred to by scholars as 5 Esdras.

you manna for food. You ate the bread of
messengers[a].

20 "'When you were thirsty, did I not split
the rock, and waters flowed out to your fill?
For the heat, I covered you with the leaves
of the trees. 21 I divided among you fruitful
lands. I cast out the Kena'anites, the
Perezites, and the Philistines from before
you. What more shall I do for you?' says
the Master.

22 "Thus says El Shaddai: 'When you were
in the wilderness, at the bitter river, being
thirsty, and blaspheming My Name, 23 I did
not destroy you with fire for your
blasphemies, but cast a tree in the water,
and made the river sweet. 24 What shall I
do to you, O Ya'aqov? You, Yehudah,
would not obey Me. So I will turn to other
nations, and I will give My Name to them
that they may guard My commands.
25 Seeing you have forsaken Me, I also will
forsake you; when you ask Me to be kind to
you, I will have no mercy upon you.
26 Whenever you call upon Me, I will not
hear you; for you have defiled your hands
with blood, and your feet are swift to
commit murder. 27 In this way, you have
not forsaken Me, but rather your own
selves,' says the Master.

28 "Thus says El Shaddai: 'Have I not
exhorted you as a father *exhorts* his sons, as
a mother *exhorts* her daughters, and as a
nurse *exhorts* her infants, 29 that you would
be My people, and I would be your Elohim;
that you would be My children, and I
would be your father? 30 I gathered you
together, **as a hen gathers her chicks
under her wings**; but now, what shall I do
to you? I will cast you out from My
presence. 31 When you offer sacrifices to
Me, I will turn My face from you; for your
appointed times, your new moons, and your
circumcisions of the flesh, have I rejected.
32 I sent to you My servants the prophets,
whom you have taken and slain, and torn
their bodies in pieces, whose blood I will
require of your hands,' says the Master.

33 "Thus says El Shaddai, 'Your house is
desolate, I will cast you out as the wind
does stubble. 34 And your children shall not
be fruitful; for they have neglected My
command to you, and done that which is
evil before Me. 35 I will give your houses
to a people that will come which, though
they have not heard of Me, yet still believe
Me. Though I have not shown signs to
them, they shall do that which I have
commanded. 36 They have seen no
prophets, yet they shall call their former
estate to remembrance. 37 I take to witness
the favor of the people that shall come,
whose little ones rejoice with gladness; and
though they do not see Me with physical
eyes, yet in spirit they shall believe the
thing that I say.

38 And now, O father, behold with glory;
and see the people that come from the east:
39 to whom I will give for leaders,
Avraham, Yitsḥaq, and Ya'aqov,
Yeshayahu, Amos, and Mikhah, Yoel,
Ovadyah, and Yonah, 40 Naḥum, and
Ḥavaqquq, Tsephanyah, Ḥaggai,
Zekharyah, and Malakhi, who is called also
the messenger of the Master.[b]

[a] 1:19 In common terms, angels. Referring to manna.

[b] 1:40 This phrase is a play on words. The Hebrew name Malakhi [Malachi] means "my messenger."

2 1 Thus says the Master, "I brought this
people out of bondage, and I gave them My
commands by My servants the prophets,
whom they would not hear, and they
treated My counsels as nothing. 2 The
mother that brought them forth says to
them, 'go your way, O my children; for I
am a widow and forsaken. 3 I raised you
with gladness, and with sorrow and
heaviness have I lost you; for you have
sinned before the Master Elohim, and done
that which is evil before me. 4 But what
shall I now do to you? For I am a widow
and forsaken; go your way, O my children,
and ask for favor from the Master.'

5 "As for me, O father, I call upon you for a
witness over the mother of these children,
because they would not keep My covenant,
6 that you bring them to confusion, and
their mother to a plunder, that there may be
no offspring from them. 7 Let them be
scattered abroad among the heathen, let
their names be erased from the earth. For
they have despised My covenant. 8 Woe to
you, Ashuwr, you that hide the unrighteous
with you! O you wicked nation, remember
what I did to Sedom and Gomorrah;
9 whose land lies in clods of pitch and
heaps of ashes; even so I will also do to
those who have not listened to Me," says El
Shaddai.

10 And the Master said to Ezra, "Tell My
people that I will give them the kingdom of
Yerushalayim, which I would have given to
Yisra'el. 11 I will also take their glory, and
give these the everlasting tabernacles,
which I had prepared for them. 12 They
shall have the tree of life for an ointment of
sweet savor; they shall neither labor, nor be
weary. 13 **Ask, and you shall receive**: pray
for few days, that they may be shortened.
The kingdom is already prepared for you;
so watch. 14 Take the heavens and earth to
witness, take them to witness; for I have
given up the evil, and created the good: for
I live," says the Master.

15 "Mother, embrace your children: I will
bring them out with gladness like a dove.
Establish their feet: for I have chosen you,"
says the Master. 16 And I will raise those
who are dead up again from their places,
and bring them out from their tombs. For
My Name is in them.

17 "Do not be afraid, you mother of
children: for I have chosen you," says the
Master. 18 "For your help, I will send my
servants Yeshayahu and Yirmeyahu, after
whose counsel I have set you apart, and
prepared twelve trees laden with various
fruits for you, 19 and as many springs
flowing with milk and honey, and seven
mighty mountains, upon which grow roses
and lilies, whereby I will fill your children
with joy. 20 Do right to the widow, judge
the fatherless, give to the poor, defend the
orphan, clothe the naked, 21 heal the broken
and the weak, do not laugh a lame man to
scorn, defend the wounded, and let the
blind man come to the sight of My glory.

22 "Keep the old and young within your
walls. 23 Wherever you find the dead, set a
sign upon them and commit them to the
grave, and I will give you the first place in
My resurrection. 24 Abide still, O My
people, and take your rest, for your
quietness shall come. 25 Nourish your
children, O you good nurse, and establish
their feet. 26 As for the servants whom I
have given you, not one of them shall
perish; for I will require them from among
your number. 27 do not be overly cautious:

for when the day of affliction and anguish comes, others shall weep and be sorrowful, but you shall be merry and have abundance. **28** The nations shall envy you, but they shall be able to do nothing against you," says the Master.

29 "My hands shall cover you, so that your children will not see Sheol. **30** Be joyful, O you mother, with your children: for I will deliver you," says the Master.
31 "Remember your children that sleep, for I shall bring them out of the secret places of the earth, and show favor to them: for I am kind," says El Shaddai. **32** "Embrace your children until I come, and proclaim favor to them: for my wells run over, and my favor shall not fail."

33 I, Ezra, received a charge from the Master upon mount Ḥorev, that I should go to Yisra'el. But when I came to them, they wanted nothing to do with me, and rejected the command of the Master. **34** And therefore I say to you, O nations that hear and understand, look for your shepherd; he shall give you everlasting rest; for he is near at hand, that shall come in the end of the world. **35** Be ready to the rewards of the kingdom, for the everlasting light shall shine upon you for evermore. **36** Flee the shadow of this world, receive the joyfulness of your glory: I call to witness my savior openly.

37 O receive that which is given to you from the Master, and be joyful, giving thanks to Him that has called you to heavenly kingdoms. **38** Arise up and stand, and behold the number of those that be sealed in the Feast of the Master; **39** those who withdrew them from the shadow of the world have received glorious garments from the Master. **40** Look upon your number, O Tsion, and make up the reckoning of those of yours that are clothed in white, which have fulfilled the Torah of the Master. **41** The number of your children, whom you long for, is fulfilled. Seek the power of the Master, that your people – who have been called from the beginning – may be set apart.

42 I, Ezra, saw upon the mount Tsion a great multitude, whom I could not number, and they all praised the Master with songs. **43** And in the midst of them there was a young man of a high stature, taller than all the rest, and upon every one of their heads he set crowns, and was more exalted, and I marveled greatly at this.

44 So I asked the messenger, and said, "What are these, my master?" **45** He answered and said to me, "These are those who have put off the garment of mortality, and put on immortality, and have confessed the Name of Elohim. Now are they crowned, and receive palms."

46 Then I said to the messenger, "What young man is he that sets crowns upon them, and gives them palms in their hands?" **47** So he answered and said to me, "It is the Son of Elohim, whom they have confessed in the world." Then I began to commend those who stood so stiffly for the Name of the Master. **48** Then the messenger said to me, "Go your way, and tell my people what manner of things, and what great wonders of Elohim you have seen."]

3 **1** In the thirtieth year after the ruin of the city, I Shealti'el (also called Ezra) was in Bavel, and lay troubled upon my bed, and my thoughts came up over my heart.

2 I saw the desolation of Tsion, and the
wealth of those who lived at Bavel. 3 And
my spirit was moved, so that I began to
speak words full of fear to Elyon, and said,
4 "O Adonai יהוה, did You not speak at the
beginning, when You fashioned the earth,
only You, and commanded the dust[a] 5 and
it yielded Adam to You, a body without a
being? Yet it was the workmanship of Your
hands, and You breathed into him the
breath of life, and he was made alive before
You.

6 "And You led him into paradise, which
Your right hand planted, before the earth
came to be. 7 And You gave him Your one
command, which he transgressed, and
immediately You appointed death for him
and in his generations. And innumerable
nations and tribes, peoples and kindred
were brought forth from him. 8 And every
nation walked after their own will, and did
wicked things before You, and despised
Your commands, and you did not hinder
them.

9 "Nevertheless, in due time You brought
the flood upon those that lived in the world,
and destroyed them. 10 And it came to be
that the same thing befell them; just as
death was to Adam, so was the flood to
these. 11 Nevertheless You left one of them,
Noaḥ with his household, even all the
righteous men that came from him.

12 "And it came to be, that when those who
lived upon the earth began to multiply, they
multiplied also children, and peoples, and
many nations, and began again to be more
wickedly than the first. 13 And it came to
be, when they acted wickedly before You,
You chose one from among them, whose
name was Avraham; 14 and You loved him,
and You showed him the end of the times
secretly by night, 15 and cut an everlasting
covenant with him, promising him that You
would never forsake his seed.

16 "And You gave Yitsḥaq to him, and You
gave Ya'aqov and Esaw to Yitsḥaq. And
You set apart Ya'aqov for Yourself, but set
aside Esaw; and Ya'aqov became a great
multitude. 17 And it came to be, that when
You led his seed out of Mitsrayim, You
brought them up to Mount Sinai. 18 You
bowed the heavens also, and shook the
earth, and moved the whole world, and
made the depths tremble, and troubled the
course of that age.

19 "And Your glory went through four
gates, of fire, and of earthquake, and of
wind, and of cold; that You might give the
Torah to the seed of Ya'aqov, and the
command to the generation of Yisra'el.
20 And yet You did not take away from
them their wicked heart, that Your Torah
might bring forth fruit in them. 21 For the
first Adam bore a wicked heart and
transgressed, and was overcome; and not
only him, but also all that are born of him.
22 Thus disease was made permanent; and
the Torah was in the heart of the people
along with the wickedness of the root; so
the good faded away, and that which was
wicked stayed.

23 "So the times passed away, and the years
were brought to an end. Then You raised
up a servant, called David, 24 whom You
commanded to build a city to Your Name,
and to offer offerings to You of Your own

---

[a] 3:4 So the Syriac and Ethiopic texts. Latin text reads, "world."

there. 25 When this was done many years,
then those who inhabited the city did evil,
26 in all things doing even as Adam and all
his generations had done, for they also
possessed a wicked heart, 27 and so You
gave Your city over into the hands of Your
enemies."

28 And I said then in my heart, "Are their
deeds any better that inhabit Bavel? Why
then does she have dominion over Tsion?"

29 "For it came to pass when I came here,
that I saw also profanities without number,
and my being saw many evil-doers during
these thirty years,[a] so that my heart failed
me. 30 For I have seen how You allow them
to sin, and have spared the wicked ones,
and have destroyed Your people, and have
preserved Your enemies; and You have not
made known 31 to any how Your way may
be understood. Are the deeds of Bavel
better than those of Tsion? 32 Or is there
any other nation that knows You besides
Yisra'el? Or what tribes have so believed
Your covenants as these tribes of Ya'aqov?

33 "And yet their reward does not appear,
and their labor has no fruit. For I have gone
here and there through the nations, and I
see that they abound in wealth, and do not
consider Your commands. 34 Therefore,
weigh our iniquities now in the balance,
and theirs also that dwell in the world; and
so shall it be found which way the scale
inclines. 35 Or when was it that they who
dwell upon the earth have not sinned in
Your sight? Or what nation has so kept
Your commands? 36 You shall find that
men who may be reckoned by name have
guarded Your statutes, but you shall not
find nations *who have done so*.[b]

4 1 And the messenger that was sent to me,
whose name was Uri'el, answered 2 and
said to me, "Your heart has utterly failed
you in regarding this world, and do you
think you comprehend the way of Elyon?"

3 Then I said, "Yes my master." And he
answered me, and said, "I am sent to show
you three ways, and to set forth three
parables before you. 4 If you can declare
one to me, I also will show you the way
that you desire to see, and I will teach you
why the heart is wicked."

5 And I said, "Say on, my master." Then
said he to me, "Go weigh a weight of fire,
or measure a measure of wind, or recall
again a day that is past."

6 Then I answered and said, "Who of the
sons of men is able to do this, that you
should ask me of such things?"

7 And he said to me, "If I had asked you,
saying, 'How many dwellings are there in
the heart of the sea?' or 'How many springs
are there at the fountain head of the deep?'
or 'How many ways are above the expanse
of the heavens?' or 'Where are the openings
of Sheol?' or 'Where are the paths of
paradise?' 8 perhaps you would say to me, 'I
never went down into the deep, nor yet into
Sheol, neither have I ever climbed up into
the heavens.' 9 Nevertheless now have I
asked you but only of the fire and wind,
and of the day, things which you have
passed through, and without which you

[a] 3:29 So the Ethiopic, Armenian, and Arabic[1] texts. Latin and Syriac read, "this thirtieth year."

[b] 3:36 That is, some individuals have guarded the Torah, but not whole nations.

cannot be, and yet have you given me no
answer of them."

10 He said moreover to me, "Your own
things, that are grown up with you, you do
not know; 11 how then can your vessel
comprehend the way of Elyon? [For the
way of Elyon has been formed without
measure.][a] How then can he that is already
worn out with the corrupted world
understand the way of the incorruptible?"

12 When I heard these things I fell upon my
face, and said to him, "It would be better
for us to not be here at all, than that we
should come here and live in the midst of
wickedness, and suffer, and not know
why."

13 He answered me, and said, "The woods
of the trees of the field went forth, and took
counsel together, 14 and said, 'Come! Let us
go and make war against the sea, that it
may depart away before us, and that we
may make us more woods.' 15 The waves of
the sea also in like manner took counsel
together, and said, 'Come! Let us go up and
subdue the wood of the forest, that there
also we may make us another country.'
16 The counsel of the wood was in vain, for
the fire came and consumed it. 17 Likewise
also the counsel of the waves of the sea, for
the sand stood up and stopped them. 18 If
you were judge now between these two,
whom would you declare right, and whom
would you condemn?"

19 I answered and said, "It is a foolish
counsel that they both have taken, for the
ground is given to the wood, and the place
of the sea is given to bear his waves."

20 Then he answered me, and said, "You
have given a right judgment; why not judge
in your own case? 21 For as the ground is
given to the wood, and the sea to his waves,
even so those who dwell upon the earth
may understand nothing but that which is
upon the earth. Only He that dwells above
the heavens may understand the things that
are above the height of the heavens."

22 Then I answered and said, "I ask you, O
master, why is the power of understanding
given to me? 23 For it was not in my mind
to be curious of the ways above, but of the
things that happen to us daily. Because
Yisra'el is given up as a reproach to the
heathen, and the people whom you have
loved is given over to wicked nations, and
the Torah of our forefathers is made of
none effect, and the written covenants are
nowhere regarded, 24 and we pass away out
of the world as grasshoppers, and our life is
as a vapor[b]; we are not worthy to obtain
kindness. 25 What then will He do for His
[set-apart][c] Name by which we are called?
These are the things about which I have
asked.

26 Then he answered me, and said, "If you
be alive you shall see, and if you live long,
you shall marvel; for the world hurries to
its end. 27 For it is not able to bear the
things that are promised to the righteous in
the times to come: for this world is full of
sadness and weakness. 28 For the evil about
which you asked me is sown, but the

---

[a] 4:11 Bracketed section indicates reading from Ethiopic, Armenian, and Arabic texts. Greek and Latin omit.

[b] 4:24 So the Syriac, Ethiopic, and Arabic texts. Latin text reads, "trembling."

[c] 4:25 Bracketed section indicates reading present in Ethiopic text, but absent from Latin, Syriac, Armenian, and Arabic texts.

gathering has not yet come. 29 If, therefore,
that which is sown is not reaped, and if the
place where the evil is sown does not end,
then the field where the good is sown
cannot come. 30 For a grain of evil seed
was sown in the heart of Adam from the
beginning, and how much wickedness has
it brought forth to this time. And how much
shall it yet bring forth until the time of
threshing come. 31 Consider now by
yourself, how great fruit of wickedness a
grain of evil seed has brought forth.
32 When the ears which are without number
shall be sown, how great a floor shall they
fill!"

33 Then I answered and said, "How long?
And when shall these things come to be?
Why are our years few and evil?"

34 And he answered me, and said, "Your
haste will not exceed that of Elyon: for
your haste is for your own self, but He that
is above hastens on behalf of many. 35 Did
the beings of the righteous not ask
questions of these things in their chambers,
saying, 'How long are we here? When will
the fruit of the threshing time of our reward
come?'

36 "And Yiremi'el the ruling messenger
answered them, and said, 'Even when the
number is fulfilled of those who are like
you. For He has weighed the world in the
balance; 37 and by measure He has
measured the times, and by number He has
counted the seasons; and He shall not move
nor stir them, until the measure be
fulfilled.'"

38 Then I answered and said, "O Adonai
יהוה, yet even we all are full of disrespect:
39 and perhaps it is because of us that the
threshing time of the righteous is kept back,
because of the sins of those who dwell
upon the earth."

40 So he answered me, and said, "Go your
way to a woman with child, and ask of her
when she has fulfilled her nine months, if
her womb may keep the birth any longer
within her."

41 Then I said, "No, master, it cannot." And
he said to me, "In Sheol the chambers of
beings are like the womb: 42 for like as a
woman that travails makes haste to escape
the anguish of the travail, so do these
places make haste to deliver those things
that are committed to them from the
beginning. 43 Then it shall be shown to you
concerning those things which you desire
to see."

44 Then I answered and said, "If I have
found favor in your sight, and if it be
possible, and if I am acceptable, 45 show
me this also, whether there be more to
come than is past, or whether the greater
part has already passed. 46 For what is gone
I know, but what is to come I do not
know."

47 And he said to me, "Stand up upon the
right side, and I shall explain the parable to
you."

48 So I stood, and saw, and, behold, a hot
burning oven passed by before me: and it
happened, that when the flame was gone by
I looked, and, behold, the smoke remained
still. 49 After this, a watery cloud passed
before me, and sent down much rain with a
storm; and when the stormy rain was past,
the drops remained in it still.

50 Then said he to me, "Consider this: as
the rain is more than the drops, and the fire
is greater than the smoke, so the quantity

which is past is greater; but the drops and
the smoke remained still."

51 Then I prayed, and said, "Do you know
if I will live until that time? Or who shall
be in those days?"

52 He answered me, and said, "As for the
tokens of which you asked me, I may tell
you of them in part: but as touching your
life, I am not sent to show you; for I do not
know it."

5 1 "Nevertheless, concerning the tokens,
behold, the days shall come, that they
which dwell upon earth shall be taken with
great amazement, and the way of truth shall
be hidden, and the land shall be void of
faith. 2 But iniquity shall be increased
above that which you see now, or that you
have heard of long ago. 3 And the land, that
you see now to have rule, shall be waste
and untrodden, and men shall see it
desolate. 4 But if Elyon grants it to you to
live, you shall see it thrown into confusion
[after the third *period*][a]; and the sun shall
suddenly shine forth in the night, and the
moon in the day: 5 and blood shall drop
from wood, and the stone shall give its
voice, and the peoples shall be troubled;
and the stars shall fall.[b]

6 "And he shall rule, whom those who
dwell upon the earth look not for, and the
birds shall take their flight away together;
7 and the Sea of Sedom shall cast out fish,
and make a noise in the night, which many
have not known, though all shall hear its
voice. 8 There shall be chaos also in many
places, and the fire shall be often sent out,
and the wild beasts shall change their
places, and women shall bring forth
monsters; 9 and salt waters shall be found
in the sweet, and all friends shall destroy
one another; then understanding will hide
itself, and knowledge withdraw itself into
its chamber; 10 and it shall be sought by
many, and shall not be found. And
unrighteousness and evil shall be multiplied
upon earth.

11 "One land also shall ask another, and
say, 'Has righteousness, or a man that does
righteousness, gone through you?' And it
shall reply, 'No.' 12 And it shall come to be
at that time, that men shall hope, but shall
not obtain; they shall labor, but their ways
shall not prosper. 13 I have permission to
show you such tokens; and if you will pray
again, and weep as *you have* now, and fast
seven days, you shall hear yet greater
things than these."

14 Then I awaked, and an extreme
trembling went through my body, and my
mind was troubled, so that it fainted. 15 So
the messenger that came to talk with me
held me, comforted me, and set me up upon
my feet.

16 And in the second night it came to pass,
that Palti'el the captain of the people came
to me, saying, "Where have you been? And
why is your countenance sad? 17 Or do you
not know that Yisra'el is committed to you
in the land of their captivity? 18 Rise up
then, and eat some bread, and do not
forsake us, as the shepherd that leaves in
the hands of cruel wolves."

---

[a] 5:4 So the Syriac and Latin texts. Ethiopic text reads, "after three months." Armenian text reads, "after the third vision."

[b] 5:5 So the Syriac, Ethiopic, and Arabic texts. Meaning of Latin text is uncertain.

19 Then said I to him, "Go your ways from
me, and do not come near me for seven
days, and then shall you come to me." And
he heard what I said, and went from me.

20 And so I fasted seven days, mourning
and weeping, as Uri'el the messenger
commanded me. 21 And after seven days,
so it was, that the thoughts of my heart
were very grievous to me again, 22 and my
being recovered the spirit of understanding,
and I began to speak words before Elyon
again.

23 And I said, "O Adonai יהוה, of all the
woods of the earth, and of all the trees, You
have chosen one vine. 24 And of all the
lands of the world, You have chosen one
country. And of all the flowers of the
world, You have chosen one lily. 25 And of
all the depths of the sea, You have filled
one river. And of all built cities, You have
set Tsion apart to yourself. 26 And of all the
birds that are created, You have named one
dove. And of all the livestock that are
made, You have provided one lamb. 27 And
among all the multitudes of peoples, You
have gotten one people. And to this people,
whom You loved, You gave *the* Torah that
is approved by all. 28 And now, O יהוה,
why have You given this one people over
to many, and have dishonored the one root
above others, and have scattered Your only
one among many? 29 And those that
opposed Your promises have trodden down
those that believed Your covenants. 30 If
You despise Your people so much, they
should be punished with Your own hands."

31 Now when I had spoken these words, the
messenger that came to me the night before
was sent to me, 32 and said to me, "Hear
me, and I will instruct you; listen to me,
and I shall tell you more."

33 And I said, "Speak on, my master." Then
said he to me, "You are greatly troubled in
mind for Yisra'el's sake: do you *think you*
love that people more than He that made
them?"

34 And I said, "No, master. But I have
spoken from grief: for my kidneys torment
me every hour, while I labor to comprehend
the way of Elyon, and to seek out part of
His judgment."

35 And he said to me, "You cannot." And I
said, "Why, master? Why was I born? Or
why was my mother's womb not my grave,
that I might not have seen the travail of
Ya'aqov, and the wearisome toil of the
stock of Yisra'el?"

36 And he said to me, "*Tell me the* number
of those who are not yet born; gather
together the drops that are scattered abroad;
make the flowers green again that are
withered; 37 open the chambers that are
closed, and bring forth the winds that in
them are shut up, or show me the image of
a voice: and then I will declare to you the
travail that you asked to see."

38 And I said, "O Adonai יהוה, who may
know these things, but He that does not
dwell with men? 39 As for me, I am
unwise: how may I then speak of these
things of which you asked me?"

40 Then He said to me, "Just as you can do
none of these things of which I have
spoken, even so you cannot find out My
judgment, or the end of the love that I have
promised to My people."

41 And I said, "But, behold, O יהוה: You
have made the promise to those who be in
the end; and what shall they do that have

been before us, or we that are now, or those
who shall come after us?"

42 And He said to me, "I will liken my
judgment to a ring: as there is no
negligence of those who are last, even so
there is no swiftness of those who be first."

43 So I answered and said, "Could You not
make them all to be at once? *Those* that
have been made, and *those* that are now,
and *those* that are to come, so that You
might show Your judgment the sooner?"

44 Then He answered me, and said, "The
creature may not haste above the creator;
and the world cannot hold all those that
shall be created, all at once."

45 And I said, "How have You said to Your
servant, that You will surely make alive, *all*
at once, the creation that You have created?
If they shall *all* be alive at once, and the
creation shall sustain them: even so it might
now also support them to be present at
once."

46 And He said to me, "Ask the womb of a
woman, and say to her, 'If you bring forth
ten children, why do you repeat several
times?' Ask her therefore to bring forth ten
children at once."

47 And I said, "She cannot. But *she* must do
it over time."

48 Then He said to me, "Even so have I
given the womb of the earth to those that be
sown in it in their various times. 49 For as a
young child may not yet bring forth, neither
she that has grown old bring forth any
more, even so have I disposed the world
which I created."

50 And I asked, and said, "Seeing You have
now shown me the way, I will speak before
You. Is our mother, of whom You have
told me, still young? Or does she now draw
near to *old* age?"

51 He answered me, and said, "Ask a
woman that bears children, and she shall
tell you. 52 Say to her, 'Why are those
whom you have now brought forth not like
those that were before, but smaller of
stature?' 53 And she also shall answer you,
'They that are born in the strength of youth
are of one fashion, and those who are born
in the time of age, when the womb fails, are
another.' 54 Consider also, how you are
smaller of stature than those that were
before you. 55 And so are those who come
after you smaller than you, as born of the
creature which now begins to be old, and is
past the strength of youth."

56 Then I said, "יהוה, I beg You, if I have
found favor in Your sight, show Your
servant by whom You visit Your creation."

6 1 And He said to me, "In the beginning,
when the earth was made, before the
outgoings of the world were fixed, or the
gatherings of the winds ever blew; 2 before
the voices of the thunder sounded, and
before the flashes of the lightning shone, or
the foundations of paradise were ever laid;
3 before the fair flowers were seen, or the
powers of the earthquake were ever
established; before the innumerable army
of messengers were gathered together, 4 or
the heights of the air were ever lifted up;
before the measures of the expanse were
named, or the footstool of Tsion was ever
established; 5 and before the present years
were sought out, or the imaginations of
those who now sin were ever estranged;
before those that have gathered faith for a
treasure were sealed: 6 then I considered

these things, and they all were made by Me alone, and by none other. And they shall be ended by Me, and by none other."

7 Then I answered and said, "What will the end of times be like? And when shall the end of the first, and the beginning of it that follows, come?"

8 And He said to me, "From Avraham to Avraham, inasmuch as Ya'aqov and Esaw were born of him, for Ya'aqov's hand held
the heel of Esaw from the beginning. 9 For
Esaw is the end of this world, and Ya'aqov
is the beginning of it that follows. 10 The
beginning of a man is his hand, and the end of a man is his heel; between the heel and the hand seek you nothing else, Ezra."

11 I answered then and said, "O Adonai
יהוה, if I have found favor in Your sight,
12 please, show Your servant the end of Your tokens, of which You showed me part last night."

13 So He answered and said to me, "Stand on your feet, and you shall hear a mighty
sounding voice; 14 and if the place you
stand on is greatly moved, 15 then do not be afraid when it speaks; for the word is of the end, and the foundations of the earth shall
understand, 16 that the speech is from them: they shall tremble and be moved, for they know that their end must be changed."

17 And it happened, and when I heard it I stood up on my feet, and listened, and, behold, there was a voice that spoke, and the sound of it was like the sound of mighty
waters. 18 And it said, "Behold, the days come, and it shall be that when I draw near to visit those who dwell upon the earth,
19 and when I will investigate those who have done injustice with their unrighteousness, and when the affliction of
Tsion is fulfilled, 20 and when the seal shall be set upon the world that is to pass away, then I will show these tokens: the books shall be opened before the expanse, and all shall see My judgment[a] together.

21 "And the one-year-old children shall speak with their voices, the pregnant women shall bring forth children prematurely, at three or four months, and
they shall live, and dance. 22 And suddenly
the sown places shall appear unsown, the full storehouses shall suddenly be found
empty, 23 and the trumpet shall give a
sound, which when every man hears, they
shall be suddenly afraid. 24 At that time
friends will make war against one another like enemies, and the earth shall stand in fear with those that dwell in it. The springs of water shall stand still, so that for three hours they shall not run.

25 "And it shall be, that whoever remains after all these things which I have told you, he shall be saved, and shall see My
salvation, and the end of My world. 26 And
they shall see the men that have been taken up, who have not tasted death from their birth; and the heart of the inhabitants shall be changed, and turned into a different
inclination. 27 For evil shall be erased, and
deceit shall be quenched. 28 Faith shall
flourish, and corruption shall be overcome, and the truth – which has been without fruit for so long – shall be declared."

---

[a] 6:20 So the Syriac text. Latin text omits "My judgment."

29 And when He talked with me, behold,
little by little the place on which I stood
rocked back and forth.

30 And he said to me, "I came to show you
these things tonight. **31** If, therefore, you
pray yet again, and fast seven more days, I
will tell you greater things than these.
32 For your voice has surely been heard
before Elyon: for He has seen your
righteous works; He has also seen your
innocence, which you have had from your
youth. **33** And therefore He has sent me to
show you all these things, and to say to
you, 'Be of good comfort, and do not fear.
34 And do not be hasty in regard to the
former times, to think worthless thoughts;
that you may not hasten in the latter
times.'"

35 And it came to be after this, that I wept
again, and fasted seven days in the same
way, that I might fulfil the three weeks
which he told me. **36** And in the eighth
night was my heart was vexed within me
again, and I began to speak before Elyon.
37 For my spirit was greatly set on fire, and
my being was in distress.

38 And I said, "O יהוה, truly You spoke at
the beginning of creation, on the first day,
and said, 'Let the heavens and earth be
made;' and Your word perfected the work.
39 And then the spirit was fluttering, and
darkness and silence were on every side;
the sound of man's voice was not yet *heard*.
40 Then You commanded a ray of light to
be brought forth from Your treasures, that
Your works might be seen.

41 "On the second day You made the spirit
of the expanse and commanded it to split
apart, and to divide between the waters,
that the one part might go up, and the other
remain beneath.

42 "On the third day You commanded that
the waters should be gathered together in
the seventh part of the earth. You dried up
six parts, and kept them, so that some of
these may be both planted and tilled, and
might serve before You. **43** For as soon as
your word went forth the work was done.
44 And immediately there came forth great
and innumerable fruit, and many pleasures
for the taste, and flowers of incomparable
color, and odors of most exquisite smell:
and this was done the third day.

45 "On the fourth day You commanded that
the sun should shine, and the moon give her
light, and the stars should be in their order;
46 and gave them a charge to do service to
man, who was yet to be made.

47 "On the fifth day You said to the seventh
part, where the water was gathered
together, that it should bring forth living
creatures: birds and fish – and so it came to
be, **48** that the silent water, which was
without life, brought forth living things as
it was commanded, that the people might
therefore praise Your wondrous works.
49 Then You preserved two living
creatures, the one You called Behemoth[a],
and the other You called Livyathan. **50** And
You separated the one from the other: for
the seventh part, namely, where the water
was gathered together, would not hold them
both. **51** To Behemoth You gave one part,
which was dried up on the third day, that he

---

[a] 6:49 Here and in v. 51, some Latin texts read, "Ḥanokh" instead of "Behemoth." This is most likely due to a copyist confusing the story of Behemoth from 1 Enoch 60, with the name of Enoch himself.

should dwell in it, where there are a
thousand hills; 52 but to Livyathan You
gave the seventh part, namely, the wet *part*;
and You have kept them to be devoured of
whom You desire, and when *You desire*.[a]

53 "But on the sixth day You commanded
the earth, that it should bring forth before
You cattle, beasts, and creeping things.
54 And You ordain Adam as master over all
the works that You made; and we all come
from him, the people whom You have
chosen. 55 All this have I spoken before
You, O יהוה, because You have said that
for us You made this world.

56 "As for the other nations, which also
come from Adam, You have said that they
are nothing, and are like spittle: and You
have likened their abundance to a drop that
falls from a vessel. 57 And now, O יהוה,
behold: these nations which are presumed
as nothing, are masters over us, and devour
us. 58 But we Your people, whom You
have called Your firstborn, Your only-
begotten, and Your fervent lover, are given
into their hands. 59 If the world is now
made for our sakes, why do we not possess
our land for an inheritance? How long shall
this endure?

7 1 And when I finished speaking these
words, the messenger which had been sent
to me the nights before was sent again.

2 And he said to me, "Get up, Ezra, and
hear the words that I have come to tell
you." 3 And I said, "Speak, my master."
Then he said to me, "There is a sea set in a
wide place, that it might be broad and vast.
4 But its entrance shall be set in a narrow
place so as to be like a river. 5 So whoever
then desires to go into the sea to look upon
it, or to rule it, if he did not go through the
narrow, how could he come into the broad?
6 Another thing also: there is a city built
and set in a plain country, and full of all
good things. 7 But its entrance is narrow,
and is set in a dangerous place to fall,
having a fire on the right hand, and a deep
water on the left; 8 and there is one only
path between them both, even between the
fire and the water, so small that there could
but one man go there at once. 9 If this city
is given to a man for an inheritance, and if
the heir does not pass through the danger
before him, how shall he receive his
inheritance?"

10 And I said, "How so, master?" Then said
he to me, "Even so also is Yisra'el's portion.
11 I made the world for their sake, and
when Adam transgressed My statutes, it
was decreed that the *time* now is done.
12 Then the entrances of this world were
made narrow, and sorrowful and toilsome;
they are but few and evil, full of perils, and
charged with great toils. 13 For the
entrances of the greater world are wide and
sure, and bring forth fruit of immortality.

14 "If, then, those who live do not enter
these difficult and worthless things, they
can never receive those that are laid up for
them. 15 Now therefore, why do you
trouble yourself, seeing you are but a
corruptible man? And why are you moved,
since you are only mortal? 16 And why
have you not considered in your mind that
which is to come, rather than that which is
present?"

---

[a] 6:49-52 See also Ḥanokh א [1 Enoch] 60:7-9.

17 Then I answered and said, "O Adonai
יהוה, behold, You have ordained in Your
Torah, that the righteous should inherit
these things, but that the wicked should
perish. 18 The righteous therefore shall
suffer difficult things, and hope for wide;
but those who have done wickedly have
suffered the difficult things, and yet shall
not see the wide."

19 And he said to me, "You are not a judge
above Elohim, nor do you have
understanding above Elyon. 20 Yes, rather
let many that now exist perish, than that the
Torah of Elohim – which is set before them
– be despised. 21 For Elohim commanded
such as came, even as they came, what they
should do to live, and what they should
observe to avoid punishment.
22 Nevertheless they were not obedient to
Him, but spoke against Him, and imagined
for themselves meaningless things.

23 "They framed cunning plans of
wickedness, and said of Elyon that He is
not, and they did not know His ways.
24 And they despised His Torah, and denied
His covenants; they have not been faithful
to His statutes, and have not performed His
works. 25 Therefore, Ezra, for the empty
are empty things, and for the full are the
full things. 26 For behold, the time shall
come, and it shall be, when these tokens, of
which I told you before, shall come to be,
that the bride shall appear, even the city
coming forth, and she who is now
withdrawn from the earth shall be seen.
27 And whoever is delivered from the
aforementioned evils shall see My
wonders.

28 For [My Son the Messiah][a] shall be
revealed with those that are with Him, and
the survivors shall rejoice four-hundred[b]
years. 29 After these years My Son the
Messiah will die, and all that have the
breath of life. 30 And the world shall be
turned into the old silence seven days, like
as in the beginning, so that no man shall
remain.[c] 31 And after seven days the world,
that has not yet arisen, shall be raised up,
and that which is corruptible sha die.
32 And the earth shall restore those that are
asleep in her, and so shall the dust those
that dwell in it in silence, and the secret
places shall deliver those beings that were
committed to them.

33 "And Elyon shall be revealed upon the
seat of judgment, and compassion shall
pass away, and patience shall be
withdrawn, 34 and only judgment shall
remain. Truth shall stand, and faith shall
grow strong, 35 and the work shall follow,
and the reward shall be shown, and good
deeds shall awake, and wicked deeds shall
not rest.[d] 36 And the pit of torment shall

---

[a] 7:28 So the Syriac and Arabic[1] texts. Ethiopic text reads, "My Messiah;" Armenian text reads, "the Messiah of Elohim;" Latin text reads, "My Son Yeshua."

[b] 7:28 So the Latin and Arabic[1] texts. Arabic[2] reads "one-thousand;" Syriac text reads "thirty."

[c] 7:28-30 Charles notes that these verses refer to a temporary Messianic era, in which the Messiah reigns for a length of time along with those in the Messianic Kingdom. After this period they all die, followed by seven days of a lifeless earth.

[d] 7:35 At this point, most Latin manuscripts omit vss. 36 – 105. However, it was noted in the late 19th Century that most of them were all copied from one source text, known as *Codex Sangermanensis*. This manuscript is missing an entire page where these verses should be located, and as such early translations (and copies) were deficient, including the 1611 King James Version. Later, with the examination of

appear, and near it shall be the place of rest: and the furnace of Gehenna shall be shown, and near it the Paradise of delight. 37 And then Elyon shall say to the nations that are raised from the dead, 'See, and understand whom you have denied, or whom you have not served, or whose commands you have despised. 38 Look on this side and on that: here is delight and rest, and there fire and torments.' Thus shall He speak to them in the Day of Judgment.

39 "This is a day that has neither sun, nor moon, nor stars, 40 nor cloud, nor thunder, nor lightning, nor wind, nor water, nor air, nor darkness, nor evening, nor morning, 41 nor summer, nor spring, nor heat, nor winter, nor frost, nor cold, nor hail, nor rain, nor dew, 42 nor noon, nor night, nor dawn, nor shining, nor brightness, nor light, but only the splendor of the glory of Elyon, by which all shall see the things that are set before them. 43 For it shall endure as it were a week of years. 44 This is My judgment and its statute; but I showed these things only to you."

45 And I answered and said "Even then, O יהוה, and I say now: blessed are those who are now alive and keep the statutes which You ordained. 46 But concerning them for whom my prayer was made, what shall I say? For who is there of those who are alive that has not sinned, and who of the sons of men that has not transgressed Your covenant? 47 And now I see, that the world to come shall bring delight to few, but torments to many. 48 For an evil heart has grown up in us, which has led us astray from these statutes, and has brought us into corruption and into the ways of death, and has shown us the paths of punishment, and removed us far from life; and that, not a few only, but well near all that have been created."

49 And He answered me, and said, "Listen to me, and I will instruct you, and I will admonish you yet again. 50 For this reason Elyon has not made one world, but two. 51 For while you have said that the just are not many, but few, and the wicked abound, hear the answer. 52 If you have exceedingly few choice stones, will you place them near lead and clay?"

53 And I said, "יהוה, how shall this be?"

54 And He said to me, "Not only this, but ask the earth, and she shall tell you; beg her, and she shall declare to you. 55 For you shall say to her, 'You bring forth gold and silver and copper, and iron also, and lead and clay: 56 but silver is more abundant than gold, and copper than silver, and iron than copper, lead than iron, and clay than lead.' 57 Judge, therefore, which things are precious and to be desired, that which is abundant or that what is rare."

58 And I said, "O Adonai יהוה, that which is plentiful is of less worth, for that which is rarer is more precious."

59 And He answered me, and said, "Weigh within yourself the things that you have thought, for he that has what is rare rejoices over him that has what is plentiful. 60 So also is the judgment which I have promised: for I will rejoice over the few that shall be saved, inasmuch as these are

---

Codex Colbertinus, the missing verses were added back in. Most Eastern versions do not lack this text.

they who have caused My glory to now
prevail, and of whom My Name is now
Named. 61 And I will not grieve over the
multitude of those who perish, for these are
those who are now like vapor, and have
become as flame and smoke; they are set on
fire and burn hotly, and are extinguished."

62 And I answered and said, "O earth, why
have you brought forth, if the mind is made
out of dust, like all other created things?
63 For it would be better if the dust itself
had not been brought forth, so that the mind
would not have been made from it. 64 But
now the mind grows with us, and because
of this we are tormented, because we perish
and *we* know it.

65 "Let the race of men lament and the
beasts of the field be glad; let all that are
born lament, but let the four-footed beasts
and the cattle rejoice. 66 For it is far better
with them than with us. For they do not
look for judgment, neither do they know of
torments or of any salvation promised to
them after death. 67 For what does it profit
us, that we shall be preserved alive, yet
suffer great torment? 68 For all that are
born are defiled with iniquities, and are full
of sins and laden with offenses. 69 If, after
death, we were not to come into judgment,
perhaps it would have been better for us."

70 And he answered me, and said, "When
Elyon made the world, and Adam and all
those who came from him, He first
prepared the Judgment and the things that
pertain to the judgment. 71 And now
understand from your own words, for you
have said that the mind grows with us.
72 Therefore, those that dwell upon the
earth shall be tormented for this reason,
that having understanding they have
worked iniquity, and receiving commands
have not guarded them, and having
obtained Torah they dealt unfaithfully with
that which they received. 73 What then will
they have to say in the judgment, or how
will they answer in the latter days? 74 For
how great a time has Elyon been patient
with those who inhabit the world, and not
for their sakes, but because of the times
which He has ordained!"

75 And I answered and said, "If I have
found favor in Your sight, O יהוה, show
this also to Your servant: whether after
death, even now when every one of us
gives up his being, we shall be kept in rest
until those times come, in which You shall
renew the creation, or whether we shall be
tormented immediately."

76 And He answered me, and said, "I will
show you this also; but do not join yourself
with those who scorn, nor count yourself
with those who are tormented. 77 For you
have a treasure of good works laid up with
Elyon, but it shall not be shown to you until
the latter days.

78 "For concerning death the teaching is
thus: when the decisive decree has gone
forth from Elyon that a man should die, as
the spirit leaves the body to **return again
to Him who gave it**[a], it adores the glory of
Elyon first of all. 79 And if it be one of
those that have been scorners and have not
kept the way of Elyon, and have despised
His Torah, and that hate those who fear
Elohim, 80 these spirits shall not enter into
habitations, but shall wander and be in
tormented immediately, ever grieving and
sad, in seven ways. 81 The first way,

[a] 7:78 See Qoheleth [Ecclesiastes] 12:7.

because they have despised the Torah of
Elyon. 82 The second way, because they
cannot now make a good returning that
they may live. 83 The third way, they shall
see the reward laid up for those who have
believed the covenants of Elyon. 84 The
fourth way, they shall consider the torment
laid up for themselves in the latter days.
85 The fifth way, they shall see the dwelling
places of the others guarded by messengers,
with great peace. 86 The sixth way, they
shall see how immediately some of them
shall pass into torment. 87 The seventh way,
which is more grievous than all the
aforementioned ways, because they shall
pine away in confusion and be consumed
with shame, and shall be withered up by
fears, seeing the glory of Elyon before
whom they have sinned while living, and
before whom they shall be judged in the
latter days.

88 "Now this is the order of those who have
kept the ways of Elyon, when they shall be
separated from the corruptible vessel. 89 In
the time that they lived in it they painfully
served Elyon, and were in jeopardy every
hour, that they might guard the Torah of the
lawgiver perfectly. 90 So this is the
teaching concerning them.

91 "First of all they shall see with great joy
the glory of Him who takes them up, for
they shall have rest in seven orders. 92 The
first order, because they have labored with
great toil to overcome the evil inclination
which was fashioned together with them,
that it might not lead them astray from life
into death. 93 The second order, because
they see the perplexity in which the beings
of the wicked wander, and the punishment
that awaits them. 94 The third order, they
see the witness which He that fashioned
them bears concerning them, that while
they lived they guarded the Torah which
was entrusted to them. 95 The fourth order,
they understand the rest which, being
gathered in their chambers, they now enjoy
with great peace, guarded by messengers,
and the glory that awaits them in the latter
days. 96 The fifth order, they rejoice, seeing
how they have now escaped from that
which is corruptible, and how they shall
inherit that which is to come, while they
see moreover the difficulty and the pain
from which they have been delivered, and
the large room which they shall receive
with joy and immortality. 97 The sixth
order, when it is shown to them how their
face shall shine as the sun, and how they
shall be made like the light of the stars,
being from then on incorruptible. 98 The
seventh order, which is greater than all the
aforementioned orders, because they shall
rejoice with confidence, and because they
shall be bold without confusion, and shall
be glad without fear, for they hasten to
behold the face of Him whom in their
lifetime they served, and from whom they
shall receive their reward in glory.

99 "This is the order of the beings of the
just, as from then on is announcer to them,
and aforementioned are the ways of
torment which those who would not give
heed shall suffer from then on."

100 And I answered and said, "Shall time
therefore be given to the beings after they
are separated from their bodies, that they
may see that of which You have spoken to
me?"

101 And He said, "Their freedom shall be
for seven days, that for seven days they
may see the things of which you have been
told, and afterwards they shall be gathered
together in their habitations." 102 And I

answered and said, "If I have found favor in
Your sight, show me further Your just
servant, who will, in the day of judgment,
be able to intercede for the wicked or to
entreat Elyon for them, 103 whether fathers
for children, or children for parents, or
brothers for brothers, or family members
for their next of kin, or friends for those
who are most dear."

104 And He answered me, and said, "Since
you have found favor in My sight, I will
show you this also. The day of judgment is
a day of decision, and displays to all the
seal of truth; even as now a father does not
send his son, or a son his father, or a master
his slave, or a friend him that is most dear,
that in his stead he may be sick, or sleep, or
eat, or be healed, 105 so shall anyone never
pray for another in that day, nor shall one
lay a burden on another, for then shall
everyone bear his own righteousness or
unrighteousness."

106 And I answered and said, "How do we
now find that first Avraham prayed for the
people of Sedom, and Mosheh for the
fathers that sinned in the wilderness:
107 and Yehoshua after him for Yisra'el in
the days of Akhan. 108 And Shemu'el in the
days of Sha'ul; and David for the plague;
and Shelomoh for those who should
worship in the dwelling-place; 109 and
Eliyahu for those that received rain, and for
the dead, that he might live; 110 and
Ḥizqiyahu for the people in the days of
Sanḥeriv: and many for many? 111 If
therefore now, when corruption is grown
up, and unrighteousness increased, the
righteous have prayed for the wicked, why
shall it not be so then also?"

112 He answered me, and said, "This
present world is not the end; the full glory
does not remain in it. Therefore have they
who were able prayed for the weak. 113 But
the Day of Judgment shall be the end of
this time, and the beginning of the
immortality to come, in which corruption
has passed away, 114 excess is at an end,
infidelity is cut off; but righteousness has
grown, and truth has sprung up. 115 Then
shall no man be able to have compassion
on him that is cast in judgment, nor to
thrust down him that has gotten the
victory."

116 I answered then and said, "This is my
first and last question: would it have been
better if the earth had not given You Adam,
or else, when it had given him, to have
restrained him from sinning? 117 For what
profit is it for all that are in this present
time to live in heaviness, and after death to
look for punishment? 118 O you Adam,
what have you done? For though it was you
that sinned, the evil is not fallen on you
alone, but upon all of us that come of you.
119 For what profit is it to us, an immortal
time is promised to us, while we have done
the works that bring death? 120 And that
there is promised us an everlasting hope,
while ourselves most miserably become
meaningless? 121 And that there are
reserved habitations of health and safety,
while we have lived wickedly? 122 And that
the glory of Elyon defends them which
have led a pure life, while we have walked
in the most wicked ways of all? 123 And
that there shall be shown a paradise, whose
fruit endures without decay, in which is
abundance and healing, but we shall not
enter into it, 124 for we have walked in
unpleasant places? 125 And that the faces of
those who have been abstinent shall shine
above the stars, while our faces shall be
blacker than darkness? 126 For while we

lived and committed iniquity, we did not
consider what we should have to suffer
after death."

127 Then He answered and said, "This is the
condition of the battle, which man that is
born upon the earth shall fight. 128 If he is
overcome, he shall suffer as you have said:
but if he gets victory, he shall receive the
thing that I say. 129 For this is the way of
which Mosheh spoke to the people while he
lived, saying, **'Choose life, that you may
live.'**[a] 130 Nevertheless they did not believe
him, nor the prophets after him, no, nor Me
when I have spoken to them; 131 so that
there shall not be such heaviness in their
destruction, as there shall be joy over those
who are persuaded to salvation."

132 I answered then and said, "I know,
master, that Elyon is now called kind, in
that He is kind to them which have not yet
come into the world; 133 and
compassionate, in that He has compassion
upon those that turn to His Torah; 134 and
patient, for He patiently endures those that
have sinned, as His creations; 135 and
bountiful, for He is ready to give rather
than to exact; 136 and of great mercy, for
He multiplies more and more mercies to
those who are present, and that are past,
and also to them which are to come;
137 (for if He did not multiply His mercies,
the world would not continue with those
who dwell in it;) 138 and one that forgives,
for if He did not forgive of His goodness,
that they which have committed iniquities
might be eased of them, the ten thousandth
part of men would not remain living;
139 and a judge, for if He did not pardon
those who were created by His word, and
erase the multitude of offenses, 140 there
would perhaps be very few left in an
innumerable multitude."

8 1 He answered me and said, "Elyon made
this world for the sake of many, but the
world to come for the sake of only a few.
2 But I tell you a parable, Ezra. Just as
when you ask the earth, it will tell you that
it provides a large amount of clay from
which earthenware is made, but only a little
dust from which gold comes, so is the
course of the present world. 3 Many have
been created, but only a few shall be
saved."

4 I answered and said, "Then drink your fill
of understanding,[b] O my being, and drink
wisdom, O my heart. 5 For you came into
the world not of your own will, and against
your will you depart, for you have been
given only a short time to live. 6 O Adonai
יהוה, grant to Your servant that we may
pray before You, and give us a seed for our
heart and cultivation of our understanding
so that fruit may be produced, by which
every mortal who bears the likeness[c] of a
human being may be able to live.

7 "For You alone exist, and we are a work
of Your hands, as You have declared.
8 And because You give life to the body
that is now fashioned in the womb, and
furnish it with members, what You have
created is preserved among fire and water,
and for nine months the womb endures
Your creation that has been created in it.
9 But that which keeps and that which is

---

[a] 7:129 See Devarim [Deuteronomy] 30:19.
[b] 8:4 So the Syriac text. Latin text reads, "Then release your understanding."
[c] 8:6 So the Syriac text. Latin reads, "place."

kept shall both be kept by Your keeping.[a]
And when the womb gives up again what
has been created in it, 10 You have
commanded that from the members
themselves (that is, from the breasts) milk,
the fruit of the breasts, should be supplied,
11 so that what has been fashioned may be
nourished for a time; and afterwards You
will still guide it in Your kindness. 12 You
have nurtured it in Your righteousness, and
instructed it in Your Torah, and reproved it
in Your wisdom. 13 You put it to death as
Your creation, and make it live as Your
work.

14 "If, then, You will suddenly and quickly
destroy what was fashioned by Your
command with such great labor, to what
purpose was it made? 15 And now I will
speak out: You are preeminent in
knowledge concerning mankind; but I will
speak about Your people, for whom I am
grieved, 16 and about Your inheritance, for
whom I lament, and about Yisra'el, for
whom I am sad, and about the seed of
Ya'aqov, for whom I am troubled.
17 Therefore I will pray before You for
myself and for them, for I see the failings
of us who inhabit the earth. 18 And now
also I have heard of the swiftness of the
judgement that is to come.

19 "Therefore hear my voice and
understand my words, and I will speak
before You." The beginning of the words of
Ezra's prayer,[b] before he was taken up. He
said: 20 "O Adonai יהוה, whose eyes are
exalted and whose upper chambers are in
the air; 21 whose throne is beyond measure
and whose glory is beyond comprehension,
before whom the hosts of messengers stand
trembling, 22 and at whose command they
are changed to wind and fire; whose word
is sure and whose utterances are certain;
whose command is strong and whose
judgment is terrible; 23 whose look dries up
the depths and whose indignation makes
the mountains melt away, and whose truth
[bears witness][c] forever: 24 hear, O יהוה,
the prayer of Your servant, and give ear to
the petition of Your creation; attend to my
words.

25 "For as long as I live I will speak, and as
long as I have understanding I will answer.
26 Do not look on the sins of Your people,
but on those who serve You in truth. 27 Do
not take note of the endeavors of those who
act wickedly, but of the endeavors of those
who have kept Your covenants amid
afflictions. 28 Do not think of those who
have lived wickedly in Your sight, but
remember those who have willingly
acknowledged that You are to be feared.
29 Do not will the destruction of those who
have the ways of cattle, but regard those
who have gloriously taught Your Torah.
30 Do not be angry with those who are
deemed worse than wild animals, but love
those who have always put their trust in
Your glory.

31 For we and our ancestors have passed
our lives in ways that bring death;[d] but it is
because of us sinners that You are called
kind. 32 For if You have desired to have
pity on us, who have no works of
righteousness, then You will be called kind.

---

[a] 8:9 The Syriac text here preserves a wordplay, while the meaning of the Latin text is uncertain.
[b] 8:19 So the Syriac and Ethiopic texts. Latin text omits "prayer."
[c] 8:23 So the Latin, Syriac, and Ethiopic. Arabic[2] reads "is established."
[d] 8:31 So the Syriac and Ethiopic. Meaning of Latin text is uncertain.

33 For the righteous, who have many works laid up with You, shall receive their reward in payment for their own deeds. 34 But who is man, that You are angry with him? Or what is mankind, that You are so bitter against it? 35 For in truth there is no one among those who have been born who has not acted wickedly; among those who have existed there is no one who has not done wrong. 36 For in this, O יהוה, Your righteousness and goodness will be declared, when You are kind to those who have no store of good works."

37 He answered me and said, "Some things you have spoken rightly, and it will turn out according to your words. 38 For indeed I will not concern Myself about the fashioning of those who have sinned, or about their death, their judgment, or their destruction; 39 but I will rejoice over the creation of the righteous, over their pilgrimage also, and their salvation, and their receiving their reward. 40 As I have spoken, therefore, so it shall be.

41 "For just as the farmer sows many seeds in the ground and plants a multitude of seedlings, and yet not all that have been sown will live[a] in due season, and not all that were planted will take root; so also those who have been sown in the world will not all be saved."

42 I answered and said, "If I have found favor in Your sight, let me speak. 43 If the farmer's seed does not come up, because it has not received Your rain in due season, or if it has been ruined by too much rain, it perishes. 44 But people who have been formed by Your hands and are called in Your own image because they are made like You, and for whose sake You have formed all things—have You also made them like the farmer's seed? 45 Surely not, O יהוה above! But spare Your people and have compassion on Your inheritance, for You have compassion on Your own creation."

46 He answered me and said, "Things that are present are for those who live now, and things that are future are for those who will live hereafter. 47 For you come far short of being able to love My creation more than I love it. But you have often compared yourself to the unrighteous. Do not do so! 48 But even in this way you will be praiseworthy before Elyon, 49 because you have humbled yourself, as is becoming for you, and have not considered yourself to be among the righteous. You will receive the greatest glory, 50 for many miseries will affect those who inhabit the world in the latter days, because they have walked in great pride. 51 But think of your own case, and inquire concerning the glory of those who are like yourself, 52 because it is for you that paradise is opened, the tree of life is planted, the age to come is prepared, abundance is provided, a city is built, rest is appointed, goodness is established, and wisdom perfected beforehand. 53 The root of evil is sealed up from you, illness is banished from you, and death is hidden; Sheol has fled and corruption has been forgotten; 54 sorrows have passed away, and in the end the treasure of immortality is made manifest.

55 "Therefore do not ask any more questions about the great number of those

---

[a] 8:41 So the Syriac and Ethiopic texts. Latin text reads, "be saved."

who perish. 56 For when they had
opportunity to choose, they despised Elyon,
and were contemptuous of His Torah, and
abandoned His ways. 57 Moreover, they
have even trampled on His righteous ones,
58 and said in their hearts that there is no
Elohim, though they knew well that they
must die. 59 For just as the things that I
have predicted await you, so the thirst and
torment that are prepared await them. For
Elyon did not intend that anyone should be
destroyed; 60 but those who were created
have themselves defiled the Name of Him
who made them, and have been ungrateful
to Him who prepared life for them now.
61 Therefore My judgment is now drawing
near; 62 I have not shown this to all men,
but only to you and a few like you."

63 Then I answered and said, "O יהוה, You
have already shown me a great number of
the signs that You will do in the latter days,
but You have not shown me when You will
do them."

9 1 And He answered me, and said,
"Measure diligently within yourself, and
when you see that some of the signs are
past, which have been told to you
beforehand, 2 then you will understand that
it is the very time in which Elyon will visit
the world which was made by Him. 3 And
earthquakes are seen in the world, and
unrest among the people; plans of nations;
wavering of leaders; unrest of princes;
4 then you will understand, that Elyon
spoke of these things from the former days,
from the beginning.

5 "For as all that is made in the world, the
beginning is evident, and the end made
clear; 6 so also are the times of Elyon: the
beginnings are made clear in wonders and
mighty works, and the end in effects and
signs. 7 And everyone that shall be saved,
and shall be able to escape by his works, or
by faith – with which he has believed –
8 shall be preserved from these perils, and
shall see My salvation in My land, and
within My borders, which I have set apart
for Me from the beginning. 9 Then they
shall be amazed, those who have abused
My ways. And those who have cast them
away in spite shall dwell in torments. 10 For
as many as in their life have received
benefits, and yet have not known Me;
11 and as many as have scorned My Torah,
while they still possessed freedom, and,
while the place of repentance was still open
to them, did not understand, but despised it,
12 *these* must know it after death by
torment. 13 And therefore you, *Ezra,* do not
be curious anymore, about how the wicked
shall be punished; but inquire how the
righteous shall be saved, those to whom the
world belongs, and for whom the world
was created."

14 And I answered and said, 15 "I have said
before, and now speak, and will speak it
also afterwards, that there are more of them
which perish, than of them which will be
saved. 16 As a wave is greater than a drop."

17 And He answered me, saying, "Just as
the field is, so also is the seed; and as the
flowers are, so are the colors also; and as
the work is, so also is the judgment of it;
and as is the farmer, so is his threshing
floor also. For there was a time in the
world, 18 even then when I was preparing
for those who now live – before the world
was made for them to dwell in – that no
man spoke against Me, 19 for there were
none. But now those that are created this
world that is prepared, both with a table
that does not fail, and a Torah which is

unsearchable, are corrupted in their ways. **20** So I considered My world, and behold, it was destroyed, and My earth, and behold, it was in peril, because of the plans that had come into it.

21 "And I saw, and spared them, but not greatly; and saved a grape out of a cluster, and a plant out of a great forest. **22** Let the multitude perish then, which was born in vain; and let My grape be saved, and My plant; for I have made them perfect with great labor. **23** Still, if you will cease yet seven days more, (you shall not fast in them, **24** but shall go into a field of herbs, where no house is built, and eat only of the herbs of the field; and you shall taste no flesh, and shall drink no wine, but shall eat herbs only;) **25** and pray to Elyon continually, then I will come and talk with you."

26 So I went my way, as He commanded me, into the field which is called Ardat[a]; and there I sat among the flowers, and ate of the herbs of the field, and its meat satisfied me. **27** And it came to be after seven days that I lay upon the grass, and my heart was vexed again, just like before, **28** and my mouth was opened, and I began to speak before יהוה Elohim.

29 I said, "O יהוה, You showed Yourself among us, to our fathers in the wilderness, when they went forth out of Mitsrayim, and when they came into the wilderness, where no man treads and that bears no fruit; **30** and You said, 'Hear Me, Yisra'el; and take heed to My words, O seed of Ya'aqov. **31** For behold, I sow my Torah in you, and it shall bring forth fruit in you, and you shall be glorified in it forever.'

32 "But our fathers, who received the Torah, did not guard it, and did not observe the statutes; and the fruit of the Torah did not perish, neither could it, for it belonged to You. **33** Yet those who received it perished, because they did not guard the thing that was sown in them. **34** And behold, it is a custom, that when the ground has received seed, or the sea a ship, or any vessel meat or drink, and when it comes to be that that which is sown, or that which is launched, **35** or the things which have been received, should come to an end, these come to an end, but the receptacles remain: yet with us it has not happened. **36** For we that have received the Torah shall perish by sin, and our heart also which received it. **37** Nevertheless, the Torah does not perish, but remains in its glory."

38 And when I spoke these things in my heart, I looked around with my eyes, and upon the right side I saw a woman, and, behold, she mourned and wept with a loud voice, and was greatly grieved in mind, and her clothes were torn, and she had ashes on her head. **39** Then I let my thoughts go to that with which I was occupied, and turned to her, **40** and said to her, "Why do you weep? And why are you grieved in your mind?"

41 And she said to me, "Leave me alone, my master, that I may lament myself, and

---

[a] 9:26 The exact identification of this field is unknown. The various versions record it differently. The version present in this text is from the Latin version. The Syriac and Ethiopic read 'Arpad' while Arabic[1] reads 'Araab' and the Armenian reads 'Ardab.'

add to my sorrow, for I am greatly vexed in
my mind, and greatly humbled."

42 And I said to her, "What ails you? Tell
me."

43 She said to me, "I, your servant, was
barren, and had no child, though I had a
husband thirty years. 44 And every hour
and every day these thirty years I prayed to
Elyon day and night. 45 And it came to pass
after thirty years that Elohim heard your
maidservant, and looked upon my low
estate, and considered my trouble, and gave
me a son. I rejoiced in him greatly: I and
my husband, and all my neighbors; and we
gave great honor to El Shaddai. 46 And I
nourished him with great travail. 47 So
when he grew up, and I came to find a wife
for him, I made him a banquet."

10 1 "And it so came to be, that when my
son entered into his wedding chamber, he
fell down and died. 2 Then we all put out
the lights, and all my neighbors rose up to
comfort me; but I remained quiet until the
following night. 3 And it came to be, when
they had all left from comforting me – so
that I might be quiet – that I rose up by
night and fled, and came here into this
field, as you see. 4 And now I have decided
not to return into the city, but to stay here,
and neither to eat nor drink, but continually
mourn and fast until I die."

5 Then I left the meditation which I was in,
and answered her in anger, and said, 6 "You
foolish woman above all others! Do you
not see our mourning, and what has
happened to us? 7 How that Tsion, the
mother of us all, is full of sorrow and
greatly humbled? 8 It is right now to mourn
severely, seeing we all mourn, and to be
sorrowful, seeing we are all in sorrow, but
you sorrow for one son. 9 Ask the earth,
and she shall tell you, that it is she who
should mourn for so many that grow upon
her. 10 For out of her all had their
beginnings, and others shall come; and
behold, almost all of them walk into
destruction, and the multitude of them is
utterly rooted out. 11 Who then should
make more mourning, her, who has lost so
great a multitude, or you, who grieve but
for one? 12 And if you say to me, 'My
lamentation is not like the earth's, for I have
lost the fruit of my womb, which I brought
forth with pains, and bore with sorrows;
13 but with the earth, it is after the manner
of the earth: the multitude present in it is
gone, as it came.' 14 Then I say to you, 'Just
as you have brought forth with sorrow,
even so the earth also has given her fruit,
namely, man, ever since the beginning to
him that made her.'

15 "Now therefore keep your sorrow to
yourself, and bear the tragedies which have
befallen you with good courage. 16 For if
you acknowledge the decree of Elohim to
be just, you shall both receive your son in
time, and shall be praised among women.
17 Go your way then into the city to your
husband."

18 And she said to me, "I will not. I will not
go into the city, but I will die here."

19 So I proceeded to speak further to her,
and said, 20 "Do not do that; instead, allow
yourself to be overcome by the tragedies of
Tsion, and be comforted by the sorrow of
Yerushalayim. 21 For you see that our
dwelling-place is laid waste, our altar is
broken down, our Temple is destroyed.
22 Our harp is brought low, our song is put
to silence, our rejoicing is at an end; the

light of our lamp is put out, the ark of our
covenant is plundered, our set-apart things
are defiled, and the Name that is called
upon us is profaned; our freemen are
despitefully treated, our priests are burned,
our Levites have gone into captivity; our
virgins are defiled, and our wives ravished;
our righteous men carried away, our little
ones betrayed, our young men are brought
into bondage, and our strong men have
become weak. 23 And more than all this,
the seal of Tsion: for she has now lost the
seal of her glory, and is delivered into the
hands of those who hate us. 24 You,
therefore, shake off your great heaviness,
and put away from you the multitude of
sorrows, that Elyon may be kind to you
again, and that Elyon may give you rest,
even ease from your travails."

25 And it came to be, while I was talking
with her, behold, her face suddenly shined
exceedingly, and her countenance glistered
like lightning, so that I was greatly afraid of
her, and wondered what this might be.
26 And behold, suddenly she made a great
and fearful cry, so that the earth shook at
the sound. 27 And I looked, and behold, the
woman was no longer before me, but there
was a city built, and a place showed itself
from large foundations. Then I was afraid,
and cried with a loud voice, and said,
28 "Where is Uri'el the messenger, who
came to me previously? For he has caused
me to fall into this great trance, and my end
is turned into corruption, and my prayer to
rebuke."

29 And as I was speaking these words,
behold, the messenger who had come to me
previously came to me, and he looked upon
me. 30 I lay as one that had been dead, and
my understanding was taken from me; and
he took me by the right hand, and
comforted me, and set me upon my feet,
and said to me, 31 "What ails you? Why are
you so restless? And why is your
understanding troubled, and the thoughts of
your heart?"

32 And I said, "Because you have forsaken
me, even though I did according to your
words, and went into the field, and, behold,
I have seen, and still see, that which I am
unable to explain."

33 And he said to me, "Stand up like a man,
and I will advise you." 34 Then I said,
"Speak on, my master, only do not forsake
me, lest I die without my hope. 35 For I
have seen that which I did not know, and
heard that which I do not know. 36 Or is my
sense deceived, or my being in a dream?
37 Now therefore I beg you, explain this
trance to your servant."

38 And he answered me, and said, "Hear
me, and I shall inform you, and tell you
concerning the things of which you are
afraid. For Elyon has revealed many secret
things to you. 39 He has seen that your way
is right, for you sorrow continually for your
people, and make great lamentation for
Tsion. 40 Therefore, this is the meaning of
the vision: 41 the woman who appeared to
you a little while ago, whom you saw
mourning, and began to comfort her –
42 though now you no longer see the
likeness of the woman, but there appeared
to you a city being built – 43 and she told
you of the death of her son, this is the
meaning: 44 this woman, whom you saw, is
Tsion, whom you now see as a city built.
45 And as she said to you that she has been
barren thirty years, so it is, because there
were three thousand years in the world in
which there was no offering yet offered in
her.

46 "And it came to be after three thousand
years that Shelomoh built the city, and
offered offerings. Then she that was barren
brought forth a son. 47 And when she told
you that she nourished him with travail,
that was the dwelling in Yerushalayim.
48 And when she said to you, 'My son,
when he came into his marriage chamber
died,' and that misfortune happened to her,
this was the destruction that came to
Yerushalayim. 49 And behold, you saw her
likeness, how she mourned for her son, and
you began to comfort her for what
happened to her. These were the things to
be opened to you. 50 For now Elyon, seeing
that you are sincerely grieved, and suffer
from your whole heart for her, has showed
you the brightness of her glory, and the
attractiveness of her beauty. 51 Therefore I
commanded you to remain in the field
where no house was built, 52 for I knew
that Elyon would show this to you.
53 Therefore I commanded you to come
into the field, where no foundation of any
building existed.

54 "For in the place in which the city of
Elyon was to be shown, the work of no
man's building could stand. 55 Therefore do
not fear, nor let your heart be frightened,
but go your way, and see the beauty and
greatness of the building, as much as your
eyes are able to see; 56 and then you will
hear as much as your ears may
comprehend. 57 For you are blessed above
many, and with Elyon are called by name,
like but a few. 58 But tomorrow at night
you shall remain here; 59 and so shall Elyon
show you those visions in dreams, of what
Elyon will do to those who dwell upon
earth in the last days." So I slept that night
and another, as he commanded me.

11 1 And it came to be the second night
that I saw a dream, and behold, an eagle
came up from the sea, which had twelve
feathered wings, and three heads. 2 And I
looked, and behold, she spread her wings
over all the earth, and all the winds of
heaven blew on her, and the clouds were
gathered together against her. 3 And I
looked, and other small wings grew out of
her wings near them; and they became little
wings and small. 4 But her heads were at
rest: the head in the middle was greater
than the other heads, yet it rested with
them.

5 I saw the eagle fly with her wings, to
reign over the earth, and over those who
dwell in it. 6 And I saw how all things
under heaven were subject to her, and no
man spoke against her, no, not one creature
upon earth. 7 And I looked, and behold, the
eagle rose upon her talons, and uttered her
voice to her wings, saying, 8 "Do not watch
all at once: sleep, everyone in his own
place, and watch by course; 9 but let the
heads be preserved for the last."

10 The voice did not go out of her heads,
but from the midst of her body. 11 And I
counted her wings that were near the other,
and there were eight of them. 12 And on the
right side one wing arose, and reigned over
all the earth; 13 and so it was, that when it
reigned, the end of it came, and it did not
appear, so that its place appeared no more.
And the next following rose up, and
reigned, and it ruled a great time; 14 and it
happened, that when it reigned, the end of
it came also, so that it appeared no more,
like as the first.

15 And a voice came to it, and said,
16 "Hear, you that rule over the earth all

this time: this I proclaim to you, before you
shall appear no more: 17 none after you
shall attain your time *of reign*, not even the
half of it."

18 Then the third arose, and ruled as the
others before, and it also appeared no more.
19 So it was with all the wings, one after
another, as every one ruled and then
appeared no more. 20 And I looked, and
behold, in time the wings that followed
were set up upon the right side, that they
might rule also; and some of them ruled,
but within a while they appeared no more.
21 Some of them were also set up, but did
not rule. 22 After this I looked, and behold,
the twelve wings appeared no more, neither
did two of the little wings. 23 And there
was nothing left upon the eagle's body,
except the three heads that rested, and six
little wings.

24 And I looked, and behold, two little
wings divided themselves from the six, and
remained under the head that was upon the
right side: but four remained in their place.
25 And I looked, and behold, these under-
wings thought to set up themselves, and to
rule. 26 And I looked, and behold, there was
one set up, but within a while it appeared
no more. 27 A second also, and it was
sooner away than the first. 28 And I looked,
and behold, the two that remained thought
also in themselves to reign; 29 and while
they thought this, behold, one of the heads
that was at rest awoke: the one in the
middle, for that was greater than the two
other heads.

30 And I saw how it joined the two other
heads with it. 31 And behold, the head was
turned with those who were with it, and ate
up the two under wings that presumed to
reign. 32 But this head held the whole earth
in possession, and ruled over those that
dwell in it with much oppression; and it
had the governance of the world more than
all the wings that had been. 33 And after
this I looked, and behold, the head that was
in the middle also suddenly appeared no
more, just as the wings. 34 But there
remained the two heads, which also in like
fashion reigned over the earth, and over
those that dwell in it. 35 And I looked, and
behold, the head upon the right side
devoured the *head* upon the left side.

36 Then I heard a voice, which said to me,
"Look before you, and consider the thing
that you see."

37 And I looked, and, behold, as it were a
lion roused out of the wood roaring: and I
heard how that he sent out a man's voice to
the eagle, and spoke, saying, 38 "Hear: I
will talk with you, and Elyon shall say to
you, 39 'Are you not the one that remains of
the four beasts, whom I made reign in My
world, that the end of My times might
come through them? 40 And the fourth
came, and overcame all the beasts that were
past, and held the world in governance with
great trembling, and the whole compass of
the earth with grievous oppression. So for a
long time he lived upon the earth with
deceit. 41 And you have judged the earth,
but not with truth. 42 For you have afflicted
the humble, you have hurt the peaceful, you
have hated those who speak truth, you have
loved liars, and destroyed the dwellings of
those who brought forth fruit, and cast
down the walls of those that did you no
harm. 43 Therefore your insolent dealing
has come up to Elyon, and your pride to El
Shaddai. 44 Elyon also has looked upon his
times, and, behold, they have ended, and
his ages are fulfilled. 45 And therefore,
eagle, you will no longer appear, nor your

horrible wings, nor your evil little wings,
nor your cruel heads, nor your hurtful
talons, nor all your vain body, 46 so that all
the earth may be refreshed, and be eased,
being delivered from your violence, and
that she may hope for the judgment and
kindness of Him that made her."

12 1 And it came to be, while the lion
spoke these words to the eagle, I looked,
2 and behold, the head that remained
appeared no more, and the two wings
which went over to it arose and set
themselves up to reign, and their kingdom
was small, and full of uproar. 3 And I saw,
and behold, they appeared no more, and the
whole body of the eagle was burned, so that
the earth was in great fear: then I awoke
because of great ecstasy of mind, and from
great fear, and said to my spirit, 4 "Behold,
you have done this to me, in that you
search out the ways of Elyon. 5 See, I am
still weary in my mind, and very weak in
my spirit; and there is not the least bit of
strength in me, because of the great fear
with which I was afraid tonight.
6 Therefore I will now seek Elyon, that He
might strengthen me to the end."

7 And I said, "O Adonai יהוה, if I have
found favor in Your sight, and if I am
declared right with You above many others,
and if my prayer does indeed come up
before Your face, 8 then strengthen me, and
show Your servant the interpretation and
plain meaning of this fearful vision, that
You may perfectly comfort my being. 9 For
Yu have judged me worthy to show me the
end of time and the latter days."

10 And He said to me, "This is the
interpretation of the vision which you saw:
11 the eagle, whom you saw come up from
the sea, is the fourth kingdom which
appeared in vision to your brother Dani'el.
12 But it was not explained to him, as I now
explain it to you. 13 Behold, the days come
that a kingdom shall rise up upon the earth,
and it shall be feared above all the
kingdoms that were before it. 14 Twelve
kings will reign in it, one after another:
15 the second of those shall begin to reign,
and shall have a longer time than any of the
twelve. 16 This is the interpretation of the
twelve wings, which you saw.

17 "And when you heard a voice which
spoke, not going out from the heads, but
from the midst of its body, this is the
interpretation: 18 after the time of that
kingdom there shall arise no small
contentions, and it shall stand in peril of
falling: nevertheless it shall not fall then,
but shall be restored again to its first estate.
19 And when you saw the eight under
wings sticking to her wings, this is the
interpretation: 20 eight kings shall arise in
it, whose times shall be small, and their
years swift. 21 And two of them shall
perish, when the middle time approaches:
four shall be kept for a while until the time
of its ending shall approach, but two shall
be kept to the end.

22 "And when you saw three heads resting,
this is the interpretation: 23 in those latter
days Elyon shall raise up three kingdoms,
and renew many things in them, and they
shall rule over the earth, 24 and over those
that dwell in it, with much oppression,
above all those that were before them:
therefore are they called the heads of the
eagle. 25 For these are those who shall
accomplish her wickedness, and that shall
finish her latter end. 26 And when you saw
that the great head appeared no more, it
signifies that one of them shall die upon his

bed, and with pain. 27 But for the two that
remained, the sword shall devour them.
28 For the sword of the one shall devour
him that was with him, but he also shall fall
by the sword in the latter days.

29 "And when you saw two under wings
passing over to the head that is on the right
side, 30 this is the interpretation: these are
they, whom Elyon has kept to His purpose:
this is the small kingdom and full of
trouble, as you saw. 31 And the lion, which
you saw rising up out of the wood, and
roaring, and speaking to the eagle, and
rebuking her for her unrighteousness, and
all her words which you have heard, 32 this
is the Messiah, whom Elyon has kept to the
end of days, who shall spring up out of the
seed of David, and He shall come and
speak to them and reprove them for their
wickedness and unrighteousness, and shall
heap up before them their contemptuous
dealings.

33 "For at first, He shall set them alive in
His judgment, and when He has reproved
them, He shall destroy them. 34 For He
shall deliver the rest of My people with
kindness: those that have been preserved
throughout My borders. And He shall make
them joyful until the coming of the end,
even the Day of Judgment, of which I have
spoken to you from the beginning.

35 "This is the dream that you saw, and this
is its interpretation. 36 Only you have been
allowed to know the secret of Elyon.
37 Therefore write all these things that you
have seen in a book, and put them in a
secret place, 38 and you shall teach them to
the wise of your people, whose hearts you
know are able to comprehend and keep
these secrets. 39 But wait here seven more
days, that there may be shown to you
whatever it pleases Elyon to show you."
And He departed from me.

40 And it came to be, when all the people
saw that the seven days were past, and I
had not come again into the city, they
gathered them all together, from the least to
the greatest, and came to me, and spoke to
me, saying, 41 "What have we done to you?
And what evil have we done against you,
that you have utterly forsaken us, and sit in
this place? 42 For of all the prophets, only
you remain with us, as a cluster of the
vintage, and as a lamp in a dark place, and
as a haven for a ship saved from the
tempest. 43 Do we not have enough evil
among us? 44 If you forsake us, how much
better had it been for us, if we also had
been consumed in the burning of Tsion!
45 For we are not better than those who
died there." And they wept with a loud
voice. And I answered them, and said,
46 "Be of good comfort, O Yisra'el, and do
not be sorrowful, you house of Ya'aqov:
47 for Elyon has remembered you, and El
Shaddai has not forgotten you forever.

48 "As for me, I have not forsaken you, nor
have I departed from you: but have come
into this place, to pray for the desolation of
Tsion, and that I might seek compassion for
the low estate of your dwelling-place.
49 And now, go your way, every man to his
own house, and after these days I will come
to you." 50 So the people went their way
into the city, as I said to them; 51 but I sat
in the field seven days, as the messenger
commanded me; and in those days I only
ate of the herbs of the field, and had my
meat of the aromatic plants.

13 1 And it came to be after seven days, I
dreamed a dream by night. 2 And behold, a

wind arose from the sea, and it stirred up
all the waves. 3 And [I looked, and behold,
the wind made something like the figure of
a man come out of the heart of the sea.][a]
And I looked, and behold, that man flew[b]
with the clouds of the heavens; and
wherever He turned His face to look,
everything under His gaze trembled. 4 And
whenever His voice went out of His mouth,
all that heard His voice melted like wax
melts when it feels the fire.

5 And after this I looked, and behold, an
innumerable multitude of men were
gathered together from the four winds of
the heavens, to make war against the man
that came out of the sea. 6 And I looked,
and behold, He carved Himself a great
mountain, and flew upon it. 7 And I tried to
see the region or place from which the
mountain was carved, but I could not.

8 And after this I looked, and behold, all
those that were gathered together to fight
against Him were greatly afraid, and yet
dared fight. 9 And when He saw the assault
of the multitude that came, He neither lifted
up His hand nor held a spear nor any
instrument of war; 10 but I saw only how
He sent out of His mouth, as it were, a
flood of fire, and out of His lips a flaming
breath, and off of His tongue He cast forth
sparks like a storm. 11 And these were all
mixed together; the flood of fire, the
flaming breath, and the great storm, and fell
upon the assault of the multitude which was
prepared to fight, and burned up every one
of them, so that suddenly nothing was seen
of the innumerable multitude, but only the
dust of ashes and smell of smoke; when I
saw this I was amazed. 12 Afterward I saw
the same man come down from the
mountain, and call to Him another
multitude which was peaceful.

13 And many people came to Him, some of
whom were glad, some of whom were
sorrowful, some of whom were bound, and
some of whom brought others as offerings;
then I awoke in great terror, and prayed to
Elyon, and said, 14 "You have shown Your
servant these wonders from the beginning,
and have counted me worthy that You
should receive my prayer. 15 Now show me
the interpretation of this dream also. 16 For
as I consider it in my understanding, woe to
those who shall be left in those days! And
much more woe to those who are not left!
17 For those who were not left shall be sad
18 because they understand the things that
are laid up for them in the latter days, but
will not attain to them. 19 But woe to them
also that are left, for that reason; for they
shall see great perils and many necessities,
as these dreams declare. 20 Yet is it better
for one to be in peril and to come into these
things, than to pass away as a cloud out of
the world, and not see the things that will
happen in the last days." And He answered,
and said:

21 " I will tell you the interpretation of the
vision, and I will also open to you the
things that you have mentioned. 22 As you
have said of those who survive [and of
those who do not][c], this is the
interpretation: 23 He that brings the peril in
that time shall keep those who fall into

---

[a] 13:3 Bracketed section indicates reading absent from Syriac text.
[b] 13:3 So the Syriac, Ethiopic, Arabic, and Armenian texts. Latin text reads, "grew strong."
[c] 13:22 So the Syriac text and Arabic[1]. Latin text omits bracketed section.

danger, those who have works and faith
toward El Shaddai. **24** Know therefore that
those who survive are more blessed than
those who die.

25 "These are the interpretations of the
vision: the man you saw coming up from
the midst of the sea, **26** this is He whom
Elyon has kept for many ages, who will
Himself deliver His creation; He will direct
those who remain. **27** And as you saw that
wind, and fire, and storm came out of His
mouth; **28** and as He held neither spear nor
any instrument of war, but destroyed the
assault of that multitude which came to
fight against Him, this is the interpretation:
29 the days are coming when Elyon will
deliver those who are on the earth. **30** And
astonishment of mind will come upon those
who dwell on the earth. **31** And one will
plan war against another, city against city,
place against place, **people against people,
and kingdom against kingdom**.[a] **32** And
when these things happen, and the signs
happen which I showed you before, then
My Son will be revealed, whom you saw as
a man ascending [up from the sea].[b]

33 And it shall be, when all the nations hear
His voice, every man shall leave his own
land and the battle they have against one
another. **34** And an innumerable multitude
shall be gathered together, as you saw,
desiring to come and fight against Him.
35 But He shall stand upon the top of the
mount Tsion. **36** And Tsion shall come, and
be made manifest to all men, being
prepared and built, as you saw the
mountain carved without hands. **37** And My
Son will rebuke the nations which have
come on account of their wickedness, with
plagues that are like a tempest; **38** and He
will taunt them to their face with their evil
thoughts, and the torments with which they
will be tormented, which are likened to a
flame: and He shall destroy them without
labor by the Torah, which is likened to fire.

39 "And as you saw Him gather to Himself
another multitude that was peaceful–
40 these are the ten tribes, which were led
away out of their own land in the time of
Hoshea the king, whom Shalmaneser the
king of the Ashuwrites led away captive,
and carried them beyond the River *Perath*,
and they were carried into another land.
41 But they took this counsel among
themselves, that they would leave the
multitude of the heathen, and go forth into
a further country, where men never lived,
42 that there they may keep their statutes,
which they had not kept in their own land.
43 And they entered by the narrow passages
of the River Perath. **44** For Elyon then
worked signs for them, and stopped the
channels of the River *Perath*, until they had
crossed over. **45** For through that country
there was a great way to go, namely, of a
year and a half; and the same region is
called Arzareth[c]. **46** Then lived they there
until the latter days; and now when they

---

[a] 13:31 See Loukas 21:10.
[b] 13:32 So the Ethiopic and Arabic texts. Syriac and most Latin texts omit bracketed section.
[c] 13:45 Arzareth – This is actually a Hebrew phrase, ארץ אחרת (*erets aḥereth*), meaning "another land." This is the exact phrase as it appears in Devarim [Deuteronomy] 29:28. This phrase also appears in the Mishnah in Sanhedrin 10:3, where R. Eliezer and R. Aqiva disagree on the meaning. According to the view of R. Eliezer, the Ten Tribes would eventually return from "another land" while Aqiva maintained they would not. In *Antiquities of the Jews 11:133*, scholar Flavius Josephus states: "the ten tribes are beyond the Euphrates till now, and are an immense multitude and not to be estimated in numbers."

begin to come again, 47 Elyon stops the
channels of the River *Perath* again, that
they may go through; therefore saw you the
multitude gathered together with peace.

48 "But those that remain of your people are
those who are found within My set-apart
border. 49 It shall be, therefore, when He
destroys the multitude of the nations that
are gathered together, He shall defend the
people that remain. 50 And then He shall
show them many wonders."

51 Then I said, "O Adonai יהוה, show me
this: why have I seen the man coming up
from the midst of the sea?"

52 And He said to me, "As one can neither
seek out nor know what is in the deep of
the sea, even so can no man upon earth see
My Son, or those that are with Him, except
in the time of His day. 53 This is the
interpretation of the dream which you saw,
and this will be explained only to you.
54 For you have forsaken your own ways,
and applied your diligence to Mine, and
have sought out My Torah. 55 You have
ordered your life in wisdom, and have
called understanding your mother. 56 And
therefore have I shown you this. For there
is a reward laid up with Elyon. It shall be,
after three more days I will speak other
things to you, and declare to you mighty
and wondrous things."

57 Then I went out into the field, giving
praise and thanks greatly to Elyon because
of His wonders, which He did time and
again; 58 and because He governs the time,
and the things that occur in their seasons.
And there I sat for three days.

14 1 And it came to be on the third day, I
sat under an oak and a voice came out of a
bush near me, and said, "Ezra, Ezra."

2 And I said, "Here am I, יהוה." And I
stood up upon my feet.

3 Then He said to me, "I openly revealed
Myself in the bush, and talked with
Mosheh when My people were in bondage
in Mitsrayim. 4 I sent him and he led My
people out of Mitsrayim; and I brought him
up to Mount Sinai, where I held him by Me
for many days, 5 and told him many
wondrous things, and showed him the
secrets of the times, and the end of the
seasons, and commanded him, saying,
6 'These words you shall publish openly,
and these *others* you shall hide.'

7 "And now I say to you, 8 lay up in your
heart the signs that I have shown, and the
dreams that you have seen, and the
interpretations which you have received.
9 For you will be taken away from men,
and from then on you shall remain with My
Son – and with those that are like you –
until the times have ended. 10 For the world
has lost its youth, and the times are
growing old. 11 For the *days of the* world
are divided into twelve parts, and ten parts
are gone already, *and* even half of the tenth
part; 12 still two parts after the middle of
the tenth part remain.

13 "Now therefore, set your house in order,
and reprove your people; comfort the lowly
among them, and instruct the wise among
them; and now renounce the life that is
corruptible, 14 and let go of the mortal
thoughts. Cast away from you the burdens
of man, put off your weak nature, 15 and
lay aside the thoughts that are most
grievous to you, and remove from these
times quickly. 16 For still worse evils than

those which you have seen shall be done
after this. 17 See how much the world shall
be weaker through age, and evils shall
greatly increase upon those who dwell in it.
18 For the truth shall go further away, and
falsehood shall draw near; for now the
eagle which you saw in the vision is
hurrying to come.

19 Then I answered and said, "I will speak
before You, O יהוה. 20 Behold, I will go,
as You have commanded me, and reprove
the people that are now *living*. But those
who shall be born afterward, who shall
reprove them? For the world is set in
darkness, and those who dwell in it are
without light. 21 For Your Torah is burned,
and no man knows the things that You have
done, or the works You shall do. 22 But if I
have found favor before You, send the Set-
Apart Ruaḥ to me, and I shall write all that
has been done in the world since the
beginning, even the things that were written
in Your Torah, that men may be able to
find the path, and that those who will live
in the latter days may survive."

23 And He answered me and said, "Go your
way, gather the people together, and tell
them not to seek you for forty days. 24 And
prepare many tablets, and take with you
Tsarea, Davaryah, Shelemyah, Eithan, and
Asi'el – these five who are ready to write
swiftly – 25 and come here, and I will light
a lamp of understanding in your heart
which shall not be extinguished, until the
things about which you write have ended.
26 And when you are finished, you shall
publish some things openly, and some
things you shall deliver in secret to the
wise. At this time tomorrow you shall
begin to write."

27 Then I went out as He commanded me,
and gathered all the people together, and
said, 28 "Hear these words, O Yisra'el. 29 At
the beginning, our fathers were strangers in
Mitsrayim, and they were delivered from
there, 30 and received the Torah of life,
which they did not guard; *and this* you also
have transgressed after them. 31 Then the
land, even the land of Tsion, was given to
you for a possession. But you yourselves,
and your fathers, have done
unrighteousness, and have not guarded the
ways which Elyon commanded you. 32 And
because He is a righteous judge, He took
from you – for a time – the thing He had
given to you. 33 And now you are here, and
your brethren are among you.

34 "Therefore if you will rule over your
own understanding, and instruct your
hearts, you shall be saved alive, and *even*
after death you shall obtain kindness. 35 For
after death the judgment shall come, when
we shall live again, and then the names of
the righteous shall be manifest, and the
works of the wicked shall be declared.
36 Therefore let no man come to me now,
nor look for me for forty days."

37 So I took the five men as He commanded
me, and we went out into the field and
remained there. 38 And it came to be the
next day that behold, a voice called me,
saying, "Ezra, open your mouth, and drink
that which I give you to drink."

39 Then I opened my mouth and, behold, a
full cup was handed to me, which was full
of water, but the color of it was like fire.
40 And I took it, and drank. And when I had
drunk of it, my heart uttered understanding,
and wisdom grew in my breast, for my
spirit retained its memory. 41 And my
mouth was opened and no longer closed.

42 Elyon gave understanding to the five
men, and they each wrote the things that
were told to them, in a script they did not
know, and they sat for forty days. They
wrote in the day-time, and at night they ate
bread.

43 As for me, I spoke in the day, and by
night I held not my tongue. 44 So in forty
day, ninety-four books were written.
45 And it came to be, when the forty days
were fulfilled, that Elyon spoke to me,
saying, "Openly publish the twenty-four[a]
books that you wrote first, and let the
worthy and unworthy *alike* read them.[b]
46 But keep the seventy *books*[c] last, that
you may deliver them to the wise among
your people. 47 For in them is the spring of
understanding, the fountain of wisdom, and
the stream of knowledge."

48 And so I did.

15 [1 "Behold, speak in the hearing of My
people the words of prophecy, which I will
put in your mouth," says יהוה, 2 "And
cause them to be written down, for they are
faithful and true. 3 Do not be afraid of their
thoughts against you; do not let the unbelief
of those that speak against you trouble you.
4 For all the unbelievers shall die in their
unbelief.

5 "Behold," says יהוה, "I bring evils upon
the whole earth; sword and famine, and
death and destruction. 6 For wickedness has
prevailed over every land, and their hurtful
works are now full. 7 Therefore," says
יהוה, 8 "I will no longer hold My peace
concerning their wickedness, which they
profanely commit; neither will I allow them
to continue in these things which they
wickedly practice. Behold, the innocent and
righteous blood cries to me, and the beings
of the righteous cry out continually. 9 I will
surely avenge them," says יהוה, "And will
receive to Myself all the innocent blood
from among them.

10 "Behold, My people are led like sheep to
the slaughter. I will not allow them to dwell
in the land of Mitsrayim now, 11 but I will
bring them out with a mighty hand and
with an outstretched arm, and will strike
Mitsrayim with plagues, as before, and will
destroy all their land. 12 Let Mitsrayim
mourn, with their foundations, for the
plague of discipline and the punishment
that Elohim shall bring upon it. 13 Let the
farmer that tills the ground mourn, for their
seeds shall fail to grow and their trees shall
be laid waste through the blasting and hail,
and a terrible tempest. 14 Woe to the world
and those who dwell in it! 15 For the sword
and their destruction draws near, and
nation shall rise up against nation[d] to

[a] 14:45 So the Syriac and Arabic[1] texts. Latin text omits "twenty-four" here.

[b] 14:45 This number 24 most likely refers to the original number of books contained in the Tanakh (OT). Five books of Moses (Torah: 5), eight prophets (including the Minor Prophets [all twelve as one volume], Major Prophets, Joshua, Judges, Samuel [one volume], and Kings [one volume]: 8), and the Writings (Psalms, Proverbs, Job, Ecclesiastes, Lamentations, Ruth, Song of Songs, Esther, Chronicles [one volume], Ezra-Nehemiah [one volume], and Dani'el: 11) for a total of 24. This enumeration is also hinted at in the Jewish Midrashic text, Midrash Qoheleth 12:12.

[c] 14:46 It is unknown whether these seventy books refer to the additional Apocryphal texts, to the so-called "Lost Books" that are mentioned throughout the Tanakh, or perhaps even to the "Translation of the Seventy" or the Septuagint (LXX) itself.

[d] 15:15 See Loukas 21:10.

battle with weapons in their hands. 16 For
there shall be sedition among men. And
growing strong one against another, they
shall not regard their king – nor the chief of
their great ones – in their might. 17 For a
man shall desire to go into a city, and shall
not be able. 18 For because of their pride
the cities shall be troubled, the houses shall
be destroyed, and men shall be afraid. 19 A
man shall have no pity upon his neighbor,
but shall make an assault on their houses
with the sword, and plunder their goods,
because of the lack of bread, and for great
affliction."

20 "Behold," says Elohim, "I call together
all the kings of the earth to turn to Me,
from the rising of the sun, from the south,
from the east, and Levanon; to turn and
repay the things that they have given them.
21 Just as they do even today to My chosen,
so I will do also, and repay them in their
bosom." Thus says יהוה Elohim, 22 "My
right hand shall not spare the sinners, and
My sword shall not cease over those who
shed innocent blood upon the earth."

23 A fire has gone forth from His wrath,
and has consumed the foundations of the
earth, and the sinners, like the straw that is
kindled. 24 "Woe to those who sin, and do
not guard My commands!" says יהוה. 25 "I
will not spare them. Go your way,
rebellious children; do not defile My
dwelling-place."

26 For יהוה knows all those who trespass
against Him, therefore He has delivered
them to death and destruction. 27 For now
evils have come upon the whole earth, and
you shall remain in them; for Elohim shall
not deliver you, because you have sinned
against Him.

28 Behold, a terrifying vision, and its
appearance from the east! 29 And the
nations of the dragons of Aravia shall come
out with many chariots, and from the day
that they set forth their hissing is carried
over the earth, so that all they that hear
them may fear also, and tremble. 30 Also
the Karmanites[a], raging in wrath, shall go
forth as the wild boars of the forest, and
shall come with great power, and join battle
with them, and shall waste a portion of the
land of the Ashuwrites with their teeth.
31 And then shall the dragons have the
upper hand, remembering their nature. If
they shall turn themselves, conspiring
together in great power to persecute them,
32 then these shall be troubled, and keep
silence through their power, and shall turn
and flee. 33 And from the land of the
Ashuwrites shall the one lying in wait
besiege them, and consume one of them,
and fear and trembling shall come upon
their army, and treason against their kings.

34 "Behold, clouds from the east and from
the north to the south, and they are very
horrible to look upon, full of wrath and
storm. 35 They shall dash against one
another, and they shall pour out a great
storm upon the earth, even their own
tempest. And there shall be blood on
account of the sword *that reaches up* to the
horse's belly, 36 and to the thigh of man,
and to the camel's hock. 37 And there shall
be fear and great trembling upon the earth.
And they that see this wrath shall be afraid,

---

[a] 15:30 Karmanites – From the Greek Καρμανια (*Karmania*). This refers to a Persian province today located near Kerman in Iran.

and trembling shall take hold upon them.
38 And after this there shall be stirred up
great storms from the south, and from the
north, and another part from the west.
39 And strong winds shall arise from the
east, and shall shut it up, even the cloud
which he raised up in wrath; and the
tempest that was to cause destruction by the
east wind shall be violently driven toward
the south and west. 40 And great clouds,
mighty and full of wrath shall be lifted up,
and the tempest, that they may destroy all
the earth, and those who dwell in it; and
they shall pour out over every high and
eminent one a terrible tempest: 41 fire, and
hail, and flying swords, and many waters,
that all plains may be full, and all rivers,
with the abundance of those waters.

42 "And they shall break down the cities
and walls, mountains and hills, trees of the
forest, and grass of the meadows, and their
grain. 43 And they shall go steadily on to
Bavel, and destroy her. 44 They shall come
to her, and surround her; they shall pour out
upon her the tempest and all wrath; then
shall the dust and smoke go up to the
heavens, and all those who are near her
shall mourn her. 45 And those who remain
shall do service to those who have put her
in fear.

46 "And you, Asia, who have partook in the
beauty of Bavel, and in the glory of her
person: 47 woe to you, you wretch, for you
have made yourself like her. You have
adorned your daughters in whoring, that
they might please and glory in your lovers,
which have always desired you whore with
them! 48 You have followed her who is
hateful in all her works and inventions.
Therefore," says Elohim, 49 "I will send
evils upon you: widowhood, poverty,
famine, sword, and pestilence, to waste
your houses to destruction and death.
50 And the glory of your power shall be
dried up as a flower, when the heat arises
that is sent over you. 51 You shall be
weakened as a poor woman with stripes,
and as one disciplined with wounds, so that
you shall not be able to receive your
mighty ones and your lovers.

52 "Would I have done so against you,"
says יהוה, 53 "if you had not always slain
My chosen, exalting the stroke of your
hands, and saying over their dead, when
you were drunk, 54 'Set forth the beauty of
your countenance'? 55 The reward of a
whore shall be in your bosom, and you
shall receive payment. 56 Just as you do to
My chosen," says יהוה, "Even so shall
Elohim do to you, and shall deliver you
into trouble. 57 And your children shall die
of hunger, and you shall fall by the sword,
and your cities shall be broken down, and
all that belongs to you shall perish by the
sword in the field. 58 And those who are in
the mountains shall die of hunger, and eat
their own flesh, and drink their own blood
on account of hunger for bread and thirst
for water.

59 "You, unhappy above all, shall come and
again receive evils. 60 And in the alley they
shall rush on the idle city, and shall destroy
some portion of your land, and ruin part of
your glory, and shall return again to Bavel
that was destroyed. 61 And you shall be cast
down by them as stubble, and they shall be
to you as fire, 62 and shall devour you, and
your cities, your land, and your mountains.
They shall burn all your forests and your
fruit trees with fire. 63 They shall carry
your children away captive, and shall
plunder your wealth, and ruin the glory of
your face."

16 1 Woe to you, Bavel, and Asia! Woe to
you, Mitsrayim, and Aram! 2 Gird up
yourselves with sackcloth and garments of
hair, and mourn for your children, and
lament: for your destruction is at hand. 3 A
sword is sent upon you, and who is he that
may turn it back? 4 A fire is sent upon you,
and who is he that may quench it? 5 Evils
are sent upon you, and who is he that may
drive them away? 6 Can one drive away a
hungry lion in the forest? Or can one
quench the fire in stubble, when it has once
begun to burn? 7 Can one turn again the
arrow that is shot by a strong archer?
8 יהוה Elohim sends these evils, and who
shall drive them away? 9 A fire shall go
forth from His wrath, and who is he that
may quench it? 10 He shall cast lightning,
and who shall not fear? He shall thunder,
and who shall not tremble?

11 יהוה shall threaten, and who shall not be
utterly broken in pieces at His presence?
12 The earth quakes, with its foundations;
the sea ascends up with waves from the
deep, and its waves shall be troubled, and
its fishes also, at the presence of יהוה, and
before the glory of His power. 13 For his
right hand that bends the bow is strong; His
arrows that He shoots are sharp, and shall
not miss, when they are shot into the ends
of the world.

14 Behold, the evils are sent forth, and shall
not return again, until they come upon the
earth. 15 The fire is kindled, and shall not
be extinguished, until it consumes the
foundations of the earth. 16 Just as an arrow
which is shot by a mighty archer does not
return backward, even so the evils that are
sent forth upon earth shall not return again.
17 Woe is me! Woe is me! Who will deliver
me in those days?

18 The beginning of sorrows, and there
shall be great mourning; the beginning of
famine, and many shall perish; the
beginning of wars, and the powers shall
stand in fear; the beginning of evils, and all
shall tremble! What shall they do in all this
when the evils shall come? 19 Behold,
famine and plague, tribulation and anguish!
They are sent as scourges for amendment.
20 But for all these things they shall not
turn from their wickedness, nor will they be
mindful of the scourges. 21 Behold, food
shall be so inexpensive upon earth, that
they shall think themselves to be in good
shape, and even then shall evils grow upon
earth: sword, famine, and great confusion.

22 For many of those who dwell upon earth
shall perish by famine; and the other, *those*
that escape the famine, shall be destroyed
by the sword. 23 And the dead shall be cast
out as dung, and there shall be no man to
comfort them, for the earth shall be left
desolate, and its cities shall be cast down.
24 There shall be no farmer left to till the
earth, and to sow it. 25 The trees shall give
fruit, and who shall gather them? 26 The
grapes shall ripen, and who shall tread
them? For in all places there shall be a
great forsaking; 27 for one man shall desire
to see another, or to hear his voice. 28 For
in an *entire* city, *only* ten shall be left; and
two in the field, who have hidden
themselves in the thick groves, and in the
clefts of the rocks. 29 As in an orchard of
olives upon every tree there be left three or
four olives, 30 or as when a vineyard is
gathered there be some clusters left by
those who diligently seek through the
vineyard; 31 even so in those days there

shall be three or four left by those who
search their houses with the sword.

32 And the earth shall be left desolate, and
its fields shall be for briers, and her ways
and all her paths shall bring forth thorns,
because no sheep shall pass through her.
33 Virgins shall mourn, having no
bridegrooms; wives shall mourn, having no
husbands; their daughters shall mourn,
having no helpers. 34 Their bridegrooms
shall be destroyed in the wars, and their
husbands shall perish from the famine.

35 Hear now these things, and understand
them, you servants of יהוה. 36 Behold, the
word of יהוה, receive it: do not disregard
the things of which יהוה speaks.
37 "Behold, the evils draw near, and are not
slack. 38 Just as a woman with child in the
ninth month, when the hour of her delivery
draws near, within two or three hours
miserable pains surround her womb, and
when the child comes forth from the womb,
there shall be no lingering for a moment;
39 even so the evils shall not be slack in
coming upon the earth. And the world shall
groan, and sorrows shall take hold of it on
every side.

40 "O My people, hear My word: make
ready for battle, and in those evils be even
as pilgrims upon the earth. 41 He that sells,
let him be as him that flees. He that buys,
as one that will lose. 42 He that occupies
merchandise, as he that has no profit by it.
He that builds, as he that shall not dwell in
it. 43 He that sows, as if he should not reap;
so also he that prunes the vines, as he that
shall not gather the grapes. 44 Those who
marry, as those who shall not have
children. Those who do not marry, as the
widowed. 45 Just as those who labor do so
in vain; 46 for strangers shall reap their
fruits, and plunder their goods; overthrow
their houses, and take their children
captive; for in captivity and famine shall
they bring forth their children, 47 and those
who traffic do so to become a plunder. The
more they adorn their cities, their houses,
their possessions, and their own persons,
48 the more I will hate them for their sins,"
says יהוה.

49 "Just as a righteous, honest, and valiant
woman hates a whore, 50 so shall
righteousness hate iniquity when she
adorns herself, and shall accuse her to her
face, when he comes, who shall defend the
ones that diligently search out every sin
upon earth.

51 "Therefore do not be like this, nor do
these works. 52 For yet a little while, and
iniquity shall be taken away out of the
earth, and righteousness shall reign over us.
53 Let the sinner not say that he has not
sinned, for he shall burn coals of fire upon
the head of one who says, 'I have not
sinned before Elohim and His glory.'
54 Behold, יהוה knows all the works of
men, their imaginations, their thoughts, and
their hearts. 55 Who said, 'Let the earth be
made;' and it was made; 'Let the heaven be
made;' and they were made. 56 And at His
word the stars were established; and He
knows the number of the stars.

57 "Who searches the deep and its
treasures; He has measured the sea, and
knows what it contains. 58 Who has shut the
sea in the midst of the waters, and with His
word He has hanged the earth upon the
waters. 59 Who spreads out the heavens like
a vault, and upon the waters He founded it.
60 Who has made in the desert springs of
water, and pools upon the tops of the

mountains to send forth rivers from the height to water the earth.

61 "Who formed man, and put a heart in the midst of his body, and gave him breath,
life, and understanding; 62 yes, the Ruaḥ of
El Shaddai. He who made all things, and searches out hidden things in hidden places,
63 surely He knows your thoughts, and what you think in your hearts. Woe to those who sin, and would try to hide their sin!
64 For יהוה will search out all your works perfectly, and He will put you all to shame.
65 And when your sins are brought forth before men, you shall be ashamed, and your own iniquities shall stand as your
accusers in that day. 66 What will you do? Or how will you hide your sins before Elohim and His messengers?

67 "Behold, Elohim is the judge: fear Him. Cease from your sins, and forget your iniquities, and do not take them up again; so shall Elohim lead you forth and deliver you from all affliction.

68 "For behold, the burning wrath of a great multitude is kindled over you, and they shall take away some of you, and feed you with that which is sacrificed to idols.
69 And those who consent to them shall be in derision and in reproach, and be trodden
under their foot. 70 For there shall be in various places, and in the next cities, a great revolt against those that fear יהוה.
71 They shall be like mad men, sparing none, but spoiling and destroying those
who still fear יהוה. 72 For they shall waste and take away their goods, and cast them
out of their houses. 73 Then shall the trial of My elect be manifest; even as the gold that is tried in the fire.

74 "Hear, O you My elect," says יהוה, "Behold, the days of affliction are at hand,
and I will deliver you from them. 75 Do not fear or doubt; for Elohim is your guide.
76 You who guard My commands and precepts," says יהוה Elohim, "Do not let your sins weigh you down, and do not let
your iniquities lift themselves up. 77 Woe to those who are fast bound with their sins, and covered with their iniquities, as a field is fast bound with bushes, and its path covered with thorns, that no man may
travel through! 78 It is even shut off, and given up to be consumed by fire."][a]

[a] 15-16 Just as it is likely that chapters 1 and 2 were penned by a later editor, so were chapters 15 and 16 like penned by a third editor. These chapters break from the flow and content of the book. Many scholars refer to these two as their own text, generally titled 6 Esdras.

Appendix A: Explanatory Notes

Being. The Hebrew (and Aramaic) word נפש (*nephesh*) is almost universally rendered as "soul" for most translations. It has also been rendered as "being" in this publication. This is true of *nephesh* and its Greek counterpart, ψυχη (*psuche*), which carries the same meaning. It should be noted, however, that these words are separate from the words for "spirit" in both Hebrew and Greek (see entry **Ruaḥ**). Simply put, humans are souls (beings), and have a spirit. In Ethiopic it is a bit more difficult, as the word used for being [soul] is the same word used for spirit: ነፍስ (*na'fas*). This is a cognate to the Hebrew *nephesh*.

Messenger. The word "angel" has been replaced with the more accurate and appropriate "messenger." The Hebrew (and Aramaic) word in question is מלאך (*malakh*), the Greek is αγγελος (*angelos*), and the Ethiopic is መልአክ (*ma'la'k*), all meaning "messenger." These words can be applied both to men (eg. Yehoshua [Joshua] 6:17 and Loukas [Luke] 7:24) and heavenly messengers (eg. Sh'mot [Exodus] 3:2 and Mattithyahu [Matthew] 1:20). As such, in order to keep a consistent translation, all instances have been rendered as "messenger."

Naḥash. The Hebrew word נחש (*na'ḥash*) is most often rendered "serpent." The word is derived from the word *nawḥash* (same word, different vowels) which means "divination." The association is most likely due to the "hiss" of whispering a spell, in connection with the noise a serpent makes. However, it is also etymologically connected to the word נחשת (*ne'ḥo'sheth*) meaning "copper." The connection with copper is believed to be on account of it being a metal used in divination, or possibly the "ringing" sound of copper resembling the "hiss" or "whisper" mentioned in the use of divination.

Regardless, the exact classification of animal (serpent, snake, etc.) is unknown, and thus has been transliterated in Genesis Retold.

Nations. The Hebrew word rendered "nation" is גוי (*goy*) and literally means "nation." It is usually used in the plural form *goyim*, which is "nations." Strictly defined, it refers to anyone that is not a Yisra'elite.

The Greek word rendered "nation" is εθνος (*ethnos*) and means the same as its Hebrew counterpart. This word is generally translated as "Gentile" but I have chosen a more literal translation.

New Moon. The Hebrew word חדש (*ḥodesh*) is usually rendered as "month." However, the word itself is derived from the word *chadash* (see entry **New**) meaning "new." As such, the word is more accurately translated as "renewal." There is also the Hebrew word ירח (*yerach*) which does mean "moon." In order to keep the translation consistent, *chodesh* has been translated as "new moon" throughout, since it specifically carries the connotation of a renewal cycle; *yerach* has been translated as "month." Note that this applies when the source text is Hebrew, primarily in Yashar.

Ruaḥ. The word "spirit" has been left alone in many cases. However, whenever it applies directly to יהוה, it is rendered as

"Ruaḥ." רוח (*Ruaḥ*) means "spirit," "breath," or "wind." Thus, to differentiate between just a "spirit" and the Set-apart Spirit of יהוה, it is rendered as the transliterated form "Ruaḥ." It should also be noted that in the Greek writings, the word πνευμα (*pneuma*) is used, but is rendered as spirit or Ruaḥ depending on what (or whom) it is applied to.

Set-apart. The common English rendering of "Holy" has been changed to "Set-apart." The Hebrew (and Aramaic) word commonly rendered as "Holy" is קדוש (*qadosh*) and means literally "set-apart." While "Holy" is usually defined as "something dedicated to God" the meaning of *qadosh* is slightly different. The Greek word in question is ἅγιος (*hagios*) and means the same as *qadosh*. In Ethiopic, this word is ቅዱስ (*k'dusa*) which is a cognate to the Hebrew *qadosh*. Likewise, rather than use a separate word for "consecrate" it is simply written as an action, without the hyphen. So the adjective – and noun – ("Holy") becomes set-apart, while the verb ("consecrate") becomes set apart.

Sheol. The Hebrew (and Aramaic) word שאול (*Sheol*) is usually rendered as "grave" or is left un-translated. Sheol is literally the grave; it is a physical place where the dead are buried. Its Greek counterpart is Αδης (Hades). The Ethiopic word used is ሲኦል (*si'ol*) which is a cognate to the Hebrew *Sheol*. All have been rendered as "Sheol."

Torah. The Hebrew word תורה (*Torah*) is best rendered as "instructions" and not the commonly translated word "law." To the Hebrew mind, Torah is always seen in a positive light. As such, Torah has simply been transliterated and not translated. The Aramaic word is, typically, אוריתא (*ora'iyta*). In Syriac Aramaic, however, the word used is actually a loan-word from Greek, which is ܢܡܘܣܐ (*n'musa*). The Greek word is νομος (*nomos*), and the Ethiopic word is ኦሪት (*'oriyt*) which is a cognate of the Aramaic *ora'iyta*. In Genesis Retold these words are usually rendered as law, except: (1) when the Hebrew text reads "Torah" and (2) when the context of the section clearly indicates that the Torah is the law being referenced.

Tsedaqqah. The Hebrew word צדקה (*tsedaqqah*) literally means "righteousness." In most Jewish writings, however, it denotes charity or alms, specifically for the less fortunate. In synagogues today there is what is known as a *tsedaqqah box*, similar to a tithe box, or donation box for charities. This term has been transliterated in the SQV to highlight its Jewish cultural significance. That is, it is not merely a charitable donation or giving of alms, but is considered a "righteous deed" that helps to sustain one's people.

Tsevaot. The Hebrew word צבאות (*Tsevaot*) is usually rendered as "armies" or "hosts." It is one of the Titles of יהוה, and is seen over 200 times in the Scriptures as "יהוה Tsevaot" though this is normally translated as "LORD of Hosts." As with most terms for Genesis Retold, I prefer the transl*iteration* over the transl*ation*. Thus, in the text, it is rendered simply as "Tsevaot."

Appendix B: Alphabets

Hebrew / Aramaic	English Equivalent (Hebrew & Aramaic)	Greek	English Equivalent (Greek)
א (Alef)	Depends on vowel	Α α (Alpha)	A
בּ (Bet) ב (Vet)	B V	Β β (Beta)	B
ג (Gimel)	G	Γ γ (Gamma)	G
ד (Dalet)	D	Δ δ (Delta)	D
ה (Hey)	H	Ε ε (Epsilon)	E
ו (Vav/Waw)	V/W/U	Ζ ζ (Zeta)	Z
ז (Zayin)	Z	Η η (Eta)	Ee
ח (Chet)	Ch [Ḥ]	Θ θ (Theta)	Th
ט (Tet)	T	Ι ι (Iota)	I
י (Yod)	Y	Κ κ (Kappa)	K
כּ (Kaf) כ (Khaf) ך (Kaf Sofit)*	K Kh [Ḥ] Kh [Ḥ]	Λ λ (Lambda)	L
ל (Lamed)	L	Μ μ (Mu)	M
מ (Mem) ם (Mem Sofit)*	M M	Ν ν (Nu)	N
נ (Nun) ן (Nun Sofit)*	N N	Ξ ξ (Xi)	X
ס (Samekh)	S	Ο ο (Omicron)	O
ע (Ayin)	Depends on Vowel	Π π (Pi)	P
פּ (Pe) ף (Pe Sofit)* פ (Fe)	P P F	Ρ ρ (Rho)	R
צ (Tsadi) ץ (Tsadi Sofit)*	Ts Ts	Σ σ (Sigma) ς (Final Sigma)	S
ק (Qof)	Q	Τ τ (Tau)	T
ר (Resh)	R	Υ υ (Upsilon)	U
ש (Shin)	S/Sh	Φ φ (Phi)	F
ת (Tav/Taw)	T	Χ χ (Chi)	Ch [Ḥ]
		Ψ ψ (Psi)	Ps
		Ω ω (Omega)	Oh

* Sofit letters are final forms. That is, they appear in this form only at the end of a word.

Ge'ez	English Equivalent	ä	u	i	a	e	ə	o	wa	yä
Hoy	H	ሀ	ሁ	ሂ	ሃ	ሄ	ህ	ሆ	-	-
Lawe	L	ለ	ሉ	ሊ	ላ	ሌ	ል	ሎ	ሏ	-
Chawt	Ch [Ḥ]	ሐ	ሑ	ሒ	ሓ	ሔ	ሕ	ሖ	ሗ	-
May	M	መ	ሙ	ሚ	ማ	ሜ	ም	ሞ	ሟ	ፙ
Śawt	Ś	ሠ	ሡ	ሢ	ሣ	ሤ	ሥ	ሦ	ሧ	-
Rə's	R	ረ	ሩ	ሪ	ራ	ሬ	ር	ሮ	ሯ	ፘ
Sat	S	ሰ	ሱ	ሲ	ሳ	ሴ	ስ	ሶ	ሷ	-
Khaf	Kh [Ḥ]	ቀ	ቁ	ቂ	ቃ	ቄ	ቅ	ቆ	ቋ	-
Bet	B	በ	ቡ	ቢ	ባ	ቤ	ብ	ቦ	ቧ	-
Tawe	T	ተ	ቱ	ቲ	ታ	ቴ	ት	ቶ	ቷ	-
Ḫarm	Ḫ	ኀ	ኁ	ኂ	ኃ	ኄ	ኅ	ኆ	ኋ	-
Nahas	N	ነ	ኑ	ኒ	ና	ኔ	ን	ኖ	ኗ	-
'Alf	Depends on Vowel	አ	ኡ	ኢ	ኣ	ኤ	እ	ኦ	ኧ	-
Kaf	K	ከ	ኩ	ኪ	ካ	ኬ	ክ	ኮ	ኳ	-
Wawe	W	ወ	ዉ	ዊ	ዋ	ዌ	ው	ዎ	-	-
'Ayn	Depends on Vowel	ዐ	ዑ	ዒ	ዓ	ዔ	ዕ	ዖ	-	-
Zay	Z	ዘ	ዙ	ዚ	ዛ	ዜ	ዝ	ዞ	ዟ	-
Yaman	Y	የ	ዩ	ዪ	ያ	ዬ	ይ	ዮ	-	-
Dant	D	ደ	ዱ	ዲ	ዳ	ዴ	ድ	ዶ	ዷ	-
Gaml	G	ገ	ጉ	ጊ	ጋ	ጌ	ግ	ጎ	ጓ	-
Tayt	Ṭ	ጠ	ጡ	ጢ	ጣ	ጤ	ጥ	ጦ	ጧ	-
Payt	P̣	ጰ	ጱ	ጲ	ጳ	ጴ	ጵ	ጶ	ጷ	-
Tsadday	Ts	ጸ	ጹ	ጺ	ጻ	ጼ	ጽ	ጾ	ጿ	-
Ṣappa	Ṣ	ፀ	ፁ	ፂ	ፃ	ፄ	ፅ	ፆ	-	-
Af	F	ፈ	ፉ	ፊ	ፋ	ፌ	ፍ	ፎ	ፏ	ፚ
Psa	P	ፐ	ፑ	ፒ	ፓ	ፔ	ፕ	ፖ	ፗ	-

Note: In Ge'ez Ethiopic, the alphabet uses different characters to indicate vowels that follow a letter. For example, the letter Af (ፍ) makes the sound of the English "F." However, when written as (ፌ) it makes the sound "FE." When written as (ፋ) it makes the sound "FA." When written as (ፏ) it makes the sound "FWA." Thus each of the letters are assigned a vowel sound based on the way the letter is written. This means the Ge'ez alphabet, though it only has 27 letters, actually has 214 different characters. Whenever a letter in the (ə) column is used, it represents the consonant itself without a following vowel. If the letter is 'Alf or 'Ayn, it generally represents a full stop.

Appendix C: New Testament Parallel Verses

The following table is a list of cross-references between the New Testament and the Apocrypha. Some are direct quotes, some are close paraphrases, and some may even be considered veiled references. Note that it cannot be established with absolute certainty that the NT writers were indeed referencing the Apocryphal works. However, knowing that they were well-known in their day, it is highly likely. This list should **not** be considered exhaustive.

New Testament Verse	Apocrypha Verse
Mattithyahu 6:14-15	Ben Sira 28:2
Mattithyahu 6:19-20	Ben Sira 29:11-12
Mattithyahu 6:23	Ben Sira 14:10
Mattithyahu 7:12	Tovi 4:15
Mattithyahu 7:16-20	Ben Sira 27:6
Mattithyahu 9:36	Yehudith 11:19
Mattithyahu 16:18	Ḥokhmat Shelomoh 16:13
Mattithyahu 22:25	Tovi 3:8; 7:11
Mattithyahu 24:15	Maqabiym א 1:54; Maqabiym ב 8:17
Mattithyahu 24:16	Maqabiym א 2:28
Mattithyahu 27:43	Ḥokhmat Shelomoh 2:18
Markos 4:5-17	Ben Sira 40:15
Markos 9:48	Yehudith 16:17
Loukas 1:42	Yehudith 13:18
Loukas 1:52	Ben Sira 10:14
Loukas 2:29	Tovi 11:9
Loukas 13:29	Barukh א 4:37
Loukas 21:10	Esdras ⲃ 13:31
Yoḥanan 1:3	Ḥokhmat Shelomoh 9:1
Yoḥanan 1:18	Ben Sira 43:31
Yoḥanan 3:13-14	Ḥokhmat Shelomoh 16:7
Yoḥanan 6:35	Ben Sira 24:21
Yoḥanan 10:22	Maqabiym א 4:59
Yoḥanan 15:6	Ḥokhmat Shelomoh 4:5
Ma'asei 12:20-23	Maqabiym ב 9:5
Ma'asei 17:29	Ḥokhmat Shelomoh 13:10
Romaious 1:20	Ḥokhmat Shelomoh 13:1
Romaious 5:12	Ḥokhmat Shelomoh 2:24
Romaious 9:21-24	Ḥokhmat Shelomoh 15:7-9
Korinthious ⲁ 2:16	Ḥokhmat Shelomoh 9:13
Korinthious ⲁ 6:9-10	Ben Sira 20:25
Korinthious ⲁ 8:5-6	Ḥokhmat Shelomoh 13:3

Korinthious ꓒ 9:26	Ben Sira 11:10
Korinthious ꓒ 10:20	Barukh א 4:7
Korinthious B 6:14-16	Ben Sira 13:15-17
Ephesious 6:14-17	Ḥokhmat Shelomoh 5:18
Timotheon ꓒ 6:15	Maqabiym ב 13:4
Ivrim 11:5	Ḥokhmat Shelomoh 4:1-11; Ben Sira 44:16
Ivrim 11:35	Maqabiym ב 7
Ivrim 12:12	Ben Sira 25:23
Ya'aqov 1:19	Ben Sira 5:11
Ya'aqov 3:13	Ben Sira 3:17
Ya'aqov 5:6	Ḥokhmat Shelomoh 2:10-20
Kepha א 1:6-7	Ben Sira 2:5
Kepha ב 2:7	Ḥokhmat Shelomoh 10:6
Galah 1:4	Tovi 12:15
Galah 2:12	Ḥokhmat Shelomoh 18:15-16
Galah 8:3-4	Tovi 12:12;15
Galah 8:7	Ben Sira 39:29
Galah 9:3	Ḥokhmat Shelomoh 16:9
Galah 19:11	Maqabiym ב 3:25; 11:8
Galah 21:19	Tovi 13:17-18

Appendix D: Glossary of Terms

Pronunciation Key							
AH	a in "father"	**AI**	eye	**EI**	ay in "pray"	**TS**	ts in "cats"
EE	ee in "tree"	**EH**	e in "pet"	**E**	e in "pet"	**OH**	o in "bone"
OO	oo in "soon"	**Ḥ/ch/kh**	Guttural "h" in Bach or Loch				

SQV	Pronunciation	Anglicized
יהוה	~	LORD
Adoni-Tsedeq	Ad-oh-nee Tseh-dek	Adonizedek
Aharon	Ah-ha-ROHN	Aaron
Aiyalon	Ai-ya-LOHN	Ajalon
Amaleq	Am-ah-lek	Amalek
Amein	Ah-mein	Amen
Aram	Ar-ahm	Syria
Aram-Naharayim	Ar-ahm Nah-hah-rah-yeem	Mesopotamia
Ashuwr	Ah-SHOO-wr	Assyria
Avarim	Av-ar-EEM	Abarim
Avihu	Av-EE-hoo	Abihu
Avimelekh	Av-ee-MEL-ek	Abimelech
Avraham	Av-RAH-hahm	Abraham
Avram	Av-RAHM	Abram
Azazel	Ahz-ah-ZEL	Scapegoat
Balaq	Bah-LAHK	Balak
Bavel	Bah-vehl	Babel / Babylon
Beersheva	Beh-ehr-SHEI-vah	Beersheba
Being	BEE-EENG	Soul
Beliyya'al	Beh-LEE-yah-ahl	Belial
B'midbar	Beh-MEED-bahr	Numbers
Benyamin	Bein-yah-MEEN	Benjamin
B'reshiyt	Behr-eh-SHEET	Genesis
Beth-El	Beith-el	Bethel
Beth-lechem	Beith-leh-chehm	Bethlehem
Bil'am	Beel-ahm	Balaam
Botsrah	Bohts-rah	Bozrah
Dammeseq	Dahm-ess-ehk	Damascus
D'varim	Deh-vahr-EEM	Deuteronomy
Devorah	Deh-vor-ah	Deborah
Diqlah	DEEK-lah	Diklah
Divrei Ha'Yamim	Dee-vrei-hah-yah-MEEM	Chronicles
Edom	Eh-DOHM	Edom / Idumea
El	Ehl	God
el	ehl	god
El Shaddai	Ehl Shah-DAI	God Almighty
Elazar	Ehl-ah-zahr	Eleazar (also Lazarus)
Elohim	Ehl-oh-HEEM	God
elohim	ehl-oh-heem	gods
Elyaqim	Ehl-yah-KEEM	Eliakim
Elyon	Ehl-YOHN	Most High
Ephesious	Eh-pheh-SEE-os	Ephesians
Ephrayim	Eph-rah-YEEM	Ephraim
Eqron	Ek-ROHN	Ekron
Esav	Eh-sahv	Esau
Ever	Eh-vehr	Eber
Eyval	Ei-vahl	Ebal
Galah	Gah-lah	Revelation
Galatas	Gah-lah-teis	Galatians
Gavri'el	Gahv-REE-ehl	Gabriel
Gichon	Gee-CHOHN	Gichon
Gilad	Gee-LAHD	Gilead
Givon	Gee-VOHN	Gibeon
Havel	Hah-vehl	Abel

Ḥam	Ḥahm	Ham
Ḥanokh	Ḥahn-OHCH	Enoch (also Hanoch)
Ḥaran	Ḥah-rahn	Haran
Ḥatsor	Ḥahts-OHR	Hazor
Ḥavilah	Ḥahv-EE-lah	Havilah
Ḥavvah	Ḥah-vah	Eve
Ḥeshbon	Ḥesh-BOHN	Heshbon
Ḥetsron	Ḥets-ROHN	Hezron
Ḥittite	Ḥeet-AIT	Hittite
Ḥivite	Ḥiv-AIT	Hivite
Ḥorev	Ḥohr-ehv	Horeb
Hoshea	Hoh-shei-ah	Hosea
Ivrim	Eev-REEM	Hebrews
Iyyov	Ee-yohv	Job
Kaldea	Kal-DEE-ah	Chaldea
Kana'an	Kah-nah-ahn	Canaan
Kerub	Keh-roob	Cherub
Kittim	Kit-TEEM	Chittim
Kolossaeis	Kol-oss-ei-iss	Colossians
Korinthious	Kor-in-thee-oos	Corinthians
Kush	KOO-sh	Cush (also Ethiopia)
Lamekh	Lah-mehk	Lamech
Lavan	Lah-vahn	Laban
Levanon	Lev-ah-nahn	Lebanon
Livnah	Leev-nah	Libnah
Livyathan	Leev-yah-thahn	Leviathan
Loukas	Loo-kahs	Luke
M'lakhim	Meh-lah-KHEEM	Kings
Ma'asei	Mah-ah-sei	Acts
Malakhi	Mah-lah-kee	Malachi
Menasheh	Meh-nah-sheh	Manasseh
Markos	Mahr-koss	Mark
Mattithyah /-yahu	Maht-tith-yah	Matthew
Messiah	Me-sai-uh	Christ
Mikha'el	Mee-kah-ehl	Michael
Miryam	Meer-yahm	Mary (also Miriam)

Mishlei	Meesh-lei	Proverbs
Mitsrayim	Meets-rah-YEEM	Egypt (also Mizraim)
Moav	MOH-ahv	Moab
Mosheh	Moh-sheih	Moses
Noach	Noh-ach	Noah
Noph	Noh-ph	Memphis
Paras	Pahr-ahs	Persia
Perets	Peh-rehts	Perez
Pesach	Pei-sahch	Passover
Perath	Peh-rahth	Euphrates
Philippesious	Phil-ih-pee-see-oos	Philippians
Pinechas	Peen-chas	Phineas
Put	Poot	Libya (also Phut)
Qadesh	Kah-dehsh	Kadesh
Qayin	Kai-een	Cain
Qedar	Keh-dahr	Kedar
Qemuel	Keh-moo-ehl	Kemuel
Qenan	Keh-nahn	Cainan
Qenaz	Keh-nahz	Kenaz
Qeturah	Keh-too-rah	Keturah
Qiryath	Keer-yahth	Kirjath
Qohath	Koh-hath	Kohath
Qoheleth	Qoh-heh-leth	Ecclesiastes
Qorach	Kor-ach	Korah
Ragesh	Rah-gesh	Rages
Reuven	Reh-oo-vein	Reuben
Rivqah	REEV-kah	Rebecca
Ruach	ROO-ach	Spirit
Sha'ul	Shah-OOL	Saul (also Paul)
Shekhem	Sheh-chem	Shechem
Sh'mot	Sh'-MOHT	Exodus
Sh'muel	Shem-OO-ehl	Samuel
Sheth	Sheh-th	Seth
Shimon	Shee-mohn	Simon (also Simeon)
Shir Ha'Shirim	Sheer-HAH-sheer-EEM	Song of Songs

Shofar	SHOH-fahr	Trumpet
Shoftim	Shohf-TEEM	Judges
Tehillim	Teh-heel-EEM	Psalms
Timotheos	Teem-oh-thei-oss	Timothy
Torah	Toh-rah	Law
Torot	Toh-roht	Laws
Tsedaqqah	Tseh-da-kah	Alms
Tsevaot	Tseh-vah-oht	Hosts
Tsidon	Tsee-DOHN	Sidon
Tsion	Tsee-OHN	Zion
Tsipporah	Tsee-por-ah	Zipporah
Tsivon	Tsee-VOHN	Zibeon
Tsor	Tsor	Tyre
Uts	Oots	Uz
Vayyiqra	Vah-yee-krah	Leviticus
Ya'aqov	Yah-akohv	Jacob (also James)
Yarden	Yahr-dein	Jordan
Yashuv	Yah-SHOOV	Jashub
Yavan	Yah-vahn	Greece (also Javan)
Yevusite	Yehv-OO-sait	Jebusite
Yechezqel	Yeh-chez-kehl	Ezekiel
Yehoshua	Yeh-hoh-shoo-ah	Joshua
Yehudah	Yeh-hoo-dah	Judah (also Judas; Judea; Jude)
Yehudim	Yeh-hoo-DEEM	Jews
Yehudite	Yeh-hoo-dait	Jew
Yeptheth	Yeh-pheth	Japheth
Yericho	Yeh-ree-choh	Jericho
Yerushalayim	Yeh-roo-shah-lah-YEEM	Jerusalem
Yeshayah /-yahu	Yeh-shah-yah	Isaiah
Yirmeyah /-yahu	Yeer-meh-yah	Jeremiah
Yishmael	Yeesh-mah-ehl	Ishmael
Yiskah	Yees-kah	Ishcah
Yisra'el	Yees-rah-ehl	Israel
Yissakhar	Yees-sah-char	Issachar
Yithro	Yeeth-roh	Jethro
Yitschaq	Yeets-chahk	Isaac
Yitshar	Yeets-hahr	Izhar
Yochanan	Yoh-chah-nahn	John (also Johanan)
Yoel	Yoh-ehl	Joel
Yokheved	Yoh-keh-vehd	Jokebed
Yoseph	Yoh-sehph	Joseph
Yoshiyah /-yahu	Yoh-shee-yahu	Josiah
Yovav	Yoh-vahv	Jobab
Yovel	Yoh-vehl	Jubilee
Zevulun	Zeh-voo-loon	Zebulun

Appendix E: Major Textual Variants

Tovi [Tobit] Chapter 6, according to the Greek text. The translation set forth in the main body text within the book itself is based primarily upon the Hebrew and Aramaic fragments. The section given here is the more traditional rendering of the Greek version.

6 1 Now as they went on their journey, they came at evening to the river Ḥideqqel, and they stayed there. 2 But the young man went down to wash himself, and a fish leaped out of the river, and would have swallowed up the young man. 3 But the messenger said to him, "Grab the fish!" So the young man grabbed the fish, and hauled it up onto the land.

4 And the messenger said to him, "Cut the fish open, and take the heart, the liver, and the gall, and keep them with you." 5 And the young man did as the messenger commanded him; but they roasted the *flesh of the* fish, and ate it. And they both went on their way, till they drew near to Aḥmetha.

6 The young man said to the messenger, "Brother Azaryah, of what use is the heart, the liver, and the gall of the fish?"

7 He said to him, "This is *the use of* the heart and the liver: if a demon or an evil spirit troubles anyone, we must burn those and make smoke from them before the man or the woman, and the affliction will flee. 8 But as for the gall, it is good to anoint a man that has white films in his eyes, and he will be healed."

9 But when they drew near to Ragesh, 10 the messenger said to the young man, "Brother, today we will lodge with Ragu'el. He is your kinsman. He has an only daughter named Sarah. I will speak about her, that she should be given to you for a wife. 11 For her inheritance belongs to you, and you only are of her kindred. 12 The maiden is fair and wise. And now hear me, and I will speak to her father. When we return from Ragesh we will celebrate the marriage; for I know that Ragu'el may in no way marry her to another according to the Torah of Mosheh, or else he would be liable to death, because it belongs to you to take the inheritance, rather than any other."

13 Then the young man said to the messenger, "Brother Azaryah, I have heard that this maiden has been given to seven men, and that they all perished in the bride-chamber. 14 Now I am the only son of my father, and I am afraid, lest I go in and die, even as those before me. For a demon loves her, which harms no man, except those who come to her. Now I fear lest I die, and bring my father's and my

mother's life to Sheol with sorrow because of me. They have no other son to bury them."

15 But the messenger said to him, "Do you not remember the words which your father commanded you, that you should take a wife of your own kindred? Now hear me, brother; for she will be your wife. Do not worry about the demon, for this night she will be given you as wife. 16 And when you come into the bride-chamber, you shall take the ashes of incense, and shall lay upon them some of the heart and liver of the fish, and shall make smoke with them. 17 The demon will smell it, and flee away, and never come again any more. But when you go near to her, both of you rise up, and cry to Elohim who is kind. He will save you, and be kind to you. Do not be afraid, for she was prepared for you from the beginning; and you will save her, and she will go with you. And I suppose that you will have children with her."

When Toviyah heard these things, he loved her, and his being was strongly joined to her.

www.ingramcontent.com/pod-product-compliance
Lightning Source LLC
Chambersburg PA
CBHW070935180426
43192CB00039B/2211